Kamikaze

By the same Author:

Kamikaze

To Die for the Emperor

Peter C. Smith

Pen & Sword
AVIATION

First published in Great Britain in 2014 by
Pen & Sword Aviation
an imprint of
Pen & Sword Books Ltd
47 Church Street
Barnsley
South Yorkshire
S70 2AS

ISBN 978 1 78159 313 4

A CIP catalogue record for this book is available from the British Library

Typeset in Ehrhardt by
Mac Style Ltd, Bridlington, East Yorkshire
Printed and bound in the UK by CPI Group (UK) Ltd, Croydon,
CRO 4YY

Pen & Sword Books Ltd incorporates the imprints of Pen & Sword
Archaeology, Atlas, Aviation, Battleground, Discovery, Family History,
History, Maritime, Military, Naval, Politics, Railways, Select, Transport,
True Crime, and Fiction, Frontline Books, Leo Cooper, Praetorian Press,
Seaforth Publishing and Wharncliffe.

For a complete list of Pen & Sword titles please contact
PEN & SWORD BOOKS LIMITED
47 Church Street, Barnsley, South Yorkshire S70 2AS, England
E-mail: enquiries@pen-and-sword.co.uk
Website: www.pen-and-sword.co.uk

See all the books of Peter C Smith at www.dive-bombers.co.uk

Contents

Telegram: From Washington to Foreign Office. Earl of Halifax d. 4.11 pm Jan 5th 1945. Received 12.5 am Jan 6th 1945. Important. Secret.

Following Personal for Prime Minister.

'I saw the President yesterday, whom I did not think looked too good.'

'He was bothered about Japanese suicidal aircraft attacks on their ships, which meant they were constantly losing forty or fifty American sailors for one Japanese, and was not very sanguine about early end of either war.'[1]

1. FO954/7B/2466.

Foreword & Acknowledgements

This book does not describe in full detail *every* action in which the Japanese suicide aircraft took part, nor the loss or damage of each and *every* ship. I would have liked to have done so, but was constrained by space limitations. There are already several books which purport to do just that, although they do seem to disagree a great deal. Nor does this book concern itself with other forms of specialised suicide weaponry that the Japanese developed late in the war, but concentrates on the aerial attackers that actually saw combat. The final three main Allied landings, in the Philippines, at Iwo Jima and at Okinawa were the focus of such attacks; while the planned invasion of Kyushu and Japan proper concentrated minds on both sides for a bloodbath that never, thankfully, took place. In order to concentrate on the subject of the book background description of these has quite deliberately been kept to a minimum.

Difficulties arise with regard to language. Not just the 'correct' way to translate many Japanese names and indicators, themselves of Chinese origin, but in interpreting the various British and American reports. Thus a Japanese Air Fleet is *Koku Kentai*; an Air Group is *Koku Sentai*, a Squadron *Hikotai* in the Army and *Daitai* in the Navy, while a three-plane section was *Shotai*, three of which made the nine-plane *Chutai*. Both the Americans and Japanese used the term Lieutenant (j.g) meaning 'Junior Grade', but the Royal Navy had Sub-Lieutenants. Not only are many English and American naval terms different (British 'quarterdecks' become American 'fantails'; British 'funnels' are American 'stacks', 'lifts' become 'elevators', 'accelerators' are 'catapults' and so on), but actual spellings differ, even when the words are the same. In quoted reports, American spelling is often quite different to the Queen's English, so 'fuse' is 'fuze', while 'manoeuvre' is all sorts of things! I have had to compromise a great deal, which will upset critics in both countries but other than repeat each such word twice, (which would prove irksome to all) once is deemed sufficient. Also, references are in the form of footnotes, which, surprising as it may seem to some armchair critics, go at the *foot* of the relevant page!

Note also, the main US Fleet units remained basically the same, with influxes of fresh ships rotating all the time, but dependant on the Commander (namely: Admiral William Frederick 'Bull' Halsey, Jr., OBE, USN; or Admiral Raymond Ames Spruance, USN; Admiral Marc Andrew 'Pete' Mitscher, USN; or Admiral John Sidney 'Slew' McCain, Sr., USN) commanding the carrier operations, the nomenclature changed from Task Force 58 to Task Force 38 and the British Pacific Fleet complied with this as Task Force 57 and Task Force 37.

It should also be noted that while the Kamikaze attacks carried out in this period were widespread, they were interspersed throughout with conventional attacks, and that for example the largest loss of life, aboard the carrier *Franklin*, was caused by a conventional dive-bombing attack and *not* a Kamikaze.

As for the moral issues which arise, I try to present the facts in an historical and also a National context. There was little meeting of minds back then between Western and Eastern values and traditions – and hasty judgements should be tempered by conditioning, of *both* sides. When a nation's back is up against the wall it can surrender or fight. Great Britain's back was firmly against the wall in June 1940, and she fought on. Japan was in a similar unenviable state in July 1945, and many wanted to fight on. If the Germans had landed on the south coast of England in 1940, Churchill has stated that he was prepared to use poison gas as one option; in 1945 America chose, in order to save lives (both Allied and Japanese incidentally) to use the Atomic Bomb; Japan chose the Kamikaze. I leave others to judge the finer points of these options in an all-out war situation.

One cannot doubt the bravery of the young men who sacrificed themselves in this way, just as one cannot but admire the bravery of the ships' crews who had to stand up to them, day-after-day-after-day. On both sides the majority of the combatants were young men, barely out of school, facing horrors we can only guess at. All tribute to them, and may our current crop of seemingly befuddled and very mediocre rulers, some of whom seem itching to make every nations' woes our own special problem, do everything possible to stay aloof from it all and prevent the same thing happening to our young generation on such a scale again.

The Author would like to thank the following for unstinted help and permission to use information and photographs here:

Lee-Ann Conchie, Information Services, Research Centre, Australian War Memorial, Canberra ACT; William Hughes Fitzhugh, publisher of *The Concord Review*, for permission to reproduce extracts from Mako Sasaki's research paper; Laura Hirst of Pen & Sword for her encouragement and backing on this difficult project; Terry Morgan for allowing me to freely quote from his memoirs; Jack Ormsby for his great kindness in relating his memoirs of the attack on the *Essex;* Jane Peek, Curator, Military Heraldry & Technology, Australian War Memorial, Canberra ACT – for her permission to quote from the papers and notes of her late father, Admiral Sir Richard Peek, RAN which were also published in *The Naval Review*, London, 1946; Bob Pisz, Library/Research Division, National Naval Aviation Museum, Pensacola, Fla; Janet (Limbaugh) Remiyac, daughter of Ben Limbaugh for arranging the interview with her father while he was in hospital; Mako Sasaki, now a successful Trans-Pacific Lawyer working in Tokyo and New York for her IB Extended Essay in History, printed in *The Cord Review*; Glenn Scroggins, Mako Sasaki's teacher, Saint Maur International School, Yokohama; the late Commander Sadao Seno, JMDF, Rtd; whose help, encouragement and wise advice down the decades will always be treasured; Professor Akira Shimizu, one of the last members of the IJNA 77th Class – many years ago we once aspired to write a much larger book on the *Tokkou* with the biographies of over 2,500 of these pilots with names, ranks, birth place, birth dates etc, but no British publisher would entertain such a huge project and it foundered; Lieutenant-Colonel Rufus B. 'Tommy' Thompson, Jr, (USMC Ret) for his kind permission to quote from his memoirs of the attack on *Nashville* and finally to Lieutenant Commander George J. Walsh, USNR, Rtd., former Helldiver pilot for his permission to use his Oral History of the attack on *Ticonderoga*. Special thanks and gratitude to Sandra Meacock for permission to reproduce her father's photos of attacks on British Pacific Fleet carriers.

During my research visits to Japan I would like to thank Vice Admiral Kazunari Doke, Commandant, Kure District, Japan Maritime Self-Defence Force, Hiroshima; Rear Admiral Sadayoshi Matsuoka, JMSDF, Superintendent, Officer Candidate School, Etajima; Rear Admiral Kazuo Takahashi, JMSDF, Chief of Staff, Commandant Kure District, Hiroshima; Captain Masato Shimada, Deputy Superintendent, Officers Candidate School, Etajima; Ryunosuke Valentine Megumi, JMSDF (Rtd), Okinawa ,for our extremely and informative discussion in London, Colonel Shogo Hattori, JASDF (Rtd) and Commander Noritaka Kitazawa, JMSDF (Rtd), formerly of the Military History Department, National Institute for Defence Studies, Tokyo, for much assistance down the years; Kohji Ishiwata, Honorary President, and founder of *Ships of the World* Magazine, Kaijinsha Corporation; Tohru Kizu, Editor-in-Chief/Director, *Ships of the World*, Kaijinsha Corporation, Tokyo; Mr Hitoshi Hasegawa, staff writer of the *Kojinsha*, for advising me via Commander Seno down the years; Mr Tetsuya Nakama, Hankyu Toho Group, of the Dai-Ichi-Hotel, Tokyo, and Hanku Hotel, Kure, for making my visits a pleasure; Mr Shuzo Inaba, who treated me with cordial tea service in his home at Kure.

Finally, I would wish to express my thanks to my editor, Martin Derry, for his rigorous and welcomed work, and very sound advice.

Peter C. Smith, Riseley, Bedfordshire, UK November 2014

Chapter One

The Spirit of *Bushido*?

'In the tradition of the *Bushido* he spoke of the glory of death, saying, I go to die for my country, it fills me with humility to have been selected by the Emperor'
Kuwahara, Rear-Admiral Torao, IJN,
Commander Third Carrier Division.

In the October of 1944, just three years after the opening of the Pacific War with the attack on the US Fleet at Pearl Harbor, Japan was facing a bleak prospect. Whereas in the opening six months of the conflict the Navy and Army of the Chrysanthemum Empire had swept all before it, humbling the western powers, the United States, Great Britain and the Netherlands with ease in a succession of easy victories, now these victories were but distant memories. The speed and completeness of Japan's initial assault had been dazzling; they had reduced the US Navy's battle line in one blow, taken the Philippines, Wake and Guam, and similarly humiliated the British Empire by rapidly sinking the capital ships *Prince of Wales* and *Repulse* with disdainful ease before conquering Hong Kong, Borneo, Malaya, Singapore and Burma, and had threatened India and raided Ceylon [Sri Lanka], and sortied across the Indian Ocean to Vichy-French ruled Madagascar, having already secured the cooperation of that same nation's colonies in Indo-China. They had destroyed all the hastily assembled American, British and Dutch naval squadrons, occupied the oil-rich Dutch East Indies, Sumatra, Java and the Celebes, invaded New Guinea and threatened Australia.

This tidal wave of easy victories had made Japan's armed forces appear invulnerable, but they were not. That illusion was first shattered by the air/sea Battle of Midway in June 1942 which had marked a turning point in Japan's fortunes[1], and the grinding attrition of the Guadalcanal and Solomon Islands campaign revealed the fragility that lay behind the cutting edge blade that was the Imperial Japanese Navy. For the truth was that, although led by an unequalled martial elite, and with the backing of an indoctrinated nation of one hundred million people dedicated to their Emperor and expanding Empire, which in recent times had known only victory and never defeat, Japan was not able to compete with the industrial might of the United States of America, whose capacity for innovation, invention and mass-production was unequalled and overwhelming.

The oft-quoted remarks of Admiral Isoroku Yamamoto, Imperial Japanese Navy (IJN), that he would guarantee six months of victory but that beyond that time could guarantee nothing were not isolated comments. In their heart-of-hearts most knowledgeable Japanese knew they ultimately could not win. That dour warrior Admiral Chūichi Nagumo, IJN, the

---

1. Smith, Peter C. *Midway Dauntless Victory: Fresh Perspectives on American's Seminal Naval Victory of World War II*, Barnsley, UK, Pen & Sword Maritime, 2007.

man who led the Carrier Task Force that represented the best of Japanese naval power, but which was destroyed in a few moments of carelessness at Midway, was himself to state: 'It is agreed that if we do not fight now, our nation will perish. But it may well perish even if we *do* fight. In this hopeless situation, survival can be accomplished only by fighting to the last man. Then, even if we lose, posterity will have the heritage of our loyal spirit to inspire them in turn to the defence of our country. We will fight to the last drop of blood.'[2]

Forced into a war that most did not want as the only alternative to a humiliating acceptance of American and British sanctions of essential oil and material supplies,[3] Japan did indeed choose war rather than bend the knee, and their astonishingly easy early victories only fed the illusion, almost universally accepted after decades of indoctrination, that they were a chosen people and that divine intervention would somehow aid their admitted expertise, and compensate for their lack of industrial power on the scale that the United States was capable of. It was wistful thinking, and doomed to failure, but few proud nations would have accepted the alternative.

Now had come the reckoning. A strange lack of resolution had taken hold of the Japanese Navy in the period 1942–43. Having won their greatest victory over a foreign power at the Battle of Tṣushima in 1905, and having been frozen at 60% of the strength of the British and American navies since the American stage-managed Washington Naval Conference of 1921, the Japanese naval high command had been fixated on the concept of 'one final battle' – a colossal once-and-for-all make-or-break naval battle (as Tṣushima had been and Jutland *ought* to have been) that would decide the nation's fate. This policy led to a determination to husband their naval strength for this one decisive moment. Thus later victories like Savo Island in August 1942 were not pressed home. The United States was in the process of building an awesome 'Two-Ocean' Fleet, a Navy that would equal that of all the other navies of the world, including the next two largest, Britain and Japan, combined. When that fleet entered service nothing would prevail against it. If the Japanese hope of a major fleet action in which the US Navy was so defeated that her people would become war-weary and sue for peace were to be achieved, then it had to be done in the period 1942–43 at the latest. After that Japan would be swamped. But the nettle had not been grasped and as the Allies took the offensive, all the Pacific outposts had been re-conquered steadily and at great cost, but remorselessly. As islands steadily fell it was the IJN that was whittled down, ship-by-ship, plane-by-plane, while American power waxed mightily. Finally, with the outer bastion of the Marianas threatened, the air-sea battle of the Philippine Sea had been fought, and in the space of two days what remained of Japanese naval air power afloat had been utterly smashed. Not for nothing was that battle known as the Great Marianas Turkey Shoot – ten Japanese planes were lost for every American. Her carrier fleet, essentially carriers without aircraft, (which are themselves merely large,

2. Imoguchi, Rikihei; Nakajima, Tadashi; Pineau, Roger, *The Divine Wind: Japan's Kamikaze Force in World War II*, Annapolis, United States Naval Institute, 1948.
3. Vice-Admiral Hoshima, Zenshiro, IJN, Chief of Naval Affairs Bureau in 1945 was once asked what single thing made war between Japan and the United States inevitable, his reply was "The stoppage of oil imports. Without them Japan could not survive." United States Strategic Bombing Survey (USSBS) Report # 5, *Oil in Japan's War*, dated February 1946.

expensive and vulnerable targets) was from then on reduced to the role of 'live bait', lures to draw away American air power while what remained of her battleship strength finally fought that long-awaited showdown battle. But it was all too late. At the Battle of Leyte Gulf, what had happened to Japanese naval air power at the Marianas re-occurred with her surface fleet – it was utterly beaten, many battleships and heavy cruisers that had been husbanded for years were sunk and crippled, and only a few managed to escape the debacle. Japan as a naval power was done.

And yet even as *finis* was being writ large in the waters of the Philippines, an event occurred that took the victorious Americans totally by surprise. What battleships had failed to achieve off Samar, a few single-engined fighter aircraft with bombs attached carried out the sinking of American carriers. The planes were frail and fragile, but their pilots were dedicated to giving their lives to achieve such results. They were volunteers choosing to die by crashing their aircraft on Allied ships. They were the Kamikazes. So successful were they deemed to have been, when the chances of conventional air attacks achieving similar results were almost zero, that this method of attack soon grew from a handful of volunteers to whole units adopting this course. And soon it was not just volunteers but whole units that were being 'volunteered' by shame, order or cohesion. Rapidly this 'unthinkable' method of warfare grew to be Japan's guiding principal and sole beacon of hope that somehow defeat could be staved off by self-sacrifice.

Earlier precedents

Japan's fighting forces had long had a reputation of fighting almost to the last man with the *Banza*i charge ending many a hopeless struggle from Guadalcanal onward. In the air specifically, there were many precedents in the form of pilots deliberately crashing their aircraft into enemy warships. Let us cite a few:

Off the coast of the Island of Luzon, an invasion convoy had been reported and an American heavy bomber was despatched from Clark Field to deal with it. Arriving over the target at 22,000 feet it dropped three 600lb bombs. Two were near misses while one, 'went right down the stack bringing their target ship, an enemy battleship, to a halt on fire and with oil spilling out of her hull'. This was electrifying news and the official Air Force Command issued the following day confirmed that a, '29,000–ton battleship' had been sunk. Furthermore the heroic pilot had deliberately smashed his heavy bomber into the ship to achieve this great feat. The press back home in the States took the story and made headlines of it. The pilot was a national hero and the fact that he sacrificed his life for his nation was accorded a mark of respect and honour.

The date was 9 December 1941, the battleship claimed sunk was the *Haruna* (Captain Takama Tomotsu, IJN), the pilot made a national hero was Lieutenant Colin Kelly, United States Army Air Force! Despite the official hype it was all a complete fabrication. The Japanese invasion convoy attacked had *no* battleship escorts, just one very small light cruiser, the *Nagara* (Captain Naoi Toshio, IJN). Far from being bombed, crashed into and sunk, she was not even scratched – while the *Haruna*, which was 1,500 miles away in the Gulf of Siam (and would be claimed 'sunk' by the USAAF many more times during the war), survived in fact until July 1945 and the very last days of the conflict. It was all totally untrue.

A certain Lieutenant Sam Marret, piloting a P-35 fighter plane earlier that same day, made a heroic attack against a Japanese transport and was killed when his target ship exploded. Again, reports released indicated that he had deliberately smashed his aircraft into the transport ship, thus sacrificing himself. Again it was all a myth and totally untrue, but back home in the States the press merged the two stories and an unstoppable legend was begun. It was not that the story was so distorted as to be farcical, that is not the point, which is, that these 'suicide' missions were regarded, when carried out by *American* pilots, as gallant sacrifices.

We can quote other examples; the United States Marine Corps pilot Captain Richard E Fleming, USMC, at the Battle of Midway, is alleged to have crashed his aircraft into the heavy cruiser *Mikuma* (Captain Shakao Sakiyama, IJN). Again this did not happen; he was shot down into the sea and no plane, either deliberately, or accidently, dove into *Mikuma*. However, that did not stop yet another legend, one that endures to this day. Fleming, like Kelly and Marret, were very brave men and did not commit suicide, but the American press and public thought all the more of them when they believed that they *had* made suicide attacks!

A rather different portrait was painted when Japanese pilots chose to crash their damaged aircraft into Allied ships. Taking as an example, the much-publicised photograph of the carrier *Shokaku*'s flight leader, Lieutenant (jg) Mamoru Seki, deliberately crashing his *Val* dive-bomber into the signal bridge of the carrier *Hornet*, comments were far from favourable, 'fiercely determined' was the least offensive.

A final example of the 'non-Kamikaze' or *Jibaku*, a spontaneous and individual suicide attack, can be cited. This time the unit involved was an Army Air Force one, and this is important as the general impression given is that all Japanese aerial suicide attacks were conducted by Navy pilots alone. This was far from the case and over 40% of Kamikaze attackers between October 1944 and the end of the war were carried out by Army pilots.

On 27 May the Allies made a surprise landing at Biak, one of the Schouten Islands off north-west New Guinea (Operation *Globetrotter*), where the Japanese had a strategic airfield, with 6th Division, US Army, being put ashore supported by US Navy Task Force 77. Ashore the Japanese Army had few aircraft available for defence, but those they had, four Kawasaki Ki-45 *Toryu* (Dragon Slayer, codenamed Nick) Type 2 twin-engined fighter aircraft armed with light 110lb bombs, under the command of Major Katsuhige Takada, IJA, Commander of 5th *Hiko Sentai*, immediately took off from Muni and made attacks on the ships offshore. Although a gallant effort, none of the four survived. Takada was reported in official Japanese reports as having attacked a cruiser and then a destroyer, and died in a suicide attack. The Japanese post-war account states that Takada, 'fearlessly crashed into an enemy warship in a 'suicide' attack. This was the first of the *Tokkou* attacks.'[4] Most American sources are totally dismissive of this claim although Professor

---

4. Japanese Monograph No. 136, *North of Australia Operation Record (January 1944–August 1945)*. Prepared by the Military History Section of the Headquarters, Army Forces East. Distributed by the Office of the Chief of Military History, Department of the Army.

S. E. Morison wrote in his multi-volume history[5] that the object of Takada's suicide dive was the destroyer *Sampson* (DD-394, Commander Thomas Martin Fleck, USN), 'The Japanese pilot made a deliberate effort to suicide crash *Sampson*; but anti-aircraft fire clipped off part of the wing, and the plane passed over the bridge and struck the water 400 yards beyond.' The crash damaged the nearby submarine chaser *SC-699* which had to be towed away with casualties. Takada's crewman, Sergeant-Major Motomiya, apparently survived the crash.

The difference between being hit by a Japanese suicide aircraft before the 'official' date of 21 October 1944, and after it, might, to most of us, seem rather academic! Others deem that 25 October was the real 'official' start date of the Kamikaze campaign. Certainly the crews of such ships might consider that armchair warriors who insist on what they deem to be a vital difference of a few days, or even a few hours, being of paramount importance, is rather bizarre. However, the crew of one ship that *was* struck by a suicide aircraft on exactly that first date, but unfortunately early in the morning and not at the 'official' time of later that same afternoon, felt rather bemused by the whole debate. Especially as Japanese sources do not agree.

On 13 October 1944 Rear Admiral Masafumi Arima, IJN, a noted aviator, then based at Clark Field, stripped himself of his symbols of rank and boarded a Mitsubishi G4M twin-engined bomber (code named *Betty*), vowing to destroy an enemy carrier and never to return. He made an attack against the carrier *Franklin*, but was shot down by the combat air patrol (CAP) before he could crash into her. Back in Tokyo, propaganda was whipped up which alleged that he had in fact carried out his attack and that he had crippled the ship, and by so doing he had 'lit the fuse of the ardent wishes of his men.'[6] Arima might not have hurt the *Franklin* but he may well have achieved the latter ambition and indeed lit the fuse! How close did Arima come to achieving his goal?

Franklin has a lucky let off

On 13 October 1944, the *Franklin* (CV-13, commanded by Captain John Malcolm Shoemaker, USN), Flagship of Rear Admiral Ralph Eugene Davidson, USN, of the Fast Carrier Task Group, was operating continuous air strikes against Japanese bases on the island of Formosa. In the late afternoon, a favourite time for the air attacks, she had recovered all her strike aircraft. Because there had been enemy snoopers in the area all day, she had assumed full Battle Stations at 16.54 as a precaution, but had stood down to Readiness III from this state at 17.27, although all her 40mm guns and the fire control stations remained fully manned, as they were between sunrise and sunset when within range of the enemy. The eight fighters of her CAP were returning to land back aboard at this time, when, without any warning from the Combat Information Center (CIC), a force of five *Betty* twin-engined bombers, each carrying a torpedo, suddenly appeared

5. Morison, Professor Samuel Eliot, *History of the United States Naval Operations in World War II, Volume 8; New Guinea and the Marianas*, Boston: 1953, Brown & Little.
6. Leckie, Robert, *Strong Men Armed; The United States Marines Against Japan*, Cambridge, Mass.: 1997. De Capo Press.

from out of a rain squall off her port side. They came in low in conventional torpedo-bomber attack mode, some 50–70 feet above the water, spaced at one-minute intervals. It was all very professionally done. One *Betty* was apparently forced to turn away by the intense barrage put up by the cruisers and destroyers on the screen, but the remaining quartet kept boring in. *Franklin*'s rudder was put over to full left and her AA guns began engaging at about 4,000 yards range. The leading plane was hit continually and began to burn as it continued in on a bearing of 270 degrees, but was not stopped. The torpedo was released at a range of 500 yards and passed under the ship's stern, while the *Betty* itself attempted to crash into the ship even though well on fire by this time and difficult to control. This aircraft hit the deck on the port side, abaft the island, then slid across the flight deck and went over the starboard beam, exploding as it hit the water. The only damage to the flight deck was caused by the Kamikaze's propellers gouging the wooden deck in several places as the plane skidded across. The *Franklin* resumed her original base course and the second and third bombers were destroyed by the barrage from the fleet and one of *Franklin*'s fighters still aloft. The fourth *Betty* made a conventional torpedo drop from off the port bow and *Franklin* went to full right rudder, and the starboard engine was backed causing the torpedo to miss about 50 feet from her bow, while the attacker was shot to pieces and after hopping over the bow, where it brushed the starboard gun sponsons, damaging two 20mm guns, it went into the water in flames. The ship's casualties were confined to one man killed and ten wounded. Three of the ship's 20mm gun mountings were temporarily put out of action, but all repairs were done by the ship's company and she did not have to withdraw from action.

Ugaki's early thoughts

Maybe suicide missions had occupied like-minded senior officers' minds still earlier. Consider the entry of Admiral Matome Ugaki for Wednesday 20 July 1944. Saipan had fallen, and Vice Admiral Chūichi Nagumo and Lieutenant General Yoshitsugu Saito, IJA, had committed *hari kiri*. On that day, as Guam was being invaded, the Admiral was aboard his flagship, the battleship *Yamato*, undergoing a night warfare practice off Singapore, many miles away from where the fighting was taking place. After the exercise he confided to his diary, 'Unless a commander leads the rest in devising, utilising new weapons, and contemplating new ideas by making use of past battle lessons and in repeated earnest training, I firmly believe that, in the end, it will be impossible to recover from our present plight.'[7] Was Ugaki even then contemplating the widespread use of suicide as a final weapon in Japan's armoury? One thing is certain; there was a widespread mind-set in existence among young and old fighting men alike. It just needed a determined man to strike the spark.

On 21 September 1944, Halsey's Task Force 58 approached to within forty miles of the Philippines and Mitscher's carriers launched four strong attacks on airfields in the vicinity of Manila, including Clark Field, which continued the following day.

---

7. Ugaki, Admiral Matome – *Fading Victory – The Diary of Admiral Matome Ugaki 1941–1945*, Annapolis, MD: Naval Institute Press, 1991.

These attacks softened up the Japanese defences and the 1st Air Fleet's counter-attacks failed to inflict any damage whatsoever. Ugaki was frustrated, writing 'If the planes are to be expended anyway, attack the enemy and perish!' He scorned the policy of husbanding strength for the main battle being planned (The *Sho-Go* Operation, Operation Victory).[8]

The Beginning

As early as 25 June 1944, Captain Motoaru Okamua, IJN, commanding 341 Air Group and Tateyama Air Base at Tokyo, told Vice-Admiral Shigeru Fukudome, IJN, Commander 2 Air Fleet that: 'In our present situation I firmly believe that the only way to swing the war in our favour is to resort to crash-dive attacks with our planes. There is no other way.' He added that, 'There will be more than enough volunteers to save our country.' He compared the tactic to a swarm of bees, 'They Sting, They Die.' The idea proved too radical then, but after the Leyte Gulf battles (23 to 26 October 1944) things looked so black that the idea was re-introduced. Two days prior to that disaster for Japan, Captain Eiichiro Jyo, captain of the carrier *Chiyoda*, sent a memo suggesting that a special crash-dive unit be formed; he volunteered to command it.

Vice-Admiral Takejiro Ōhnishi, IJN, who had been overseeing the Bureau of Aviation Ordnance at Naval Headquarters in Tokyo, attended a top-level conference chaired by Commander Tamai Asaichi, IJN, on 14 October 1944, to make a stunning suggestion. He is alleged to have announced that 'In my opinion, there is only one way of assuring that our meagre strength be effective to a maximum degree. That is to organize attack units composed of Zero fighters armed with 500lb bombs with each plane to crash dive into an enemy carrier. What do you think?'[9] Although most were taken aback by the extremity of the measure proposed, Ōhnishi's option was universally accepted by the meeting as policy with hardly any dissenting voice. Ōhnishi was ordered to put his policy into practice forthwith. Accordingly Ōhnishi was appointed to command the 1st Air Fleet based in the Philippines. He took up his new post on 17 October.

Within two days, following the discussions, approval had been given to adopt suicide attacks and volunteers were called for immediately from the 201st *Kokutai* (Air Group) based at Clark/Mabalacat airfield, so serious had Japan's position become. On 20 October the Special Attack Corps formed its first unit from these volunteers commanded by Lieutenant Commander Tadashi Nakajima, IJN. He named it the *Yamato* unit which was equipped with eight Mitsubishi Navy Type 0 (Allied code name *Zeke*, commonly known as Zero) single-engined fighter aircraft adapted to carry bombs. These flew to Cebu and were ready for operations the following day as the First Kamikaze or *Shimpū* (Divine Wind – so named after two opportune Typhoons, which legend had it had providentially arisen and destroyed two huge invasion fleets sent by Kublai Khan against Japan in 1274 and in 1281) Special Attack Corps. In all, twenty-four pilots and aircraft in four units,

8. Ugaki, Admiral Matome – *Fading Victory – The Diary of Admiral Matome Ugaki 1941–1945,* Annapolis, MD: Naval Institute Press, 1991.

9. Morris, Ivan, *The Nobility of Failure,* New York: 1975. Random House.

named after the four *Tai* symbols of Japanese spirit, as expressed by the poem of Norinaga Motoori, as the *Asahi, Shikishima, Yamato* and *Yamazakura*, were established.

Ugaki celebrated the establishment of the first Kamikaze units on the eve of the decisive Leyte Gulf battle; an entry in his diary of Saturday 21 October revealed just how pleased he was that this was to be done. 'In view of the present situation, the First Air Fleet is going to organise a Kamikaze Special Attack Corps with twenty-six carrier fighters of the 201st Air Group, all of its present strength, of which thirteen are suicidal ones. They are divided into four units. They intended to destroy enemy carriers without fail – at least put them out of order for a while – before the thrust of the surface force, when they come to the sea east of the Philippines. Oh, what a noble spirit this is! We are not afraid of a million enemies or a thousand carriers because our whole force shares the same spirit.'[10]

The *Shikishima* unit attacks

Lieutenant Yukio Seki took off from Mabalacat airfield, eager to conduct his voluntary suicide attack four times between the 20 and 24 October, but on each occasion had been forced to return having failed to find a suitable target.

At 16.25 on 21 October, two *Zekes* took off from Cebu with a solitary escorting fighter. Later one of the Kamikaze planes and the fighter returned to base without sighting a suitable target. The *Zeke* of Lieutenant (j.g.) Yoshiyasu Kuno did not come back.

Two days later a second attack was launched from the same base with another pair of *Zeke* suicide aircraft, and these also vanished without trace. No Allied ship was attacked by the three missing aircraft. On 25 October a greater effort was made in conjunction with the naval battles under way in Leyte Gulf. A fifth attempt was made, with the aircraft of the *Shimpu Tokubetsu Kōgekitai*[11] taking their departure at 07.25 local time to hunt for American forces east of the Philippines. At 10.10, according to Japanese observers, the Americans were located. In a later translated and published account, this US fleet consisted of four or five battleships escorted by in excess of thirty cruisers and destroyers on a northerly course with a CAP of twenty fighters overhead. Thirty minutes later came a report of a second group, composition not listed, bearing 085 degrees about 90 miles from Tacloban. On this occasion sorties were mounted, not only from Cebu, but from Mabalacat and Davao also. And this time there were results and spectacular results at that. Two days later the *Zeke* suicide aircraft were joined by Navy Type 99 dive-bombers, (code name *Val*) of Attack Unit 701 and the assaults increased in intensity.

---

10. Ugaki, Admiral Matome – *Fading Victory – The Diary of Admiral Matome Ugaki 1941–1945*, Annapolis, MD: Naval Institute Press, 1991.
11. Mainichi Shinbunsha, *Bessatsu Ichiokunin no Showa-shi-Tokubetsu Kōgeki-tai-Nihon no Sen-shi Bekkan 4*, Tokyo: 1979, Mainichi Shinbunsha. The Japanese armed forces used the briefer title *Tokuetsu Kōgekitai* – Special Attack Force, while the more general Japanese public reduced this to *Tokkōtai* or *Tokkō*, which meant all organised suicide attacks. The terms *Kamikaze* – Divine or God Wind – and *Shimpu* were considered synonymous, but only the latter term took hold in the West.

Not until 5 November did the Japanese Army Air units join in these attacks, according to Dr. Yashuo Izawa.[12] But many Australian and American sailors well might think otherwise.

Australia damaged by suicide attack

Another disputed attack, which many American historians simply refuse to acknowledge as a Kamikaze attack at all, took place on 21 October 1944. The invasion launched to re-take the Philippines had begun the day before, with the ships of the US 7th Fleet giving full support to General Douglas MacArthur and his troops ashore. A strong Royal Australian Navy (RAN) contingent was part of this fleet and included the heavy cruisers *Australia* and *Shropshire,* destroyers *Arunta* and *Warramunga,* the frigate *Gascoyne,* landing ships *Kanimbla, Manoora* and *Westralia,* and Harbour Defence Motor Launch *HDML1074* which surveyed the beaches.

Early that morning (a memorial day for the RAN, it being Trafalgar Day) the fire support ships were up-anchoring when they were surprised by a lone aircraft. This was identified as a Navy Type 99 Aichi D3A2 *Val* naval dive-bomber but was more probably an Army Type 99 Mitsubishi Ki-51 *Sonia* light bomber, which, in possessing a distinctive fixed undercarriage, was frequently mistaken for a *Val*. Several Ki-51s from the Air Force's 6th Flying Brigade *(Hiko Dan)* made attacks from Lipa and San Jose airfields that day, and claimed to have hit and set afire a 'transport ship.'

Whatever its origins, this aircraft suddenly appeared low over the water from the direction of the land unannounced and passed between the two heavy cruisers. Fire was opened, which was apparently hitting and this lone aircraft turned away to the west. It was reported that it appeared to skim the sea but pulled up, turning back towards the ships once more while still heavily engaged by all guns that would bear. Bearing a charmed existence, this '*Val*' then passed along *Australia*'s port side before turning in and steering straight for the cruiser's bridge, strafing the decks as it approached. The 4–inch and 2–pdr pom-pom on this side of the cruiser were 'wooded' by the close approach and would not bear for a time, but when they could resume fire they did so, either killing the pilot or putting him off his aim. Either way the *Val* hit the ship's foremast just below the crow's nest, which had two supporting struts fractured while the mast itself bent with the impact. This collision had the effect of spinning the plane by the wing-root and it went into the sea at 06.05, but not before its fuel tanks detonated in the air directly overhead. Flaming aviation fuel ('Avgas' in American parlance) and burning aircraft parts rained down on the ship's open bridge, its air defence position and exposed upperworks, causing horrendous burns and wounds among those unlucky enough to be caught in the open. The Type 273 radar lantern fell down onto the compass platform while both the high angle directors and the director control tower were put

12. Japanese Monograph No.84, *Philippines Area Naval Operations Part II* (October–December 1944). Prepared by the Military History Section of the Headquarters, Army Forces East. Distributed by the Office of the Chief of Military History, Department of the Army.

out of action. *Australia*'s commanding officer, Captain Emile Frank Verlaine 'Dishy' Dechaineux, DSO, RAN, received a shard of hot metal through his stomach as he sat in his chair. He was carried below but died soon afterward. The ship's Navigation Officer, Commander John Rayment, RAN, was also mortally wounded. The senior officer of the RAN squadron, Commodore John Collins, RAN, and Commander Richard Peek, RAN, the gunnery officer, were also hit and badly burned. In total thirty officers and men died agonisingly then or of their wounds later, while twenty-six others were badly injured, and thirty-eight more were seared and blackened unrecognisably. Collins and Peek survived, but command of the RAN Squadron devolved upon Captain Charles Allred Godfrey Nichols, MVO, DSO, RN, of the *Shropshire*. As for *Australia*, her resulting fires were soon brought under control and within half-an-hour much of the wreckage had been cleared away and she was subsequently sent back to Manus escorted by *Warramunga*.

That this was a deliberate Kamikaze attack was totally dismissed by American historian Samuel E Morison, who claimed, 'This was not an organised attack.'[13] and most other American historians agree with his verdict. But in a detailed analysis, submitted many years later, Richard Peek, by then a Rear-Admiral, was adamant that it *was* indeed a deliberate suicide attack. Peek wrote:

'At that time there were still people who charitably believed that the aircraft crashed onto us by mistake, but among those of us who saw the incident, there was no doubt as to the pilot's suicidal tendencies.'

He described the attack thus:

'The 'plane, a *Val*, was one of a small group which had appeared out of the dark of a western land horizon in the first light of dawn, all of which were engaged briefly as they flew overhead, and were lost in the half light. Our *Val* was next seen diving at an angle of 10–15 degrees from almost directly astern and at a visibility range of perhaps 2000 yards. Because of the stern approach, the 8–barrelled pom-pom would not bear, although one of them managed to 'jump' the safety training stops, and get away a few rounds at an angle of sight of about 45 degrees and above. Apart from this fire, two single 40mm using eye-shooting, and two single 20s with Mark 1C sights, engaged the aircraft with no appreciable result, although the pilot's aim was slightly upset so that he hit the foremast with his wing root and went on over the side instead of falling aboard and adding to the fires.'[14]

---

13. Morison, Professor Samuel Eliot, *History of the United States Naval Operations in World War II, Volume 12 – Leyte – June 1944 – January 1945*, Boston: 1958, Brown & Little.
14. Australian War memorial- Private Record: MSS-703, Folder number: 1 of 1, DPI: 300. Peek, R, *Guns Versus Suicide Bombers*, Conflict W2, AWM file: 91/0572. Reproduced by permission of copyright holder.

It was certainly on this day that a trio of A6M *Zeke*s were despatched from Cebu on a Kamikaze mission, albeit later that afternoon. This mission was one of several that proved abortive; two of the aircraft returned without making attacks and one failed to return. This latter aircraft was piloted by Reserve Lieutenant (j.g.) Kōfu Kuno, of *Hikōtai* 301 *Yamato-tai* (Spirit of Japan) unit from Cebu, whom the Japanese themselves list as having died conducting a 'Special Attack' that day.

In retrospect, and as stated above, it now appears more likely that the attacker may have been a Ki-51 *Sonia* of the 6th Flying Brigade *Hiko Dan* operating out of San Jose, Mindoro Island. They had been practicing attacking shipping, not their usual role, but were still not very good at ship recognition. Six of these aircraft were despatched that morning, of which three failed to return. It is thought that of the three pilots killed, either First Lieutenant Takeo Morita or Sergeant Chōbei Itano was the one who attacked *Australia*. Another such unit, the 65th Fighter Regiment (FR), sortied from Lipa airfield and one failed to return. A third possibility is a sortie by three other Ki-51s of the 66th FR, of which two failed to return while the survivor claimed to have set afire a 8,000–ton 'transport ship', which the three-funnelled *Australia* might well possibly have looked like to an Army pilot unfamiliar with ship targets. In short this suicide attempt is thought to have been another example of the *Jibaku*.

Guns versus Suicide Bombers

Admiral Sir Richard Peek later submitted a detailed analysis of the attack, which contained many very pertinent comments which, had they been studied at the time, might have been very helpful. He summarised his experience thus:

(a) The only sure way of stopping suicide aircraft is to burst a heavy AA shell close to them. Whether VT [variable-time] fuse is as effective as firing by Automatic Barrage Unit (ABU) is debatable. I have seen aircraft continue to come in low through numerous 5in VT bursts and on one occasion saw a diving aircraft disintegrated by a 4 inch shell (possibly 8 inch) fire by ABU, but on another occasion I have seen a 5in VT shell do exactly the same, to a torpedo bomber at about 200 feet.

(b) It is possible to stop low level suiciders [verbatim] by close range fire, but close range fire at diving targets seems ineffective, though it is possible that effectively aimed fire may force the aircraft to miss. For this purpose multiple remote power director controlled 40mm (or pom poms) are essential.

(c) 20mm, although they saved the bridge personnel in the final attack, are virtually useless in cruisers and above facing suicide bombing, and the only use for these weapons in cruisers and above appears to be a last card against dive bombers.

(d) It is essential to keep every gun firing at the aircraft [to] the last minute. This seems very obvious and elementary, but the attacks are very terrifying – each man feels each aircraft is personally aimed at him, and if the aircraft are not fired at they cannot miss.

(e) All possible personnel should be kept off the upper deck – supply parties, cipher, radar and W/T staff off watch, medical parties and every person without a definite upper deck action station should be kept below. Not only does this reduce the casualties, but it has the advantages that your potential spare gun crews are not terrified unnecessarily, and it does away with people on the upper deck who have nothing to think about except their own safety and whose rushes for cover must effect any gun crews and lookouts who are at all shaken.

(f) Finally, at the end of five suicide hits we were still able to fight. True, our speed was limited to a safe 17 knots and we were short of hands, but the guns and engines were all working and we were able to carry out our bombardment missions. I doubt whether five hits by any other weapon could have caused such a minimum of damage.'

However, *Australia* was not the only warship attacked prior to the first 'official' mission. The light cruiser *Reno* (CL-96, Captain Ralph Clonts Alexander, USN,) was damaged on 14 October by a suicide aircraft crashing and exploding on the quarterdeck (or fantail in US parlance). Her number six, twin-5in turret was partially incapacitated by the blast, but the turret officer kept the guns firing and when approached by other suicide aircraft, *Reno* claimed to have destroyed four of them. On 24 October the transport vessel *Augustus Thomas*, Master Alfred A Pedersen, which was at anchor that morning, was struck by a twin-engined *Betty* bomber while the ancient US Navy tug *Sonoma* (ATO-12) was secured alongside taking on fresh water. The aircraft hit the transport dead amidships and her cargo of aviation gas and ammunition, plus a deck cargo of landing mats for the airfield ashore, ignited. *Augustus Thomas*, (MC 2151) an Army Transport Service (USAT) chartered Liberty Ship, suffered no casualties and was subsequently beached by the tugs *Chowanoc* (ATF-100) and *Whippoorwill* (ATO-169). One of the *Betty*'s wings slammed into the *Sonoma* and two bombs fell between the two vessels, followed by two large explosions. Another tug, *Chockasaw* (ATF-83), and *LCI-72* closed her starboard side to fire-fight and take off her wounded. An attempt to beach her on Dio Island failed and she sank that afternoon. Also lost that day was *LCI (L)-1065* which was struck on her quarterdeck by an Army Type 97 Mitsubishi Ki-21 heavy bomber (codename *Sally*) that had been set on fire by anti-aircraft gunnery. Fierce fires broke out and one officer and six men were killed and five others of her crew were listed as missing. Also hit while anchored in San Pedro Bay was the *David Dudley Field* (MC0470, Master Albion M Burbank). None of these victims of individual suicide attacks 'counted' as Kamikaze attacks apparently. But the ships were sunk and the men were just as dead.

Chapter Two

The Kamikazes Make their Mark

'… if they are on land, they would be bombed down, and if they are in the air, they would be shot down. That's sad. Too sad. To let the young men die beautifully, that's what *Tokko* is. To give beautiful death, that's called sympathy.'

Ōhnisi, Admiral Takijiro, Commander, First Air Fleet

Let us briefly skip ahead of our story to the aftermath of the traumatic naval battle off Samar, during the Leyte Gulf series of conflicts.

St Lo – the first Kamikaze escort-carrier victim.

Often described in history books as the 'first' true Kamikaze attack, the escort carrier *St Lo* (CVE-63 Captain Francis J McKenna, USN,) was sunk on 25 October 1944 after the heroic actions off Samar during the complex, but decisive, Battle of Leyte Gulf. This little 8,188–ton escort carrier was one of the numerous *Casablanca* class and had formerly been assigned the names *Chapin Bay* and then *Midway*. She could carry twenty-seven aircraft and her only defensive armament was a single aft-mounted 5in gun, eight twin-40mm guns and twenty single 20mm Oerlikons. Originally part of a fifty-strong group mass-produced by Henry J. Kaiser as convoy escorts, most of them which actually served in the Pacific operated as close-air-support providers for amphibious landings and protection of the subsequent beachheads ashore, and were nicknamed 'Jeep' carriers. It was while acting in this role during the recovery of the Philippines that Rear-Admiral Thomas L. Sprague's Task Group 77.4, one of the Group's 'Taffy' sub-units, were involved inadvertently in holding off Vice-Admiral Takeo Kurita's battle fleet of four battleships, thirteen cruisers and nineteen destroyers after they broke through the San Bernadino Strait unopposed and headed for the American invasion transport fleet.

As the various *Taffys*[1] came under heavy shellfire from the Japanese fleet, *St Lo* was busy launching aircraft to contribute to the non-stop counter attacks being made by the desperately outnumbered American ships against the approaching Japanese 2nd Fleet ('Central Force') under Admiral Takeo Kurita, who were intent on their destruction. And, despite being straddled by heavy shells, she managed to launch four torpedo bombers and fifteen strafing fighters from 07.18, and even opened fire with her solitary

---

1. *Taffy* 1, *Taffy* 2, etc – From each Task Group's distinct voice radio call signs.

5in gun. Amazingly Kurita, victory well within his grasp, withdrew his forces and up to that point *St Lo* had suffered no damage.

At 10.10, thinking the worst of their ordeal had passed, the carrier stood down from General Quarters (GQ) and ten minutes later men started to relax in relays while some returning aircraft were landed aboard. It was shortly after this, at 10.51, that gunfire was heard and AA shell bursts observed ahead, as were many aircraft off the starboard bow approaching at heights varying from 1,000 to 3,000 feet. A group of hostiles was tracked as it moved swiftly down *St.Lo*'s starboard flank. As the hostiles passed through the Task Group, one of them, identified in the Combat Report as a '*Zeke* 52, with a bomb under each wing', was hit by AA fire from the nearby *White Plains* (CVE-66, Captain Dennis Joseph Sullivan, USN,) and veered off its previous course at 10.51. This machine continued in a right turn and approached the *St.Lo*'s stern very rapidly. He was taken under fire by the aft starboard AA weapons, without any apparent further effect.

At 10.53 this *Zeke* roared over the ramp at a height of less than 50 feet and then, 'he appeared to push over sufficiently to hit the deck at about number 5 wire, 15 feet to the port side of the centre-line. There was a tremendous crash and flash of an explosion as one or both bombs exploded. The plane continued skidding up the deck leaving fragments strewn about but, doing little physical damage and its remnants went over the bow.'[2] However, the bombs carried by this aircraft proved lethal as they penetrated into the ship and exploded on the hangar deck below. At once huge fires broke out among the stowed aircraft there and the ship's own gasoline fuel supply. These fires spread rapidly and her bomb and torpedo magazines were engulfed, both blowing up with shocking explosions that gutted the ship. It was not clear whether the bombs had been released prior to this aircraft striking the deck.

At first Captain McKenna thought that his command had escaped serious damage. 'There was a hole in the flight deck with smouldering edges which sprang into flames.' The crew ran out hoses and began attacking these flames, but then it was seen that smoke was erupting through the hole and also belching out from either side of the ship, indicating a big fire on the hangar deck, which was at this point out of contact from the bridge. Ninety seconds later there was a severe explosion from the hangar deck, the detonation bulging the flight deck upward, and blasting smoke and fire through the hole. This first blast was followed almost at once by a second huge detonation which erupted to the rear of the original aperture and rolled the flight deck back like a sardine can. Yet a third heavy blast followed, hurling the forward elevator up out of its shaft and opening more of what remained of the flight deck. All power went off and the stern half of the ship was invisible from the bridge due to the fire and smoke, so much so that McKenna thought for a while it had actually broken off!

The *St Lo*, however, was still making way as her engine rooms continued to function but it was clear the ship was doomed and 'stop engines' was sounded as well as the call to stand by to abandon ship. Once *St Lo* had slid to a halt, 'abandon ship' was ordered and this was conducted in a calm and orderly manner with the wounded being lowered from the forecastle. Last away were Bugle Master Leonard Neale, Lieutenant-Commander

---

2. *St Lo* Action Report, Battle of Samar 25 October 1944, dated 23 November 1944.

Charles W Centner, USN, the Air Officer, and finally Captain McKenna. The rent and torn *St Lo* herself had initially listed heavily to port, but the later explosions appeared to have blown the starboard bottom of the ship out, causing her to heel back over to starboard and she sank, stern first, at 11.25.

Meanwhile more heavy detonations from below followed in rapid succession, number six was described as 'particularly violent' and number seven as a 'very violent explosion which threw much large debris into the air.' Explosion number eight was thought to have been the main bomb storage blowing up and it spread wreckage from the ship over a wide area of the ocean, inflicting further casualties among those in the water. There were also three underwater explosions, one heavy, two light after the *St Lo* had vanished beneath the waves, her grave being in position 11 degrees 10 minutes North, 126 degrees 05 minutes East. Men in the water were rescued by the destroyer *Heermann* (DD-532, Commander Dwight M. Agnew, USN,) who plucked 150 from the sea, and destroyer escorts *John C. Butler* (DE-339, Lieutenant Commander John E. Pace, USN,) *Raymond* (DE-341, Lieutenant Commander A. F. Beyer, Jr., USN,) and *Dennis* (DE-405, Lieutenant Commander S. Hansen, USN,) who herself rescued 434 men, although one of the injured died from his wounds.

The whole attack was witnessed by Chief Warrant Officer Hiroyoshi Nishizawa, who reported back to Tacloban that an enemy task force had been the target and that all five Kamikazes, led by Commander Yukio Seki, as the first such *Gunshin* (War God) at 10.45, attacked; Seki himself plunging into a carrier. His fellow *bakusō* pilots were Ensign Iwao Nakano, Ensign Nobuo Tani, Chief Petty Officer Hajime Nagamine and Chief Petty Officer Shigeo Oguro. Nishizawa was reported as saying a second pilot chose the same ship and also hit her, and that debris was blown high into the air. He also reported, according to the same source, that a second carrier was also hit and started to burn, while a light cruiser was also struck and sank 'instantly'. The final aircraft was reported not to have succeeded.[3]

While *St Lo* had certainly been a victim, the light cruiser was an entirely imaginary vessel, *no* light cruiser was attacked, or even approached by Kamikaze aircraft on this day whatsoever. So which ships were the *Shikishima* unit's victims?

Kalinin Bay takes punishment

Yet another casualty this fateful day was the *Kalinin Bay* (CVE-68, Captain Thomas Binney Williamson, USN). Like the *White Plains*, she had earlier been hit by shells from Admiral Takeo Kurita's 'Centre Force', which included among its many powerful warships, the battleships *Musashi* and *Yamato*. This was just part of a multi-pronged all-out attack on the American beachhead at Leyte Gulf by the Japanese fleet, but Kurita's ships alone had penetrated through to engage the escort carrier groups operating off the bridgehead. With victory seemingly within his grasp, however, Kurita reversed course, but not before he had inflicted considerable damage on the defending US warships. While the Japanese surface ships pulled out, that very same day the Kamikazes began their

---

3. Inoguchi and Nakajima, *Divine Wind, op cit,* pp 59–60.

attacks in force and it was against the American escort carriers, many already damaged, others still unscathed, that a quartet of suicide aircraft concentrated their venom. Two of these aircraft were shot down dangerously close in by the defensive barrage, while another got through and rammed the flight deck on the port side causing significant damage, killed five men and wounded fifty more. The fourth Kamikaze also got through and smacked into her after-port funnel. Despite this battering the *Kalinin Bay* did not sink although she had severe structural damage. She was sent back to Manus where she arrived on 1 November and was patched up sufficiently for her to sail home to San Diego where she was fully repaired between 27 November and 18 January 1945.[4]

The *Kitkun Bay* also further damaged

The final escort carrier Kamikaze casualty was the *Casablanca* Class 'Jeep' carrier *Kitkun Bay* (CVE-71, Captain John Perry Whitney, USN) which was attacked by an aircraft identified as an *Oscar* (Type 1 Nakajima Ki-43 *Hayabusa* [Peregrine Falcon]) or a *Zeke* 52 at 18.57. This aircraft just missed the bridge and hit the forward port catwalk of the ship, where one man was killed and sixteen wounded. Rear Admiral Ralph Andrew Ofstie, USN, aboard the carrier, recorded her attacker as a *Tony* (Type 3 Kawasaki Ki-61 *Hien* [Flying Swallow]). He also recorded that the ship suffered a small gasoline fire.[5] The resultant fire and flooding were brought under control, but her total casualty count was sixteen killed and thirty-seven wounded. She was withdrawn listing to Manus. Subsequently she was sent back to Pearl Harbor, and by 17 December she was repaired and able to resume operations once more – although the Kamikazes were not finished with her yet.

White Plains damaged

The *White Plains* (CVE-66, Captain Dennis Arthur Weller, USN) was another escort carrier from this same group, which had already been hit and damaged by gunfire from Japanese surface forces off Samar, when two Kamikazes took her for their main target. Her gunners scored telling hits on one of these aircraft which subsequently dove on and sank the *St.Lo*. The other Japanese aircraft was also heavily damaged while making an approach and went flaming into the water close astern of the *White Plains* herself. The impact threw a considerable amount of debris and splinters that peppered the ships upperworks and flight deck, but did not do any serious additional damage. Eleven men were injured but there were no deaths. The shell damage she had already received proved far more serious and necessitated the *White Plains* being sent back to San Diego for major repairs from 27 November onward. By 19 January 1945 she was fully effective once more and returned to full combat duties.

---

4. Action Report *Kalinin Bay*.
5. Action Report *Kitkun Bay*.

Summary of the first 'official' attack

One carrier sunk and two more sufficiently damaged that they had to be withdrawn from battle, for the expenditure of five aircraft. This debut showed promising results and to many Japanese it seemed to indicate that the Kamikaze method had some merit as an act of war. Whatever the moral compass of the young men 'body crashing' (*Tai-Atari*) to immortality, purely and objectively *as an act of war* those first results appeared to be what nowadays would be called 'cost effective.'

Admiral Kimpei Teraoka, IJN, Commander of the 1st Air Fleet, later stated:

> 'Conventional methods of warfare are no longer adequate. Since death is the inevitable fate of the young eagles, they should be allowed to die in the most worthwhile way. We must steel our hearts in order to win the war. It is necessary that the names of those who volunteer for this death mission be reported beforehand to the Imperial GHQ, in order that they prepare themselves with dignity and maintain a cool head.' He added: 'No, it would be better to work through their immediate superiors in view of the consequences. If the fighter pilots can first be organized, other units will automatically follow suit. If the air forces carry this out, they will in turn inspire the surface forces. If the entire Navy is inspired with this spirit, the Army too will no doubt follow in line. It was finally concluded that in order to save the country there was no other method than the crash-dive tactic. Further it was agreed that Admiral Ōhnishi, the incoming commander, would assume complete responsibility for the formation of the Special Attack Corps.'[6]

One American post-war view of these volunteers, arrogantly expressed, was totally dismissive, describing them thus, 'aviators manifestly unable to hit much of anything with bombs or torpedoes, would make up in guts what they lacked in skill'[7] However, Yukio Seki was regarded by his contemporaries as one of Japan's best remaining aviators, skilled in the art of dive-bombing, so much so that he had become an instructor at the Kasumigaura Training School. So such casual blanket allegations, even by the most distinguished of historians, need considerable examination and would seem to reflect the fact that some modern western assumptions were still as unenlightened in 1975 as they were uncomprehending in 1945. The same US historian, however, was forced to acknowledge that: 'the organization of the Kamikaze Corps had enormously increased the effectiveness of Japanese air power.' It was also stated that, 'In Halsey's fleet during November 1944, Kamikazes crashed into seven carriers, killing nearly 300 Americans and wounding hundreds more. In Kinkaid's fleet during the same period they hit two battleships, two cruisers, two attack transports and seven destroyers, one of which sank. Following three suicide crashes on his ships on November 25, Halsey withdrew

---

6. USSBS Interview, Admiral Kimpei Teraoka.
7. *The Naval Academy Illustrated History of the United States Navy;* Potter, E. B. 1975, Ty Crowell Company. New York, NY.

TF 38 temporarily to Ulithi to make repairs and to give his exhausted aviators a chance to rest.'[8]

The Japanese draw on aircraft and men to extend the technique

Once the Kamikaze concept had so convincingly proven itself in combat, many Japanese commanders were eager to extend its usage further. There were already a number of Nakajima-constructed A6M2b (*Zeke*) Model 21 *Bakusen* fighter-bomber conversions which could carry a single 500–lb bomb on an extra bomb rack below the fuselage. These were intended as replacements for the *Val* dive-bombers, which lacked the speed to be effective in their designed role and thus lent themselves for adoption as Kamikaze aircraft. The Model 52 and Model 52–*Koh Zekes*, constructed by both Mitsubishi and Nakajima, were even faster and stood the best chance of penetrating the American CAP, and most were expended in the suicide role. But in the end, losses were so enormous that practically any type of warplane, even floatplanes and trainers, were thrown into the melting pot and expended with their pilots, some of whom were barely trained at all in combat. In fact, with regard to the matter of pilots willing to volunteer for such missions, there proved to be no shortage. Contrary to most popular recorded histories, it was not just the officer class who proved willing to lay down their lives for their Emperor, but the ordinary conscript as well. As Yuki Tanaka revealed in the study *Japan's Kamikaze Pilots and Contemporary Bombers: War and Terror*, by far the greatest number of Kamikaze pilots were not college graduates but Petty Officers and NCOs straight from Navy and Army flight training units of whom 1,732 such Navy personnel died in suicide missions as against 782 officers; while it was a similar story in the Army where 708 NCOs died in Kamikaze attacks as against 621 officers. That officer cadets are generally depicted in such classics as *Kike Wadatsumi no Koe (Listen to the Voices from the Sea)* is because their diaries were preserved while those of the NCOs are not available to study.

Santee pounded

Returning to the events of 25 October 1944, the *Santee* (CVE-29, Captain Robert Edwin Black, Jr., USN) took damage from both above and below the waves almost at the same time. By a strange coincidence the ship was stuck by a Kamikaze at 07.40 that day, and it and its bomb went through to the hangar deck, killing sixteen men and wounding others. A fire was started, but this was very efficiently fought and was under control within a very short period. Not surprisingly, given the mayhem aboard at this time, when the Japanese submarine *I-56* (Lieutenant-Commander Gon Yamato) hit the carrier with a single torpedo at 07.56, it was mistaken for the detonation of a depth-charge which had been jettisoned by the carrier as a safety measure. Several compartments were flooded by this torpedo and *Santee* listed six degrees. Counter-flooding corrected this, but, with all eyes focussed aloft, no thought was given to

---

8. The *Naval Academy Illustrated History of the United States Navy;* Potter, E. B. 1975, Ty Crowell Company. New York, NY.

submarine attack. The repair teams managed to get her damage under control by as early as 09.35 and she even began to fly aircraft on and off once more. Eventually though, she was sent back to Seeadler Harbor and then to San Diego where more thorough repairs were carried out, enabling her to rejoin the fleet at the end of January 1945. Amazingly, even when examined in dry-dock, the real cause of her underwater damage was not then realised and only a post-war analysis revealed that she had been struck by a Kamikaze *and* a torpedo: truly, to survive both, *Santee* proved to be a tough little ship.

Suwannee at Leyte, Gulf October 1944

As part of TG77.4.1, the *Suwannee* (CVE-27, Captain William David Johnson, USN) part of Taffy 1, was badly damaged at 07.40 on the 25th by an A6M2/5 of the 201st *Kokutai*, the *Shikishima* unit, from Mabalacat/Clark, armed with a 500lb bomb. However, she may possibly have been selected for attack some days prior to this. On 21 October it was recorded that a total of six *Zekes* had been launched at 06.30 and three failed to return. Offshore, *Suwannee*'s air group had been kept busy in supporting American troops on Leyte from the 20th onwards as American landing operations had continued apace and continued on into the following day, but, at 07.55 on 21 October, an unidentified aircraft was reported by *Suwannee*'s radar and the CAP was vectored out to intercept, although the fighters were recalled before any 'Tally-ho' (signifying they had made a confirmed airborne sighting) was made. *Suwannee* then prepared to land-on her aircraft and turned to a course 340 degrees (True) into the wind at 18 knots to carry this out.

At 08.24 enemy fighters, with their wheels down to mimic American aircraft in the landing circuit, were identified astern of the escort carrier group. They were identified as *Zekes* and they closed upon the *Santee* to strafe and bomb her, but they missed and turned to attack *Suwannee* instead. These machines headed westward at an estimated 300 knots only about fifty feet above the waves as *Suwannee* went to General Quarters. At 08.34 these aircraft were sighted bearing 260 degrees about six miles out and closing fast, at an altitude of about 75 feet. The ships' guns destroyed one of the attackers and the CAP nailed the second. *Suwannee* only made a slight adjustment to her course as she was not attacked. No recorded Kamikaze attacks followed until four days later, but as the 20th had been the day of Seiki's first abortive mission, so, an unanswered question still remains had he been among the Japanese aircraft sighted on the 21st?

Returning to the fateful 25th, bogies were reported on the screen at 07.38, while TG77.4.1 was landing aircraft, and three Kamikazes, identified as *Zekes*, were visually sighted two minutes later. One of these was off *Santee*'s port quarter at an altitude of 8,000 feet and this aircraft made a 20 degree approach, crashing into the *Santee*'s forward flight deck. The second *Zeke* appeared within half-a-minute circling astern of *Suwannee* and was hit by the ship's gunfire. This attacker 'spiralled down, smoking slightly and then rolled over into a 45 degree dive heading for *Sangamon*. The only 5in shell fired from *Suwannee* hit the plane when it was about 500 feet from *Sangamon*, causing the plane to swerve slightly and crash into the water on *Sangamon*'s port side.' The third of the trio was sighted astern of *Suwannee* circling in the clouds at 8,000 feet. It was hit by AA fire and started to burn. As it did so the *Zeke* rolled over, 'putting it slightly on the starboard beam, dodged a pursuing F6F, then came straight down, hitting at 08.04 about 40 feet forward of the after elevator, slightly to the starboard side, making a hole in the flight deck about 10 feet in diameter.' This particular aircraft, piloted it is thought, by Petty Officer Tomisaku Kastsumata, hit the ship and the engine burst through the flight deck, leaving a ten-foot hole. The *Zeke*'s bomb, carried below its fuselage and released moments earlier, was estimated to be of 500lb, and exploded between the flight and hangar decks. It tore a hole 17 feet in diameter in the hangar deck starting a fire, and damaged the main deck where its blast failed to penetrate a welded seam; several arrestor wires were also destroyed on the flight deck. The aircraft's engine penetrated to the main deck. *Suwannee* had been given no time to take evasive action. The fires were quickly quenched, but the after elevator was inoperable and the ship had to be manoeuvred from the steering-engine room following the failure of both the gyro and main steering. Yet again the resilience of these little ships was remarkable, for by 10.09 the flight deck damage had been temporarily repaired and air operations were resumed. At 11.45 another *Zeke* made an attack on the *Petrof Bay* (CVE-80), Captain Joseph L 'Paddy' Kane, and *Suwannee* fired on it. This plane missed and escaped unharmed.

Suwannee's bomb disposal officer reported that no evidence had been recovered as to the bomb's fuses, tail assembly or bomb filler. The bomb and plane penetrated the flight deck with the bomb detonating about three feet above the hangar deck plates. Resulting splinter damage was extensive, with holing up to six inches in diameter and penetration up to 250 feet from impact through steel plate. He was of the opinion that the bomb was carried in an armed condition.

Amazingly the ship's crew dealt with this hit so effectively that she was able to continue launching air strikes against the Japanese fleet later the same day and also contributed to the dawn attacks the following morning. An outstanding achievement.

At 12.38 on 26 October another Kamikaze, also armed with a 500lb bomb, exacted revenge. This attacker dove into *Suwannee*'s forward elevator, destroying it. Three minutes later another Japanese aircraft scored a direct hit in the catapult machinery space at frame 84, with a 220lb bomb. The catapult was destroyed as was its associated machinery. Between these two direct hits, severe fires broke out both on the flight deck and in the hangar deck. The flimsy flight deck buckled with the intense heat and thirteen of her aircraft were destroyed in the blaze. This left the carrier inoperative, her bridge wrecked and abandoned, with temporary control directed from Battery II.

The ship's bomb disposal officer later reported that the bomb was seen to be released just prior to the Kamikaze striking the deck, with distinct holes of both plane and bomb about 20 feet apart. The bomb detonation was instantaneous, without penetration. The nose fuse and part of the bomb's nose section were recovered, which indicated a 500lb weapon. Victims of this second attack included *Suwannee*'s skipper, Captain Johnson, who was seriously wounded while in total *Suwannee*'s crew lost five officers and eighty enlisted men killed with a further thirteen officers and eighty-nine enlisted men wounded, with two officers and fifty-six enlisted men missing in action. *Suwannee* lay dead in the water only briefly however and was soon got underway again to rejoin the formation.

Examples of extreme heroism aboard the stricken ship were many. The Executive Officer's Report cited the case of one such anonymous hero, an uninjured enlisted man, positioned on the forecastle, which had been cut off from the rest of the ship by the flames. 'After several calls to have medical supplies brought to the forecastle for those seriously injured were unproductive of results, the enlisted man informed C.M. Barr, Aviation Chief Electrician's Mate (ACEM) that he would try to get through the flames to get medical supplies because he could no longer stand the sufferings of the wounded. Despite Barr's efforts to stop him, the man climbed to the 20mm mounts just forward of the flight deck and when Barr lost sight of him, was climbing toward the flight deck. Seconds later a TBM directly in his path exploded and the man was seen holding on to the starboard side of the flight deck with one leg blown off. Moments later he fell into the water and was not seen again. Every effort to ascertain his name has proved unavailing. It is a justifiable assumption that many similar cases occurred.'

One of the many who gave similar examples of bravery was CSF (AA) William S. Brooks, who was making his way forward along the hangar deck when he was knocked unconscious and injured in the abdomen by the force of the explosions. 'Upon regaining consciousness he crawled under the planes to the valves controlling the water curtain and the forward sprinkler system, and opened them, thus preventing a fire on the forward elevator, which had been smashed down to hangar deck level, from spreading to the gassed planes on the hangar deck which in all probability would have made the fire uncontrollable, resulting in the loss of the ship.'

The success of the Kamikazes were accredited to:

(a) Ships operating as close as 30 miles to large land masses resulted in the radar screen being blocked in bearing up to 180 degrees.
(b) Failure of the actual 'fitting' fade charts in use, even though fade charts in use were constructed and based on many radar calibration runs.[9]

It had been a startling, if not stunning, debut. The Kamikaze attacks, frightening and dangerous as they appeared, had caught the Allies by surprise. Worse was to come.

---

9. Above quotations from *Suwannee* Action Reports in CVE27/A16–3(3) (95–hlr) dated 6 November 1944.

Chapter Three

The Rising Tide

'The pilot did not start out on his mission with the intention of committing suicide. He looked upon himself as a human bomb which would destroy a certain part of the enemy fleet for his country. He considered it a glorious thing.'

Lieutenant-General Takijirō Kawabe,
Deputy Chief, Imperial General Headquarters

The whole point of the suicide attack was to inflict as much damage as possible on the enemy, so it made more sense to attack the transports packed with troops rather than heavily armed warships. On occasions this was understood; often it failed to be.

Ugaki recorded in his diary for Tuesday 31 October 1944: 'The Kamikaze Special Attack Corps attacked the enemy task force east of Suluan Island yesterday, and inflicted firm damage to three carriers and one battleship, of which one CV was reported surely sunk.' The diary entry for 1 November recorded: 'A plane of the *Baika* (Plum Blossom) unit of the Kamikaze Special Attack Corps sighted a battleship or a cruiser sailing south in Panaola Strait and hit the roof (*sic*) of her foremast, causing a big fire.'[1]

Liberty Ships targeted

The third day of November saw a suicide attacker crash into the *Matthew P. Deady*, (MC 0545, Master K. D. Frye) while this Liberty ship was lying in Tacloban Bay. At 05.30 the aircraft had made a dive-bombing run without scoring any hits, and then circled around aft and returned to machine-gun the ship. The bomber then dived into the port side of the *Deady* and exploded on top of No.2 20mm mounting, with one wing ploughing into No.1 mounting, the detonation igniting the acetylene and oxygen-tank deck cargo. Heavy casualties among the US Army troops aboard left fifty-seven men dead or missing and more than one hundred others wounded. The unfortunate gunners of the Navy Armed Guard suffered two dead and four horribly burnt.[2] The *Matthew P. Deady* was the first troopship to be hit by suicide aircraft, though not the last.

On 4 November the US Maritime Commission (MARCOM) turbine-engined Type C1–B cargo ship, *Cape Constance* (Master Axel Eichel Uldall), with a cargo of motor fuel,

---

1. Ugaki, Admiral Matome – *Fading Victory – The Diary of Admiral Matome Ugaki 1941–1945*, Annapolis, MD: Naval Institute Press, 1991.
2. Armed Guard Report, ss *Matthew P. Deady*, *Report of Voyage of Matthew P. Deady, K. D. Frye, Master*, dated 3 January 1945.

was anchored in Nakagsuklu Wan ('Buckner Bay', so named by the invading Americans in honour of US Army General Simon Bolivar Buckner) when she was targeted by a Kamikaze which 'ripped its wings off when it struck our mainmast and bounced off the deck boards into the sea alongside.'[3]

Further transport losses

Although it takes us out of sequence, further transport losses can be summarised thus. On 12 November five combat transports were damaged by Kamikaze attacks at Leyte. Had the Japanese concentrated their assaults against such thin-skinned and (relatively) defenceless targets, instead of repeatedly attacking heavily armed and armoured warships, they may have achieved a better return on their efforts. The ships concerned were the *Alexander Majors* (MC 2262), *Thomas Nelson* (MC0030), *Leonidas Merritt* (MC 1564), both the latter being USAT vessels, *Jeremiah M. Daily* (MC 1724) and *Benjamin Ide Wheeler* (MC 0675).

The experience of the *Alexander Majors* (Master John Michael Griffin) was typical. She was loaded with a cargo of army trucks, tractors for airfield building, oil and gasoline as well as 407 US Army personnel. She was attacked while lying offshore from Dulag Harbour. That afternoon, around 17.18, a force of ten *Zekes* attacked the anchorage and the fat juicy targets lying there. One *Zeke* selected the *Majors*, but a hit from a 5in round from her Armed Guard knocked this aircraft up in the air so that it was deflected past the starboard wing of her bridge and into the ship's main mast. The impact detonated the bomb, and both plane and bomb detonated in the air above the vessel. Numbers' 2 and 3 hold covers were both blown off and the deck cargo of fuel ignited set the fore part of the ship ablaze. Fortunately the bulk of the Army passengers had already disembarked and only thirteen remained on board or else loss of life would have been heavy. As it was the blaze was brought under control although the *Majors* lost two men dead and sixteen wounded. She survived, was patched up and later returned to San Francisco on 15 September 1945, and repaired before being sold into commercial service.

Other ships were hit harder; the *Thomas Nelson* (MC0030, Master Olaf Winnes) was carrying Army personnel and equipment for the 345th Bomb Group, but unloading was repeatedly delayed as the airstrips ashore were not ready to receive them. Thus, when at lunch time on 12 November she was hit aft by a suicide plane, the loss of life was heavy, with more than 225 Army personnel killed, wounded or missing in addition to five of her Armed Guard killed and two wounded. Much heroism was displayed amongst this carnage.[4] As bad was the damage done to the *Jeremiah M. Daily* (Master Harry J Mannering), with 800 Army personnel on board. At 14.16 four single-engined enemy aircraft approached over Samar Island. At about three miles range this group broke up into two pairs and commenced shallow dive-bombing attacks at an angle of 45 degrees before one of them crashed into a Liberty Ship one mile off. The report read: 'The

---

3. Roush, Jr, Colonel John H., *World War II Reminiscences*, San Rafael: 2013 Privately Published.
4. Brokaw, Tom, *The Greatest Generation*, 1998: New York, Delta/Dell Publishing.

other plane pulled out of the dive at 150 feet and dropped one or two bombs on a ship lying 1000 yards on the subject vessel's starboard bow, then swerved at mast height and crashed into the forward starboard corner of the wheelhouse of the *Daily*. Both of these planes were apparently undamaged when they commenced their suicide dive. The only gun in action of the *Daily* was the No.5 20mm (forward starboard wing of bridge) which expended fifteen to twenty-five rounds. The plane crashed through the bridge protection into the wheelhouse and a bomb (surmised to be incendiary from holes burned in deck) was believed to have been knocked loose and exploded by a guy wire to the booms on No.3 hatch, which were lowered. Flaming gasoline and parts of the plane were showered about causing a number of casualties among the troops on deck forward, and also igniting a quantity of range fuel, which was stored abreast No.3 hatch, port side, blocking the port alleyway'. On the ship's bridge deck, the wheelhouse, chartroom, Master's office and quarters, and all bridge equipment, were completely destroyed by impact and fire from the exploding aircraft. The radio room and equipment, Armed Guard Officer's and Radio Operators quarters were also almost immediately destroyed by the explosion and burning gasoline.[5] Again the Army passengers suffered with 100 of their number killed and forty-three injured while the Armed Guard gunners lost six more men. Among the casualties were the Captain, the Chief Engineer, the Third Officer, the Radio Officer and the Armed Guard lieutenant. In addition to these ships the repair ships *Egeria* (ARL-8, Lieutenant A H Wilson) and *Achillies* (ARL-41, Lieutenant Clarence Cisin) also received damage. *Achillies* was hit by a Kamikaze on 5 November and suffered forty-three dead or missing plus many wounded, while on 12 November the *Egeria* shot down a Kamikaze, which crashed just 25 feet off her port side and seriously damaged a Landing Craft Infantry (LCI), secured alongside.

A British viewpoint on American Escort carriers

Commander F. Harry E. Hopkins, RN, the British Naval Liaison Officer with the US Pacific Fleet, called on Admiral Sir James Somerville. From his observations of the actions off the Philippines he was scathing about the design of American escort carriers (CVE). 'He criticises the design of the US CVEs on the score that the flight decks are much too light and these are penetrated by the falling engines of suicide bombers after the latter have been shot to pieces in the air. Through the holes made by the engines, burning oil runs down into the hangars and causes the fires which have been so prevalent after all these attacks.'[6]

According to Admiral Chester Nimitz's biographer, Harry Hopkins endeared himself to one and all (Somerville described him as 'a very bright lad') and especially to Nimitz himself. When Admiral Sir Bruce Fraser suggested replacing him with a Vice-Admiral Nimitz protested that Hopkins was doing a fine job. Fraser responded that the Admiralty felt it was more appropriate to assign a more senior officer to the role now that the British

---

5. *Jeremiah H. Daily*, Summary of Statements by Survivors of Enemy Attack on. ComTwelve conf. Ltr. Serial 0138, dated 11 January 1945.
6. Somerville, British Admiralty Delegation Desk Diary, entry for 27 December 1944.

Pacific Fleet (BPF) was about to operate. Nimitz's response was apparently, 'Make Hopkins an admiral.' Potter wrote, 'The Admiralty compromised. They made Hopkins an Acting Captain and left him with CinCPac for another six months.'[7]

Franklin damaged again off Samar

Reverting to attacks upon warships once more, after her earlier close calls, the carrier *Franklin* was the target of suicide attackers again on 30 October while she was approximately 100 miles to the east of Samar Island, on stand-by to give air support to the Leyte operation. Part of Rear-Admiral Ralph Eugene Davidson's Task Group 38.4, which consisted of the carriers *Belleau Wood* (CVL-24), *Enterprise* (CV-6), *Franklin* (CV-13) and *San Jacinto* (CVL-30), she was steaming at 15 knots and in Condition 'Baker' or second degree readiness. The visibility was twelve miles with unlimited ceiling and a light sea. Forty-five fighters had been readied on *Franklin*'s flight deck, all fully fuelled and armed, with the same number of aircraft fuelled, though not yet armed, in the hangar below. All these machines had wing or belly drop tanks full of aviation fuel, but there were no bombs or torpedoes in the hangar deck. *Franklin* began catapulting off the first range of twelve fighters at 14.05 but, with impeccable timing, the Japanese were on the mark and at 14.10 bogies were picked up on the radar scopes at a range of thirty-seven miles. The carrier went to Torpedo Defense, all AA weapons were closed up in readiness, and a destroyer which had been refuelling alongside her hastily cast off and clawed for some sea-room. The ship went to General Quarters at 14.19 and the launch of the last dozen fighters was completed a minute later. By 14.23 *Franklin* went to Condition Able – first-degree readiness – and increased speed to eighteen knots; the carrier was thus as ready as she could be.

The enemy was now visible, a group of six single-engined aircraft – *Judys* or *Zekes*? Opinions differed. Approaching very fast, three of them selected *Franklin* as their target. The leading Kamikaze missed completely, the pilot was probably dead in his seat as it went into the ocean some twenty feet from the port side. The second attacker, complete with bomb, came in at 14.26 in a twenty degree slant approach and hit the flight deck just right of the centreline at frame 127. The aircraft went right through the flight deck, opening it up with an aperture between frames 125 and 128, 12 feet by 35 feet and bulging the deck upward. The Kamikaze plunged on through the gallery decks, forcing the after elevator up by two feet and jamming it crossways across the elevator shaft. The aircraft finally penetrated down into the hangar, its 500lb general purpose (GP) bomb detonating at gallery deck level as it passed through. At the time of this catastrophic hit, only five of the eight repair parties had reported ready, and the three not in place at the time of impact included the hangar team known as Repair I.

The third of the trio of attackers passed low over *Franklin*, dropping a bomb which missed by thirty feet and which did no damage. This aircraft then carried on and

---

7. Potter, E. B. *Nimitz*, 1976. Annapolis, MD Naval Institute Press. The BNLO with the 7th Fleet during the Philippines period was Commander John Frederick Beaufoy Brown, RN. His papers are held at the Liddel Hart Centre for Military Archive; Box ref: GB99 KCLMA Beaufoy Brown.

crashed into the *Belleau Wood*. But aboard the *Franklin* the damage had been done and resulted in ghastly carnage. The blast and fragments from the impact wrecked the gallery deck spaces and raging fires broke out among the aircraft ranged on the flight deck and those in the hangars which intensified almost immediately as their fuel tanks ignited and rapidly spread with nobody to fight them. The fuel vapour spread below the hangar deck, exploding at intervals. On the flight deck eight aircraft were manhandled over the side while the remaining aircraft were incinerated, and fire and flames gutted No.5 and No.7, 5in gun mounts. Heroic efforts by fire-fighters managed to confine this holocaust to within frames 115 and 150, and by 15.30 the flight deck fires were out, although the wooden decking continued to smoulder. In the hangar deck the detonation had wrecked No.3 bay water sprinklers, and demolished water curtains and dense smoke made evacuation by the survivors nightmarish. The main conflagration station on the hangar deck had its windows blown in, forcing all personnel to immediately evacuate the position. These hangar fires remained unchecked for half-an-hour until fire crews could even commence work on containing them and the area was untenable save for persons wearing full breathing gear. However, the armoured hangar deck remained inviolate.

Not until 16.25 were the hangar decks fires doused while the gallery deck inferno was not quenched until ten minutes later. Because the initial blast had instantly wrecked the inner flame seal door on the third deck level, a fire was started here and the same blast flashed down the trunking to the elevator pit on the fourth deck level, likewise killing the man trying to close the armoured hangar deck hatch and burning aviation fuel ran down the hatch spreading the fire and smoke yet deeper into the ship. A gasoline vapour explosion on the second deck resulted about ten minutes later which dished the third deck down while simultaneously bowing the second deck upward, each by about one foot. A smaller explosion on this deck caused a similar dishing in both directions near the general workshop. The gallons of water used to fight these fires caused flooding in some fire rooms and the *Franklin* took on a 3–degree list to starboard which was later overcompensated by counter-flooding to become a 2–degree list to port before being stabilised. Dense smoke overcame many fighting the fires and several were incapacitated despite using breathing apparatus. The carrier's casualty list was not light, fifty-six officers and men killed, and fourteen injured. Despite this carnage (the fires aboard *Franklin*, described as of 'tremendous proportions and intensity' were the worst to that date from which the affected vessel survived) the damaged carrier was able to steam all the way back to the United States where she was repaired at Puget Sound Navy yard, Washington State, in a remarkably short time, being fully operational and back on her war station by 26 January 1945.

One lesson noted was that in both the actions in which she was hit by suicide aircraft, *Franklin* developed a list to starboard due to the huge amounts of water which accumulated on the hangar deck and in the starboard compartments beneath. This water carried with it a surface film of burning gasoline and this was thereby spread throughout the 2nd, 3rd and Hangar decks, thus spreading the conflagration further and very quickly. It was thought that had counter-balancing to port been initiated at an earlier stage, this spread of flammable liquid would have been contained sooner. A similar effect was noted in the case of the *Intrepid*.[8]

---

8. USS *Franklin* (CV13) Suicide Plane Crash Damage Formosa – 15 October 1944. War Damage Report No.56. Preliminary Design Section, Bureau of Ships, Navy Department, dated 15

Belleau Wood (CVL-24) hit

On 30 October, an aircraft that was part of the Kamikaze group that approached Task Group 38.4 at about 18,000 feet, and which dropped a bomb close to *Franklin* as noted above, was identified as a *Judy* (Navy Type 33, Yokosuka D4Y1 *Susei* [Comet]) which, after releasing a single bomb, pulled up and made its Kamikaze dive into the *Belleau Wood* (Captain A. M. Pride, USN) at 14.27. The AA gunners hit but could not stop her and the Kamikaze fell on the flight deck aft. The light carrier had a deck park of twelve Grumman F6F Hellcat fighters of VF-21[9] and Grumman TBM-1C Avengers from VT-21.The enemy machine struck home among them, exploding, holing the flight deck and setting these aircraft alight, ultimately destroying them all. There followed a series of explosions and fierce fires, and smoke rolled over the ship.

The nine light carriers (CVL) of the *Independence* Class were of around 11,000 tons displacement and were really a stop-gap type built at New York Shipbuilding, Camden, on the hulls of *Cleveland* class light cruisers when the US Navy's carrier position looked at its most critical in late 1942. As such they were narrow with a restricted capacity of just forty-five aircraft, but they were fast and thus able to keep up with contemporary task forces, unlike the much slower CVEs. CVLs had a flight deck pierced by two centreline elevators, H-IVC catapults and eight arresting wires aft. Their weakness was that their wooden flight and hangar decks lacked any armour protection. Their tiny bridges were cramped and their defensive armament was basic, consisting of a few 40mm and 20mm mountings.

Belleau Wood was perhaps fortunate that the Kamikaze had dropped its bomb before impact. Even so, it took the best part of three hours to get the fires under control and ninety-two officers and men were killed with a further fifty-four injured. The destroyer *Patterson* (DD-396, Lieutenant-Commander Walter A Hering) alone rescued sixteen men who had been blown over the side of the ship, though sadly two of these died aboard her and were buried at sea the following day. The light carrier remained able to steam and reached Ulithi for temporary repairs before sailing via Pearl Harbor for San Francisco, which she reached on the 29th. She was repaired at Hunters Point, and her near-useless 20mm mountings were replaced by additional 40mm weapons. By 7 February 1945 *Belleau Wood* was back at Ulithi once more and ready to resume operations with Task Force 58.

On Saturday 4 November Ugaki wrote: 'At 1330 *Sakon* Unit of Special Attack Corps sighted two carriers and ten others at a point 140 miles bearing 90 degrees off Cape Encant. One plane hit a CV with superstructure on her starboard. A few minutes after an induced explosion, her stern began to go down. Another hit a CVL and set her on fire.'[10] The CV referred to was the *Lexington*, McCain's flagship, and he had to shift flag and send her back to Ulithi.

September 1946.

9. For an explanation of US Navy and Marine Corps air unit designations, see the Glossary on Page TO BE DETERMINED LATER.

10. Ugaki, Admiral Matome – *Fading Victory – The Diary of Admiral Matome Ugaki 1941–1945*, Annapolis, MD: Naval Institute Press, 1991.

Destroyer *Claxton* damaged

The *Fletcher* Class destroyer *Claxton* (DD-571, Captain Miles Hubbard, USN) was screening the Seventh Fleet Task Group operating in Leyte Gulf during the morning of 1 November. The sea was calm, with a light breeze and excellent visibility although there were some scattered high cumulus clouds. The destroyer was at General Quarters, with Condition One Easy set as there were warnings of incoming bogeys. According to Lieutenant (j.g.) [Junior Grade] Charlie Nelson, USNR, who was the *Claxton*'s Damage Control Officer, the ship had been at General Quarters, fully closed up and ready for action, for a matter of days and the crew was showing signs of fatigue. Nelson advised Captain Hubbard accordingly and the CO decided to make things a bit more bearable aboard by ordering one watertight door in each living compartment to be left open. The doors so affected were staggered from port to starboard allowing some fresh air to circulate through the destroyer. The danger was that the deck in the living spaces aft was at the waterline on these ships and any damage there might flood the after third of the vessel.

When the *Val* dive-bomber was first observed coming hard at the ship, the alarm sounded off for Condition One and Nelson was in the CIC just forward of the mast. He was relieved by the Executive Officer and began to run to his battle station in DC Central. The Captain put the *Claxton* into a hard starboard turn and as the enemy aircraft closed in, hits could clearly be seen being made by both 5in and 40mm weapons but these failed to deflect her from her chosen course. Nelson wrote later how he vividly remembered seeing 'that round spinner on the prop and those two wheels that hung below the fuselage that were coming straight toward me.' When the *Val* struck the *Claxton*, one wing scythed into the high 40mm mount aft, cutting off the first loader's head, but the bulk of the aircraft failed to impact and missed the ship. However, the 500lb bomb it carried did detonate and blew open a 15ft hole in the ship's starboard quarter, opposite the after 5in upper handling room. The explosion was fierce, wrecking that compartment and blowing out all the watertight doors in the after living spaces and killing one of the handlers while fragments spread across a wide area and killed or badly wounded many more. The heel of the ship thus far kept the hole out of the water but with all watertight integrity aft of the rear engine room gone it was essential to try and keep her that way. However, further attacks were developing and the officer of the deck (OOD), Bill Hogan, ordered full left rudder to avoid another hit, and water flooded in.

Nelson recalled how the petty officer closed the hatch which, in theory, kept the water out and the guns firing, but which effectively sealed him and his companions in with little hope of escape should the *Claxton* go down. However, Nelson recorded that he and Gunners Mate Gail Fiscus escaped by swimming into the upper handling room and exiting via the powder scuttle of the after 5in mounting. That achieved, Nelson went up to the bridge to report the situation. He estimated that the *Claxton*'s geometric metacentre (GM) had been reduced to just 0.02ft which meant that she was excessively tender and might roll over and capsize at any time should any undue action at all take place. Very little margin remained before the ship would fail to right herself at the end of each roll. The ship's chief engineer asked the captain to counter-flood forward to bring the hole in the after hull out of the water, but Nelson requested this not be done as it might prove fatal for stability.

Eventually, through some sound and dangerous work by Assistant Damage Control Officer Ensign John Tiedeberg, the patches made from four mattresses tied to a sleeping bunk bed-spring were affixed over the hole, and once in place pumping began and the stern was raised – without rolling the ship over – and she was pumped dry, an action that took a full six hours of hard work following which *Claxton* began to make her way back to the transport area.[11]

Meanwhile neither friends nor enemy had been idle.

Abner Read sunk

On the afternoon of 1 November, another *Fletcher* Class destroyer, the *Abner Read* (DD-526, Commander Arthur Montgomery Purdy, USN) was screening the *Claxton*, which had been damaged earlier as described. *Abner Read* had sent over her doctor, corpsmen and a damage control party to *Claxton*, and was zig-zagging at 15 knots across the bows of the crippled destroyer and was at Material Condition 'Baker', with her engineering plant split.[12] At 13.39 her radar picked up approaching bogies at ten miles range, closing fast and GQ was sounded off, and Condition Able set. Within a short time two *Vals* were clearly visible through the intermittent clouds at 60–degrees relative bearing at a height of 6,000ft. Commander Purdy kicked *Abner Read* into full right rudder and her engines went to full ahead flank speed[13] while all guns that could bear opened fire. The destroyer's 40mm and 20mm fire were accurate and heavy, but the two forward 5in guns had only time to get off six rounds. The leading dive-bomber was undeterred and dived at the ship, despite being hit and in flames, and continued even as its port wing was shot off. The aircraft dived steeply into No.3 40mm mounting and the after torpedo mounting, before careering over the ship's port side. The aircraft's starboard wing struck the 40mm director platform on the starboard side of the after funnel, the breech end of the after torpedo-tubes (which were trained 275–degrees relative) and port side 20mm mounting which was knocked over the side of the ship. What was described as 'an intense fire' at once broke out and quickly spread. The bomb carried by this aircraft went through the forward starboard side of the after funnel about 5ft above the top of the deckhouse and penetrated into the after fire room uptakes, where it detonated with enormous force. The explosion knocked men off their feet in both the fire room and after

---

11. USS *Claxton* (DD-571) First Person – Charlie Nelson: *Fanaticism in Warfare: The First Organized Multi-Aircraft Suicide Attack.* Destroyer History Foundation.
12. Warships of this era were constructed with at least two engineering plants in order to minimise the risk of a single major hit causing total disablement. The layout of the engines, pumps and associated equipment, along with electrical generating equipment, piping etc, were purposely misaligned to reduce the one-hit-all-down scenario, and each could be disconnected into independent units in an emergency, with each propulsion section able to operate its own propeller shaft. This would be sufficient to keep the ship under way, albeit at much reduced speed. When full power is not required, one set could be disconnected ('split') until required.
13. 'Flank speed' is a term used by the US Navy to indicate a vessel's actual maximum speed at top acceleration in very short bursts of power to avoid imminent danger when under air attack.

engine room, where the main distribution board short circuited starting electrical fires as well as blowing in the forward starboard bulkhead, killing many men.

Both engines were rung to 'Stop' to try and prevent the motion of the ship fanning the fires aft, but only the forward engine room was able to respond with all connections further aft gone. Meanwhile the second *Val* had also made its dive and was engaged by the main 5in battery under director control and No.1 40mm mounting, who between them knocked it into the sea close by without causing any damage to the ship. Meanwhile the fires were raging with flames and smoke, forcing the abandonment of both No.3 5in gun and Nos.3 and 4 40mm mounting, as well as the after fire room (after both boilers had been secured) and the after engine room. 'Here many personnel were injured but all managed to escape via the scuttle. All these spaces, plus the adjacent living compartment and No.3 handling room, and then the entire topside aft of the rear funnel to abaft No.3 5in gun were subsequently engulfed in flames.' The after stack was reported to resemble 'a blast furnace emitting roaring flames and burning fragments.'[14] As the fires raged the aft repair party were 'hopelessly marooned – without light, power or fire main pressure.' Thus they had little choice but to set the depth-charges to safe, lead out hoses, open the sprinkler valves in the rear magazines and then abandon ship. As fires threatened the ship's torpedo-tubes, with the aft mounting on fire and the forward mount hazarded by intense heat and flame, the order was given to jettison them all from the port beam. However, only the forward mount could comply and all five torpedoes were fired with tripping latches retracted so that they all sank immediately upon launch. The aft mounting, as stated, was a sea of fire and this cooked off the impulse charges with all five 'fully ready and highly erratic' torpedoes being fired off intermittently.[15] All five torpedoes duly appeared to run erratically toward the horizon, presenting a lethal hazard to neighbouring vessels. The nearby battleship line was duly warned and turned away, and no ship was struck although *Abner Read* almost torpedoed herself when at least some of the errant torpedoes re-appeared off the ship's port bow close to the surface, with one circling to within five yards of the ship.

With the after deckhouse fully ablaze, the ready-use ammunition began to cook off on Nos.3, 4 and 5 40mm mountings, port and starboard 40mm mountings, No.3 upper handling room, and port and starboard K-gun impulse charge stowage. The enormous heat, the exploding ammunition and lack of fire main pressure rendered the gallant efforts of the fire fighters null and void, and almost every man was injured. Within three minutes of the hit the *Claxton* attempted to go alongside and help assist, but the conditions were such that she aborted the first attempt and began picking men out of the water, and hauled no less than 187 aboard.

Ten minutes after the Kamikaze first hit her, *Abner Read* suffered a very large explosion under the waterline aft centred on No.3 lower handling room, and the whole ship shook and

---

14. War Damage Report No. 51, Destroyer Report: *Gunfire, Bomb and Kamikaze Damage, including Losses in Action 17 October, 1941 to 15 August 1945*, dated 25 January 1947, Preliminary Design Section, Bureau of Ships, Navy Department, Washington DC.
15. Nelson, watching from aboard the *Claxton*, wrote that they were fired by hand with a mallet by the torpedoman while he was engulfed in flames.

listed sharply to starboard, jamming the main director. This blast opened up a large hole in the starboard side at frame 160 and plating could be seen projecting outboard beneath the water. Aboard the destroyer *Killen* (DD-593, Commander Howard Grant Corey), which was standing by, it was thought that the *Abner Read* had blown up, and flames were seen spreading rapidly. Fearing further magazine explosions, the Captain ordered 'abandon ship', but this was rescinded before it was completed as the inpouring sea helped quench some of the flames and the forward 5in and 40mm guns were re-manned. Nonetheless the situation was fraught and the whaleboat, all available life rafts and 5in powder tanks (utilised as makeshift floats) were lowered into the water, and remaining personnel brought up from below decks. This respite proved only temporary however; *Abner Read* was doomed. As she continued to settle aft, more explosions took place in increasing severity and frequency. By 13.50, about a quarter-of-an-hour after being struck, the destroyer had assumed a 20–degree list and 'abandon ship' was ordered again. The bulk of the crew were off after seven minutes and by 14.15 she was over on her beam ends to starboard, finally going down stern first at 14.17 in 35 fathoms, leaving a large fuel-oil fire on the surface of the sea which burnt for several hours.

There was a great deal unresolved about *Abner Read*'s loss. For a start Kamikaze attacks were relatively new at that time; secondly it was the very speed of her loss that resonated and, thirdly, the way that the fire and flames spread throughout the ship so quickly caused much unease. Eyewitness accounts varied considerably and did not help much once she had gone. Whether the *Val* that hit her was actually carrying a bomb or not was another issue. Eyewitnesses aboard the destroyer *Ammen* (DD-527, Commander James H. Brown, Jr. USN), who were able to get a good look as they were firing at this Kamikaze, later reported that it released no bomb prior to striking. On the other hand Nelson aboard the *Claxton*, recalled that the *Val* did carry a bomb and that this exploded into the port 40mm magazine where it ignited gasoline that rapidly spread all over that area, and that this, 'combination of the bomb blast and the flash gasoline fire set off the 40mm ammunition.' He added that, 'exploding 40mm ammunition penetrated the five-inch magazine setting it ablaze, blowing the bottom out of the ship.' Again *Abner Read*'s commanding officer and the Divisional Commander (her former CO, Captain Herald F. Stout, USN) suspected that this *Val* was carrying some type of incendiary material, akin to napalm-thickened gasoline. An alternate theory was that the fires were fed by fuel oil spilling from lines in the bilges ruptured by the initial explosion, or pumped out into hot fire boxes when the fire room was hastily evacuated in total darkness. This theory was lent credence by the 'blast furnace' description of the after funnel and by the fact that oil fuel burned on the water for a long time after the ship had gone down. The after-action summary emphasised that the inability to cope with this fire 'was not due to a lack of courage on the part of the fire-fighters, all of whom were burned or wounded by fragments from exploding ammunition, but rather to the intensity of the fire and the unexplained failure to get adequate pressure on the fire main.' What is known is that normally some six hundred 5in projectiles containing about one-ton of explosive were usually stored in C-301–M, and that study of photographs of the massive detonation and subsequent mushroom cloud that followed and structural damage corresponded to 'that to be expected from a mass detonation of a substantial portion of the projectiles' rather than a mixture of steam and water vapour as in a boiler explosion. The conclusion was that the fire reached the lower handling room via open hatches or burning oil which leaked in from the GC tanks after the impact and blast on the main deck.

On 1 November two further destroyers had been damaged: the *Anderson* (DD-411, Commander John Adrian Sharp, Jr.) and the *Killen* (DD-593). The former was hit at 18.12 by an *Oscar* on her port side with the loss of sixteen crew killed. She had to be sent back to San Francisco for major repairs. *Killen* was attacked by no less than seven aircraft, she destroyed four of them but one scored a direct bomb hit to port, killing fifteen men. She, in turn, had to be sent home, being later repaired at Hunter's Point, California. In addition a third destroyer was hit on 11 November; the *Ammen* (DD-527, Commander James Harvey Brown, Jr.) being struck on her bridge by a twin-engined *Frances,* which killed five of her personnel and damaged both funnels. Nonetheless she was able to continue her duties for a while before being repaired locally.

Further major warships attacked

On 5 November, while off Luzon, the *Essex* Class carrier *Lexington* (CV-16, Captain Ernest Wheeler Litch, USN) was hit by a Kamikaze aiming for her bridge. The aircraft impacted adjacent to the ship's island and totally wrecked it with many casualties. Several fires broke out but were mainly contained within twenty minutes thanks to heroic efforts by her crewmen. She was then able to resume normal operations prior to returning to Ulithi for more permanent repairs and had returned to front line action once more by 1 December.

More transports hit

On 17 November the Attack Transport *Alpine* (APA-92, Master George G K Reilly) and the *Gilbert Stuart* (MC 1628, Master John Kiehl)[16] were damaged and they were joined by the C1 Cargo ships *Alcoa Pioneer* (MC 5361) suffered five crew members killed and the *Cape Romano* (MC 0240) which had nineteen dead, when both ships were hit by Kamikazes while at anchor San Pedro Bay on 19 November as the casualty toll steadily mounted.

The turn of *Essex*

At 12.56 on 25 November 1944, a *Judy* Kamikaze of the Yoshino Special Attack Corps based at Malabacat East Field (the first Kamikaze base), piloted by Yoshinori Yamaguchi, struck the carrier *Essex* (CV-9) off Leyte. This machine was one of two *Judys* sent on suicide missions that day along with six A6M5 *Zekes*. The dive brakes on this aircraft were in the down position, as used when dive-bombing, but its approach was shallow and it may well be that the brakes were down due to flak damage rather than activated by the pilot, while the self-sealing port-wing fuel tank was trailing fuel vapour and smoke.

---

16. MC – in full the United States Maritime Commission was established as an independent Federal Agency in 1936 and charged with replacing 500 obsolete American merchant vessels with a new standard type of fast cargo ship. These ships were leased to the American shipping companies and acted as reserve auxiliary units.

Yamaguichi released a bomb prior to impact that missed the target, however, his *Judy* hit directly, causing almost total casualties from two of the 20mm gun mountings. One of these mounts was manned by coloured sailors and the other by white, but all died together in that fireball or later. Jack Ormsby was First Powder man on No.4, 5in mounting that day and later related his story, and gave me his express permission to use it here while adding additional information. 'I observed the Kamikaze attack from my vantage point about 90 feet forward of the hit. I was standing on the rearing gear housing of Gun 4. My head stuck up just far enough to see everything until the fireball was about 60 feet in diameter. It seemed quite small.' He continued:

'Many pictures of it make it look like the explosion takes in the entire island structure; it is misleading. If you examine movies of it, you will see it is all smoke and the ship moves into the smoke. The picture was lifted from a frame of motion picture film and they picked a frame that looked the most dramatic. Sorry gang but that's show biz. I only had to duck a few inches when I saw black fragments of the airplane coming at me and it all went over my head. After it was all over, and we came back to the gun, we found the upper half of the Kamikaze pilot lying on the deck between Guns 2 and 4. His parachute was out of its pack under him which became a shroud when two gun crew members used it to pick up the body and keep blood off their hands while they heaved it over the side.

'You can see the explosion for yourself; get a CD of *Victory at Sea*, Volume 25 *Suicide for Glory*. When you come to the Kamikaze hitting *Essex*, click one frame at a time. At 24 frames per second you will count about 36 frames, meaning that the explosion lasts about one and a half seconds. When the flash starts dimming the explosion is over, the rest is just smoke. Then you will see *Essex* move into that smoke, that takes another 36 frames, one and half seconds more. At that time the island looks engulfed in an explosion when it is just engulfed in smoke. Not to minimize the damage and killing, I just want to show that reading history is not like being there. Even pictures do not tell the whole story.

'I can attest to the fact that the 20mm gunners fired into the *Judy* until it ploughed into them. In spite of what the history books report it, did not kill all the gunners instantly. Four of the gunners walked to the Marine – manned 40mm gun mount that sat between the 20mm battery and Gun 4. The man leading the others was around 6 feet [tall]. He asked me where the battle dressing station was and I led them to it only about fifteen feet away, just off our gun deck. If we had been required to wear flash gear, the way Captain Roscoe Bowman demanded, I believe all four of them would have lived. They died within minutes while waiting to be taken care of. They were taken out on stretchers in a sitting position.

'Don't believe any stories of trying to pick someone up and the flesh coming off the bone. The flash of an explosion is only a fraction of a second. It would take twenty minutes in a microwave to cook flesh that much. That is why that thin metallic woven flash gear will protect you, but only for seconds.

'I didn't see the fire that destroyed the tyre repair shop. I did, however, walk past it going to the mess hall less than an hour later. Except for that one spot there wasn't fire damage anywhere on the hangar deck, not even water damage. There were a couple of F6Fs with their fabric covered control surfaces burned, but I was told by

Damage Control that one of the men from the loading room that loaded magazines for the 20mms rode the deck plate that opened down like a sardine can lid, dumping a man through the open hanger curtain. He was on fire and ran across the hanger deck, and jumped off the starboard side. I can't swear to that story because I didn't see it, but I did see the burned elevator and rudder surfaces as the burning man touched them, weaving through the planes spotted forward on the hanger deck.

'I cannot swear to this but I believe that the 20mm guns were the only guns firing, although 5in mount No.1 got off one round less than a second before the Kamikaze hit. Probably in panic or a feeling that someone should do something. I would not have been standing on top of Gun No.4 if we had been on red alert. I would have been standing on the gun platform with a 5in powder in my hands. I often stood there to watch the activity on the flight deck. The diving *Judy* was a complete surprise to everyone. Remember, the 40mm and 20mm guns only need one man on each gun to commence firing. The 5in guns need a minimum of four men to get off more than one unaimed round.

'Most accounts claim there was only a pilot in the *Judy*, but myself and ten others from my gun crew knew better. None of us knew that there would ever be a controversy. I guess everyone thought everything was known about it at the time. There was no investigation, or at least nobody ever talked to me about it. I always thought that maybe it might not have been a Kamikaze because of the two bodies, and both of them wearing parachutes. I have always judged it to be an impromptu suicide technically, but Kamikaze would not be improvised. Many accounts claim it was a Zero. Knowing of the second body I would say, only if they have two-man Zeros!

'I tried to prove that the body found on our gun deck was the pilot. My reasoning is that the aircraft's gas tanks are always in the centre of the airplane. So the explosion would throw the pilot up and forward and the second man up and back, because he was behind the explosion.'[17]

Some ships seemed to act as Kamikaze magnets and received hits time and time again.

On 27 November, the light cruiser *Denver* (CL-58, Captain Albert MacQueen Bledsoe, USN), a vessel that had already been slightly damaged when near-missed by a bomb during a conventional air attack on 28 October, was again attacked, this time by a Kamikaze, whose bomb also near-missed the cruiser but which nevertheless still wounded four of her crew. Another ship in receipt of attention from multiple Kamikazes was the carrier *Intrepid* (CV-11, Captain Joseph Francis Bolger, USN). She had already received her baptism of fire from this source on 30 October when a fully ablaze suicide aircraft struck her port upper deck, detonating among the AA positions there. The explosion killed ten men and wounded a further six. Operationally she was back to full capacity within a few hours. But, just after midday on 25 November, she was hit by two Kamikazes in the space of five minutes, and lost six officers and fifty-nine crew killed and one hundred injured. Her fires were brought under control, but the next day she had to be sent back to San Francisco for major repairs.

---

17. Jack Ormsby, *Account of Kamikaze attack on Essex* and supplementary information to the Author, 7 September 2009.

Val or *Sonia*?

In almost all the descriptions of Kamikaze attacks undertaken by 'fixed-undercarriage, single-engined aircraft', it is assumed that the attackers were Aichi *Val* Navy dive-bombers. The *Val* had earned itself a formidable reputation earlier in the war, being one of the most successful Japanese aircraft used against shipping. It had a record in the period of 1941–42 that was second-to-none in the Pacific, despite the fact that it was relatively slow and only carried a 500lb bomb, which was only half the bomb-load of the contemporary US Navy SBD Dauntless and, in Europe, the equally slow, but equally accurate and deadly, Junkers Ju 87 *Stuka*. This reputation was fearsome, but it was mainly due to the excellence and skill of their aircrew rather than the machine itself.[18] However, with the introduction of superior interceptors, like the Grumman F6F Hellcat and the Chance-Vought F4U Corsair, their day was clearly done as conventional dive-bombers, despite which they were to achieve many successes as Kamikazes, especially off Okinawa, later on in the campaign.

Off the Philippines, however, it might equally have been the Army light bomber, known to the Allies as the *Sonia*, that was more often than not involved. Like the *Val* the *Sonia* was a single-engined light bomber, with a fixed undercarriage. Not only was it visually very similar, even if built with a different role in mind, but its speed, payload and performance was very much akin to the *Val*, although the *Val* was superior in all respects as an aircraft, as the following table illustrates:

Details	Mitsubishi Ki-51 *Sonia*	Aichi D3A2 Val
Crew	2	2
Length	9.21m (30ft 2⅜in)	10.2n (33ft 5½in)
Wingspan	12.1m (39ft 8⅜in)	14.37m (47ft 2in)
Height	2.73m (8 ft 11½ in)	3.8m (12ft 7½ in)
Wing Area	24.0m² (259ft²)	34.9m² (375.6ft²)
Weight (Empty)	1,873kg (4,129lb)	2,570kg (5,666lb)
Weight (Loaded)	2,798kg (6,169lb)	
Weight (Max takeoff)	2,920kg (6,415lb)	4,122kg (9,100lb)
Engine	1 x 709kW (950hp) Mitsubishi Ha-26–11 air-cooled radial	1 x 969kW (1,300hp) Mitsubishi Kinsei 54 air-cooled radial
Speed (Max)	424km/h @ 3,000m (229mph @ 9,840ft)	430km/h (267mph)
Range	1,060 km (660 miles)	1,352 km (840 miles)
Service Ceiling	8,270m (27,130ft)	10,500m (34,450 ft)
Wing Loading	117kg/m² (23.8 lb/ft²)	
Climb	5,000m (16,400ft in 10 min)	8.62 m/s (1,869.685 ft/m)
Defensive armament	2 x 12mm (.5in mg)	2 x 7mm (0.303 in mg)
Bombs	1 x 227kg (500lb)	1 x 227kg (500lb)

---

18. See Smith, Peter C, *Aichi D3A1/2 Val*, Ramsbury, Marlborough, UK. The Crowood Press, 1999 and also *Jungle Dive Bombers at War*, London, John Murray, 1987.

Cabot struck

The light carrier *Cabot* (CVL-28, Captain Walton Wiley Smith, USN), also received damage on 25 November when a Kamikaze smashed into the port side of her flight deck. The port gun director, and several guns and mountings, were erased by the impact. Then another Kamikaze followed the first toward her; being heavily hit by defending fire the disintegrating aircraft slammed into the water very close alongside the ship. Blazing pieces of the machine came inboard on this side adding to the existing carnage there: combined the two strikes accounted for some sixty-two officers and men killed and injured. The *Cabot* was nonetheless able to maintain her place in line and, once makeshift patching up had been carried out, even to operate some flights. She returned to Ulithi on 28 November where she was repaired and was back in the war again by 11 December.

Further suicide attack victims.

The toll amongst the support ships off the landing areas also steadily mounted. On 27 November the *SC-744* was sunk, while damaged ships included the battleship *Colorado* (BB-45, Captain Walter Scott Macaulay), which lost nineteen crewmen killed by a Kamikaze, necessitating a return later to Manus for repairs, and light cruiser *St. Louis* (CL-49, Captain John Bradford Giggs, Jr.) which shot down one Val but was hit by a second and suffered the death of sixteen of her crew. Damage was heavy and she too had to return to California for repairs. Another light cruiser, *Montpelier* (CL-57, Captain Harry Draper Hoffman, USN), also became a victim. She was patrolling off Leyte Gulf on 27 November 1944 when she was slightly damaged by a torpedo bomber which made a suicide attack. Two days later, the battleship *Maryland* (BB-46) was hit and had thirty-one crewmen killed; she later had to undergo major repair at Pearl Harbor. That same day the destroyers *Saufley* (DD-465) and *Aulick* (DD-569) were both hit by Kamikazes in Leyte Gulf, the former suffering much hull damage and the latter, attacked by six aircraft and hit by one of them, lost thirty-two of her personnel and had to be sent back to Mare Island for repair.

December 5th saw the loss of the *LSM-20* while the destroyer *Mugford* (DD-389) was struck by a *Val*, which killed eight men, and had to be sent back to Mare Island. On 6 December, the destroyer *Drayton* (DD-366) was hit and slightly damaged but was hit again more severely on the 7th, with six dead, and had to limp back to Manus, while *LSM-23* was also damaged.

The third anniversary of the Pearl Harbor attack saw more victims in attacks on shipping off the Ormoc beachhead, the destroyer *Mahan* (DD-364) and fast transport *Ward* (APD-16), (which, as a destroyer, had fired the first American shots of the war) were both damaged and consequently both had to be sunk. *LSM-318* was also lost this day. Finally, on 10 December, the Liberty ship *William S. Ladd* (MC-2084, Master Nils Anderson) and PT-323 were both sunk and *LCT-1075*, which was alongside the Liberty ship *Marcus Daly* (MC-1697, Master Alvin W Opheim) was heavily hit. Flames from the landing craft subsequently spread to the *Daly* which then had to be beached. The destroyer *Hughes* (DD-410) was also damaged off San Jose. Three days later the Japanese were claiming to have sunk a further five LSTs and five Liberty ships. Ugaki, over-confident as always, was recording that twenty-five enemy vessels had been destroyed. It was not *that* bad of course, but, even so, it was a depressing scenario for the Americans.

Chapter Four

A Mauling at Mindoro

'For the sake of the country,
I am going as if Blossoms are falling,
the scent of cherry blossoms
in Naha, Okinawa, please reach Japan.'

Akira Sarumi

The light cruiser *Nashville* (CL-43, Captain Charles Edward Coney, USN), was flagship of the expeditionary force tasked with retaking Mindoro. It was hoped that the construction of airfields there would provide ample land-based air power to help support the proposed liberation of Luzon. The squadron proceeded via the Surigao Strait and the Sulu Sea; their own air cover was provided by both the escort carrier groups and airfields on Leyte, from which US Marine squadrons were able to fly their powerful F4U Corsair fighters as protection. However the Japanese were able to mount strong air attacks on this force, including Kamikaze strikes, and both the *Nashville* and the destroyer *Caldwell* (DD-605, Lieutenant-Commander J F Newman) were damaged and forced to withdraw while the destroyer *Reid* (DD-369) was sunk. On 13 December two more destroyers, *Haraden* (DD-585, Commander Halle Charles Allen, Jr.) and *Caldwell* (for the second time), were hit and damaged, the latter being forced to withdraw.

Eyewitness aboard the *Nashville*

Lieutenant-Colonel Rufus B. 'Tommy' Thompson, Jr, (USMC Ret) was serving aboard the *Nashville* that day and gave this graphic account of the Kamikaze attack which gives a good idea of the speed and suddenness of it all. 'It was known that there were still many operational Japanese airfields located on Mindanao, Negros and other small islands flanking our route. So, we were at our General Quarters stations immediately after getting underway. With the exception of my assistant, 2nd Lt. Poul Finn Pedersen, USMC, 1st Sgt Alton B. Chambers, USMC, and myself, all of the Marines were stationed amidships on the boat deck manning the 40mm and 20mm anti-aircraft weapons. Lt. Pederson was the assistant anti-aircraft control officer stationed in the foremast (forward superstructure). 1st Sgt. Chambers was in charge of the two quad 40mm guns located on the fantail, and manned by our wardroom cooks and mess men. I was the anti-aircraft control officer stationed in the mainmast (aft superstructure). Two quad 40mm guns manned by sailors were located just below my station, one on the port and one on the starboard side. The first day and night were quiet with no air alerts or other warnings, so we had been placed on One Easy, which meant half of the personnel on station could rest or take a short break. I believe it was about 9 or 10 am on December 13, 1944, a light cloudy day, that we received an IFF [Identification Friend or Foe] radar alert. Scanning the sky I saw two F4Us well to the rear and crossing the stern of the *Nashville* to my right (port side of the *Nashville*) in level flight at about 1500 elevation. (One report I have read estimated the elevation to be about 5000 feet). I think my estimate was more accurate because I was able to identify the planes as Marine F4Us. This was all observed in a second or two.

'Seeing the F4Us, we thought the IFF was a false alarm but all of a sudden a plane, that apparently had been closely following the F4Us, veered off and dove for our ship coming directly from our stern. First Sgt. Chamber's crew was the only one able to fire a few rounds as the plane banked into the port side clipping its right wing tip on the Quad 40mm below me. The plane slammed into the port side of the boat deck and into two 5in AA guns on the main deck. One bomb exploded there, and another bomb was catapulted from the left wing of the plane over to the starboard side of the boat deck, where it also exploded, knocking out the two 5in guns there. The 5in ammo ready boxes on both sides were open and much of that ammo exploded. The forward superstructure received some damage, causing the AA control located there to be evacuated. The brunt of the explosion was forward, leaving only superficial damage to the after superstructure. Fire raged on the main deck and boat deck in the mid-section of the ship until the Damage Control team was able to extinguish it. The Kamikaze plane, which was surprisingly still in one piece, and pilot were pushed over the side with other debris to clear the decks. With AA control forward out of action, I established communications with the few AA gun crews that were still operable, alerting them to be on the lookout for any more enemy planes. Fortunately, none appeared. I don't recall how long it was before someone relieved me at my station so I could check on my Marines.

'The devastation was beyond belief. All of my Marines manning the AA weapons on the boat deck and the sailors manning the 5in guns in the mid-ships area on both the starboard and port side were wounded or killed. The wounded were evacuated to emergency medical facilities established in the officers' wardroom and the crew's mess hall for treatment, and the KIAs were moved to the hanger deck. The Landing Force Commander and his staff, who weren't wounded or killed, were transferred to the light-cruiser USS *Boise* (CL-47) as I recall. The *Nashville*, escorted by two escort ships, immediately returned to San Pedro Bay, Leyte, where the wounded and dead were transferred to Army medical facilities ashore for treatment or burial. We had no time to sort out the personal belongings of the wounded to send ashore with them. However, I did transfer the individual personal records of the wounded ashore with them to the Army Medical Field Hospital.'[1]

Lieutenant-Colonel Thompson recalled that of the forty men in his detachment, nineteen were killed and only three Marines remained uninjured: Colonel Thompson himself, Second-Lieutenant Poul Finn Pedersen and First Sergeant Alton B Chambers.

---

1. Lieutenant-Colonel Rufus B 'Tommy' Thompson, Jr. (USMC, Ret.) Memoir, *My Tour Aboard the USS Nashville (CL-43) – 1943–1945*, reproduced with express permission of the author himself.

Despite his injuries Ben Limbaught was one of the Marines who survived that horrendous attack, one of the very first and therefore among the most shocking attacks. Now a sprightly ninety plus I talked to him on 5 May 2013 while he was in his hospital bed in Florida after a bad fall, but his memory of the incident was crystal clear. 'I was originally from Chicago, and became a Pfc (Private, First Class) in 3 Marine Corps in the Fleet Marine Force and was serving as a gunner aboard *Nashville* that day. I was wounded in this incident. How I survived when most of my buddies died all around me I will never know. I had joined up as a very young man and in our boot camp there were thirty-eight of us boys who had all enlisted for the duration and stayed together for eighteen months, during which time we saw lots of combat with the 7th Fleet helping MacArthur's advance between June 1943 and December 1944. There was a poem written at the time: 'By the grace of God (and a few Marines), MacArthur returned to the Philippines'. Although the photo of him wading ashore took several 'takes' before he was fully satisfied with it!'

'Our cruiser squadron was *Nashville, Boise, Phoenix* and the RAN heavy cruisers *Australia* and *Shropshire*. I had witnessed *Australia* take a suicide aircraft into her earlier, that was the first we knew about them. Out of those thirty-eight close-knit team mates, twenty-eight died that day and ten were wounded, along with two NCOs and two officers.[2] 'It was mid-afternoon, the sky had big cumulus clouds and a CAP was overhead. The aircraft suddenly dove out of these clouds from the ship's side where I was stationed at the No.13 starboard 20mm mount, in the shade. We only had helmets on, no blast gear. The Kamikaze struck us about forty feet in front of the boat deck and our ready-use ammunition boxes blew up, and big fires started. It all happened very fast, a big boom, and my friends were blown all over the place. I emerged with six to eight shrapnel wounds and my eardrum blown out. I was lucky and with another survivor we later were called upon to ID the bodies of our friends laid out on the ship's fantail. Bad burns on most and young kids, a sobering thing to do. No trauma counselling in those days of course! You got on with it. Many could only be identified by the insignia on what remained of their uniforms.

'After the attack we were transferred to a Hospital Ship at Manus while the *Nashville* herself, after having undergone emergency repairs at Leyte, was sent back to New Caledonia and eventually reached Bremerton to refit. A few of the Marine survivors re-joined her there and she got back into the Pacific later ending up at Singapore. Post-war she was sold to Chile. I attended two crew reunions, the 1985 one at Orlando and the 1990 at Nashville. I ended the war with a Purple Heart, the South Pacific and America Ribbons and two Bronze Stars, one with the inscribed 'V'.'

Other victims

Although the actual landing itself, which took place on 15 December, went ahead, the follow up supply convoys were targeted by suicide aircraft and between that date and the 21 December many ships fell victim to them. On 15 December *LST-472* and *LST-738* were both sunk, the escort carrier *Marcus Island* (CVE-77, Captain Charles

---

2. Ben Limbaugh to the Author, 5 May 2013.

Frederick Greber) and destroyers *Ralph Talbot* (DD-390), *Paul Hamilton* (DD-590) and *Howorth* (DD-592) were all damaged. The *Marcus Island* was barely harmed in an attack by two *Zekes* that morning, one of which just grazed her flight deck and caused a few minor injuries. Three PT-boats[3] were also struck, *PT-300* being sunk on 18 December, while *PT-84* and *PT-223* were damaged. On 21 December it was the turn of the destroyer *Foote* (DD-511) which was damaged while *LST-460* and *LST-749* were both sunk. Over the New Year period the *John Burke* (MC 0609, Master George F Mentz, the while ship and crew being vaporised) was sunk, the destroyer *Bryant* (DD-665) and the *William Sharon* (MC 2106, Master Edward Macaughey) were damaged on 28 December, while on the 30 December the *Armadillo* Class Liberty ship Station Tanker conversion, *Porcupine* (IX-126), (Lieutenant Daniel M. Paul), was hit on successive days and finally sunk. Damaged ships included the destroyers *Pringle* (DD-477) and *Gansevoort* (DD-608), and the *Orestes* (IX-73, Captain Kenneth N Mueller).

Rescuing the *Gansevoort*

The *Gansevoort* (DD-608, Lieutenant-Commander E. A. McFall, USN), a *Benson* Class destroyer, presented a unique case with regard to Kamikaze damage. Part of Destroyer Squadron (DesRon) 48, she was part of the escort of a large supply convoy, dubbed the Mindoro Resupply Unit, heading for Mangarin Bay, Mindoro via the Surigao Strait. Concentrated air attacks were mounted by the Japanese against this large force with attacks almost round-the-clock between the 28 and 30 December. The *Gansevoort* contributed to the convoy's defence and claimed to have destroyed five Japanese aircraft and aided in the destruction of a dozen more. Losses to the ninety-odd ships were restricted to three Liberty ships, the *John Burke* (MC0609), *William Sharon* (MC2734) and *Francisco Morazan* (MC2106), plus *LST 750*. The intensity of these attacks can be gauged by the fact that *Gansevoort* went to General Quarters on forty-nine occasions in this 72–hour period, with the resultant strain and tension on her crew.

During the afternoon of 30 December, *Gansevoort*, which had already shot down two Japanese aircraft that morning, was finally hit by a Kamikaze that struck on the port side of her main deck after bombing the aviation fuel tanker *Porcupine* and setting her ablaze. The resultant detonations blew this deck upward and cut off all contact with the stern of the destroyer, as well as severing all electrical power and steering and many fires broke out. Boiler Rooms 3 & 4 were damaged and she took on a six-degree starboard list. Thirty-four of her officers and men were killed or injured. Aided in fire-fighting by the destroyer *Wilson* (DD-408) and *Philip* (DD-498), the *Gansevoort* was finally towed to the PT-Boat anchorage at Mindoro, adjacent to the burning *Porcupine* which had been hit again and burnt out. The spread of the fires aboard this vessel necessitated the moving

---

3. PT Boats were the approximate American equivalent of the British MTB (Motor Torpedo Boats) or MGB (Motor Gun Boat) and had no armour protection to speak of, but relied on speed.

of the *Gansevoort* to a safer haven at White Beach and most of her surviving crew were landed ashore while attempts were made to salvage her.

There was no repair facilities at the anchorage, but *Gansevoort* was so damaged amidships that she was unable to proceed without a great deal of work and it had to be done within her own limited resources. Her engineering spaces were a shambles. Not daunted, the Engineering Officer, Damage Control Officer and twenty volunteers stayed aboard the destroyer under constant threat of further air raids and patiently effected repairs to her damaged hull. The upper flange of the hull girder in the way of the damage was restored despite lack of suitable materials. The team managed to thus restore longitudinal strength in the mid-length of the ship enough for her to be moved to a more suitable forward area facility.

This good work lasted a month and she was finally considered suitably seaworthy for a longer tow on 2 February. She was subsequently moved to San Pedro Bay and then to Ulithi for further repairs which lasted until 21 April. The *Gansevoort* eventually completed the long voyage home to San Francisco via Pearl Harbor under her own power, arriving on 19 May. This was not the end of her saga; she left San Diego on 3 October and reached New York on 20 October, and then sailed to Charleston Navy Yard where she was paid off on 1 February 1946 as part of the Atlantic Reserve Fleet, surviving at Orange, Texas, until March 1972 before being sunk as a target.

Two further casualties were suffered in January. The destroyer *Shubrick* (DD-639) was assailed by two Kamikazes on the 6th, one of which caused her load of depth-charges to detonate, killing thirty-five of her crew. She was subsequently ordered to the West Coast for repair but ultimately was deemed unworthy of repair and scrapped. The destroyer-escort *Gilligan* (DE-508) was hit by a Kamikaze on 12 January and suffered twelve dead, but her damage was light; she was repaired at Pearl Harbor and resumed operations later.

Heavy Cruiser *Minneapolis* minimally damaged

The *New Orleans* Class Heavy Cruiser *Minneapolis* (CA-36, Captain Harry Browning Slocum, USN) had slight-brush with a Kamikaze on New Year's Day 1945, being attacked by a single aircraft at 14.37. This aircraft, unidentified, crossed the ship's bow and flew down her port side under heavy fire from the close-range weapons. She was eventually shot down very close to the ship's starboard bow, having carried away the starboard minesweeping paravane and grazing the deck. Two of her crew suffered injuries in this incident.[4]

On 2 January, the oiler *Cowanesque* (AO-79, Commander L S McKenzie) was hit and damaged in San Pedro Bay. She was attacked by three single-engined Kamikazes – two of which were destroyed by AA fire, but the third struck her and started large fires aboard. Fortunately, the bomb the aircraft was carrying failed to detonate, and was gallantly retrieved and dumped overboard, while the blazes were finally brought under control. Two of her crew were killed and two wounded, but the oiler was back on task refuelling the ships of the fleet in very short order.

---

4. USS *Minneapolis* CA36, Serial 005, USS *Minneapolis (CA36), Report of Participation in Bombardment of Lingayen Gulf, 6–10 January 1945, inclusive*, dated 17 January 1945.

VT (Proximity) fuses

One gunnery innovation that was to have an increasingly beneficial influence in countering the Kamikaze was the so-called 'Variable Time' (VT) fuse. This was a cover name for what was really a radar proximity fuse and comprised four minute vacuum tubes with associated circuits. One tube acted as an oscillator and antenna, two were amplifiers that measured the low frequency signal and the fourth tube was a gas-filled thyratron which trigged the electrical detonator when the target was at optimum distance. This miniature radar set was both small enough to be inserted into a standard 5in/38 calibre AA shell, the standard 'heavy' anti-aircraft weapon of US Navy Battleships, Fleet Carriers and Cruisers, and the main armament of their destroyers. This assembly was not just small; it was resilient enough to withstand rough handling, storage and firing at sea. The device worked with the shell casing and fuse ring working as a dual dipole antenna, while the nose-cap acted as the receiver. An inbuilt battery was provided which had its electrolyte activated when the shell was fired after a few milliseconds, ensuring that it was clear of the gun and the ship before it became armed. No longer did AA shells have to be physically set and detonation points guessed at because, when the shell was close enough to the target, it automatically reacted with the detonator and the shrapnel burst was activated.[5]

Original research into the VT fuse was done in Great Britain by Sir Samuel Curran and W.A. Butemont, but it was subsequently shared with the USA and developed by a team under Merle A. Tove at Johns Hopkins University Applied Physics Laboratory (APL). It was tested at sea by the light cruiser *Cleveland* (CL-55) in August 1942 when a 52% success rate was achieved, and once the Allies had developed it the Americans put it into mass-production and it was steadily improved. The Command-in-Chief, Fleet Admiral Ernest Joseph King, USN, always a pronounced Anglophobe, was extremely reluctant to supply the Royal Navy with this device for use in the Pacific, despite its origins.

Ommaney Bay sunk

On 3 January 1945, in order to carry out Operation *Mike 1*, a powerful force left San Pedro Bay, Leyte. At 17.17 on 4 January the Bombardment and Fire Support group, together with Task Group 77.4, were approaching the Mindoro Strait and west of Panay

---

5. Its operation was described by the US Navy thus 'the fuse contains a continuous wave high-frequency transmitter. Reflection of the radio wave back to the fuse is received, and interacts with the outgoing impulses to cause a Doppler 'ripple'. Suitably amplified, this 'ripple' energizes a thyratron tube, which acts as an electronic switch. This releases the electrical energy stored in a charged condenser which, in turn, operates an electrical detonator called a squib. The blast from this squib operates a standard detonating fuse, which sets off the main explosive charge in the projectile. The whole process requires an infinitesimal fraction of a second'. The same source claims that this invention was 'proposed by the Navy in August 1940, was developed by the National Defense Research Committee of the Office of Scientific Research and Development. By September 1942, the project had progressed to a point where the Navy had VT fuzes in production.' There was not a word about any of the original British input.

with the Lingayen Fire Support Unit (CTU 77.2.2) plus six CVEs in the van and the San Fabian Fire Support Unit (CTU 77.2.1) plus six more CVEs about fifteen miles astern. The combined force commanded by Vice Admiral Jesse Barrett 'Oley' Oldendorf, USN, (flying his flag in the battleship *California*, BB-44) totalled six battleships (with Rear Admiral George Lester Weyler, USN, in *New Mexico* BB-40), twelve CVEs, four heavy cruisers, two light cruisers, thirty-nine destroyers, twelve APDs and three AOs.

An incoming bogey was reported as attempting to attack the leading group and to have been intercepted by the CAP, but suddenly a Kamikaze, which was identified as a *Judy*, appeared over the rear group and dove straight into the flight deck of the *Ommaney Bay* (CVE-79, Captain Howard Leyland Young, USN). Severe fires broke out which rapidly got out of control. Ultimately the escort carrier had to be abandoned and was sunk but not before one of her aircraft torpedoes cooked off and the resulting blast killed two crewmen on a neighbouring ship. In total *Ommaney Bay* had ninety-three men killed. She was finally put down with torpedoes from the destroyer *Burns* (DD-588).

HMAS *Australia*, which was stationed on the *Ommaney Bay*'s port bow, received no warning of close bogies on the bridge or Aircraft Defence Position (ADP), and when the diving aircraft was first sighted by lookouts it was high on the port side, at about 4,000ft and turning to starboard to commence its final dive. Captain J. Armstrong, RAN, reported that: 'Undoubtedly HMAS *Australia* was caught unawares and though the lesson was taken to heart, it was most regrettable.'[6] Vice-Admiral McCain later used this as an illustration of how surprise was achieved. 'At 17.02 the ship went to General Quarters upon receipt of a report of a bogie, bearing 270 degrees (T), distance 45 miles, closing the formation. The bogie was tracked in from 75 miles to 45 miles, where it was lost in geographic returns from the area. The Army CAP was vectored to intercept and later reported shooting down one twin-engined plane. At 17.15 visual reports were received of enemy planes overhead, in the sun. At 17.16 an enemy plane, believed to have been a twin-engined Kawasaki Ki-48 (Sokei) *Lily* or *Frances*, was sighted by this ship's lookouts, coming out of the sun at about 8,000 feet, parallel to the course of the formation. The plane was taken under fire by 40mm batteries from USS *New Mexico*. Less than five seconds later the plane had peeled off into a dive on an opposite course coming in over the port bow of the *Ommaney Bay* in a dive of 45 degrees. The plane struck the ship on the starboard side of the flight deck, just aft of the island structure.'

At 17.15, what was identified as a *Hamp* was seen almost directly above the destroyer *Barton* (DD-722, Commander Edwin Boardman Dexter, USN), on a bearing of 030 degrees at an altitude of 3,500 feet and heading toward the centre of the Group. Nobody fired on this aircraft until it was almost over the centre of the formation, when *California* opened fire with every AA gun she had. It was an impressive sight, but too late and no hits were seen. This audacious pilot had achieved total surprise and proceeded to go into his suicide dive, taking the *Lunga Point* (CVE-94, Captain George Arthur Tappan Washburn, USN) as his target. The pilot deserved better, for his aiming was just off and the aircraft went into the sea very close alongside the carrier, fortunately without

---

6. Commanding Officer HMAS *Australia*, Action Report – *Mike 1* Operation, D.40/202/9 dated 22 January 1945.

causing any damage or casualties.[7] His companion, who achieved equal surprise, made no such mistake with his attack on *Ommaney Bay*. From the stricken carrier a similar story of complete surprise was recorded, although the attacker was identified in Captain Howard L. Young's report as 'an undetected twin-engined Kamikaze' which approached the carrier 'out of the sun nearly dead ahead.' This aircraft tentatively identified as a *Frances* [Yokosuka P1Y, *Ginga*, (Milky Way) twin-engined bomber] was one of the largest aircraft used up to that date for the Kamikaze mission its normal bomb load would have been two 500lb bombs. Whatever the true identity of the attacker it strafed the ship as it approached, its bullets contributing to what was to come as aircraft on the deck, in particular an Avenger torpedo-bomber parked aft of the ship's island, began to burn and petrol began spewing out from other damaged aircraft. The Kamikaze then aimed at the ship's small island structure, just clipping it before penetrating down and aft through the after end of the open bridge. 'The after end of the open bridge was destroyed and all superstructure above collapsed.'[8] The aircraft went right through the starboard side of the flight deck where it touched off a huge blaze among the ready-use AA ammunition, and finally ended up on the No.1 starboard sponson. It was said to have been carrying two bombs, one of which, estimated to have been a 500lb delayed-action fuse, detonated among the fully armed and fuelled planes at the forward end of the hangar. 'All the aircraft here were fuelled to capacity and the ship's own gasoline system was purged with inert gas. Cofferdams around gasoline tanks were also charged with inert gas.'[9]

The second bomb travelled deep into the vessel and exploded in the ship's oil tanks, knocking out the forward boilers. The resulting fires were deadly, burning aviation gas sprayed all around the hangar spaces, which soon filled with smoke, and the after machinery rooms were also quickly rendered completely untenable by smoke and scalding steam. The fire in the hangar spread rapidly as the mains pressure was rendered inoperative, and the water curtains and sprinkler system failed to operate as a result. For forty minutes the fires raged out of control and, it being obvious the ship was doomed, abandon ship was ordered. Within a few minutes the fires reached the torpedo warheads which detonated and blew away the entire after part of the flight deck. 'Nine torpedoes, complete with warheads, were stowed in racks on the hangar deck, six to port and three to starboard. Dinner was about to be served in the wardroom and supper was being served to the crew.'[10] Nearby destroyers closed amidships to pass fire hoses, but were unable to do so due to the intense heat being generated by the hangar deck inferno. One destroyer came alongside the starboard bow to embark survivors, but had to immediately back away when the blazing carrier drifted down on her and damaged the port wing of the destroyer's bridge sponson. The evacuation continued from both the forecastle

---

7. Captain W. L. Freseman, USN, Commander Destroyer Squadron 60 Action Report. Serial 013 OF6–60/A16–3, dated 2 February 1945.

8. C.O. *Ommaney Bay*, Action report letter CVE79/A16–3, Serial 001, dated 4 February 1945.

9. C.O. *Ommaney Bay*, War Damage Report letter CVE79/L11/A9, Serial 002 dated 3 February 1945.

10. *Ommaney Bay* -War Damage Report, *op cit*.

and fantail aft, with the Captain as last man away at 18.12. When the torpedo warheads ignited at 18.18, the after flight deck collapsed and the ship was burning from stem to stern. The destroyer *Burns* (DD-588, Commander Jacob Thompson Bullen, Jr., USN) was ordered to sink the blazing hulk by torpedo and at 19.58 she fired a single missile which struck amidships and *Ommaney Bay*, her back already weakened by the fire and explosions, she immediately broke in half and went down. She took with her ninety-three dead from her crew and air group, plus, as previously recorded, two men aboard one of the nearby destroyers who were killed by debris when the stored torpedoes blew up.

Another appalling loss this day was the ammunition ship *Lewis L. Dyche* (MC-2532, Master John W Platt) which was hit amidships at 08.20 by a *Val* while anchored off Mindoro. The detonation immediately set off her cargo and she blew up with a shocking explosion. An eyewitness aboard the minelayer *Monadnock* (CM-9, Lieutenant-Commander Frederick O. Goldsmith, USNR) stated that this enormous fireball 'completely disintegrated the *Dyche*' and killed every man aboard. Her casualty list was forty-one crew and thirty Naval Armed Guard gunners.

The destroyer minesweeper *Long* (DMS-12, Lieutenant Stanley Caplan USN), a former *Clemson* Class 'four-piper' destroyer, was attacked by a *Zeke* in Lingayen Gulf on 6 January. The Kamikaze made a low approach and, although hit, struck the ship about one foot above the waterline under her bridge. The ship had to subsequently be abandoned and, in that state, was hit by a second Kamikaze later. She finally sank in the early hours of 7 January.

Heavy Cruiser *Louisville* takes a hit

At 17.14 on 6 January, the *Northampton* Class heavy cruiser *Louisville* (CA-28, Captain Rex LeGrande Hicks, USN), flying the flag of Rear Admiral Theodore Chandler, USN, commander of Cruiser Division 4, was taken as the main target for a pair of Kamikazes. Chandler had only hoisted his flag on 8 December, having been moved over from Battleship Division (BatDiv-2). One of these aircraft was immediately hit by AA fire and crashed into the ocean near one of the screening destroyers, but the second passed through the screen. *Louisville*'s gunners were unable to open fire until the enemy had cleared the destroyers and by then there remained but a few moments to chop him up. 'All *Louisville* guns that could bear were shooting. [The] plane was smoking, but kept on coming, headed straight for the foremast structure. By swinging the ship hard to port, the CO diverted the blow from the comparatively fragile and vulnerable foremast structure to Turret 2 and the pilot house. All guns' crews continued to shoot until the plane struck.'[11] The Commander of DesRon 90 recorded that this Kamikaze hit on the *Louisville*'s bridge structure,[12] but *Louisville*'s own report stated that the aircraft itself detonated on the starboard side forward, while one of the two bombs it was carrying blew a hole in the deck and the other wrecked the side of the chart house. Captain Hicks

---

11. Serial 005A, Action Report USS *Louisville* (CA-28) in Seizure and Occupation of Luzon Area, 2 January to 12 January 1945, dated 12 January 1945.
12. Action Report DesRon 90.

was badly burned by the blast and command of the ship devolved onto Executive Officer Commander W. P. McCarty, USN. In total *Louisville* suffered fifty-eight casualties in this attack.

HMAS *Arunta* has a close call

By 5 January the Bombardment and Fire Support Group, Task Group 77.2 (TG.77.2), commanded by Vice-Admiral Jessee Barrett Oldendorf, were pushing towards Luzon's west coast in preparation for the Lingayen Gulf landing operations on the 6th and were within 120 miles of Manila itself for most of the hours of daylight. This was tantamount to putting your head into the lion's mouth, it seemed to many, and the Japanese saw it both as a provocation and an invitation. The day was therefore bound to be one of battle and was described by the Captain of *Australia* as 'a day of continuous air alerts with reports of up to 69 bogies being taken in from the ships' radar.'[13] Although there were many red alerts it was not until late in the afternoon that the big Kamikaze raids came in. One of the early victims was the Australian *Tribal* Class destroyer HMAS *Arunta* (I-30, Commander Alfred Edgar Buchanan, RAN). *Arunta*, which with her sister ship *Warramunga* formed Desron 56, was on the screen of the leading group of TG 77.2, stationed just off the *Louisville*'s port beam, when, at 17.35, when the ships were nearing their objective, this attack came in. In her Captain's Action Report this was described thus: 'Two bandits were sighted on the port bow heading straight towards us. Speed was at once increased to 25 knots and fire was opened with barrage set to 3,000 yards.'

Tribal Class destroyers, groups of which were built for the Royal Navy pre-war and the Australian and Canadian Navies during the war, had been designed to carry eight low-angle 4.7in guns in four twin open-shield mountings as anti-surface target weapons, although the Australian ships only carried three plus a twin 4in AA mounting. The maximum elevation of the 4.7in guns was only 40 degrees, and were thus inferior to both American and Japanese destroyer guns of the same era. But the approach favoured by many Kamikaze pilots, at low level, enabled *Arunta*'s main armament to play its full part in defence. Each mounting had a rate of fire of twelve rounds per minute. Both *Arunta* and *Warramunga* had been equipped with American radars by this time, carrying both the SC-2 air-search and target direction, and also the curved SG surface-search microwave sets. The US Navy was fortunate enough to be so resource rich that they could provide a degree of insurance against damage or other failure by mounting a minimum of two air-search radars (SC-2 and SK sets) in all its fleet and light fleet carriers. (One unexpected bonus with regard to the *Independence* class was that, due to their small island/bridge profiles, of the two radar sets, at least one was mounted on a stub mast instead of both being grouped together as on the larger carriers – which occasionally provided a better signal reception.) The Action Report continued: 'One of the enemy planes veered to the right. The other headed straight for our bridge. The wheel was put hard a starboard and,

13. D.40/202/9, Commanding Officer HMAS *Australia*, Action Report – Mike 1. Operation. Dated 22 January 1945.

thanks to the extreme manoeuvrability of the *Tribal* class destroyer, the plane missed by feet. It plunged into the sea alongside the Gear room on the port side. The plane, a Zero, carried a bomb, estimated to be around 50lb. The subsequent explosion holed the ship's side in several places and severed the electrical leads to both steering motors.

'The ship continued to circle with the wheel hard a starboard for about five minutes, as while enemy planes were still attacking, I was anxious to keep moving. Before long, however, it was necessary to stop the main engines as the pumping system was failing, and to shut off steam in order to isolate an exhaust steam pipe that had been holed in the gear room. When the steam cleared sufficiently, the Gear room was found to be flooded to the water line and the forced lubricating oil system damaged by several holes both in the steam and oil lines. The Gear room and the Engine room, which had been partly flooded, were pumped dry and the work of repairing the steam and oil lines by welding and brazing proceeded.' The *Arunta* suffered two men killed and five wounded in this attack, one of the fatalities, Able Seaman Henry Louis Sellick, being buried at sea on the 5th, and that of Stoker Petty Officer Richard Allan Hand the following morning.

The other ships of the Task Group had also been heavily engaged with the enemy and had moved off before *Arunta* was got underway again, but the *Allen M. Sumner* Class destroyer *Ingraham* (DD-694, Commander John Francis Harper, Jr., USN) remained behind as escort, and slowly circled her until the main engines were ready and other emergency repairs had been affected. *Arunta* got underway again at 22.55 and worked up to 25 knots, and although both ships were attacked later by conventional aircraft, no further damage was done. Both Australian destroyers were therefore able to carry out their assigned role as Minesweeper Support Unit (TU 77.2.9) in Lingayen Gulf between 6 and 8 January.

Manila Bay damaged

On 5 January it was also the turn of the escort carrier *Manila Bay* (CVE-61, Captain Fitzhugh Lee, USN). She had been at General Quarters since 16.50 and set Material Condition Able, the highest state of readiness, as there had been repeated aerial clashes with numerous Japanese aircraft for an hour. *Manila Bay* had just launched eight fighter aircraft as CAP and the carrier group was steaming at fifteen knots. Japanese warships had also been sighted and *Manila Bay* was busy preparing a torpedo-bomber strike against these, with air cover, and, as a result, some twenty-three of her aircraft that remained aboard were being refuelled and armed in readiness for this mission.

At 17.46, six Kamikazes selected the group as their targets and approached at low level above the surface of the ocean from out of the setting sun, from off the port beam. Two of these, identified as *Zekes*, selected *Manila Bay* and made what was later described as 'an expert approach.' Both oncoming aircraft weaved and strafed as they bored in at high-speed. When approximately one thousand yards out, both machines made sharp pull-ups into climbing turns and then made steep dives into the *Manila Bay* from about 800 feet altitude. Both aircraft were heavily hit by AA fire from the carrier and her escorts, the second machine being more affected. Its pilot had probably been killed as it appeared to be aiming at the bridge, which received only a glancing blow that carried away the starboard yardarm, and then crashed into the sea. The first aircraft, however, continued straight and true, despite any damage, to crash right through the flight deck at the base of the ship's island and into the radar transmitter room, starting large fires both there and in an adjacent radio room, while leaving petrol-fuelled fires burning on the flight deck, gallery deck and among aircraft parked in the hangar deck. Here three fully fuelled TBMs were set ablaze. The remaining fire sprinklers performed efficiently and heroic work below by the fire-fighting teams in breathing apparatus and asbestos suits, using fog and foam, managed to confine the blaze.

All the ship's radio, radar, telephone and public address system circuits were destroyed as were one sprinkler system and a hangar deck water curtain. There was a sixteen-foot hole blown in the flight deck and the forward elevator was jammed and buckled, while bomb fragments caused extensive damage below. The engines remained unharmed and fully functional, although when the electric circuits went out they caused the engine room telegraph indicator to drop to the 'Stop' position, which the engine room staff obeyed so the ship came to a halt for fifteen minutes before the error was rectified. *Manila Bay* took on a 4–degree list to port, but by 18.20 she was underway once more with all fires out and steering by her engines. By 19.00 she was able to resume her place in the formation. Her crew suffered the loss of fourteen men killed and fifty-two wounded in this action, but *Manila Bay* was back conducting air operations within 24 hours. It was a remarkable achievement

Australia damaged yet again

Part of the same group that devastated the *Manila Bay* also gave the *Australia* close attention as her Action Report recorded: 'At least six Enemy planes were sighted on a relative bearing of Red 86, just above the water and were taken under fire by all ships. One went into the water abreast the destroyer screen and one altered course to pass astern, what happened to it is not known. The remainder came in weaving low and fast despite intense AA fire. They crossed ahead of HMAS *Australia*, two within 100 yards. One went on to score a hit on the CVE *Manila Bay* and another executed a very steep turn to the right, and, ending in a vertical dive, hit HMAS *Australia* on the port side of the upper deck amidships at 17.35. This plane carried a bomb which was responsible for a number of casualties. The fate of the remainder was not seen. The resulting fire was quickly subdued.'[14] Max Grey, an Able Seaman aboard, gave a graphic account of what took place: 'The bridge was still alright in the second encounter, but there were a lot of the on-deck gun crews – all out in the open – and the anti-aircraft guns. They never had a hope. One of my mates from my hometown, Smithton, was on one of the guns and the gun was completely written off (*sic*). Nothing left of the thing. It was blown to pieces.'[15]

14. D.40/202/9, Commanding Officer HMAS *Australia*, Action Report – Mike 1. Operation. Dated 22 January 1945.
15. Australian War Memorial – Public Record: MSS1946; Folder number: 1 of 1; DPI: 300. Grey, Maxwell David (H1953, AB, RAN). *An Interview with Max Grey*, W. Geof Jay, 10 December 2–5. Recollections of Service Life Series.

Commodore Harold Farncomb was to record that actual material damage was slight, although the ship's funnels, crane, decks and ammunition lockers were damaged to some extent, while the biggest setback to her fighting efficiency was the fact that Port 2, 4in twin mounting was put out of action for a short period, as were Nos.4 and 6 40mm Bofors. It was the manpower losses that *Australia* suffered that were the most serious aspect. Among the twenty-five men killed and thirty wounded were the whole of P/2 mounting's gun crew, eight members of P/1's gun crew and many Bofors' gun crews as well as the captains of both the port and starboard multiple 2–pdr pom-poms, and most of the upper-deck ammunition supply parties. Included in the numbers were three officers killed and one wounded. These losses were replaced by redistributing the remaining crew and the heavy cruiser continued to function.

Savo Island lights up

A unique form of defence was adopted by the *Casablanca* Class escort carrier *Savo Island* (CVE-78, Captain Clarence Eugene Ekstrom, USN) when she was targeted by a lone Kamikaze on 5 January. As well as every gun that would bear, a searchlight was trained upon the oncoming aircraft at full intensity in an attempt to blind, or at least disorientate the pilot. Maybe it worked, maybe not, but the fact was that the aircraft, which was again aiming at the island, missed and just nudged the ships radar mast before going into the sea. A bent aerial was the sole damage received and flight deck operations were not even interrupted.

Small ships suffer

The destroyer escort *Stafford* (DE-411, Lieutenant V. H. Craig Jnr, USN) was damaged at this time. With two companions, *Goss* (DE-444, Lieutenant Commander Claude Siceluff Kirkpatrick, USN) and the *John Butler* Class destroyer escort *Ulvert M. Moore* (DE-442, Lieutenant Commander Franklin Delano Roosevelt, Jr., USN), the *Stafford* was screening the *Casablanca* Class escort carrier *Tulagi* (CVE-72, Captain Joseph Campbell Cronin, USN). At 17.47 an attack developed with eight *Zekes* approaching out of the setting sun and low down over the water. Fire was opened by all the ships at a range of about 8,000 yards and four of the attacking aircraft peeled away to starboard. The remaining quartet pressed on toward the carrier. Intense fire destroyed two of these machines, one passed by and was shot down by F4F Wildcat fighters, while the fourth hurtled at full speed into the *Stafford*, impacting and detonating amidships on her starboard side, just abaft her funnel. The ship immediately lost way and water flooded into her boiler room. All surviving members of her crew were taken aboard the *Ulvert M. Moore* except for a small emergency contingent, who fought to keep her afloat. To keep some stability all the topside depth-charges, K-guns (depth-charge throwers) and the loading machinery were jettisoned. She was badly damaged and had two men killed and twelve more injured, but remained afloat. Later her crew, other than the wounded, re-embarked and on 11 January the ship sailed for San Pedro Bay, Leyte, which she reached five days later and subsequently dry-docked.[16]

---

16. *Dictionary of American Naval Fighting Ships* (DANFS), Washington Navy Yard, DC.

Other casualties included the destroyer *Helm* (DD-388, Commander Albert Francis Hollingsworth) damaged and a miscellany of other small ships, including the *Orca* (AVP-21), *Apache* (AT-26) and *LCI(G)-70* damaged, while on 6 January the destroyer-minesweeper *Long* (DMS-12, Lieutenant Stanley Caplan) was hit and she sank the next day.

The *New Mexico* hit on her bridge

Meanwhile the invasion proceeded with the heavy bombardment group taking up positions off San Fernando to Poro Point, and the minesweeping destroyers and vessels worked at clearing the mouth of Lingayen Gulf while five APDs with Underwater Demolition Teams and their high-explosives were kept out to seaward until needed. In line ahead the big ships formed up at 10.20, with the two Australian heavy cruisers leading the line, and, next astern, the battleship *New Mexico* (BB-40, Captain Robert Walton Fleming, USN) which, as stated, was flying the flag of Rear Admiral George L. Weyler, as flagship of BatDiv 3.

Enemy shore batteries proved ineffective, but an attack by three *Val* dive-bombers was made on *Warramunga* at 10.22, which she fought off without loss on either side. The bombardment commenced at 10.41 at 16,000 yards range. The first Kamikaze reaction was slow in coming, isolated reconnaissance machines were sighted from 11.20 onward and the CAP shot down a lone *Val* at 11.53. Around midday a single Kamikaze from a group of four, with a 500lb bomb under its belly, suddenly dove on the battleship from astern, plunging into her port navigation bridge where the bomb detonated, causing carnage among those assembled there.[17] The ship's commander, Captain Fleming, Lieutenant-General Herbert Lumsden, a former armoured division commander in North Africa and who had been sent by Premier Winston Churchill as Special Military Representative to General MacArthur, and Sub-Lieutenant (S) Morton, RN, as well as William Henry Chickering, a war correspondent with *Time* magazine, were all killed instantly on the bridge of the *New Mexico*, but Admiral Sir Bruce Fraser, C-in-C designate of the British Pacific Fleet, standing on the other side of the bridge, was miraculously unharmed, saying later he only received 'a bit of a bang in the ears.' It was doubly poignant in that Lumsden got on very well with MacArthur, and Fraser had requested Lumsden's presence aboard to witness the bombardment and that Morton was Fraser's Secretary. Command of the battleship descended upon the Executive Officer, Commander John T. Warren, USN. Although two of the ship's AA positions had been wrecked she continued to operate and provide bombardment support, despite the loss of twenty-nine men killed and a further eighty-seven injured in this strike. A medical sidelight on this tragedy was that because *New Mexico* remained under attack for the following four days, the crew had to remain closed up for action. Captain Ian Jones stated that, 'Only at night could the health care teams render definitive care to those wounded in the initial attack. It was not possible to evacuate the wounded from the ship for thirteen days.'[18]

17. USS *New Mexico* (BB-40) Deck Log, 6 January 1945.
18. Jones, Captain Ian, RFD, MB ChM, MHA, GradCertED, FRCOG, FRANZCOG, FACS, RANR – *Surgery on ships: constraints and difficult realities.*

Within ten minutes *New Mexico* was hit again, this time by an *Oscar* which dove on the port bow, causing little damage and no casualties, nor did a brief strafing run on her add to her difficulties. Others were not so fortunate. The Captain of the *Allen M. Sumner* reported that: 'The Kamikazes made full and clever use of their close proximity to the land to the utmost advantage of concealment until just prior to their assaults, and many made their dives from out of the sun as well.' Some five Japanese aircraft were claimed shot down at this time, and some missed their targets by the closest amounts. The destroyer *Walke* (DD-723 Commander G. F. Davis, USN), with the minesweeping group was attacked by four planes which approached simultaneously on the starboard side. 'Two were shot down, one crashing within fifty feet of the fantail; the third swung around to the port side and sliced into the bridge structure in the vicinity of the sea cabin. The bomb passed through the CIC, but did not explode. The bridge was enveloped in a gasoline fire and many casualties resulted. The fourth plane was also shot down.'[19] The *Walke* suffered severe damage from this hit, the main battery and torpedo directors, and the two forward Mk. 51 directors were both badly damaged, the Mark 12 and SC radars suffered only minor damage, but all the ship's radio equipment other than TBL (High Frequency) and MAN (Very High Frequency) transmitters were rendered inoperative. There was also much structural damage to the pilot house and the captain's sea cabin. Commander Davis himself was very badly wounded and died later along with eleven other members of his crew, while thirty-five men were wounded.[20] However, by 12.40 *Walke* had reported that all her fires were under control, and although the CIC and main director remained inoperative, her engine rooms were not damaged.

The *Allen M. Sumner* (DD-692, Commander Norman John Sampson, USN) herself was attacked by three more aircraft, one after the other, with the smallest of intervals between them. The leading pair were both driven off by the destroyer's fierce AA defence, but the third of the trio was made of sterner stuff. This machine approached from the ship's port bow, and actually dove right through the rigging and struck No.2 funnel a glancing blow, before crashing on to the after quintuple 21in torpedo mounting. The bomb carried by this machine detonated as the plane hit. Number 3 twin 5in turret and No.4 20mm mounting were both damaged, while the after torpedo-tube mounting and two other 20mm guns were totally demolished. A fire broke out in No.2 magazine, which required flooding to bring it under control. There was an eight-foot hole blown in the ship's main deck at frame 158 and compartment 203 flooded with water, oil and debris. The ships degaussing equipment was rendered non-functional.[21] The battleship *West Virginia* (BB-48, Captain Herbert Victor Wiley, USN) was also damaged at this time and was by no means the only battleship to receive such a blow.

---

19. Captain W. L. Freseman, USN, Commander Destroyer Squadron 60 Action Report. Serial 013 OF6–60/A16–3, dated 2 February 1945.
20. Roscoe, Theodore, *United States Destroyer Operations in World War II*, Annapolis, 1953. Naval Institute Press.
21. Degaussing equipment. Basically a cable girth or belt emplaced around the ship carrying an electric current to provide protection against magnetic mines.

Battleship *California* heavily hit

On 6 January the battleship *California* (Captain S. B. Brewer, USN), with Vice-Admiral Oldendorf aboard, was providing shore bombardment at Lingayen Gulf when, at 17.19, two *Zeke*s suddenly appeared from out of the loom of the land where they had remained hidden, and made a parallel approach to the bombardment line, before turning into their attack still skimming the ocean. Both aircraft were taken under intense fire in the few moments remaining and one was destroyed close in, but the other, although repeatedly seen to be hit, made a steep climb and dove down across the starboard beam, striking the ship at the mainmast. Simultaneous with this and the enormous detonation that followed, one of *California*'s 5in guns in No.4 mounting misfired and exploded inside the turret. Both these explosions resulted in large fires which took considerable time to control. Casualties were high with six officers and twenty-six men killed outright, three missing and thirteen died later of their injuries. In addition 155 further officers and enlisted men were wounded, many being burnt. Much of her after gun battery was put out of action and her battle efficiency was reduced by twenty-five per cent. Undeterred she made temporary repairs on the spot and remained to carry out her critical mission of shore bombardment until the job was done.[22]

Louisville (CA-28) damaged again

The *Louisville* (CA-28) was attacked again by no less than six Kamikazes of which four were destroyed, but the fourth of the group, a *Judy* dive-bomber, crashed into her starboard flag bridge structure at 17.14. Among the many casualties was Rear-Admiral Theodore Chandler, USN, commanding Cruiser Division 4, who received terrible burns. His Orderly, Marine Walter Joseph Siegel, USMC, and forty-one naval personnel, were killed while fifty-six were wounded. Despite his horrible injuries Chandler continued to issue orders[23] and assisted in manning the fire hoses to stem the worst of the fires, before taking his turn in line for treatment. He suffered from scorched lungs which proved fatal. In spite of everything the medical team could do, the Admiral died the next day. The structural damage to *Louisville*, added to the previous day's attack, was extensive but she continued in action and was not withdrawn to make temporary repairs until later. Subsequently she was despatched to Mare Island Navy Yard, California, for an extensive repair.

One of *Louisville*'s survivors reported that the body of the Kamikaze pilot, Tadasu Fukino, almost naked save for a white cloth around his groin, was lying some ten feet from the 8in turret with the top of his head missing. His corpse was unceremoniously dumped over the side by the fire-fighters and his brain followed separately soon after![24]

---

22. USS *California* (BB-44), Serial 0030, *Report of Damage Sustained by Ship During Enemy Aircraft Attack at 1720(I) 6 January while en route to Lingayen Gulf Landings, Suicide Plane Crash the Cause*, dated 25 January 1945.
23. Admirals lead from the front. Ships' bridges being the most favoured targets of the Kamikaze with the results we have seen. Not for Navy leaders a cosy bunker miles behind the front line.
24. Duffy, John, *The Wonderful World of John Duffy: An Autobiography*, 1997, privately published Palisades Park, New Jersey. A further development was that Fukino's Aunt, Ms Hino, and his youngest sister contacted Duffy via the journalist K. Tatsuno, who once trained Kamikaze

Columbia seriously damaged, but continues in action

Meanwhile the *Cleveland* Class Light Cruiser *Columbia* (CL-56, Captain Maurice Edwin Curtis, USN) joined the supporting warship squadron in readiness for the landings in Lingayen Gulf. On 6 January, as she was engaged in the pre-invasion softening-up bombardments, her twelve 6in guns were commencing, Japanese suicide attacks began. The *Columbia* was in the thick of it, being near-missed by one suicide aircraft and then in quick succession, hit fair-and-square by two more. '*Columbia* was first crashed close aboard by one of the Kamikaze planes, then was struck on her port quarter by a second. The plane and its bomb penetrated two decks before exploding with tremendously damaging effect, killing 13 and wounding 44 of the crew, putting her after turrets out of action, and setting the ship afire. Prompt flooding of two magazines prevented further explosions, and impressive damage control measures enabled *Columbia* to complete her bombardment with her two operative turrets, and remain in action to give close support to underwater demolition teams.'[25]

Australia hit once more

HMAS *Australia* had been carrying out bombardments with her 8in guns during the 6th, hitting targets as required at Poro Point and San Fernando in the morning, but all the time it was reported that there were numerous suicide attacks taking place, the battleship *New Mexico* being struck and the Australian-manned *London* Class heavy cruiser *Shropshire* (83, Captain Charles Alfred Godfrey Nichols, RN) near missed. The afternoon was no different; if anything the Kamikaze attacks intensified as the day wore on and in the later afternoon it became *Australia*'s turn again, when, 'At 17.34 a *Val* dived on the ship from the starboard quarter and, flattening out, hit the ship on the upper deck between S.2 and S.1 4in gun mounts. This plane also carried a bomb which, from fragments found aboard, appeared to have been converted from a large calibre shell.'[26] A fire broke out at the point of impact and forced the temporary shutting down of 'A' boiler room, but this was quickly got under control. S.2 mounting was put out of action, the gunnery controls

pilots, after he had given a television interview in which he described Kamikaze pilots as brave men to do what they did. But he refused to meet the sister or to give back the piece of the aircraft's wing he had brought home and kept. Hino herself wrote a book for Japanese children in 1997 trying to explain their motivation to the newer generation of Japanese. *(Tsubasa no kakera: Tokkou ni chitta Kaigun yobi gakusei no seishun (Wing fragment: Youth of Navy reserve students who died in special attack),* 1997, Tokyo. Kodansha.

25. DANS entry for *Columbia*. There are several ship biographies concerning this ship – see – Greg Shooner, *America's Gem- The Story of USS* Columbia *CL-56 1941–1946.* Self-published 2012; Captain Cary Hall, USN (Rtd.), *The War Cruises of USS* Columbia, Beverly Hills, FL, for USS *Columbia* Association, 1987 and also *USS* Columbia *Memories,* self-published November 1988; Reprint – *Battle History of the USS* Columbia: *The "Blue Book",* USS Columbia Association, Beverly Hills, FL; and see also Ron Burt, *Kamikaze Nightmare,* his brother Pete Burt was a survivor of the *Ommaney Bay* aboard *Columbia* at the time.
26. D.40/202/9, Commanding Officer HMAS *Australia,* Action Report – Mike 1. Operation. Dated 22 January 1945.

and ammunition lockers for this mounting were destroyed, and the air-warning radar was out of action for twenty-five hours. Once again there were casualties amongst the gunners, fourteen men were killed and twenty-six wounded which included all the crew of the unfortunate S.2 gun and most of those serving S.1. This left *Australia* with just one 4in HA mounting in action on either side.

Destroyer *Newcomb* damaged

The *Newcomb* (DD-586, Commander Ira Ellis McMillan, USN) was a *Fletcher* Class destroyer which had already seen considerable action and was destined to see much more. She had been part of the screen for the light cruiser *St. Louis* (CL-49, Captain Ralph Henry Roberts, USN), acting in support of the minesweeping operations, and, on conclusion of that task was steering to join a night retirement group[27] when she was attacked by no less than seven suicide aircraft. The first attack occurred around 18.00 when the *Newcomb* was attacked by two aircraft which were identified as Tonys. The first machine was heavily hit and crashed close off the port quarter of the destroyer just twenty-five yards out. Debris from the crash came inboard, killing two of her crew and wounding fifteen others[28] and heavily damaged the ship's bridge wings, flying bridge and fire-control director. Captain McMillan was wounded while the pair who died were Signalman Ray Collins, hit in the hip by shrapnel (he died later on the wardroom table) and Fire Control Man Ed Schoenneberg, who was struck down on the flying bridge – his chest blown open by a large section of shrapnel. Included among the wounded were Quartermaster John Mulqueen, whose legs took the brunt of his wounds and a lookout, Robert Schultz, who was blown overboard with only his steel helmet (with holes through) remaining aboard! Another version, however, has it that Schultz dived from the bridge rather than being blown up and landed in the sea close to the body of the Kamikaze pilot as the ships steamed away, still under heavy attack. He trod water in the shark-infested sea for fourteen hours before being rescued the following day without a mark on him! The damage to the fire-control director affected *Newcomb*'s gunnery accuracy until it was able to be repaired.

The first aircraft to actually score a *direct* hit struck her after funnel, which put the after fireroom out of operation and caused a blaze in the upper handling room of No.3, 5in mounting. This was followed by a second direct hit by an aircraft (one which was carrying a 1,214lb bomb, that ploughed into the ship amidships near the torpedo workshop. The explosion wrecked both engine rooms and immobilised *Newcomb*. The devastation in the 'midships area was widespread: the after funnel, both torpedo mountings, upperworks, deckhouses, 40mm mountings and their ready-use magazines were all blown over the side. The razing of the upperworks was compounded by the fact that the main deck

---

27. Having operated close to shore during daylight hours such groups of vessels moved further out to sea during the hours of darkness to guard against potential surface attacks.
28. One eyewitness claimed that the damage was actually inflicted by 'friendly fire' from a neighbouring destroyer that failed to check fire quickly enough as this aircraft, which evidently had intended to hit *Newcomb*'s bridge, passed along her starboard side under fire.

between frames 108 and 135 was fractured, the starboard side being heaved upward and the port side forced down, all of which was worsened by the fierce fires that broke out.

A third direct hit was taken with this aircraft smashing into the forward funnel, its flaming petrol spreading aft to add to the conflagration already raging in the body of the destroyer. The destroyer *Leutze* (DD-481, Commander Berton Aldrich Robbins, Jr., USN) gallantly came alongside at 18.11, despite the raging inferno, in an effort to assist fire-fighting, but before he could act, a fourth Kamikaze came in aiming at the bridge. Heavily hit by defending AA fire this machine was knocked off course and impacted on what was left of the amidships deck. Meeting no resistance this aircraft slid across the *Newcomb* and into the quarterdeck of the *Leutze* before exploding. The damaged *Leutze* was forced to back off, with eight casualties among her crew, and at 18.30 the destroyer *Beale* (DD-471, Commander Doyle Murray Coffee, USN) took her place. She managed to pass fire hoses across to aid the fire-fighting and by 19.00 *Newcomb*'s fires were under control, being finally extinguished half-an-hour later. As for the remaining three attackers, they were destroyed before they could reach the ship.

The *Newcomb*'s damage above the waterline was obvious; the central section of the ship had been virtually erased, while below she was just as badly hurt. The keel was buckled at frame 120 for two feet and was projecting some six inches below the base line. There was a 5ft x 2½ft hole opened at frame 119, six feet to port of the centreline. There were two 1ft x 1½ft holes at frames 120 and 121, five and six feet to starboard of the centreline. There was a 1ft diameter hole at frame 118, an 8in diameter hole at frame 119, a 6in diameter hole at frame 123, many small projections of plating at frame 120 and leaking shell plating seams from frames 120 to 130. There was up to 6in distortion of the shell plating on both sides from frame 100 to 140. Both bulkhead 110 and 131 were destroyed, flooding B-2, B-3 and B-4 to the waterline while bulkhead 92 was bulged and damaged with minor leakage into B-1-1.[29] The fact that *Newcomb* was not only still afloat after this, but that she able to be towed into Keramo Retto from 20.30 throughout the night and reached that anchorage safely at 09.30 speaks volumes for her construction. She was built at Boston Navy Yard- they should be proud of their workmanship.[30]

The ordeal of the *O'Brien*

The Allied navies continued their probing of the Japanese defences at Lingayen Gulf, prior to the planned Allied invasion of Luzon, which itself was scheduled to take place on 9 January. Underwater obstacles and mines were slowly and methodically dealt with to clear the offshore area before the landing ships approached. While these tasks were

29. NARA, Seattle. Record Group 181, Entry 59A-271 13th Naval District Bremerton, Washington. *General Correspondence 1947–48. Structural Repairs in Forward Areas During World War II* – BuShips Booklet, Washington, December 1949.

30. After being patched up in dry-dock, *Newcomb* did return home. She was never the same ship again and was struck from the Navy List in 1946, and broken up in early 1947, as indeed were many other badly damaged ships in the immediate post-war period which were condemned as not being worth the cost of repair.

carefully and deliberately carried out, the warships attempted to give adequate cover and protection to the vulnerable ships employed in this work.

Two destroyers, the *Richard P. Leary* (DD-664) and the *Walke* (DD-723), were both damaged in the same area on 6 January. The *Leary* suffered only slight damage from a twin-engined Nakajima J1N1–S *Gekko* (Moonlight), 'Irving', Kamikaze which just brushed the forward 5in gun turret before crashing into the sea. The destroyer also shot down a Nakajima B6N *Tenzan* (Heavenly Mountain) *Jill* in the same attack. The *Walke* was more seriously hurt. Attacked from a low-level by four *Oscar* fighters, she shot down two of them, but the third crashed into the port side of her bridge and, although the bomb she was carrying failed to explode, it passed right through the structure near the CIC and caused enormous damage. The destroyer's skipper, Commander George F. Davis, USN, was extremely badly burnt but continued to command until his ship was safe; he later died of his injuries and was awarded the Medal of Honor. The fourth *Oscar* was also destroyed close alongside the ship. Despite her damage, the *Walke* remained on station until 9 January when she returned to Mare Island Navy Yard for repairs, and later rejoined the fleet off Okinawa.

The destroyer *O'Brien* (DD-725, Commander William Woodward Outerbridge, USN) was, at 14.10, ordered to give gunfire support to the minesweeping group by replacing the damaged *Walke* and, in compliance with this, was proceeding up the swept channel heading north-west at 14.32. She was just passing the destroyer *Barton* (DD-722), heading in the reverse direction toward the anchorage (to hospitalise a very badly burnt crewman who unfortunately later died), when the two ships passed each other at a distance of about 500 yards. This very tempting dual target was selected by at least two *Zekes* which had used smoke clouds from the burning shore installations to screen their approach.

The leading aircraft selected *O'Brien* as his target while only one of *Barton's* 20mm guns had time to open fire as this aircraft dove. The Kamikaze struck the port propeller guard at the rear of the destroyer, knocking a hole in the ship's side which started a fire in an adjacent compartment and let in a considerable amount of water. The second *Zeke* attacked *Barton* from the ship's quarter in a steep diving attack. 'Although taken under fire by all guns that could bear, and hit repeatedly, it seemed to be impossible to deflect the plane's course. It passed very close to the radar antenna and struck the port anchor a glancing blow as it crashed into the water. The plane came so close that the bridge, pilot house, and even the director were covered with water, gasoline and debris from the plane.'[31] The *O'Brien's* only material damage was a 15 x 10 feet hole in the area of frame 196 with four compartments flooded, while the degaussing gear and a depth charge rack were both damaged. Calls were made to Commander, Task Group 77.2, (CTG.77/2) for the urgent need for air cover for the minesweeper groups supporting destroyers, but before any friendly aircraft reached them the *Barton* was under attack once more. This aircraft was identified as a twin-engined *Frances* which made its approach from the starboard quarter and was first sighted by the ship's lookouts at 4,000 yards. Every

31. Captain W. L. Freseman, USN, Commander Destroyer Squadron 60 Action Report. Serial 013 OF6–60/A16–3, dated 2 February 1945.

battery that could train opened fire and they blew away a section of the port wing and set fire to the port engine. This damage apparently prevented the pilot from making a final turn into the ship due to a lack of control, and he passed over the quarterdeck at a height of thirty feet and hit the sea in flames some fifty yards off the port bow of the *Barton*, which was weaving at flank speed throughout the attack.

Among other ships hit in other Kamikaze attacks on the 6th were two old former destroyers, the fast transport conversion *Brooks* (APD-10, Lieutenant-Commander Charles Vern Allen), which was struck on her port side and had her forward boiler room flooded with three men killed, and the fast minesweeper conversion *Southard* (DMS-10), which was hit by another Kamikaze whose engine embedded itself into the ship while the fuselage tore a large chunk of her upper deck away. *Brooks* was a write-off, being towed to San Pedro, California, and de-commissioned, but *Southard* carried on working following emergency repairs.

Death of a Veteran

One of the oldest ships still serving in the US front line was the *Palmer* (DMS-5), once one of the famous 'four-piper' destroyers built at the end of World War One. She was of the 1,060-ton *Little* Class and was first commissioned just as the Great War ended with the Armistice in November 1918, being designated as Destroyer 161 (later DD-161). She served in both the Atlantic and Pacific Fleets until May 1922 when she was placed in reserve and there she remained for the next eighteen years. In August 1940, with the German occupation of Europe an accomplished fact, Britain standing on her own, and with Japan occupying much of China and a looming menace in the Pacific, she was recommissioned in a new role, that of a fast minesweeper and redesignated as DMS-5. When the USA entered the war some years later, *Palmer* served at the invasion of Vichy-held French Morocco in 1942–3 and then sailed right around the world to perform her unglamorous, but essential, duty at the invasion of the Marshall Islands early in 1944, Saipan and Guam, and then in October, at Leyte.

By 1945 her ancient hull was over a quarter-of-a-century old, creaking at the seams, yet still needed. For the reconquest of Luzon *Palmer* formed part of the dedicated minesweeping force that cleared the path for the fleet through the minefields of Lingayen Gulf. In the late afternoon of 7 January, at 15.00, *Palmer* experienced an explosion in her engine room and was forced to stop. On-board repairs were affected to keep her old engines cranking over until, at 18.40, a lone aircraft made an attack against *Palmer*; the aircraft, described as big and slow (and later identified as a twin-engined *Frances*), dropped two large bombs and apparently made an attempt to crash into the ship's bridge according to one eyewitness.[32] The ship's 20mm AA weapons set the plane on fire and her Captain, Lieutenant W. E. McGuirk, USN, turned his ship into the attack forcing the Kamikaze pilot to misjudge. The aircraft overshot, but not until after his bombs had been released, and was immediately shot down by AA fire from the other ships in the

---

32. Willard E. Miller, *The War Years: XXN The Death of the Palmer*. Notes dated 7 January 1953.

group, and crashed into the sea instantly. The old *Palmer* was hard hit, the after section of the ship and the port side of her hull were blown open. She sank within six minutes, her radar still turning as she went down. The crew managed to lower the whaleboat and a raft, others jumped into the sea. Two men were killed outright, thirty-eight wounded, some of whom died later aboard the light minelayer *Breese* (DM-18, Commander Donald Noble Clay, USN)[33] and *Hopkins* (DMS-13, Commander Douglas B Payne, USN),[34] or the battleship *Colorado* (BB-45, Captain Walter Scott Macauley, USN), to where they were transferred. Twenty-six others were listed as missing in action (MIA) from a total complement of 120.

In addition the light cruiser *Boise* (CL-47, Captain Wilard Merril Downes) received slight damage from a *Zeke* which carried out a Kamikaze attack but was shot down, crashing close alongside with some parts of the aircraft landing aboard. The Attack Transport *Callaway* (APA-35, Captain Donald Carrol McNeil) was hit on the bridge by a Kamikaze on 8 January, suffering twenty-nine dead and many wounded, but she carried on with the operation, while at 05.55 on 8 January *LST-912* received damage from a *Val* Kamikaze which rammed into the vessel after being heavily hit by AA fire, killing four of her crew.

---

33. The former *Wickes* Class four-piper destroyer DD-122.
34. The former *Clemson* Class four-piper destroyer DD-249.

Chapter Five

Taking Stock

'I am actually a member at last of the Kamikaze Special Attack Corps. My life will be rounded out in the next thirty days. My chance will come! Death and I are waiting. The training and practice have been rigorous, but it is worthwhile if we can die beautifully and for a cause.'

Ensign Heiichi Okabe, Shichisei Unit 2

As successive operations and landings were made from January 1945 onward, in order to widen and expand the Allied foothold in the Philippines, Japanese resistance was bolstered by successive Kamikaze attacks. The role of providing close-range air support for the troops ashore ensured that the escort carriers that had borne the brunt of the earlier attacks now found themselves firmly back in the firing line once more. Off Iwo Jima, thirty-two aircraft of the Kamikaze Special Attack Corps 2nd *Mitate* Unit sank one escort carrier and damaged five other ships.

Kitkun Bay damaged twice more

Having returned to the fray after her earlier battle damage from both surface fire and suicide aircraft, the *Kitkun Bay* was again battered by both on 8 January. At 18.57 that evening a suicide aircraft, identified as an *Oscar*, on fire and disintegrating after flying through a heavy barrage from several ships, hit the water and slid into the carrier's port side amidships on the waterline, opening her engine room up to the sea. Flooding reduced her to one engine and she took on a heavy list. Almost at the same time a 'friendly' 5in round from a nearby destroyer exploded on the *Kitkun Bay*'s opposite side inflicting further damage. Between the two hits the carrier suffered sixteen dead and a further thirty-seven injured.

Her damage necessitated her withdrawal all the way back to San Pedro which she eventually reached on 28 February where, over the next two months, she was extensively repaired. Although she survived her ordeal and was intended to return to full combat duties, *Kitkun Bay*, like her sister ships *Wake Island* (CVE-65, Captain James Robert Tague), *Kalinin Bay* and *Tulagi*, did not survive long in the post-war fleet, their damage ensuring they went early to the breakers in 1947.

The *Kadashan Bay* takes a hard knock

The 8th also saw *Kadashan Bay* (CVE-76, Captain Robert Nesbit Hunter, USN), take an *Oscar* amidships, right below the bridge. This caused considerable damage, started fires and she flooded; fortunately there were no dead from this attack and the ship was brought back under control after ninety minutes. She could only fly off her remaining aircraft to operate from nearby carriers, while *Kadashan Bay* herself was sent back to Leyte to carry out emergency repairs. Finally she was sent back to San Francisco, and her rebuilding took place between 13 February and 8 April.

Australia takes more punishment

This day also saw the much-battered *Australia* targeted once again. It may possibly have been that the unique three-funnelled layout of the *County* Class proved unmistakeable, or that the number of funnels signified to some Japanese attackers some special significance that attracted them like bees to honey. Whatever the reason *Australia* was once more a victim.[1] The first attack occurred just after dawn when, at 07.20, a twin-engined *Dinah* (Mitsubishi Ki-46 *Shiki)* was seen approaching at low-level off *Australia*'s port quarter. The cruiser was the rearmost ship of the Allied line and she opened fire, but at the same time four Grumman Wildcat fighters from the CAP swooped down and intercepted very bravely, one fighter following the *Dinah* through the ship's barrage and being shot down with the pilot bailing out. The Kamikaze was finally knocked down just twenty yards from the cruiser, 'and skidded into the ships side doing little damage.' This Kamikaze caused no casualties fortunately, but they were not done with *Australia* yet!

The next attack developed almost immediately, and at 07.39 another *Dinah* came in from the same quarter and it too was destroyed by the fleet's AA barrage, going into the water just a few yards from the ship, but again sliding into her and striking *Australia* on the waterline just beneath the bridge. An aircraft engine complete with propeller came inboard. This aircraft was carrying a single heavy bomb, which detonated close alongside or in contact with the hull and blew a 14 by 8 foot hole in her side. An oil tank and a provision room were opened up to the sea and the bulges were also flooded, causing *Australia* to list five degrees to port. Shrapnel from the explosion caused much superficial damage but, remarkably, once again there were no casualties to the ship's company from this fourth Kamikaze to strike the *Australia*. The damage control teams managed to arrest the spread of the water, and bulkheads were shorn up and the mission was resumed, although speed was reduced to fifteen knots. As extra AA protection in her reduced defence state, the *Australia* was allocated the destroyer *Moale* (DD-693, Commander Walter Manley Foster, USN) as her special protector for the rest of the day. She was one of the new *Allen M. Sumner* Class vessels, large 2,610–ton ships, with a main armament of six 5in/38 guns in three twin turrets and twelve 40mm AA guns.[2]

---

1. In April 1942, two ships of this class, *Cornwall* and *Dorsetshire*, had been the objects of one of the most successful Japanese dive-bombing attacks of all time when they were set upon by eighty of Lieutenant Commander Takashige Egusa's Aichi D3A1 *Vals* and sent to the bottom in a matter of minutes south of Ceylon (now Sri Lanka). Another, *Canberra*, had been one of the victims of the infamous Savo Island battle, also in 1942. The Japanese Navy had a penchant for the *County* Class it would appear.
2. The *Sumners* were the same length as the *Fletcher* Class and there was some debate at the time as to which class gave the best defence, the five single mountings of the *Fletchers* being able to engage five separate targets simultaneously, while the *Sumners* with their twin mountings could only engage a maximum of three.

The LSI *Westralia* (F-95, Lieutenant-Commander Eric Walton Livingston) was hit and damaged, but bigger targets were on the Kamikaze menu as January progressed.

Battleship *Mississippi* attacked

Battleships were hit by Kamikazes from the earliest attacks, but of course, such weapons would never sink a battleship, although they could cause minor damage if they hit the right place, ie the bridge. If they struck an armoured deck or a turret the paint might singe, but that would be the extent of the harm. Nonetheless, the older battleships were instrumental in laying down heavy bombardments which smashed Japanese defences ashore, and so were priority targets. Also, as they operated close inshore they were easier to reach and surprise than the task groups further out to sea. One such veteran was the *Mississippi* (BB-41, Captain H. J. Redfield, USN).

On the morning of 9 January 1945, *Mississippi*, one of the battleship group, was using her twelve 14in guns to bombard Japanese defence works around Calasiao and Dagupan in Lingayen Gulf. Such mighty shells were instrumental in keeping enemy defences to a minimum and allow the invading troops to land ashore with few casualties. Inevitably, though, their success stung the Japanese into a strong reaction. Around 13.03 a conventional attack was made on the fleet from one of four aircraft, identified as *Vals*, escorted by four single-engined fighters that approached from out of the sun, but the bomb missed. The attack was followed, almost immediately, by four aircraft, identified as *Vals* working from Tuguegarao Field, which made suicide runs on the heavy-ship line from out of the sun once more. The *Mississippi* was targeted by one of these Kamikazes which approached at high speed in a dive. The ship's AA fire hit this aircraft, stopping the engine and it then levelled off into a shallow gliding attack, crossing the battleship's forecastle, strafing as it came, and causing some casualties among exposed personnel. This aircraft clipped the ship's port upperworks and passed below the level of the bridge, before thundering into No.6 port AA mounting and exiting over the *Mississippi*'s port side into the water. Some fires broke out in the wake of this passage and some superficial damage was done to the ship. The bomb released by this machine detonated some sixteen feet out from her hull with a shock that knocked crewmen over on the quarterdeck and fragments perforated her anti-torpedo bulges ('blisters' in US parlance), flooding four of the upper and two of the lower ones, which gave the *Mississippi* a temporary list to port of 1½ degrees.[3] The fires were brought under control and the battleship resumed her duties. She continued to operate off the landing beaches until 10 February and was credited with destroying another Japanese aircraft heading for the transport anchorage the following day. Casualties aboard *Mississippi* from this strike amounted to twenty-two men killed, while five officers and fifty-seven men of her own crew, and seven survivors from the *Ommaney Bay*, were injured. The fires were soon put out and the wounded tended in the sick bay which remained fully operational.

---

3. USS *Mississippi* BB41, Serial 015. Action Report – *Bombardment Operations in Lingayen Gulf, Luzon, Philippine Islands During Period 6–9 January 1945 and including Collateral Supporting Actions and Operations During Period 3–18 January 1945*, dated 30 January 1945.

Columbia again damaged

The already badly-damaged light cruiser *Columbia* was again an early victim on the 9th. She was in action with what remained of her main battery, covering the hordes of landing craft streaming in toward the beaches and was thus restricted in her freedom to manoeuvre. At 07.45, what was reported to be a *Tojo* fighter (Nakajima Ki-44 *Shōki*) made a Kamikaze assault and crashed into the ship's main 6in forward battery director, knocking it completely over the side with the aircraft following it into the sea. The bomb it was carrying, estimated to be a 1,214lb weapon, detonated on impact with the forward superstructure where the forward fire control stations were wrecked, with all the ship's air defence and gunnery officers wounded. Control of her AA armament devolved on the assistants who were able to maintain both her bombarding and defensive firepower. This hit started what was described in her report as 'a serious fire.'[4] These fires were eventually contained but *Columbia* had lost two dozen dead with a further ninety-seven wounded in various degrees, and which were evacuated to the Attack Transport *Harris* (APA-2, Captain Marion Emerson Murphy, USN).[5] After this second severe battering, the gallant *Columbia* underwent emergency repairs at San Pedro Bay, Leyte, and eventually underwent full repairs and upgrading on the West Coast, and, incredibly, she was back in fighting trim once more at Leyte by 16 June 1945.

Another Kamikaze hits *Australia*

After the previous damage had brought about a reduction in her defensive capabilities, *Australia* had been inspected alongside the Fleet Ocean Tug *Apache* (ATF-67) and the conclusion reached that nothing by way of temporary repairs could be done for four or five days. *Australia* therefore remained with Task Unit 77.2.1 for the next day's work and she had carried out limited bombardment work during the morning.

At 13.11 a pair of bogeys were seen approaching at high speed from the east towards *Australia*, 'one dived past the ship and hit USS *Mississippi*, the other came in from ahead after a curving dive, and attempted to hit the bridge and fore controls. He, however, missed his aim and, diving under the fore yard, his wingtip caught on a mast strut which swung him into the foremost funnel and over the side. There was no other material damage than cutting off the top third of the funnel, which necessitated closing down two boilers in A Boiler room, and damage to radar and W/T aerials, which were quickly repaired. There were no casualties. A hole was cut in the damaged funnel by the next day and all boilers were again in action.'[6]

---

4. USS *Columbia* CL56, Serial 06/23, *Action Report – Lingayen Gulf, Luzon, Period 1–9 January 1945*, dated 22 January 1945, Enclosure A.
5. *Harris* was originally the old pre-war passenger liner *Pine Tree State* which was later taken over and became the troop-carrying ship *President Grant* (AP-8) early in the war before conversion to her final role in 1943.
6. D.40/202/9, Commanding Officer HMAS *Australia*, Action Report – Mike 1. Operation. Dated 22 January 1945.

Australia sailed with the *Louisville, Columbia* and *Arunta*, all damaged, that evening for Leyte and repairs. As the Commodore recorded at the time: 'During the operation HMAS *Australia* was hit five times by suicide bombers, and except for the hole in the ship's side and the casualties among AA crews, her fighting efficiency was not impaired beyond the capacity of temporary repairs. In the matter of casualties we were lucky, as other ships with only one or two hits had more casualties. Two of the attackers were definitely put down before hitting the ship, two did not appear to be affected by our AA fire and one missed his aim, which may have been due to AA fire. I consider that the same number of hits from bombs or torpedoes would probably have done much more damage.'[7] As for better defence, the Commodore recommended the fitting of multiple short-range weapons in place of the numerous single mountings and that this would do much to assist in repelling or at any rate deflecting the suicide form of attack.

Effects and recommendations from DesRon 60

It is interesting to compare the reactions of the *Australia*'s captain with those of Captain William L. Freseman, USN, of DesRon 60, also on the receiving end of no less than fifty of these first devastating Kamikaze attacks. He gave a most detailed and clear analysis of his experiences along with detailed recommendations of how to counter them in future. These deserve to be examined in detail and quoted at length for the accuracy of their forecasting.

He began by stating that 'The menace of enemy suicide crash planes should not be under-estimated and we should not delude ourselves into believing that it was a temporary expedient of the enemy that will disappear at a later date.' He considered that the closer the Allies got to the Japanese home islands and the more desperate the plight of the enemy, 'the greater will be the number of suicide planes encountered.' The expressed view that the suicide attacker had less chance of 'getting home' than any other type of aerial attack was profoundly disagreed with. On the contrary, he wrote, 'The percentage of hits is far greater than any other type of bombing, and, like other types of bombing, the chance of 'getting home' on a small ship is dependent to a great extent on the location of the hit. A suicide plane can sink a destroyer or small ship if the suicide plane carries bombs. The majority of small ships hit are generally badly damaged and suffer many personnel casualties.'

He pointed out the 'tremendous effect on morale, and consequently on the fighting ability of a ship, if the crew is not properly trained and does not possess the necessary fighting spirit.' On this morale aspect Freseman was refreshingly blunt. 'It is a mistake to attempt to minimize too much to the crew the effect of suicide crash planes, particularly if crash dives have been observed. The men and the officers know the results in damage and casualties. Rather the fact should be plainly pointed out to them that the suicide plane is a weapon of considerable effect which will be encountered henceforth, and which must be defeated by skill, determination, and courage.' He considered that in destroyers

---

7. D.40/202/9, Commanding Officer HMAS *Australia*, Action Report – Mike 1. Operation. Dated 22 January 1945.

and small ships, the effectiveness of the suicide attack was determined by the action of the commanding officer. Freseman's observations on the tactic and characteristics of the Kamikaze attacks can be summarised as below.

Whenever possible, the initial approach by the Kamikaze toward the selected target area offshore was made from the direction of any nearby land, relying on the land mass echoes on the ships' scopes to confuse or even nullify accurate radar detection. Should a strong CAP be present overhead, the favoured method of suicide attack was at high speed flying close to the sea while weaving and jinking to make gun-laying difficult. Very few attacks were made at dawn, the Japanese usually waiting until sunset when the protecting fighters were withdrawn and visual sighting of incoming aircraft was most difficult. When attacking during full daylight, again a low-level approach was favoured, alternately a steep dive, as in a conventional dive-bombing attack, was made, the latter method being used when there was abundant cloud cover over the target zone for the aircraft to hide in and elude the CAP. Such an approach also avoided the flak defences of the outer screening destroyers, which often destroyed or hindered Kamikazes making a low-level approach. Whether by dive or low-level, however, maximum speed was utilised in most cases giving little time for directors to lock on to the aircraft. Lone ships, or small ill-defended vessels, proved tempting targets which made radar picket duty especially hazardous. It was noted that, in the case of destroyers, the Kamikazes tended to aim at the base of the ship's bridge structure. This choice gave optimum chance of knocking out command personnel, controls and communications, and homing in on the central turning point of any ship manoeuvring at speed. Although Freseman did not say so, with carriers, the priority target among the large ships, the bridge also featured, but lifts or deck parks were also favoured. Beam attacks appeared to be the most favoured final approach, the assumption being that this gave the attacker more chance of avoiding concentrations of AA guns due to directors being masked or blinded.[8]

The Kamikaze avoided dog-fighting with CAP fighters of course;the aim was to make the fastest low-level entry into the target ship as possible and the ships' gunners therefore had difficulty as often friendly aircraft, intent on the chase, inevitably flew into the ships' barrages. It was also noted that another method to confuse the defence was for groups of three or four Kamikazes to separate and make individual attacks, dividing gunfire and the CAP. Even if damaged the Kamikaze would always attempt to crash into the closest ship,

---

8. This had also been the favoured method of approach for dive-bombers of all nations, but the added emphasis given to this approach by the Kamikaze emphasised it. The British *Battle* class destroyers, indeed, had all their main armament concentrated forward, and only AA batteries were installed astern, which led to much criticism at the time. Only one actually arrived in the Pacific in time for this gun layout to be assessed, but she was never taken under attack. The First Sea Lord, Admiral Sir Andrew Cunningham, RN, was scathing about this decision post-war, writing after a trip aboard the new *Solebay*: (R70, Lieutenant-Commander George Ian Mackintosh Balfour, RN) 'these '*Battles*' fulfil my worst expectations. An erection like the Castle Rock, Edinburgh, on the bridge. They call it a director, and all to control four guns firing a total broadside of about 200 lbs. We must get back to destroyers of reasonable size and well –gunned.' Admiral of the Fleet Viscount Cunningham of Hyndhope, *A Sailor's Odyssey*, London: 1951. Hutchinson.

whatever it might be. There was, of course, no deterrence as would have worked against conventional air attack; they had to be knocked down to be stopped.

The early suicide attackers usually carried a 500lb bomb which they either released just prior to impact, or dropped it on one target while crashing on another for maximum effect. Those making steep dives tended to overshoot the target. But it was Freseman's final sentence that summarised the feeling of destroyer crews. 'When an individual ship is attacked simultaneously or in quick succession by a number of suicide planes, it is practically impossible to avoid being hit, except by strong support from close supporting ships.'

There were also suggestions for how small warships, like destroyers, might counter such attacks in the future. Some were fairly obvious, like going to full flank speed when under attack, and bringing the gunnery director and every possible gun to bear as quickly as possible. The warning here was not to neglect other aircraft that might 'sneak in undetected.' To enable these aircraft to be spotted in time, additional 'overhead' lookouts in addition to the usual air lookouts were recommended, as well as actively attempting to avoid an impact by the use of high-speed manoeuvring and tight turns.

It was found that sometimes the gun director could not acquire the target fast enough, and local control of the guns was seemed to be the answer, with gun captains given the authority to open fire immediately on any hostile aircraft. This included firing over friendly ships, if the threat justified it, without hitting the ships themselves. A dangerous option, not always successfully done.[9] When a destroyer was taking violent evasive action at high speed, the fire-control radars could lose the target on the scope, which reduced effective defensive fire. Freseman wrote, 'The answer is, of course, installation of improved type fire control radars, similar to Mark 12.' However he also noted that in small ships the primary ship control, fire control, CIC and communications were all concentrated in the bridge structure, which meant a hit there would knock most if not all of them out at once, even if the ship did not sink. Turning the ship's stern to the attacker could lessen this vulnerability.

Lone ships, notably those on isolated radar picket duties, proved the most vulnerable. The juicy fat transports – laden with troops and equipment, or the carriers, with their fuel and bomb-laden aircraft, would have been a better return for Kamikaze pilots, but the temptation to hit the first ship seen often proved irresistible and the pickets paid the price in blood no matter how gallantly led or fought. 'They may shoot down two or three planes, but if the attacks continue, the ship will probably be hit. If destroyers are desired on picket stations during daylight, at least two and preferable three should be stationed as a unit, even then, he felt, only if considered essential. For destroyers screening Task Groups it was recommended that, 'Only a heavy concentration of accurate fire from all batteries of all ships within range, stationed not further than 1000 to 1500 yards apart,

---

9. This ploy had been used by the Royal Navy in the Mediterranean since 1940, but off Sumatra on 24 January 1945, the anti-aircraft cruiser *Euryalus* (C167, Captain Richard Oliver-Bellasis, RN) had accidently put several 5.25in rounds into the carrier *Illustrious* (R2, Captain Charles Edward Lambe, RN), killing twelve men and wounding twenty-one. As noted earlier, some US ships suffered similar incidents in the heat of battle.

will provide a measure of security.' Furthermore it was felt that, due to the speed of a Kamikaze attack, and the difficulty of getting the main 5in battery on the target, 'one or two mounts should be prepared to fire only Mark 32 fused projectiles, in local control if necessary.'

It was not felt that using director-controlled 24in or 34in searchlights during daylight attacks would confuse (presumably by dazzling) the pilots. Nor was reliance on 20mm weapons which, he noted, had been 'of little or no assistance in repelling suicide planes', adding, 'The replacement of 20 mm batteries with 40mm, where space and weight conditions permit, is very desirable.' He emphasised that the enemy would continue suicide crashing and that 'the 20–mm batteries do little to stop it.'

If the Kamikaze could not be stopped then precautions taken to lessen the needless waste of lives aboard the target destroyer included ensuring that all bridge personnel not engaged with fire control should take cover wherever they could, and that all exposed personnel should be made to wear flash-proof clothing. The separating of damage control parties throughout the ship was essential and they should keep under cover until required.[10]

No ships were sunk by suicide attacks in the three-day period 10–12 January 1945, although the list of damaged vessels included the destroyer escort *Le Ray Wilson* (DE-414, Lieutenant-Commander Matthew Vaughan Carson, Jr.) which shot down a Kamikaze on 10 January; unfortunately the aircraft's starboard wing came inboard and killed six crewmen. On the same day the Attack Transport *Dupage* (APA-41, Captain James William Daugherty) was hit in her port side by a Kamikaze which started severe fires, killed thirty-five men and wounded 136 others. On the next day Kamikazes hit the high-speed transport *Belknap* (APD-34, Lieutenant Ralph Childs, Jr.) which struck her funnel, disabled her engines and killed thirty-eight crewmen while wounding forty-nine more. She was towed to Manus and then to Philadelphia Navy Yard, where she was written off. On 12 January the destroyer escorts *Richard W. Suesens* (DE-342, Lieutenant-Commander Robert Wallace Graham) and *Gilligan* (DE-508, Lieutenant Carl Edward Bull) were both damaged, the *Gilligan* taking a Kamikaze directly into her No. 2 40–mm mounting which left her with twenty-two gunners dead or MIA. The *Suesens* went to her aid and, while rescuing some survivors from the water, was also attacked by a Kamikaze which she destroyed but the aircraft hit the water close alongside and flaming debris swept aboard to wound eleven of her crew. The Liberty ships *Otis Skinner* (MC-2130, Master Edson Baxter Gates), *Kyle V. Johnson* (MC-2948, with the loss of one of her crew and 128 soldiers), *David Dudley Field* (MC-470, Master Albion M Burbank) and *Edward N. Westcott* (MC-2072, Master Lars Hanson) all took hits during this period, while the transport *War Hawk* (AP-168, Commander Thompson H Stanley), which had already been badly damaged by a *Shinyo* suicide boat on the 10th, was again damaged on the 11th, when flaming debris from a Kamikaze showered the ship's bow area. Also damaged by suicide aircraft that day were *LST-700* and *LST-778*.

---

10. Captain W L Freseman, USN, Commander Destroyer Squadron 60 Action Report. Serial 013 OF6–60/A16–3, dated 2 February 1945.

Salamaua damaged

At 08.58 on 13 January 1945, the escort carrier *Salamaua* (CVE-96, Captain Joseph Irwin Taylor, Jr., USN) was surprised by a *Frank* (Nakajima Ki-84 Type 4 *Hayate* [Gale]), which was laden with a pair of 500lb bombs. The aircraft and one of its bombs caused serious fires on the CVE's flight and hangar decks which rapidly spread further into her interior. The second bomb was a dud that went through the ship to exit out of the starboard side of the hull at the waterline, causing instant flooding of the starboard engine room resulting in a consequent loss of power, steering and internal communications. Casualties included fifteen dead and more than eighty men injured. *Salamaua* stopped and effected temporary repairs before being detached that same evening for Leyte Gulf, where she was made sufficiently seaworthy to return to San Francisco for further repairs which were made between 26 February and 21 April. She was stricken from the Navy List in 1946.

The Attack Transport *Zeilin* (APA-97, Commander Thomas Benjamin Fitzpatrick) was damaged on 13 January by a Kamikaze which aimed at *Mount Olympus* (AGC-8, Captain John Henry Saultz), but missed and instead hit the *Zeilin*. The aircraft detonated a large cargo of incendiaries causing several large fires to break out, while the engine of the Kamikaze penetrated diagonally through her upperworks and into the bowels of the ship. She suffered seven men dead, three MIA and thirty wounded.

Summary of Kamikaze operations in the Philippines, October to January 1945

Between 25 October 1944, when the first *organised* Kamikaze attack took place, and January 1945, prior to Ugaki taking over command of the Navy's Kamikaze operations, about 400 IJN Kamikaze pilots sacrificed their lives off the Philippines and Taiwan. In February 1945 Vice Admiral Ugaki, Commander of the 5th Naval Air Fleet, assumed command of the Navy's Kamikaze operations and subsequently presided over the deaths of 2,100 IJN Special Attack flyers. These are the hard statistics, but what of the human cost?

Chapter Six

Trapped Below Decks

'Please congratulate me. I have been given a splendid opportunity to die. This is my last day. The destiny of our homeland hinges on the decisive battle in the seas to the south where I shall fall like a blossom from a radiant cherry tree.

I shall be a shield for His Majesty and die cleanly along with my squadron leader and other friends. I wish that I could be born seven times, each time to smite the enemy.

How I appreciate this chance to die like a man!'

Petty Officer First Class Isao Matsuo, 701st Air Group to his parents

On 21st January 1945 the *Niitaka* force was despatched from three separate bases, Shinko, Taibu and Taitung, to strike an enemy task group reported south-east of Formosa. It totalled just six *Suisei* dive-bombers and four *Zeke* fighters as Kamikazes with seven *Zeke* fighter escorts. A tiny force of which some turned back. The remainder pressed on and made their attacks.

Just what was it like to be on the receiving end of a Kamikaze attack on a fleet carrier? Lieutenant Commander George J. Walsh, USN, was a distinguished dive-bomber pilot flying the Curtiss SB2C Helldiver on numerous missions during the latter stages of the Pacific War. He was used to dishing it out to the enemy, but on one momentous occasion he was on the receiving end while serving with his squadron, VB-80, aboard the fleet carrier *Ticonderoga* (CV-14, Captain Eugene Willard Kiefer, USN).

Task Force 38, operating in three Groups, had attacked Japanese airfields on Formosa, the Pescadores and Sakishima-Gunto, the latter two being island groups located approximately west and east of Formosa respectively. The Japanese responded violently to these attacks. On 21 January, further attacks on Formosan airfields took place with 1,164 sorties and in response the *Niitaka* Group despatched eight Kamikazes escorted by five fighters. Both *Ticonderoga* and the destroyer *Maddox* (DD-731, Commander James Sturgis Willis, USN) were hit and damaged by this force. In the early afternoon a Kamikaze achieved total surprise when it dived out of cloud and penetrated *Ticonderoga*'s flight deck abreast of No.2, 5in turret, with its bomb detonating just above the floor of the carrier's hangar deck just below. Some of the aircraft parked on the flight deck ignited and fierce fires swept the ship and the resulting damage control measures, including vast amounts of water, caused the carrier to assume a startling ten-degree starboard list. Captain Kiefer counteracted this by ordering the damage-control teams to flood the port compartments until she assumed a ten-degree list to port. The resulting swing from starboard to port shifted the blazing aircraft, and most slithered harmlessly off the flight deck and over the side of the ship.

But the enemy were not finished. While fire-fighters swung into action and blazing airplanes were being dumped overboard, a second Kamikaze penetrated the defences and impacted close to the ship's island. Yet more parked aircraft caught fire, crewmen on deck were mown down and Captain Kiefer wounded. Captain Harmon Vedder Briner, USN, took over temporarily. It took until 14.00 to bring the fires under control. In all 143 officers and men died while 202 were wounded. Incredibly, within two hours the blazes were under control and she was able to move again by 16.00. Ultimately she was sent back to Puget Sound Navy Yard, arriving there on 15 February. Her repairs took until 20 April and by early May she was back on station and conducting strikes against the Marshall Islands.

Survival and death aboard the *Ticonderoga*, 21 January 1945

George Walsh kindly made this graphic account available to the author especially for this book.

'After getting back into the Pacific, we were much relieved but continued striking. January 21 was a beautiful day. We set out for Takao and did some damage. The fleet was only 70 miles from Formosa, the fleet almost in sight of land. We returned early and my wing men informed me that my tail hook was not operating correctly. I landed last and crashed into the barriers, feeling pretty good that only the prop was damaged as the plane nosed up.

'Down in the ready room the usual routine of briefing and kidding kept spirits high as the second op readied to go out. I got into my uniform and had a sandwich. Suddenly GQ [General Quarters] alarms sounded and before the gong stopped, guns were firing spasmodically. A crunching smash and shuddering concussion knocked us from our feet. We grabbed life jackets and as smoke poured in the ventilators, donned gas masks. Those in the rear opened the rear doors, those in the front, the front door. Smoke and heat poured in from each before they were shut. Immediately the lights went out and the smoke thickened. Men from the rear rushed forward crying, "You can't get out that way." Pilots from the front rushed back yelling. "You can't get out that way," meeting in waves in the middle of the ready room. Confusion, but no panic. Many tried the doors again, to be driven back by the heat. Finally desperation drove me to the front just as a voice called over our squawk box, "Go aft on the port side." I opened the door and felt my way aft until a blast of intense heat stopped me. It was the opening from the hangar deck. The bomb had hit 10 yards from the ready room up forward and set the hangar deck planes aflame. Despair! Then Commander Ernest M Moore, leading a chain of groping men, caught up and pushed me past the hottest point although I was afraid of falling into a hole.

'Our red emergency lights were futile in the smoke, merely giving the impression of fire. We came to a closed hatch which I twisted wrong so that it locked instead of opening. The crowd pressed against me yelling to find the trouble. I swung the hatch open and we stumbled aft till we found our way into the catwalk and fresh air. The light of day never looked so good. On deck we were afraid everyone hadn't gotten out. They had, despite several close calls. Benny collapsed in the passage and was stepped on before he was dragged out. The Skipper gave up and was rescued by a torpedo pilot. Center and Price, the last to get out, just sat down in chairs and said, "Well this is it. We go down here." However, they raised themselves and traced our escape route.

'Back on the after end of the flight deck, with smoke pouring out from the guts of the ship, those who were overcome were revived and a muster taken. Some pilots began to go forward to fight fires and carry wounded. Smoke was everywhere. Before any progress could be made the second plane came in through a hail of fire, smashing into the island as we all crouched and watched. Flame shot several hundred feet into the air, as the ship shuddered again. Many felt an impulse to jump overboard. Many did. Some were picked up by destroyers.

'Bombs were jettisoned and planes pushed over the side as fast as men could work. The VT Ordinance Officer, Nicholas Stillwell, heaved a 500–pound bomb over and many of 250lbs. Up in the island few were alive, alive in a hell of burnt and mutilated flesh. Commander Irwin Chase, Jr. held the Captain's jugular for 25 minutes till a doctor arrived. The few others alive began giving first aid and soon stretcher parties were at work gathering all, for the wounded and dead looked alike. William Tirrell and Price gathered seven cases only to find five dead.

'On deck fire fighters battled courageously among shattered bodies. Word was passed to the bridge, "Unless the ship gets a port list, it is going to blow up." Three times, "Open the sea cocks was ordered." The proud vessel shifted over dangerously, the plume of smoke signalling other Japs, "Here we are. Come and finish us off." We stripped the planes of life rafts, parachutes and first-aid kits. Then came another volley of gunfire as the third Jap Kamikaze came in only to be shot down off the bow.

'Out of control *Ticonderoga* drifted from the group, but in an impressive display of seamanship and loyalty, the Task Group of three carriers, battleships, cruisers and destroyers manoeuvred perfectly to surround us with a wall of ships, taking the Big 'T' as fleet guide. Then, amid the fear of further attack, the dirty work began. The fires were put out and the injured collected. The heroism and patience displayed was something none of us will ever forget, but the cost was horrible. 150 dead or missing and over 200 seriously injured. As the sun went down that day all breathed a sigh of relief and the unhappy ship began the trek for Ulithi.

'The proud 'T' was burnt and smoked. A hundred holes in the deck, buddies dead or dying. The island was torn and scarred, living wounded, black and burned. Most of the planes were gone. Our ready room was a shambles. Even the phonograph record, *The Sheik of Araby*, by the Hoosier Hot Shots, had melted down on the console. Pearson, Mullaney and Perkins were critically wounded. Andy, Laster and Monson were burned. All of us were shaken and shocked.

'At Ulithi a damage assessment board came on and the wounded were transferred to the *Solace* and *Samaritan*. The Air Group began to think of going home. Everyone from the Navy Commander down wanted to. (At the moment we did not know our fate). Out of the weary blackness, a ray of light appeared Lieutenant-Commander John 'Dugan' Doyle came back.

'Bill Tirrell was on the bridge of the *Ticonderoga* on January 21st, 1945, when the second Kamikaze crashed into the island. His story of the action was dramatic and colourful. Although I heard it many times I cannot recite it as he could from first-hand experience. He was in the hospital with terminal cancer when we agreed to tape his story. However, I went on a trip and by the time I got back he was gone. I've always been sorry that his great adventure of the war died with him so I will tell it for him as best I can.

'Lt. William H. Tirrell's battle station was on the bridge, where his duty was to identify incoming aircraft as friend or foe. In other words he was responsible for ordering every gun on the ship to open fire on an incoming plane and his ability to distinguish our own aircraft from the various Japanese models was unmatched. There had been occasions when our own planes were shot down by friendly fire. Bill had picked out an inside corner of the bridge as his shelter in the event a Jap penetrated our anti-aircraft barrage. On January 21st, after the first Kamikaze crashed through the deck of the *Ticonderoga*, a second Kamikaze dove toward the island through a wall of anti-aircraft fire and an explosion was imminent. Bill dove into his corner, felt a heavy impact the length of his body, followed by the explosion, flames and smoke. He pushed loose and struggled to his feet.

'Unknown to him, Captain Dixie Kiefer had selected the same shelter and dove in on top of Bill. The captain was wounded in thirty-three places but he protected Bill from getting a scratch.

'Out of the smoke a figure approached Bill in flames. It was Commander Robert L Miller, who ordered in proper Annapolis form, "Lieutenant, I'm on fire. Put me out!" Bill carried out the order, but the commander died there on the bridge, as a bloody Dixie struggled to his feet. Bill Tirrell survived the war and entered my life again in later years.

'Ev Wehr was also at the island structure and was fatally wounded. Ev was a dive-bomber pilot who had gone through all the training with us and the shakedown cruise. After the stress of his first combat missions he turned in his wings. He could not take it, and was kept aboard ship for possible retraining as a landing signal officer. He died in Rex Pearson's arms after Rex had been seriously wounded himself. Rex had been below decks when the first Kamikaze struck. He was trapped by flames and climbed out a porthole where he was spotted by some of the deck crew who lowered a line to him. He climbed up and sought shelter near the island with Wehr.

'As the second Kamikaze struck, Rex put a nearby pail over his head, which saved his life. He was handicapped for life with a metal plate in his skull. On our audio tape Rex reports Wehr as saying "Rex I'm dying, I'm dying." These were Ev Wehr's last words.

'Ev might have been better off if he had continued flying. On the other hand Lieutenant Edward Ed Bagley kept flying even though he had a strong premonition that he would be killed. Ed's only brother had died early in the war as a Navy pilot. 'Bags' attended daily Mass with Father Denis O'Brien. However, as he had feared, he was lost in an attack over Luzon.'[1]

---

1. Lieutenant-Commander George J. Walsh, USNR, Rtd., July 2001. *Memoirs*. Reproduced with the permission of the author.

Reaction of the Emperor

Although Hirohito maintained a lively interest in the progress of the war, and indeed, managed to influence events far more than many imagined at the time, few hints and clues were to be found of his true feelings. His biographer[2] uncovered several of them. The Emperor was known to have viewed the propaganda cine film *The Divine Wind Special Attack Force Flies Off* in 1944 and, on 1 January 1945, Hirohito and his Empress were shown examples of the last ritual meals consumed by Kamikaze pilots prior to their final missions. Bix also translated a statement made by the Emperor's military aide, Yoshihashi Kaizō, in which the latter recalled that during a discussion of a particular Kamikaze mission, 'the Emperor stood up and made a deep, silent bow. I was pointing at the map and His Majesty's hair touched my head, causing me to feel as though an electric current had run through my body.'[3]

Another example of the Emperor's thinking, far from showing such tacit approval were interpreted by some as to be the exact opposite. It was recorded how, that when informed of the attack by the *Shikishima* Kamikaze unit, a cable was received from Admiral Takejiro Ōhnishi which was read out to the assembled aircrew. "When told of the special attack, His Majesty said – 'Was it necessary to go to this extreme? They certainly did a magnificent job."[4] Ōhnishi was said to have been upset at this pronouncement, implying as it did, Royal criticism of the implementation of the Kamikaze concept. But, as with all his utterances, the Emperor was deliberately ambiguous.

Renewed assaults

There was a lull in Kamikaze operations and the only vessels to be damaged by isolated attacks were *LST-700* (near-missed on 12 January with three dead and two wounded among her crew) and, on 5 February, the transport *John Evans* (MC-1712, Master George Brimble) was damaged. However, all would change again when, toward the end of February, Kamikazes re-appeared in force as the reconquest of the Philippines continued with the Allied landings at Lingayen Gulf, Luzon.

On 9th February Rear-Admiral Ugaki was appointed Commander-in-Chief of the newly activated 5th Air Fleet, based at Kanoya. Iwo Jima was attacked by Task Force 58 with Spruance replacing Halsey on 26 January.

Off Iwo, the escort carrier *Bismarck Sea* would be sunk and the massive *Saratoga* knocked out of the war.

Loss of the *Bismarck Sea*

While operating off Iwo Jima on 21 February, the *Bismarck Sea* (CVE-95, Captain John Lockwood Pratt, USN) was hit twice by Kamikazes which inflicted serious damage. The

---

2. Bix, Herbert P. – *Hirohito and the Making of Modern Japan.* New York/London. Harper Collins. 2000, pps 482–483.
3. Bix's translation of Yoshihashi Kaizō, *Jijū bukan toshite mita shūsen no kiroku,* pp 97.
4. Inoguchi, *Divine Wind, op cit,* pp 64.

first went into the ship from the starboard side and penetrated a magazine causing huge fires that began to rage out of control. Then a second Kamikaze plunged into her after lift shaft, knocking out all the fire control teams and equipment. As a result the fires spread through the ship and she had to be abandoned. She sank within ninety minutes with the loss of 318 of her crew. Among the rescue vessels, the destroyer escort *Edmonds* (DE-406, Lieutenant Commander Christopher Sylvanus Barker, Jr., USN), alone, managed to rescue 370 of her survivors. To the *Bismarck Sea* goes the unhappy distinction of being the very last US aircraft carrier to be sunk in World War II.

'*Sara*' survives

At over 888 feet in length, the *Saratoga* (CV-3) fielded the largest flight deck in the world in 1945 and this vast expanse was the target of no less than six *Zeke* Kamikaze aircraft on 21 February 1945. Under the command of Captain Lucian Ancel Moebus, USN, the carrier had been acting as Flagship of Task Unit 55.2.4 but, as an aircraft carrier dedicated to operating dedicated night-fighter aircraft, she was detached to join the amphibious forces and carry out night patrols over Iwo Jima, and night heckler missions over Chi-chi Jima with an escort of just three *Fletcher* Class destroyers: *McGowan* (DD-678, Commander William Ruffin Cox), *McNair* (DD-679, Commander Montgomery Lientz McCullough, Jr.) and *Melvin* (DD-680, Commander Barry Kenworth Atkins). It may have been thought this was sufficient for night operations, but unfortunately it proved totally inadequate when she was caught at 17.00 that afternoon as she was still sailing to her assigned operating area.

Meanwhile the thirty-two strong mixed aircraft group of the 2nd *Mitate* unit from the 601st *Koku Sentai* under Lieutenant Hiroshi Murakawa, with twelve *Zeke*s, twelve *Judy*s and eight torpedo-armed aircraft, had sortied from Katori, refuelled at Hachijo Jima and headed out to the fleet besieging Iwo Jima. On arrival Lieutenant (jg) Akira Iijima chose as his target the biggest flight deck he could see. From *Saratoga*, the cloud base was reported as 'low' and a group thought to consist of six bogeys (but there were actually more) was reported as a mixture of *Judy*s and *Zeke*s which cleverly used the cloud to make a concealed approach from the east. These aircraft attacked the carrier in quick succession and hit her seven times (four aircraft actually striking the vessel while others hit her with three bombs released prior to the aeroplane's actual demise) within the space of three minutes. Two Kamikazes were hard hit by defensive fire and were shot into the sea without causing any damage while two more, despite being shredded by the AA gunners, each hit the water off her starboard side where their momentum caused them to flip into the ship itself, opening two sizeable holes and starting severe fires. The fifth aircraft to hit struck a crane, while the sixth smashed into the forward flight deck setting fire to aircraft there as well as her teak deck. Additionally, three bombs from these last two aircraft pierced '*Sara*'s' hull causing fierce fires to erupt in her hangar deck. Casualties aboard totalled 123 killed and missing. While fire-fighting continued, at 19.00, yet another Kamikaze materialized – this time its bomb struck the ship while the aircraft slid over the flight deck and into the sea.

The carrier's captain recorded: 'Opened fire. Planes (1 or 2) strafed ship while coming in fast. No.1 plane hit and on fire, crashed into starboard side, frame 104, penetrated into hangar deck. Violent explosion. No.2 plane, hit and on fire, hit water and bounced into starboard side, frame 147, at water-line. Violent explosion. 5 degree list to starboard. No 3 plane shot down clear of the ship. No. 4 plane from astern updeck dropped bomb into anchor; windlass through port catapult and crashed into water. 17.03. No 5 plane, hit and burning, headed for the bridge, carried away antennae and signal halyard, crashed into port catapult and exploded violently. No.6 plane hit and burning, crashed into airplane crane on starboard side, dropped bomb at frame 25, starboard flight, parts of plane landing in number one gun gallery, rest of plane went over the port side.'[5] By 20.15, such was the efficiency of her control teams, the fires were under control and she was able to embark aircraft. However, this famous old carrier was effectively out of the war for, although she withdrew to Eniwetok to be patched up and was later repaired at Bremerton during the period 16 March to 22 May, she was subsequently only used as a training carrier.[6]

Lunga Point survives a second assault

Having survived a near miss by a Kamikaze once, *Lunga Point* (CVE-94, Captain George Arthur Tappan Washburn) was assailed by a group of four *Jill* torpedo-bombers on 21 February in what *seemed* like a conventional attack. All these aircraft made their torpedo drops, and by skilful use of the helm *Lunga Point* avoided them. However, thwarted in his intent, one of the pilots apparently decided to put things 'right' by ramming the carrier instead. He misjudged, probably his decision was a last-minute thing and not properly thought through. In any event the *Jill* hit the bridge superstructure with one wing tip, then slid along the flight deck and into the ocean. The ship only received minor damage and the whole thing was over in seconds. *Lunga Point* dusted herself down and carried on operating her aircraft, having notched up two near misses without loss.

Smaller ships hit by Kamikazes which survived during this period included the net cargo ship *Keokuk* (AKN-4, Commander Robert Paul Lewis), which was hit in an evening raid on 21 February by a *Jill* which ploughed into her starboard side, killing 17 of her crew and wounding 44 more. After being patched up locally she carried on working, while *LST-809*, which was hit amidships by a *Jill* off Iwo Jima and heavily damaged, was towed to the Kerama Retto anchorage where she sank on the 7th. Losses had been minimal, but before the Americans congratulated themselves the Japanese soon demonstrated that they had yet more tricks up their sleeves in the suicide aircraft field.

Raid on Japan, March 1945

On 14 March 1945, Task Force 58, under Vice-Admiral Marc Mitscher, set out to make a pre-emptive strike against Japanese air power in the home islands. The US Fleet was now large enough and powerful enough to carry out this mission with confidence, but it was not to remain immune.

---

5. *Saratoga* (CV3), Serial 007, Action Report for period 0900(K) to 2130 (K) 21 February 1945, dated 26 February 1945.
6. DANFS, *Dictionary of American Naval Fighting Ships*, Vol. 6, page 341.

During the Philippines period Vice-Admiral Raymond Spruance had, naturally, studied the Kamikaze methods and their impact on operations, and had expressed the view that this form of attack was 'very sound and economical warfare' and was of a type of combat 'especially suited to the Japanese temperament.'[7] However, he did not think these methods would be used much against US ships during the planned Iwo Jima and Okinawa operations. He was soon to be disabused of this naive view.

In response to the heavy American attacks launched against airfields on Kyūshū on 18 March, a force of four dozen Kamikazes was despatched from Vice-Admiral Ugaki's 5th Air Fleet. Only thirty of these aircraft succeeded in locating the massive US Task Force and they inflicted considerable damage. As the British Pacific Fleet Liaison Officer (BPFLO) subsequently reported: 'The enemy air reaction to our presence 90 miles from their coast was slight in the number of aircraft employed but effective in the damage caused.' All through the morning hours Japanese single-engined aircraft were in the clouds above the US fleet. With seven-tenths cloud extending down to as little as 3,000 feet, the cloud cover was used by the Japanese intelligently. Mitscher reported: 'It was a trying period as little, if any, warning was being given by the radars in the Force and at times the first indication of an aircraft approaching was a visual sighting from the close screen.'

Three American carriers were struck during this period. The *Yorktown-II*, (CV-10, Captain Thomas Selby Combs) suffered minor damage to her island when a bomb exploded outside the structure, killing four men and wounding eighteen; *Enterprise* CV-6, Captain Grover Budd Hartley Hall) was similarly hit, with her island and some electrical circuits being damaged. Her casualties were eleven men killed and twenty-two injured. The *Intrepid* (CV-11, Captain Giles Ezra Short) was near-missed with only minor damage and a few casualties. The CAP had meanwhile despatched eleven enemy aircraft during the day. The cloud lifted slightly as the day wore on and only one further attack was made, although the picket destroyers gave good visual warnings of this raid by three aircraft, and all of them were shot down by the fleet's gunfire without damage to any vessel.

The following day the exchanges continued, with the Americans launching heavy strikes against Japanese warships at Kure and Kobe, and around the Inland Sea. In retaliation a force of thirty-nine Kamikazes found the most northerly formation, Rear-Admiral Davidson's TG 58.2, some twenty miles ahead of the rest of the Task Force. The *Franklin* (CV-13, Captain Leslie Edward Gehres) was caught midway through launching her air strike. Two hits resulted and massive fires were started, and observers saw six enormous explosions. Casualties were 724 men killed and 265 injured. Captain Jones records that of those that died 210 were due to burns, 133 of smoke and gas induced asphyxia.[8] The

7. Buell Thomas B. – *The Quiet Warrior*, Annapolis, Maryland, Naval Institute Press, 1974, pp 344.
8. Jones, Captain Ian, RFD, MB ChM, MHA, GradCertED, FRCOG, FRANZCOG, FACS, RANR – *Surgery on ships: constraints and difficult realities*.

cruiser *Santa Fé* (CL-60, Captain Harold Carlton Fitz) and *Pittsburgh* (CA-72, Captain John Edward Gingrich) rescued 1,700 of her crew. *Franklin* required rebuilding from the second deck upward.

The *Wasp* (CV-18, Captain Oscar Arthur Weller) was hit by a 1,600-lb bomb which penetrated through to her second and third decks, before detonating and starting a large fire. She suffered 101 men killed and 269 injured and wounded, and had one boiler room flooded, which reduced her speed to twenty-eight knots, but the fires were brought under control and reported able to operate aircraft an hour after being hit. The only other casualty was the *Halsey Powell* (DD-686, Commander Sidney Douglas Buxton Merrill), a *Fletcher* Class destroyer which was alongside the carrier *Hancock* (CV-19, Captain Robert Ferdinand Hickey) when the attack commenced. Aiming for the *Hancock*, the Kamikaze missed and crashed into the stern of the destroyer. She suffered nine dead and thirty-plus injured, and her helm jammed. Her after battery of 5 inch guns were put out of action and she was forced to withdraw to Ulithi, where she arrived safely on 25 March.

Lessons learnt from this chastening experience were that fighter direction was still far from satisfactory. Task Force 58 gave up on 'Jack' patrols[9] for early warning, they were deemed 'unworkable.' Instead reliance was mainly placed on destroyer pickets placed on appropriate bearings about thirty miles out from the centre of the task force. A pair of such ships were utilised with their own CAP of up to twelve fighters. The BPFLO noted that: 'Their worth was proved, nine enemy aircraft being destroyed by the CAP, four more being shot down by gunfire. They gave numerous early warnings of approaching enemy aircraft.'

By contrast radar warning information was described as 'meagre', with no warning of the incoming hostiles until they were within gun range in at least 50% of cases. The sheer mass of aircraft airborne coupled with many 'fade' areas in the high-frequency radars meant that operators were unable to identify single aircraft. The answers were either more fighters to swamp any attack, or lower-frequency radar sets be installed. Mitscher suggested, 'A British cruiser with a Type 79 radar might possible solve the problem temporarily. As a stop-gap high altitude warning set, the APS6 is being installed hurriedly in all carriers. Its performance, however, is not likely to give the necessary information to allow the CAP to deal with fast single aircraft, beyond the fact that enemy aircraft are overhead.'

Picket Placement for Operation *Iceberg*

While General Douglas MacArthur's forces continued subduing the Philippines, thus keeping his much publicised promise 'to return', the US Navy, under Admiral Chester W. Nimitz, Commander-in-Chief, Pacific (CINCPAC), was charged with the invasion and occupation of Okinawa Gunto, the largest island of the Ryukyu Retto (archipelago). This piece of real-estate was regarded as the final stepping stone on the road which was to lead ultimately to the Allied invasion of the Japanese home islands. Both sides knew

---

9. 'Jack' Patrols were low-altitude air protection patrols carried out by British short-range Seafire fighters. For a while they had filled in the gap between the radar picket ships and the fleet itself.

of its significance and both committed the maximum forces for the battle. The Japanese employed 110,000 men, all of whom were deeply 'dug-in' and prepared to die to a man. A series of massive Kamikaze attacks were also part of the plan – designed to cripple as many Allied ships as possible. On their part the Allies prepared a huge invasion force, which included some 1,300 ships. At sea these Allied forces were divided into the 5th Fleet, with Task Force 51, which comprised the landing ships, troop and supply ships, and supporting bombarding ships, escort carriers for close air support and all their escorts. In addition there was the main carrier striking forces and fleet units, namely, Task Force 58 and the British Pacific Fleet, Task Force 57,[10] with fleet and light carriers, battleships, cruisers and destroyers. The latter's job was to eliminate as far as possible all the Japanese airfields on Formosa to the south and Kyushu to the north, and along the island chains that linked them, and prevent the enemy flying in air reinforcements.

The Allied fleets duly readied themselves in the light of knowledge gained in the Philippines. In particular radar pickets for the forthcoming invasion of Okinawa were carefully prepared. They were later adjudged to have been 'an unqualified success' and among their achievements were: 1, early radar reporting; 2, fighter direction at extended distance from objective; 3, shooting down enemy planes; 4, breaking up enemy raids with gunfire and 5, rescuing personnel from crashed planes. But, as before, a very heavy price was to be exacted for these achievements. In priority, these destroyers were first-and-foremost radar guard ships, an outer shell to warn the fleet of incoming hostiles, but they, also, were required to be fighter direction (FD) ships to steer the airborne CAP toward the enemy bogies in order of priority, or, as AA gunfire support ships to the relief fighter director (RFD) ships, and as RFD ships when required in the event of the incapacitation of the assigned FD destroyer.

The optimum distance out from the main fleet or target ships was considered to be 75 miles by the Commander of Cruiser Division Six. Being so distant gave the maximum warning of course and as such was ideal, but being so isolated was certainly no sinecure for these little ships, which, unlike the aircraft carriers or the transports, had no battleships, battle-cruisers and cruisers with their massed AA batteries to shield them should the CAP fail. They were on their own. The only solution was the quick capture of outlying islands to the north of Okinawa and the rapid establishment there of shore-based radar stations to take over the role from the picket destroyers. This ideal proved far from easy to accomplish, however, and until it was achieved the destroyers had to 'take it.'

To cover the north-eastern approaches to Okinawa fifteen radar picket stations (RPS) were specified, each spaced out so that it was feasible for one radar picket to pass on contact reports to the next without losing radio contact. It was a tight-mesh network so that all the protecting fighters, fleet and light fleet carriers of the task groups, the escort carriers of the support fleet and the US Marine Corsair squadrons ashore, once established on captured airstrips in strength, could be quickly vectored to block any threatened approach to the mass of assault shipping that lay off the beachhead.

---

10. See Smith, Peter C., *Task Force 57, The British Pacific Fleet 1944–45*, 1969: 1st Edition London, 5th Edition Manchester due 2015. Crécy Publishing.

Each of the fifteen RPS ships provided the officer in tactical command (OTC) with the ability to more easily identify the 'hot points' that could be allocated resources (pickets, support ships and CAPs) as the situation varied and developed. The limitation was, of course, the availability of sufficient suitable ships to fill the required number of RPS slots deemed necessary. The US Navy had constructed, and was still constructing, destroyers at an unprecedented rate, and of the highest quality, more than 400 between 1940 and 1945, but even this huge number had many duties to perform, and not only in the Pacific. Even the might of the US Fleet, five or six times the size of the whole Royal Navy by 1945, was still finite and stretched at this time. There were also not enough Fighter Direction destroyers as yet fitted out to fill every slot, so allocation had to be carefully planned and kept constantly under review. As a fall-back position, destroyers already allocated as anti-submarine screen vessels or anti-surface craft patrol destroyers, could be assigned radar picket duty if the situation required it, although these were not always the most suitable vessels for the job. The British and Commonwealth destroyers had particular problems as they were almost entirely equipped with low-angled 4.7in guns, with a maximum elevation of only 40 degrees and useless against dive attacks, even at this late stage of the war, due to a pre-war lack of vision, whereas American and Japanese warships had long been equipped with very effective 5in, dual purpose, high elevation, weapons throughout the war. This ensured that the British had to consider utilising some of their all too few anti-aircraft cruisers to supplement their own picket destroyers, which left their carriers with that much less protection.

The Americans also had the luxury of quantities of small auxiliary ships, in particular LCS(L) vessels, and numbers of these were assigned to each destroyer pairing as back-up and rescue vessels. They were not much help in repelling Kamikaze attacks but performed very usefully in the latter role, so much so they became ironically (if fondly) nicknamed 'Pall Bearers' by the destroyer crews.

Under COMPHIBSPAC OP PLAN Ai-45,[11] the radar pickets patrolled their assigned zones by steaming a circular area with a 5,000–yard radius, usually at a speed of fifteen knots so as to conserve fuel, although their captains were given the freedom to vary this speed according to local conditions. While on patrol, continuous radar and visual air and surface watch was maintained the whole 24 hours of each day. They also kept a constant sound search from beam to beam, using 3,000–yard keying.[12] Picket destroyers were given

---

11. Command, Amphibious Forces Pacific Fleet, Subordinate Command Operational Plan Ai-45.
12. This acoustic-searching was done with echo-ranging equipment, the QGB – (which, under the US Navy Model Lettering System stood for – Q = Sonar Ranging – G = Magnetostriction-split-lobe type – B – IFF (Identification Friend or Foe) – and was built by the RCA Victor company – see *List of Naval Radio, Radar and Sonar Equipment arranged by Navy Model Letters* – SHIPS 242A, Electronics Division, Bureau of Ships, Navy Department, Washington 25 DC, 1 January 1945). Fitted to the picket destroyers, briefly this was a retractable dome with electronic hoist and training, enclosed in a water-proof box when not in use. It was comprised of console with a transmitter, receiver, and indicating range recorder and a bearing deviation indicator. The equipment operated over frequencies of 20, 22, 23 and 26 kilocycles (kc), and to change frequencies the transducer had to be programmed by inputting ('keying') either via (a) the range recorder, which had two scales available, one at 1,500 yards radius the

orders that they were to open fire on all unidentified planes which came within a range of 12,000 yards, whether they had a good solution or not. Any contacts had to be reported immediately, via talk-between-ships (TBS) and the local air warning (LAW) net, with a receipt being required from the OTC. In reporting such contacts, Point 'Bolo' was used exclusively as a reference point, this being Bolo Point on Okinawa's East China Sea coast, where an airfield had been constructed. The supporting LCS(L)s, having no sophisticated radars of their own, also had to be kept in the loop. The picket destroyers were almost constantly at General Quarters, with the consequential heavy drain on the stamina of their crews, and thus the continual relief of such units was another planning requirement.

Picket destroyers utilised a range of radio equipment to enable their findings to be broadcast efficiently and quickly, and were listed as follows:

1. The Inter-Fighter Detector Circuit which was 2097kcs voice or 37.6mcs. Frequency Modulation (FM) where within range.
2. The CAP circuit which was VHF142, 74mcs.
3. Officer in Tactical Command (OTC) Tactical via TBS, 72.1mcs.
4. Local Air Warning Net – an Air Warning, Hunter-Killer and Radar reporting circuit, 3115kcs.
5. Screen Tactical – MN or other appropriate FM voice circuit.
6. Task Force Common circuit, which was self-explanatory.
7. Strategic Information – High-Frequency ('Honolulu- Fox') circuits depending on type.
8. Fleet common – on 34.8mcs. (listen)
9. Expeditionary Force Fox – 483 Continuous Wave (CW)

Okinawa – Task Force 58 Operations

As explained earlier, and in the Foreword, from 26 April 1944, an American Fifth Fleet had been set up as a separate unit, initially commanded by Admiral Raymond Spruance. When Admiral William F. Halsey periodically relieved Spruance, the name of this fleet automatically changed to the Third Fleet – one commander and his staff commanding the fleet while the other commander and his staff were planning the next operation, thus fooling the Japanese into thinking there was more than one major fleet, when in truth, generally the same warships were involved. Thus, under Spruance at this time, the main fighting force was Task Force 58, while when Halsey took over for his spell, these ships became Task Force 38.

---

other at 3,750 yards; (b) the tactical range recorder; (c) the hand key on the console; or (d) an automated device known as a multivibrator. In order not to waste the recorder paper when no target was located, the multivibrator automatically took over and it had two rates – one at a scale of 3,000 yards and the other at 5,000 yards. It was the former of these two that was adopted in this instance. This method, although far from infallible, had the advantage of being more sensitive to moving objects (i.e. aircraft) than stationary objects (i.e. land masses) and thus somewhat negated the Kamikaze practice of using mountains, and such, to shield them from radar detection.

With the landings on Okinawa scheduled to take place on 1 April 1945, the depleted and re-organised Task Force 58 sailed for Area *Rooster* on 22 March with three task groups instead of four. Strikes commenced on 23 March and initial Japanese air counter-attacks were negligible. The following day, however, Kamikazes appeared over the invasion beaches and the Fleet Flagship, the heavy cruiser *Indianapolis* (CA-35, Captain Charles Butler McVay III), was hit and Commander 5th Fleet had to shift his flag to the battleship *New Mexico* (BB-40, Captain John Meade Haines). Attack transports and other ships were also hit at this time.

After refuelling, the Task Force returned to the fray on 3 April and Task Group 58.3 took up a position sixty miles west of the northernmost tip of Okinawa, along with TG 58.2 which continued to support the troops ashore. It was not until 6 April that the Japanese launched an 'all-out' effort against the fleet when, during that morning, hostile aerial traffic became heavy and seven machines were shot down. As part of the escort to the crippled cruisers *Canberra* (CA-70, Captain Richard Benjamin) and *Houston* (CL-81, Captain William Wohlsen Behrens) – dubbed Cripple Division 1, both of which had been damaged by aerial torpedoes off Formosa – the light carrier *Cabot* (CVL-28, Captain Walton Wiley Smith) became the subject of several assaults. Attacks commenced at 12.45 when she was near-missed by a Kamikaze that skimmed her flight deck; similarly, two further cruisers were near-missed while thirty enemy aircraft were destroyed.

Task Force 58 itself was, as per normal standard operating practice, comprised of several Task Groups, and in Task Group 58.1 three carriers were near-missed, one of them, *San Jacinto* (CVL-30, Captain Michael Holt Kernodle), was slightly damaged. A destroyer, acting as a link between the task groups and picket destroyers, and thus isolated and lacking any support, was struck by a Kamikaze but remained afloat. The picket destroyers themselves shot down many attackers, one destroyer claiming three aircraft shot down, while their CAP claimed a further eight. In all 198 Kamikaze attacked from the Kyushu airfields and 41 returned to base. Of the remainder thirty-five were shot down by ships gunfire and fifty-five by fighter defences. In total, twenty-seven hits were made and the picket destroyers *Bush* (DD-529, Commander Rollin Everton Westholm) and *Colhoun-II* (DD-801, Commander George R Wilson) went down while the *Emmons* (DMS-22, Commander Eugene Noble Foss), which was hit by five Kamikazes on the 6th, was abandoned and sunk by the *Ellyson* (DMS-19, Commander Robert W Montrey) early on the 7th. In addition the destroyers *Leutze* (DD-481, Commander Leon Grabowsky), *Newcomb* (DD-586, Commander Ira Ellis McMillan) and *Morris* (DD-417, Commander Rexford Vinal Wheeler, Jr.), and destroyer-escort *Witter* (DE-636, Commander Alan Davis), were so badly damaged that they were soon scrapped post-war. Also sunk was *LST 447* while the destroyer-minesweeper *Rodman* (DMS-21, Commander William Henderson Kirvan), the minesweeper *Defense* (AM-317, Lieutenant-Commander Gordon Abbott) and destroyer *Mullany* (DD-528, Commander Albert Otto Momm) were badly damaged but repairable. The destroyers *Howorth* (DD-592, Commander Edward Sitt Burns), *Hyman* (DD-732, Commander Rollo Neill Norgaard) and *Haynsworth* (DD-700, Lieutenant-Commander Stephen Noel Tackney), and the destroyer-escort *Fieberling* (DE-640, Commander Edward Earle Lull), were damaged and slight damage was done to the destroyers *Bennett* (DD-473, Lieutenant-Commander Jasper Newton McDonald), *Hutchins* (DD-476, Lieutenant-Commander Caleb Barrett Laning) and *Harrison* (DD-573, Lieutenant-Commander Walter Vincent Combs, Jr.). The ammunition ships *Logan Victory* (MC-0582, Master Edson Baxter Case), sunk on 6 April, and *Hobbs Victory* (MC-0599, Master Kenneth F Izant), sunk on 7 April, were also destroyed by suicide attackers.

Intelligence

The evidence appears to indicate that the Allies were completely surprised by the advent of the Kamikaze. They are not even mentioned in David Kahn's epic history *The Codebreakers*, Chapter 17 of which, *The Scrutable Orientals,* should cover this area. Nor did the 'Revised and Updated' edition brought out in 1996.[13] Michael Smith claims that 'The Australian intercept operators were able to plot the flight patterns of the aircraft and volunteer pilots coming in from Japan via Formosa. Many were shot down before they even reached their air base,'[14] but this was after the attacks had been underway for some time there seemed little or no foreknowledge from Allied Intelligence sources.

Both the 5th US Fleet and the British Pacific Fleet embarked radio intelligence ('Y' units) consisting of two officers and fourteen intercept operators whose task was to monitor air-ground communications frequencies and warn of impending Kamikaze attacks. One of the most successful of the British contingents was under Lieutenant John Silkin which was embedded aboard the battleship *King George V*. Silkin's reports stated 'We were dealing with a beaten and disorientated enemy, whose sole power of retaliation lay in his suicide bombers. These last hopes were foiled, largely by the watch kept by Y parties.'[15] This might be over-egging the cake but they certainly played a part.

---

13. Kahn, David, *The Code-Breakers: The Comprehensive History of the Secret Communication from Ancient Times to the Internet,* New York; 1996, Scribner. Ken Kotani's *Japanese Intelligence in World War II* , New York & Oxford: 2009, Osprey Publishing, offers more coverage and is much better, but even then devotes very little space to the Kamikaze. One quotation, from *Atushi Oi, Kaijo Goei-sen* (*Defensive Battle on the Sea*), Koyosah: 1953, is very illuminating. Commenting on the fact that the Japanese High Command totally ignored all their Intelligence Reports, Captain Kaoru Takeuchi, Chief 5th Section, 3rd Department, Navy General Staff, said, 'The staff of the Operations Department are inexcusable. Totally disregarding our opinion, they insist that the US task force was routed. They are insane! It's unbelievable that the insane officers have their own way' Oi claimed that they 'always neglected our intelligence.' When Japanese Intelligence officers produced proof via Signals Intelligence (SIGINT) and Open Source Intelligence (OSINT) from US origins that proved ships had *not* been sunk, (because if the ships were still communicating then obviously they were still afloat) and gave realistic estimates of what the Kamikaze attacks had actually achieved, their views were dismissed out of hand as bad for morale! Again, there was nothing new in this, Churchill had treated Captain Arthur George Talbot, RN, the Director of Anti-Submarine Warfare, in exactly the same way regarding U-Boat losses, and post-war, Talbot's lower figures had proved to be *exactly* correct while Churchill's unsubstantiated claims were shown to be wildly over-exaggerated. The Redman brothers' notorious treatment of Joe Rochefort mirrored this attitude in the USN. No matter for politicians, the facade had to be maintained, uncomfortable facts discarded!

14. Smith, Michael, *The Emperor's Codes: Bletchley Park's Role in Breaking Japan's Secret Cyphers,* London: 2010, dialogue.

15. See National Archives, Kew, London – ADM 223/494/495/496/497/498 & 499 – NID 0050468/43 – *Intelligence – Far East and Pacific -1944-1945.*

Chapter Seven

The *Tan 2* Operation

'Flowers of the special attack are falling,
When the spring is leaving.
Gone with the spring,
Are the young boys like cherry blossoms?
Gone are the blossoms,
Leaving cherry trees only with leaves.'

Rear-Admiral Mantome Ugaki

This mission can be traced back for over a year when, in February 1944, the Japanese began planning a night bombing attack on the US Navy 5th Fleet's anchorage at Majuro, Marshall Islands, code named Operation *Yu-Go*. It was highly ambitious in scope, involving a combined strike by 500 carrier-borne and 300 land-based aircraft as well as seven submarines which would send in amphibious tanks and Japanese Navy Special Landing Forces to destroy shore installations.

On Sunday 17 February Ugaki noted in his diary that Operation *Tan* was being planned, aimed at hitting the US fleet on its return to the vast Ulithi anchorage. 'It calls for one-way attack with twenty-four land bombers. Special care should be taken in executing this operation.'[1] Setbacks soon followed. On Monday 26 February Ugaki recorded how, 'A *Ginga* bomber crashed after take-off this morning on its test flight and three were killed. It was doubly regrettable as they were members of the *Azusa* Corps of Operation *Tan*.'[2] With the death of Fleet Admiral Mineichi Koga in a flying accident on 31 March 1944, this complex and daring assault operation withered for want of leadership. A much smaller operation was drawn up in its place by Captain Mitsuo Fuchida, IJN, of 1 Air Fleet, codenamed the *Tan* Operation. Lieutenant-Commander Takashige Egusa, IJN, was to lead a night aerial attack with the new *Frances* twin-engined bombers against the same anchorage. Aerial reconnaissance was undertaken in June on several occasions, but before the attack could be made the US Fleet left Majuro and sailed for the invasion of the Marianas. Egusa's elite group of torpedo planes were subsequently all shot down attacking the carriers at dusk a few days later and Egusa himself was killed.[3]

---

1. Ugaki, Admiral Matome – *Fading Victory – The Diary of Admiral Matome Ugaki 1941–1945*, Annapolis, MD: Naval Institute Press, 1991.
2. Ugaki, Admiral Matome – *Fading Victory – The Diary of Admiral Matome Ugaki 1941–1945*, Annapolis, MD: Naval Institute Press, 1991.
3. See Peter C. Smith – *Fist from the Sky – The biography of Takashige Egusa IJN*, 2006 Manchester: Crécy Publishing Limited; 2006 –Mechanicsburg, PA: Stackpole Books; 2009– Tokyo: PHP; 2009 –Prague: Naše Vojsko.

With the fall of the Marianas the main US Fleet anchorage for the drives north moved to Ulithi in the western Caroline Islands. A revised version of the *Tan* operation was drawn up by Commander Ryosuke Nomura, IJN, again utilising the *Frances* bomber, but this time in a suicide mission. Although the plan, codenamed *Tan-2*, would stretch the aircraft and crews to the limit, involving as it did a very long flight to the target from their base at Kyushu, almost ten hours it was estimated, albeit as a one-way mission, it received the enthusiastic backing of Admiral Matome Ugaki, IJN, Commander of the 5th Air Fleet. Accordingly, on 7 March 1945, the *Azusa Tokubetsu Butai* (*Azusa* Special Attack Unit)[4] was set up in readiness for the first opportunity.

Twenty-four *Frances* bombers from the 762 Naval Air Group were assigned to the task, and five of the big four-engined Kawanishi H8K2 flying boats, (codenamed *Emily* by the Allies), which had a range of almost 4,000 nautical miles, were assigned from the 801 Naval Air Group to lead in the suicide planes, and to supplement land-based weather reconnaissance aircraft, Nakajima C6N *Saiun* (Painted Cloud), known to the Allies as *Myrt*, fast single-engined machines, normally carrier-based, of the 141 Naval Air Group flown from Kisarazu to Truk for the purpose. Seven *Myrts* were duly despatched but two aborted, one came down in the sea *en route* and one crashed on landing, leaving just three operational, but without the specialised fuel required at the Truk base they would be unable to participate. Three submarines, *I-58* (Commander Mochitsura Hashimoto, IJN), *HA-106* (Lieutenant Akimasa Okakita, IJN) and *I-366* (Lieutenant (jg) Takami Tokioka, IJN), were to support the mission, the former to act as a radio beacon, the *HA-106* to rescue any ditched aircrews and *I-366* to take specialist equipment to ready the stranded *Myrts* and make them viable again.

The *Myrts* were then sent on scouting missions over Ulithi, to which Task Force 58 had returned on 4 March. Five days later, while at a conference, Admiral Ugaki was interrupted by a report from one of these aircraft which listed the presence of six fleet carriers and nine light fleet carriers at Ulithi, with four more carriers entering the atoll from the north-east. Here was a worthy target indeed and Ugaki recorded in his diary, 'Judging that most of the enemy task forces had returned there, I decided to carry out the second *Tan* operation tomorrow. Seemingly with the same idea, the Combined Fleet ordered X-day, the day of activating the operation, set as 10 March.'[5] The weather deteriorated considerably that day with a gale blowing from the China coast, but by the morning of Saturday 10th it had somewhat abated. Ugaki went to the command post at 05.45 and ordered the *Azusa* Unit to carry out the attack and drank a toast to them in sake, 'a gift from the Emperor.' He reminded the aircrews that being chosen for the mission was a great honour, but that he appreciated the hardship involved, saying 'I am now seeing you off with my deepest emotion and gratitude.' He also read a similar exhortation from the Combined Fleet which urged the young aircrew that this was a 'Divine Chance' and ending with the words, 'Go forward, all of you, pledging yourself to defend our sacred land by surely destroying the arrogant enemy by ramming yourself

---

4. *Azusa* was the yellow Catalpa tree from which Shinto devotees believed a magic bow, which could fend off all evil spirits, was made.
5. Ugaki, Admiral Matome – *Fading Victory – The Diary of Admiral Matome Ugaki 1941–1945*, Annapolis, MD: Naval Institute Press, 1991.

into them.' However, due to confused further reconnaissance reports the operation was again suspended until the 11th. Ugaki invited the aircrew to dinner that evening and found that they displayed a 'noble and lofty spirit' on the eve of their last mission.

On Sunday 11th accordingly Ugaki went to the Kyūshū Air Group at 08.00. The weather was now fine but the reconnaissance mission was delayed in taking off, as too was one of the leading attackers due to engine problems. This meant that the twenty-four *Gingas* departed at 09.00, twenty minutes later than planned, heading south from Cape Sata. They were under the overall command of Lieutenant Naoto Kuromaru. Sunset at Ulithi was 18.52 and, as the day wore on Ugaki awaited news of the mission. 'Though some radioed back their [need to] return due to engine problems, most of them seemed to go on all right. From about 17.45 I went into a shelter to wait for their reports, but no news came in. Time passed notwithstanding until it was thought to be quite dark over there. Yet nothing was heard except reports of emergency landings.' Then, at 18.58, a signal was received claiming that surprise had been achieved and a second, at 19.03, stated 'the whole force will charge in sure hits.' Further encouraging signals came in, 'I am going to hit a regular [fleet] carrier' and at 19.06 'One hit on a regular carrier' and a minute later, 'I am going to hit' and at 19.08 'A surprise attack was made.' Hearing these Ugaki was encouraged that the attack had indeed been a success. 'I was finally relieved from anxiety.' The American air raid alert had sounded at 19.07 and remained until 19.55, and this was duly noted as further proof that the attackers had hit the target despite all the difficulties encountered.

So the attack was made, but what are we to make of the following derogatory comment made by the translator of the Ugaki Diaries, Masataka Chihaya, about his fellow countrymen?, 'Of 24 *Gingas* from Kanoya, at least six reached Ulithi after dark and tried to attack. They made so little impression that neither Samuel Eliot Morison's *Victory in the Pacific* nor the official biography of Spruance [Thomas B Buell, *The Quiet Warrior*], who was present, mentions Operation *Tan*.' While it is undeniably true that *Tan* was certainly not an outstanding success, was it the total and abject failure this account insists? What *really* took place?

Of the twenty-four aircraft of the *Azusa* force that flew over the rescue submarine *HA-106* off Minami-Daito Jima four hours after taking off, five had to turn back because of engine problems and these forced landed there. Three further *Gingas* crashed into the sea and survivors were searched for by the *HA-106* over a period of three days. Meanwhile one of the *Emily* reconnaissance aircraft disappeared (it later landed back at base in Japan) while the other, piloted by Warrant Officer Goro Nagamine, had penetrated as far as Okino-Torishima where it encountered tropical storms and lightning, and had picked up the radio beacon transmissions from the *I-58* before it turned back and landed at Meleyon around 15.30. There was no aviation fuel on the island and so the *Emily* had to be destroyed. The remaining *Gingas* met the same tropical storms and strong head winds which caused several changes of course and altitude, and steadily burnt up what was an already critical level of fuel in the process. Gradually their numbers diminished until just six were left. Four of the six had to make force landings on Yap at this time being out of fuel. After progressing almost to Yap the two survivors changed course and headed toward Ulithi some 120 miles distant. They made a high-level approach before dropping chaff and then conducted a very low altitude final approach. They found the American fleet totally unprepared, with crews in Condition of Readiness II, Material Condition 'Yoke'. Radar Guard was being maintained by just one ship, the carrier *Hancock* (CV-19, Captain Robert F Hickey, USN), and also by Air Defense Command on Falalop Island, and it was not until 20.05 that Air Flash Red was broadcast to all ships by the Atoll Commander Ulithi over the TBS system.

The fleet carrier *Randolph* (CV-15, Captain Felix Baker, USN) was anchored at the fleet base at Ulithi, when at 20.07, a *Frances* twin-engined bomber carrying a 1,600lb bomb hit the starboard side aft, just below the flight deck. This aircraft made its final approach at low altitude and high speed from a bearing relative to the ship of 120–140 degrees. The angle of glide was very slight, if at all. Impact occurred at the edge of the flight deck on the starboard side of the ship some fifteen feet from the stern. The aircraft's bomb, which was probably released just prior to impact, penetrated the ship's hull and interior bulkheads for several feet before exploding. The exact point of detonation seems to have been at frame 203, about twenty feet inboard to starboard of the CO_2 Transfer Shop. A deck-side radio antenna mast was sheared off by the aircraft near its base and parts of the plane were observed to fall into the water. Other pieces of the *Ginga* itself dropped through the hole blown in the flight deck by the explosion, and other pieces were found strewn across the flight deck. This included a landing strut which imbedded itself into the starboard edge of the flight deck. A 56ft x 58ft hole was blown in the flight deck aft. Fire rooms and engine spaces immediately started filling with smoke via the supply vent trunking, and gas masks and air-hose masks had to be used by personnel. This dense smoke was drawn from the vent trunk onto the third deck spaces and delayed the manning of the Damage Control Station by ten minutes. On the hangar deck the sprinkler system quickly kicked in, but the entire after end of the ship abaft frame 202 was ablaze from main deck to flight deck. Ready-use ammunition from the 40mm mountings aft began to explode and the intense heat set off 20mm rounds in the shell clipping room on the gallery deck. Several aircraft parked aft were destroyed by fire.

The fires were not brought under control until about 22.00 and it was not until 06.00 when all fires were extinguished. Below decks, water draining away from the firefighting flooded some compartments on the second deck and the carrier heeled three degrees to starboard, this list being rectified at 23.57, but she then rolled almost two degrees to port at 02.30. The damage to the flight deck aft meant that air operations could not be conducted, two radios ceased working and the after 40mm mountings were destroyed.

It was estimated that the aircraft had carried a mixed bomb load estimated at one single 500lb bomb, with a B-3–A short delay (0.025 sec) fuse, plus one or two smaller 140lb bombs with very short delay fuses. The large bomb which hit the ship caused 'an explosion of a high order' and all the bomb fragments found were small in size. One of the smaller bombs exploded in Radio Room V, destroying it, having travelled some six to eight feet.[6]

Randolph's casualties were twenty-five dead and 106 wounded. Although these losses may have aroused no reaction from those translators and the historians he cited, they

6. USS *Randolph* (CV-15) War Damage, Report of. BuShips ltr C-FS/111–1(374), dated 10 April 1945. 50/jhw.

were considerable and avoidable. The repairs to the vessel were carried out *in situ* and she was ready for action again on 7 April.

The second *Ginga* also attacked but it aimed at the baseball diamond which was illuminated, on the islet of Mog Mog and used as a fleet recreation facility, mistaking the lights ashore for another fleet carrier at anchor: it blew up harmlessly there.

The euphoria back in Japan rapidly evaporated. The next day another *Myrt* made a reconnaissance over Ulithi and, far from seeing widespread devastation, reported that the number of carriers had actually increased there was no busy traffic of small craft or any sign of sunken vessels. Ugaki recorded bitterly, 'It turned out to be a complete failure.' The damage to *Randolph* went unreported by both friend and foe alike it seemed and the Japanese Admiral, as was his wont, blamed himself for the failure, which, he saw in retrospect was flawed from the start. 'In general, this plan of covering such a great distance with such a plane itself seemed to be against the odds.' Ugaki painstakingly analysed the action and drew the following conclusions for its failure:

1. that the time of the unit's departure was delayed an hour;
2. the delay to the lead aircraft's take-off delayed them another half hour;
3. they made a detour *en route*;
4. their speed was only 160 miles per hour.

He made no mention of the bad weather conditions encountered or the engine failures. What he did say was: 'Most of these should be attributed to their leader's poor conduct, for which I should be held responsible.' He later gained a trifle of consolation by knowing that, 'a sufficient number of crews for manning about ten *Ginga* land bombers were saved by emergency landings.' Some Allied historians have described the Japanese Admirals at this time as the 'wicked Old Guard'[7] trying to prolong a lost war by any means available.[8]

---

7. See for example, Eric M. Bergerud , *Fire in the Sky: The Air War in the South Pacific*, Boulder, Colorado: 2000. Westview Press.
8. Winston S. Churchill, the former British wartime Premier, described the situation in Japan at this time in this manner: 'The professional diplomats were convinced that only immediate surrender under the authority of the Emperor could save Japan from complete disintegration, but power still lay in the hands of a military clique determined to commit the nation to mass suicide rather than accept defeat. The appalling destruction confronting them made no impression on this fanatical hierarchy, who continued to profess belief in some miracle which would turn the scale in their favour.' – Churchill, Winston Spencer, *The Second World War*, 6 Volumes, London, 1951. Cassel & Co. But of course Churchill, with a politician's selective memory, conveniently forgot that almost the identical fate was predicted for Great Britain when he took over the reins of power in 1940, with all her allies defeated or deserting her in favour of close collaboration with Hitler and a victorious German army standing along the coast of Europe from the North Cape to the Spanish border. Then it had been Churchill whose stirring words prevented a nation from accepting the victor's terms when the whole world (and most especially Kennedy the American Ambassador) had written Britain off. That defiance had made him a legend and almost a saint among some, but exactly the same attitude from the Japanese appeared to many westerners to be tantamount to infernal. Of course Churchill himself had always had a blind spot as regards Japan, his ignoring of her potential

Ukagi most certainly considered himself a patriot trying to save his nation and far from being indifferent to the loss of his young aircrew described in his diary how it was not because he was unfeeling that he could send them off to die 'with a smile in these days' but that, 'I had made up my mind to follow the example of those young boys some day.'[9] He was to be as good as his word.

However, he was far from alone. Even 'moderate' Japanese expressed views in favour of the Kamikaze actions, for example Jiro Horikoshi, respected designer of the Navy Type 0, or Zero, fighter, contributed an article, *Compliment to the Kamikaze Special Attack Forces*, one of ten such hymns of praise by prominent personages, to a book on the suicide forces, in which he wrote, 'We have reached the limits of human intelligence and have selfishly tried all kinds of methods to make effective adjustments to our limited human and material resources so that new arms could emerge. As I have witnessed the birth of the Zero, I know there is nothing to fear, since we have created an aircraft worthy of its task and the Kamikaze Special Attack Forces to do the job that must be done.'[10] This was but part of the general indoctrination of the Japanese public practiced during the *Shōwa* Dynasty (1926–1945).[11] One historian wrote: 'By Emperor Shōwa's reign, the military had the real authority.'[12] A modern Japanese historian stated: 'Systematic and organized education made such efficient 'brainwashing' possible. In public schools, students were taught to die for the emperor. By late 1944 a slogan, *Jusshi Reisho*, meaning 'Sacrifice Life', was taught. Most of the pilots who volunteered for the suicide attacks were those who were born late in the Taisho period (1912–1926) or in the first two or three years of Shōwa. Therefore, they had gone through the brainwashing education, and were products of the militaristic Japan.'[13] That is far from saying that Kamikaze volunteers were robots of the same mind-set or background, or otherwise all of a kind; this was far from the case. Mako Sasaki's research brought to light such diverse young men, with ages that ranged from seventeen to thirty-five. Many were college students or graduates and deep thinkers, especially when their exemption from the draft was abandoned under the *Gakuto Shutsujin* scheme. University graduates from Tokyo, Keito, Kyoto and Waseda Universities were among them, more worldly-wise and liberal in attitude. Some Japanese today claim that no such Tokyo students became Kamikaze pilots, but the testimony of

---

against the advice of his naval advisors led directly to the disaster of the loss of the battleship *Prince of Wales* and battle-cruiser *Repulse* and, ultimately, to the total loss of her Empire in the East. Also, Churchill himself stated categorically, that his main purpose was, 'victory – victory at all costs, victory in spite of all terror; victory however hard the road may be' a not so dissimilar thought to that expressed by the Japanese at this similar critical juncture of events. See also Grenfell, Captain Russell, RN, *Unconditional Hatred: German War Guilt and the Future of Europe*, New York: 1953, Devin-Adair Company.

9. Ugaki, Admiral Matome – *Fading Victory – The Diary of Admiral Matome Ugaki 1941–1945*, Annapolis, MD: Naval Institute Press, 1991.
10. Various contributors, *Kamikaze Special Attack Forces*, Osaka, 1944. Asahi.
11. Crown Prince Hirohito became Emperor Shōwa on 25th December 1926. The term *Shōwa* can be translated as either 'Brightness', 'Harmony or 'Illustrious Peace'.
12. Scoggins, Glenn (compiler), *Japanese History Source Book*, Yokohama, 1993.
13. Sasaki, Mako, *Who Became Kamikaze Pilots, And How Did They Feel Towards Their Suicide Mission?* Ralph Emerson Prize, 1997, *The Concord Review, Inc.* 1999: Concord.

Kazuo Watanabe, Assistant Professor at that University makes clear that they *did*.[14] As well as traditionalists following the Zen way, there were also Christians and atheists who were happy to become Kamikaze pilots. Second Lieutenant Ryoji Uehara, from Keio University, considered himself a democrat and a radical one at that. He was not sorry to see Nazi German follow Fascist Italy into defeat. Even such a one as this professed in his last days that he 'was greatly honoured to be chosen as a Kamikaze pilot.'[15] Or take the case of Second Lieutenant Fumihiro Mitsuyama. It was revealed that he was in fact Korean, real name Tak Kyong-Hyong. The down-side is that he was not a volunteer but had circled 'desire earnestly' to go on the selection sheet and was selected.[16] Many young pilots who were 'volunteered', or coherced into volunteering by peer pressure or worse, felt differently as Emiko Ōhnuki-Tierney demonstrated.[17]

A few American writers, such as Ruth Benedict,[18] have studied both the origins, the myths and facts of the Kamikaze spirit, with a high degree of, if not empathy, at least understanding, but most Occidentals remain aghast and baffled as to how a tiny volunteer movement could move so swiftly into a massed, organised self-sacrificial slaughter. What we do not understand, we fear, and few in the West, even now, understand the *Bushido* Code as it was practiced between 1944 and 1945.

Further actions

On 18 March Task Force 58 deployed two mixed radar picket groups, with several destroyers giving a small degree of mutual support and with supporting 'pall bearers' to render aid and assistance if any were hit. The two groups were stationed about thirty miles to the north and west of the main fleet which was operating approximately ninety-three miles east of Kyushu. A semi-continuous CAP of between four dozen to a maximum of 120 fighters, both Navy and shore-based Marine Corsairs, was maintained during daylight hours, but even this proved insufficient to guarantee immunity. It was acknowledged that a less vulnerable option was to establish shore-based radar watch positions on the outlying islands making the deployment of destroyers less essential, but this took a disproportionate amount of time for the Army to achieve. Not until 21 April was the radar station at Hedo Cape, Okinawa, operational, while that on Lejima didn't function again until the 23rd.

14. Watanabe, Kazuo, *Vacillating Youth*, article in *Nipon Dokusho Shimbun*, dated 9 September 1946 – cited in Inoguchi, Captain Rikihei and Nakajima, Commander Tadashi with Pineau, Roger, *The Divine Wind: Japan's Kamikaze Force in World War II*, Annapolis:1958, United States Naval Institute Press.
15. Chiran Ko-jo Nadeshiko Kai, *Chiran Tokko Kichi*, Tokyo: 1979, Bunwa Shoho.
16. Masako Aihoshi, *Hana no Toki was Kanashimi no Toki*, Kagoshima: 1992, Takagi Shoho.
17. Ōhnuki-Tierney, Emiko, *Kamikaze Diaries: Reflections of Japanese Student Soldiers, Chicago: 2006*, University of Chicago Press.
18. Benedict, Ruth, *The Chrysanthemum and the Sword: Patterns of Japanese Culture*, New York: 1946, Houghton Miffin Company.

Intrepid damaged once more

After her repairs on the West Coast, *Intrepid* (CV-11), now commanded by Captain Giles Ezra Short, USN, had resumed full operations once more, but on 18 March the Kamikazes again found her irresistible and she was attacked by a twin-engined *Betty*. Nicknamed the 'flying lighter' because of its tendency to easily catch fire when struck by shell or bullets, the *Betty* was true to this derisive label and was pounded by the ship's gunners, exploding in a spectacular fireball about fifty feet off *Intrepid*'s bows. Chunks of fuselage, other debris and burning fuel cascaded onto *Intrepid*, some of which penetrated down to the hangar deck and started fires, although they were quickly brought under control and flight operations resumed once more. The ship's casualties totalled two dead and forty-three wounded.

At 07.10 the next day, 19 March, the carrier *Wasp* (CV-18, Captain Oscar Arthur Weller, USN) was attacked by a suicidal *Jill* from out of high cloud. Taken under fire at 4,000 yards, this aircraft was eventually hit by a 5in VT shell at 2,500 yards and then hit many more times thereafter. The carrier's helm was put hard over to starboard and the aircraft came down in the sea close alongside the deck-edge lift on the port side. The bomb carried by this aircraft penetrated the flight deck down to No.3 deck before detonating and causing significant casualties. A second attack was made by a *Jill*, but the defensive barrage hit it fair and square, and it too struck the sea off of the port side deck-edge lift without causing any damage. Even so, the *Wasp* had 101 men killed and 269 crewmen wounded in the first attack. Another casualty that day was the destroyer *Halsey Powell* (DD-686, Commander Sidney Douglas Buxton Merrill, USN), which was hit by a *Zeke* that had attempted to crash into the *Hancock* (CV-19), but which overshot and struck the destroyer which had just finished fuelling alongside. Her steering gear was damaged and she was almost run down by the *Hancock*, but after fighting off further attacks was escorted to safety by the destroyers *Stephen Potter* (DD-538, Commander George Read Muse) and *The Sullivans* (DD-537, Lieutenant-Commander Ralph Jacob Baum).

Devilfish attacked

Attacks by Kamikazes on submarines were indeed a rare event. One that did take place occurred on 20th March 1945 off the Volcano Islands in position 25 degrees 36 North, 137 degrees 30 E. The *Balao* Class submarine *Devilfish* (SS-292, Lieutenant-Commander Stephen Statford Mann, Jr., USN) was surprised by a *Zeke* while simultaneously submerging and passing over a shelf a mere 50 feet below. Parts of the plane struck the uppermost portion of her periscope housing damaging the two periscopes both mechanically and optically. Additionally, the SJ radar mast was ruptured at the top allowing water to enter the conning tower in large volumes, its bilges filled and water poured down into the control room. Consequently, with most of her radio, radar and sonar equipment destroyed, damaged, or shorted-out by the inrush of salt water, it proved necessary to terminate the patrol.

Abortive *Ōhka* mission

What was planned as the debut of a new weapon was put into operation by the Japanese on 21 March 1945. The rocket-powered, manually piloted Yokosuka MXY-7 *Ōhka* flying bomb was to be sent against Task Group 58.1's carriers, *Bennington, Hornet, Wasp* and *Belleau Wood*. A force of sixteen *Betty* bombers adapted to carry these weapons was assembled under Commander Goro Nonaka while two more of the twin-engined aircraft were to act as guides and observe results, of which much was expected. No less than fifty-five *Zeke* fighters from the newly re-constituted 201st Air Group were assigned as fighter escorts to punch through the defensive CAP and allow the *Ōhka*s to be launched. The rocket bombers themselves were led by Lieutenant Kentaro Mihashi.

As with so many Japanese missions at this period, it all went badly wrong. No less than twenty-five of the *Zekes* had to turn back due to mechanical problems and when the force was intercepted by sixteen Hellcats seventy miles from the Allied Task Force, and while still well short of their launch position, the *Betty* pilots prematurely launched their hapless cargoes in a futile effort to escape destruction. In the fierce fight that followed, all the *Bettys* were lost along with ten of the remaining *Zekes*: no *Ōhka* was able to attack any ship.

The mission was a total and expensive flop, yet incredibly the Japanese claimed it had been a brilliant success and that no less than *eight* American carriers had been sunk, but it was all a fiasco. They were to continue to delude themselves in this manner to the very end.

Chapter Eight

Okinawa the First Phase

'We live in the spirit of Jesus Christ, and we die in that spirit. This thought stays with me. It is gratifying to live in this world, but living has a spirit of futility about it now. It is time to die. I do not seek reasons for dying. My only search is for an enemy target against which to dive.'

Ensign Ichizo Hayashi, a Kyoto graduate, a Christian
and member of the Genzan (Wonsan) Koku Sentai

A big effort mounted on 27th March 1945 by Kamikazes against the mass of shipping assembling off Okinawa resulted in damage to two battleships: *Nevada* (BB-36, Captain Homer Louis Grosskopf) and *Tennessee* (BB-43, Captain John Baptist Hefferman), the light cruiser *Biloxi* (CL-80, Captain Paul Ralph Heineman) and destroyer high-speed transports *Gilmer* (DD-233 APD-11, Commander John S Horner), *Kimberly* (DD-521, Commander James Dickson Whitfield, Jr.), *O'Brien* (DD-725, Commander William Woodward Quterbridge). Additionally, destroyer-minesweeper *Dorsey* (DMS-1, Lieutenant John Michael Hayes), destroyer-minelayer *Robert H. Smith* (DM-23, Commander Henry Farrow), destroyer-escort *Foreman* (DE-633, Lieutenant-Commander Charles A Manston), destroyer-minesweeper *Southard* (DMS-10, Commander John Edward Brennan), along with *Skirmish* (ACM-303, Lieutenant Bruce Leverington Hyatt) and *Knudson (*APA-101, Captain R D Williams) were also hit. Other pre-landing casualties included the heavy cruiser *Indianapolis (*CA-35), *Adams* (DM-27, Commander Henry James Armstrong, Jr.), *LSM-188* and *LST-724* which were all damaged on 31 March.

When the invasion finally commenced on 1 April the Kamikaze effort was redoubled and several ships were struck, among them the battleship *West Virginia* (BB-48, Captain Herbert Victor Wiley), destroyer *Callaghan* (DD-792, Commander Charles Marriner Bertholf) and four attack transports, the *Archenar* (AKA-53, Commander H R Stevens), *Alpine* (APA-92, Commander George G K Reilly), *Tyrrell* (AKA-80, Lieutenant-Commander John L McLean) and attack transport *Hinsdale* (APA-120, Commander Edward F Beyer) as well as *LST-884*. Among the attackers were six *Betty* bombers carrying *Ōhka*s, but again they do not appear to have hit any of the ships that were struck by suicide aircraft that day and none of the *Betty*s survived either.

The British Experience

On 1 April 1945 the British Pacific Fleet (BPF) employed suppressing the Japanese staging airfields along the Sakishima Gunto island group to the south, was itself under persistent attack throughout the day. At 06.50 radar detected incoming bogeys approaching from the west at a distance of seventy-five miles and a height of 8,000ft, closing at 200 knots. Fighters already airborne were called in to deal with this and additional fighters flown off. This raid split up while some forty miles out and Corsairs shot down one, Seafires two more, and finally a fourth was destroyed by Hellcats. The Fleet had gone to 'Flash Red' condition at 07.05 and a single-engined aircraft carried out a low-level machine-gun attack on the carrier *Indomitable*, killing one and injuring six others before carrying on to strafe the battleship *King George V* (B4, Captain Thomas Edgar Halsey), without any effect. This was probably meant as a diversion and, at 07.27, a *Zeke* carrying a 500lb bomb made a dive into the carrier *Indefatigable* (R-7, Captain Quintin Dick Graham, CBE, DSO, RN), striking the base of the island structure and dishing her steel flight deck across an area of 15 square feet to a depth of three inches without penetrating it. The explosion killed eight and injuring sixteen of her crew. Lieutenant-Commander Pat Chambers, RN, the Flight Deck Officer, related to the author what occurred thus:

'We heard a few bursts of fire from Bofors and Oerlikons from *King George V* close by us and, as usual, we started to put on flash gear and tin hats. Doc Alan 'Beefy' Vaughan was sitting on the sick bay couch and Lieutenant (A) William G Bill Gibson, standing next to me, looking out of the scuttle. I was fully rigged for action with the exception of my left glove – I was just pulling it on, an action which turned me half to the left. This little turn was just as well for me, because at that moment there was the most shattering explosion and the sickbay disintegrated in a sheet of flame.

'I was spun head over heels, over and over, or so it felt, until I got hold of a bit of jagged corner-post, by which I heaved myself clear. In the steam and the din there was no sign of my two companions who had been laughing and joking a moment before. There was just a mass of dead and wounded in the area and one of my DLCOs (Deck Landing Control Officer, nicknamed 'Batmen' in the Royal Navy), Sub-Lieutenant Peter Roome, helped me out onto the flight-deck and down a small ladder which led to a cabin flat. In one of these I passed out.

'The picture I retain of the scene is quite vivid; the starboard wing of the Japanese plane burning on the Island abaft the funnel and a great gap from there to the flight-deck where the whole lot had blown up, leaving a hole about eight feet long in the Island sickbay. Our Kamikaze had had a bomb of about 250 pounds on him. [Author's note – it was actually a 500lb weapon]. The explosion put the flight deck out of action for a period, but the armoured deck was not penetrated, only dented, and flying operations, albeit on a reduced scale, were soon continued with the landing aboard of her Seafire CAP within forty minutes, and proceeded throughout the day. Repairs were carried out between 2 April and 1 May.

At 07.55 another Japanese attacker, being chased by a fighter, dropped a 500lb bomb which near-missed the destroyer *Ulster* (D23, Lieutenant-Commander Ronald John Hansen, DSO, DSC, RN). One account claimed that 'she took a Kamikaze into her Iron Deck' but this was pure hyperbole.[1] Her hull was opened

1. Poolman, Kenneth, *Illustrious*, London, William Kimber, 1955.

up on her starboard side abreast the funnel, and two men were killed and one seriously wounded. The blast blew open the bulkhead between the engine-room and after boiler room, and both compartments flooded. She was unable to steam but the ship remained stable and her armament fully operational. The destroyer *Quiberon* (D-20, Commander G. S. Stewart, RAN) stood by her and later the light cruiser *Gambia* (C-168, Captain Maurice James Mansergh, RN) took her under tow to Leyte for repairs

Later that afternoon a second attack broke over Task Force 57, after a low-flying bogie was detected at 17.30 fifteen miles to the north-west. Defending Hellcats lost the incoming aircraft in the cloud but it was replaced by several more hostile aircraft which suddenly appeared over the fleet and as they commenced their attacks they were taken under intense gunnery from the fleet. Despite this, one machine made a determined dive against the *Victorious* (38, Captain Michael Maynard Denny). The carrier's close-range weapons scored hits and the ship herself was put under full helm in an avoiding manoeuvre that threw the kamikaze pilot off target with only his wing tip connecting with the ship, which was sufficient to send it spinning into the sea close alongside – its bomb detonating harmlessly on impact. Among the debris from the attacker which was blown aboard the carrier were manuscript instructions to the pilot, which, upon translation, included the priority of targets for suicide attacks. This interesting data was duly passed on to the intelligence centre for further dissemination to the fleet.[2]

Admiral Vian's thoughts on Pickets

The long-established practice of the Japanese of following returning Allied aircraft back to the carriers so that they blended in with them on the radar screens and confused the defences, was one problem that Allied commanders tried to address as plans for Operation *Iceberg* became a reality. On the last day of March, 1945, the anti-aircraft cruiser *Argonaut* (C-161, Captain William Patrick McCarthy, RN), along with the destroyer *Wager* (D30, Lieutenant-Commander Roland Chisnell Watkin, RN), were detached from the British Task Force and the following day took up a patrolling position 300 degrees, thirty miles out from the fleet centre to act as pickets in an attempt to thwart this enemy practice. Vice-Admiral Philip Louis Vian explained thus:

'H.M.S. *Argonaut* was chosen for this purpose as having the most suitable radar. Picket work must, in some measure, be difficult and risky: it requires first class radar, effective fighter-direction, personnel who are well able to indent enemy aircraft and a good armament. The destroyer, or destroyers, with her should also be very capable of beating off air attacks.'[3]

The *Argonaut* had been previously taken in hand for extensive refitting as a Command Ship in January 1944 and her radar comprised equipment for control of 10cm radars.

---

2. ADM199/1041; Enclosure No.II to V.A.B.P.F. No. 1092/4 of 9th May, 1945–Secret. Operation *Iceberg*, pp 5.
3. ADM199/1041; Enclosure No.II to V.A.B.P.F. No. 1092/4 of 9th May, 1945–Secret. Operation *Iceberg*, pp 4.

She carried Type 293 and 277 radar for surface warning and height-finding, plus fire-control radar which gave excellent forward close-range control. She also carried IFF (Interrogation) equipment and had a VHF Direction-Finding set. Her main armament comprised eight 5.25in guns in four twin turrets, three quadruple 2–pdr pom-poms while her 20mm Oerlikons had been replaced by eight 40mm Mk III Bofors.

The *Wager*, and later her sister ship, *Whelp* (D33, Commander George Anthony Francis Norfolk, RN), which was also used on this duty.[4, 5, 6]

These destroyers' radar outfits comprised a 50–cm band Search Radar Type 285 to control the main armament, a Type 282 to control the Bofors and Type 291 as an Air Warning outfit carried on a pole mainmast aft, with IFF atop the lattice mast.

The campaign intensifies

On 2 April the fast transport *Dickerson* (APD-21, Lieutenant-Commander Ralph Emerson Loonsbury, Jr) was hit and damaged, having 51 of her crew killed, including her C.O.. She was towed to Kerama Retto, but proved unsalvageable and the hulk was scuttled. Also several transports *en route* to the beachhead were damaged by suicide attacks. These ships were all from TRANSRON-17 and were all hit on the same date and in the same area, position 26⁰ N, 127⁰ 17' E. The *Henrico* (APA-45, Captain W C France) was struck by a twin-engined *Frances*, and suffered forty-nine men killed, including the ship's captain and the Army divisional commander, and two of his troop commanders; the *Chilton* (APA-38, Captain Hugh Weber Torney) also struck by a *Frances* which went into No.3 hatch causing fires; the *Goodhue* (APA-107, Captain Lewis D Shard, Jr.), which took no less than 144 casualties, including 44 dead; and the *Telfair* (APD-210, Commander Lye O Armez), fortunately with no loss of life. In addition the amphibious vessels *LCI(G)-568* and *LST-599* were hit. Next day things got worse.

---

4. Only twelve British destroyers had been built with dual-purpose guns in fully enclosed gun houses (four *Laforey* Class and eight *Milne* Class), and although the first half-flotilla of a new type of 2,400–ton destroyer, the *Battle* Class, were being readied to join the BPF, only one arrived on station before the end of hostilities, the *Barfleur* (D-61, Commander Michael Southcote Townsend, DSO, DSC, OBE, RN), while the *Armada* (D-73, Lieutenant-Commander Robert Augustus Fell, RN), *Camperdown* (D-62, Lieutenant-Commander James John Simon Yorke, DSC, RN), *Trafalgar* (D-75, Lieutenant-Commander Anthony Follett Pugsley, DSO, RN), and *Hogue* (D-74, Commander A St. Clair-Ford, DSO, RN)] were still *en route* to the Pacific when hostilities ended.

5. See Pugsley, *Destroyer Man*, London, 1957. The *Wager* and *Whelp* did have a twin 40mm Bofors with Hazemeyer.

6. This was a *pre-war* Dutch fire-control package with the instruments carried on the mounting with which guns, optical instruments and their operators were stabilised by gyro control of a three-axis mounting, the control of fire being fully tachymetric. It was only belatedly adopted by the Royal Navy after much argument. Their only other anti-aircraft weapons were four twin 20mm Oerlikons, this calibre of weapon being largely discredited by this time as firing too small a shell to stop a committed Kamikaze attack.

Wake Island damaged

The *Wake Island* (CVE-65), still commanded by Captain Tague, was targeted at 17.44 on 3 April by two single-engined suicide aircraft. The first machine misjudged his attack and passed close over the carrier's flight deck, and went into the sea hard alongside her port bow where it and its bomb detonated causing severe shock damage to her forward hull. Within half-a-minute the second aircraft, aiming at the carrier's bridge, missed by a hair's breadth and also went into the water some ten feet off. This explosion was devastating. A hole some 45 feet by 18 feet was torn in the carrier's hull under the waterline and the shell plating cracked between the first and second decks, and bent and buckled elsewhere. *Wake Island* rapidly began to flood, the water spreading compartment by compartment with the sea flooding the main condensers. As a result some 70,000 gallons of oil fuel and 30,000 gallons of fresh water were contaminated; by 18.24 the flooding had eventually shut down the forward engine totally.

Debris from this aircraft and shrapnel from its bomb also came inboard above the waterline while the bulk of the aircraft was hurled into the ship's gun tubs and onto her flight deck. Incredibly the ship suffered no casualties at all from this combined impact. The damage control teams were thus able to go about their business with considerable skill and had the situation in hand by 21.40, with both engines connected. However, the damage was such that she had to withdraw the following day to effect temporary repairs at the anchorage at Kerama Retto. These were sufficient for her to sail to Apra Harbor, Guam, here she arrived on 10 April for a ten-day full repair. On 21 April the *Wake Island* was able to sail back to the Okinawa area once more and resume full operational duties.

Also on this day, the destroyer-minesweeper *Hambleton* (DMS-20, Commander George Albert O'Connell, Jr.) was damaged by Kamikaze attack but continued working. On 6 April the minesweeper *Ransom* (ACM-283, Lieutenant-Commander William N McMillen) was slightly damaged while rescuing survivors from the *Emmons* (DMS-22, Commander Eugene Noble Foss-II), *Rodman* (DMS-21, Commander William Henderson Kirvan) and *Gladiator* (AM-319, Commander Robert W Costello).

British Pacific Fleet 3 April 1945

The BPF was detected by Japanese aircraft, at 08.50 on the morning of 3 April, which escaped into cloud. Later that morning a *Frances* was destroyed by Hellcats so it was obvious that company could be expected before the day was out and, sure enough, at around 17.00, bogeys were detected on radar. The Japanese deployed airborne jamming techniques to block the British fighter-direction frequencies, which indicated some detailed planning had gone into their mission, but although it initially caused some inconvenience most FAA pilots soon switched frequencies and the CAP shot down one D4Y3 *Judy* dive-bomber from the incoming group. A second *Judy* made an attack through cloud targeting *Illustrious* (87, Captain Charles Edward Lambe), 'who took radical avoiding action. Engaged by AA fire this aircraft was probably hit and her wingtip hit the carrier's Island, spinning the aircraft into the sea where the bomb exploded. Only slight damage and no casualties were caused.' Two more from this group were taken under fire by the destroyers of the 4th Flotilla on the screen, who knocked one down which crashed in flames on the horizon, while the other *Judy*, chased by Corsairs and Hellcats, was forced to jettison its bomb and flee, although it too was shot down in flames. A further *Judy* seen orbiting the fleet some ten miles out was also intercepted by Corsairs and destroyed for a most satisfactory outcome.[7]

The *Kikusui* Operations

Between the end of March and June 1945, the Japanese launched a total of ten major attacks against the Allied invasion fleet and the covering Task Forces off Okinawa under the generic title *Kikusui*. The term originated from the ancient *Noh* song *Kikujidou*, which featured in the *Ryouma-shinsou* of *Taiheiki*. It celebrated the 'fountain of youth' sought by Buntei, Emperor of Wei. This was found, the song recorded, by the discovery of a 700–year old hermit, Jiduo, who had distilled it from the *sui* (water) of the chrysanthemum (*kiku*). The word became the family motto of the Okusukou family, signifying the longevity of that line, but was adopted by the Kamikaze Corps as symbolising the achievement of eternal youth by youthful sacrifice to the Chrysanthemum Throne.

In the ten main attacks some 9,400 aircraft sorties were made and 1,320 machines were lost. 1,840 of these sorties were suicide missions of which 960 participating aircraft were destroyed, either by the Allied defences or by striking their targets. 185 of these missions were *Ohka* launchings, of which 118 of the participating 'mother' aircraft were lost, while 368 of these missions were made by fighter-bombers of which 284 were lost. It was a major effort to hold Okinawa, but one that ultimately failed, although it claimed many victims and caused enormous damage to Allied shipping.

Illustrious finally put out of the war

Among the many victims of these *Kikusui* assaults was the famous aircraft carrier HMS *Illustrious*. She was attacked by a *Judy* which failed to connect properly with her bridge other than to glance off the Type 272 radome, which tipped the aircraft and its bomb into the sea close alongside. The bomb detonated causing a mining effect which tore open the carrier's outer hull, cracked several frames, and exacerbated old damage and old wounds incurred earlier in the war. Although she continued to operate her aircraft, with her speed reduced to nineteen knots, she was, in effect, crippled and unfit for continued front-line combat. Nor could *Illustrious*' problems, deep-rooted as they were, be repaired even in Australia – she required the full facilities of a British dockyard. Accordingly *Illustrious* steamed out of the war and headed back to the UK. She finally reached Rosyth on 27 June and commenced a four-month repair, although long before that was completed the war reached its conclusion and she was subsequently downgraded to become a training carrier, and did not re-commission, even in that role, until a year later.

---

7. ADM199/1041; Enclosure No.II to V.A.B.P.F. No. 1092/4 of 9th May, 1945–Secret. Operation *Iceberg*, pp10.

Indomitable scratched

On 4 April the *Indomitable* (R-8, Captain John Arthur Symons Eccles, RN) was slightly damaged by a Kamikaze that belly-flopped adjacent to the ship's island structure, damaging the radar antenna of her port amidships directors, but the aircraft disintegrated and skidded overboard along with its bomb, which detonated in the sea without damage to the ship.

Hancock hit

The carrier *Hancock* (CV-19) was again damaged by Kamikaze attack on 7 April. This aircraft careered across the flight deck and smacked right into a group of parked aircraft while its bomb detonated on the carrier's port catapult. The resulting fires were quenched within thirty minutes and air operations recommenced in under an hour, but sixty-two men died and a further seventy-one were injured in this attack. She was eventually detached back to Pearl Harbor on 9 April where she was repaired in time to rejoin the fleet by 13 June. The battleship *Maryland* (BB-46, Captain J D Wilson), destroyers *Bennett* (DD-473, Lieutenant-Commander Jasper Newton McDonald) and *Longshaw* (DD-559, Lieutenant-Commander Theodore Robert Vogeley), destroyer escort *Wesson* (DE-184, Commander Hermann Reich) and minesweeper *YMS-81*, Lieutenant Peter F Beville were all damaged.

The toll continued; on 8 April destroyer *Gregory* (DD-802, Commander Bruce McCandles) was damaged; on 9 April destroyer *Sterett* (DD-407, Commander Gordon Bennett Williams) and *LCT-876* were both hit and damaged, while on 10 April the *Samuel S. Miles* (DE-183, Lieutenant-Commander Henry G Brousseau) was also damaged.

British Pacific Fleet (BPF), 3 April 1945

In view of the enormous scale of Kamikaze attack being directed against the other task groups off Okinawa by Formosa-based aircraft, Vice-Admiral BPF decided to extend his operations for a further day. He reasoned, 'even if we could do little more than occasionally strike at the Sakishima Gunto we should anyhow provide an alternative target to take some of the weight.' The 13th April therefore found the BPF back in operation. At 05.40 a bogey was detected and ten minutes later four fighters were scrambled. This Japanese group comprised four *Val* dive-bombers with a radar-equipped search plane (a type termed by the Allies as a 'Gestapo') in attendance. One *Val* turned on its navigation lights and fired an incorrect signal flare before making a conventional dive-bombing attack on *Indomitable*. Its bomb missed and this machine, although engaged, escaped unscathed. A second *Val* was hit by AA and destroyed while the other two failed to attack. A second group, this time comprised of *Zekes*, approached at 06.40 but was intercepted by Corsairs who shot down two of them, the rest retiring.[8]

---

8. ADM199/1041; Appendix V to V.A.B.P.F. No. 1092/4 of 9th May, 1945–Secret. Operation *Iceberg*, pp17.

Wild over-estimation by Japanese – Ugaki's Diary

While recording the actual success obtained by the Kamikaze method of attack, and acknowledging its limited effectiveness, it must always be remembered that the Japanese High Command was totally misled by the reports coming back from the scene of the action. Vast over-estimations of the results being obtained were believed and circulated, with, one senses, a desperation to believe which a more careful study of the true facts would have dissipated completely. Thus they continued to lead themselves up the *cul-de-sac* of suicide missions as being the answer to their many problems. We are fortunate to have available the Diary of Ugaki where the most obvious manifestation of this wistful thinking is laid bare.

The Japanese commanders, Navy and Army, combined to plan a massive resistance campaign for the defence of Okinawa which they had expected. At the heart of Operation *Ten-Go* as it was named, was a whole series of massive Kamikaze attacks, designed to overwhelm the Allied defences by sheer weight of numbers and inflict the maximum possible casualties on the attackers. These attack waves were known as *Kikusui* (Floating Chrysanthemum – a reference to the emblem of the Royal House).

On Thursday 5 April, as the Okinawa battle was underway, Ugaki recorded: 'A briefing of *Kikusui* No.1 Operation was held in the morning with all commanders concerned present,' and the next day he gave a detailed account of the operation as it appeared to him. 'We didn't know the result of our attack except the reports of "I am crashing on a carrier", but judging from the enemy telephones in hurried confusion and requests for help it was almost certain that we destroyed four carriers.' He described the battles vividly, 'the first wave of our fighter force, twenty-seven planes, lured enemy fighters high up in the sky, while the second, third, and fourth (each wave had the same number of planes as the first) took command of the air over Okinawa and Army fighters (approximately forty) flew back and forth on the line of Amamio-shima, thus facilitating the advance of special attack planes. Besides, Army Headquarters reconnaissance aircraft dropped radar-deceiving tapes (i.e. 'chaff' or 'window') to the east.'

'The attack against the enemy task force resulted in rounding up the enemy from the south while at the same time we managed to have the large enemy force come toward Minami-Daito-jima. Taking advantage of this opportunity, over 110 naval special attack planes, those belonging to the Tenth Air Fleet, detoured to the west and hurled themselves against the enemy fleet at Okinawa. Ninety Army special attack aircraft of the Sixth Air Army charged in at about the same time, and those of the Eight Air Division and First Air Fleet also made coordinated attacks.

'The sea around Okinawa thus turned into a scene of carnage, and a reconnaissance plane reported that as many as 150 columns of black smoke were observed, while others described it as difficult to observe them. Judging from the radio-equipped planes' reports of their reaching the objectives without enemy fighter interference, most of them seem to have succeeded.'[9]

---

9. Ugaki, Admiral Matome – *Fading Victory – The Diary of Admiral Matome Ugaki 1941–1945*, Annapolis, MD: Naval Institute Press, 1991.

Kikūsūi Missions at Okinawa						
Kikūsūi		Kamikaze Sorties Flown			Allied Ships	
Kikūsūi	Date	Navy	Army	Total	Sunk	Damaged
1	6–7 Apr	230	125	355	4	24
2	12–13	125	60	185	1	14
3	15–16	120	45	165	1	9
4	27–28	65	50	115	0	9
5	3–4 May	75	50	125	3	14
6	10–11	70	80	150	0	5
7	24–25	65	100	165	1	9
8	27–28	60	50	110	1	6
9	3–7 Jun	20	30	50	0	7
10	21–22	30	15	45	0	5
Total		860	605	1465	11	102
Extra suicide sorties		140	45	185	*	*
Formosa sorties		50	200	250	*	*
Grand Total		1050	850	1900	25	*

*The detailed breakdown of these totals is unknown, but what *is* known is that an extra fourteen Allied ships were sunk from both the Extra and Formosa-originated causes combined.

Similar massive self-delusion is apparent on 7 April and on the day that the Japanese battleship *Yamato* was destroyed during her own suicide sortie, Ugaki was recording in his diary that: 'About thirty various kinds of special attack planes were directed to the enemy task forces, and unexpectedly they were well distributed among enemy carriers, including the newly discovered one, not to speak of those damaged ones. Six *Suisei a*nd eleven *Ginga,* all radio-equipped, reported ramming enemy vessels, while fighter-bombers, together with two Army reconnaissance aircraft converted into bombers, rammed enemy ships without any words. The interception of enemy radio exchanges also indicated that two ships were sunk and two others damaged, so I believe that today's attack either sank or destroyed several enemy vessels.' He added, 'The result of the damage inflicted on the enemy since this morning to the west of Kaena, southwest of Itoman and south of Okinawa: Sunk: two battleships, two unidentified ships, three large types, two small types, five transports and one unidentified vessel. Damaged: one battleship. Set on fire: one destroyer, six transports, two small types, and nine unidentified ones.'[10] Ugaki wrote: 'If most of the special attack planes succeeded in hitting targets, more damage must have been inflicted on the enemy, dealing him a heavy blow. Fifty army *Tokkou* planes also made suicide attacks today.'

10. Ugaki, Admiral Matome – *Fading Victory – The Diary of Admiral Matome Ugaki 1941–1945,* Annapolis, MD: Naval Institute Press, 1991.

On 9 April details recorded by 32nd Army were set down claiming that their special attackers had hit US naval groups at 15.30 and the tally of claims was:

1. Sunk instantly: three cruisers, five destroyers, three minesweepers, one unidentified ship.
2. Sunk: three destroyers, seven unidentified ships.
3. Damaged and set on fire: two battleships, six cruisers, two destroyers, two minesweepers, one unidentified ship.

Total: thirty-five ships. Besides, many burning transports were sighted on the sea west of Cape Zaha. Together with those previously stated, these add up to sixty-nine ships, in addition to many losses of transports. The great success of *Kikusui* No 1 Operation was thus clarified.'

This was pure fantasy. In believing such reports it is no wonder the Japanese commanders pressed ahead with the Kamikaze attacks. In truth *no* ships were sunk on 9 April. The destroyer *Sterett* was attacked by five aircraft and struck by one; damaged but no casualties. Nonetheless the Japanese Naval General Staff was convinced this was the way forward. They told the Combined Fleet that efforts were under way to replenish planes and fit them for 'special attacks' and that the *Ten* No.1 operation would be launched.

Kikusui No.2 Operation was scheduled for the 10th and a briefing was held on the afternoon of the 8th. However, on Tuesday 10th, Ugaki had to postpone this due to bad weather. In due course ten such *Kikusui* mass suicide missions were mounted during the course of the Okinawa campaign, as listed in the table on the previous page.

Enterprise survives a double strike – but only just

For every direct hit from a suicide aircraft many Allied warships were damaged or severely shaken up by very near misses. The difference between the two was often a matter of feet, sometimes by misjudgement by a suicide pilot or sometimes the intensity of the defending AA fire deflecting aircraft by sheer impact of shell. A good example of this is shown by the experience of the famous carrier *Enterprise* (CV-6, Captain Grover Budd Hartley Hall, USN), veteran of many earlier Pacific battles, including her pivotal role at Midway in 1942.

Early in the afternoon of 11 April, *Enterprise* was part of Task Group 58.3 operating northeast of Okinawa. At 13.45 two big groups of bogeys were seen closing at high speed from the north and at 14.08 *Enterprise* opened fire at two aircraft that had selected her as their target. One aircraft was destroyed off the carrier's starboard quarter at a range of 1,500 yards but it had attracted the bulk of the defensive fire and the second, subsequently identified as a *Zeke*-52, was able to penetrate through to make its attack dive. This aircraft struck *Enterprise* on her port side right aft at the two rear quadruple 40mm gun platforms, Nos.8 and 10. The outboard gun shields and the semi-circular platforms were either sheared away or bent by the impact of the aircraft itself. Incredibly the guns themselves were undamaged, although parts of aircraft were found in the gun tubs. The 500lb bomb the Kamikaze carried detonated below the water at the turn of the bilge near the after machinery spaces; the resultant blast caused heavy shock damage. Numbers 3 and 4 main generators, Nos.3 and 4 main engines and Nos.3 and 4 shaft spring bearings were forced inward and upward, and the former broke loose from their foundations. The explosion 'lifted the ship bodily and whipped it violently, and this whipping snapped the SK radar antenna struts and broke off six feet of the starboard yardarm.

About one hour later, at 15.00, a *Judy* made a dive and although the aircraft itself went into the water about 45–50 feet off the carrier's starboard bow and the bomb exploded in the water, further underwater damage resulted. The main drain line of the external gasoline system was opened up from frame 141 to frame 152. A fighter sitting on the starboard catapult was set on fire which spread to the flight deck – the captain ordered the catapult fired which ejected the burning Hellcat into the sea: that was the quickest way to solve that problem. A piece of the *Judy*'s wing came inboard and was recovered from the flight deck which enabled it to be correctly identified. Casualties were remarkably light; one man was blown overboard but later rescued unharmed while five others received wounds and injuries. These blows did not affect her operational status by much. Five more suicide planes were subsequently shot down by the fleet's AA defences close to the *Enterprise*, but she was not taken under further assault after that. She left a trail of oil for about an hour but continued to operate with her task group for three more days before she was sent back to Ulithi for a sixteen-day refit and repair. She resumed her station off Okinawa again on 6 May.[11]

Other ships struck and damaged, though not sunk, by the Kamikaze hordes that day included the new battleship *Missouri* (BB-63, Captain William McCombe Callaghan), four destroyers: *Hale* (DD-642, Commander Donald Worrall Wilson), *Bullard* (DD-660, Commander Eigel Thorton Steen), *Kidd* (DD-661, Commander Robert Mannion Kenney) and *Hank* (DD-702, Commander George Mitchell Chambers) along with the destroyer escort *Samuel S. Miles* (DE-183, Lieutenant-Commander Henry G Brosseau) and *LCS (L)-36*. The 12 April was another vicious day with the old battleships *New Mexico* (BB-40, Captain John Meade Hains), *Idaho* (BB-42, Captain H J Grassie) and *Tennessee* (BB-43, Captain John Baptist Heffernan) damaged. *LSC(L) (3)-33* also fell victim to a Kamikaze hit on 12 April at Picket Station No.1, when a *Val* crashed into her starboard side; she subsequently blew up under fire from the destroyer *Purdy* after the LSL's crew had abandoned ship.

The *Purdy* in heavy action

Part of the toll exacted on that morning of 12 April was the *Allen M. Sumner* Class destroyer *Purdy* (DD-734, Commander Frank L. Johnson, USN). The destroyer had already seen the effects of a Kamikaze strike at close range, having rendered fire-fighting assistance to the destroyer *Mullany* (DD-528, Commander Albert Otto Momm) when, as related, she was hard hit on the 6th. The attacker was Takeichi Minoshima, a former

---

11. USS *Enterprise* CV6 *War History Narrative*. Damage Report No. 59: 14 May 1945, Bureau of Ships, Navy Department, Washington DC.

farmer's son, flying a Nakajima Ki-43, who was killed as he made his final dive. On that occasion *Purdy* had conveyed many of *Mullany*'s badly-wounded crewmen back to Kerama Retto anchorage, and witnessed the horrifying results of burns and fire.

On her return to the front line *Purdy* was allocated to Radar Picket Station No.1 along with the *Fletcher* Class destroyer *Cassin Young* (DD-793, Commander John Williams Ailes-III, who had succeeded Commander Earl Tobias Schreiber in October), some sixty miles north of Okinawa, in the area dubbed 'Coffin Corner' by the picket crews. In the early afternoon the weather conditions were excellent, with maximum visibility, an unlimited ceiling, a light swell and a ten-knot wind. One division of the CAP was overhead and *Purdy* herself was at Condition II (watch-and-watch) to enable half the crew to go to lunch turn-and-turn about. This meant, in effect, that in each of her three twin 5in turrets one gun was manned at all times, as were two 40mm quad mountings, the Mk.63 fire control system, two 40mm twin mountings and the Mk.51 director. Two boilers were operational giving sufficient power for 27 knots while the other two boilers were on stand-by at full readiness should extra power be required urgently, and there was partial ventilation and flushing of the circulation systems with some of the living compartments accessible; in effect one degree down from Condition 'Able'.[12] Both destroyers simultaneously located a bogey at 13.10 bearing 34 degrees (True) at a range of 74 miles and closing. The enemy was dropping bundles of 'chaff' as an electronic countermeasure which dispersed into a slowly dropping cloud that could confuse Allied radar screens. Cut to specific lengths, these aluminium strips had the effect of causing multiple echoes which effectively 'blinded' radar defences to temporarily provide a 'window' (as the strips were also known) of opportunity in which enemy aircraft might approach their targets to within visual range without interception.

Purdy went to General Quarters at 13.13, but this first raid ignored the pickets and continued on a course of 170 degrees (True) from the ships at a range of 65 miles. The rest of the CAP was hastily recalled from the northward and was immediately vectored out to intercept these hostiles which had already passed ahead of the defending fighters and no contact was made. Almost immediately a second large group (Raid 2) was picked up on a bearing of 230 degrees (True), range eighty miles, and the CAP was instructed to make contact with these.

The number of enemy aircraft rapidly built up and became overwhelming as two more big groups (Raids 3 and 4) were located approaching from the north. This time the pickets were not ignored. At fifty miles distant, Raid 3, which comprised an estimated ten *Zekes* – though it soon transpired that in fact there were many more than ten – split into smaller sub-groups (becoming Raids 5, 6, 7 & 8) on a bearing of 000 while Raid 4 continued on its original bearing of 345 degrees (True) at forty-five miles distant on a course of 230 degrees. These latter were assumed to be the aircraft that attacked the destroyer *Mannert L. Abele* (DD-733, Commander Alton Enoch Parker) shortly afterward and sank her. Raid 5 continued south passing *Purdy* to the east and Raid 6, located at 015 degrees

12. *Battle Experience – Radar Pickets and Methods of Combating Suicide Attacks off Okinawa – March–May 1945*. Secret Information Bulletin No. 24. United States Fleet- Headquarters of the Commander in Chief, Washington DC.

(True), forty-two miles out on a course of 140 degrees, faded from the screen and was never re-located, but was thought to have attacked the ships of Radar Picket Station 2.

Raids 7 & 8 were a different matter however. Both were located simultaneously at thirty-five (56.km) and forty-five miles (72.4km) range respectively on a bearing of 005 degrees (True). The *Purdy* had her Mk.12 fire control radar (Mk.27 director) coached onto Raid 7 by the air support controller (ASC) and picked up the target in full radar control on bearing 034 degrees (True) at a distance of just twenty miles; groups of Kamikazes were making radical course alterations from the point of initial contact until the Mk.28 pick-up, and the gun action commenced at 13.37. At this time *Cassin Young* was leading the *Purdy*, with a spacing of 600 yards between the two, and they commenced firing at a single Kamikaze that came in from the starboard bow, engaging at a range of 10,000 yards with full automatic, partial radar-controlled gunnery. Due to the interference of smoke and blast from the guns *Purdy* twice checked fire to clear visual sighting. *Cassin Young* started firing at the same target with the range down to 6,000 yards. This aircraft carried out a high dive-bombing attack on the *Cassin Young* from the starboard bow and released its bomb from very close range, which exploded in the sea to starboard. The aircraft survived and pulling up from its dive, across the bows of *Cassin Young*, circled to port and then made a low-level suicide run into her port quarter, crashing into her. *Purdy* had checked fire against this aircraft when the bomb had been released to avoid hitting her companion ship, but recommenced engaging this *Zeke* with No.41 twin and No.43 quadruple 40mm mountings at 5,000 yards range, the former under control of the main battery director and the latter with radar pick-up at 8,000 yards distant. A 20mm battery commenced firing at 2,000 yards . From then on all manner of aircraft were identified as they swarmed in, *Zekes*, *Kates*, *Oscars* and *Vals*, with D3A2 *Vals* predominating. By now there were enemy aircraft everywhere, and while eight groups specifically attacked *Purdy*, several others passed very close to her on their way to attack other ships nearby.

Raid 8 came in at 13.42 on a bearing of 270 degrees (True), being sighted off the starboard quarter visually. At the same time friendlies were contacted on the SC radar some ten miles south-east of the ships. The *Purdy* opened fire at 8,000 yards range with a few rounds of 5in against five *Vals* of Raid 8. This caused some of the dive-bombers to attack a supporting LCS, scoring a near-miss, while the CAP closed and accounted for two more *Vals* from this group. Meanwhile another *Val* had made a suicide run at *Cassin Young* coming in from the port bow this time. Both destroyers continually hit this aircraft as it hurtled in, knocking it off course or killing the pilot, so that this machine hit the port yardarm and SC radar antenna of the *Cassin Young* before heavily impacting the ship on the main deck and sliding over the side. The *Cassin Young* was penetrated in her forward fireroom and began to belch black smoke from this location.

While this drama was taking place a third attack was made, this time by a *Val* which selected the *Purdy* as her intended victim. This machine was visually sighted off the starboard quarter at a range of 12,000 yards coming in very low over the sea and out of the sun. When the Kamikaze that hit the *Cassin Young* went into the sea, the *Purdy* checked main battery fire and the 5in guns hastily switched target to this new menace. Fully automatic fire was opened at 8,000 yards but No.43 quadruple 40mm, initially being 'gated'[13] at 9,000 yards, could not join in until the range was down to 5,000 yards under control of the Mk.63 fire control system. Heavily hit, this aircraft winged over and went into the water ablaze about 2,500 yards out from the ship. Meanwhile the *Cassin Young* changed course at 14.07, steering south at 25 knots and *Purdy*, acting in accordance to her close support role, conformed with that course in order to give her companion covering fire. However, Captain Charles A. Buchanan, USN, Officer in Tactical Command Radar Pickets, (CDD 126) directed *Purdy* to resume her radar picket station and accordingly, she turned back north, leaving *Cassin Young* retiring in the opposite direction towards Kerama Retto. *Purdy* was now on her own and at this juncture received the report that a further fifty bogies were closing from the north.

The next Kamikaze was not long in coming, a *Val*, which had detached itself from the many groups of enemy aircraft in the vicinity, was seen approaching from starboard at 14.42, while the CAP was busily engaged in shooting down several others. Evading airborne interception this *Val* attacked in a steep glide from the starboard side (050 degrees (True). Fire was commenced against this aircraft at 6,000 yards range until the CAP closed the target, when fire was checked to avoid hitting friendly aircraft. The fighters were clearly seen chopping lumps out of this aircraft, but this failed to deter the approach which continued straight and true against *Purdy*, strafing as it came. Machine-gun bullets were clearly not going to stop such a determined attack and, at 1,500 yards, the 5in, 40mm and 20mm all re-commenced firing in a last-ditch attempt to knock this aircraft down and finally had effect. The *Val* swerved violently to the right and went into the sea close off the port bow. Attacker No.5 was picked up on the radar at 14.50 while yet ten miles out, with visual contact at eight miles range two minutes later. Several shell bursts were loosed off in order to draw the attention of the CAP to this attacker, and it is thought that this aircraft was annihilated by the 5in battery at this time, as no friendly aircraft were close when it went into the water. Other Japanese aircraft were seen being destroyed by the CAP later. Another hostile, No.6, broke from the general aerial brawl above the ship and headed for *Purdy* from off the port bow. Every gun that would bear engaged this aircraft which crossed *Purdy*'s bow from port to starboard, made a steep bank and, narrowly missing number three 5in turret aft, hit the sea close aboard the destroyer's port quarter. At 15.00 the seventh, and what proved to be the last Kamikaze, came in. This was yet another *Val* which crossed the ship from the port to starboard bow, all the time under fire from a trio of friendly fighters and again being constantly hit by them to no avail. The pilot broke away from his tormentors and, smoking badly, made a 20–degree angle attack approach into the *Purdy* from off her starboard bow. Five inch gunfire was opened at a range of 9,000 yards, but was checked to avoid friendly aircraft again. When it became clear that this aircraft would not be halted, fire was resumed at 6,000 yards with every gun that would bear.

Purdy's captain later pointed out that at the time of this final attack, both the forward 5in mount and the after 5in mount had just about fired off every one of their Mark 40 fused projectiles and were beginning to transfer replacements from the No.2 mounting (which

13. 'Gated' – gun arc blocked by ships' own superstructure – The British used the term 'wooded' to describe this same thing.

itself had been firing Mark 18 fused projectiles by doctrine). Commander Johnson was of the opinion that this lack of special fuses made the difference between being struck by the Kamikaze and being able to destroy her attacker during its final approach, the pilot of which was obviously killed or incapacitated as the *Val* struck the sea some twenty feet off the starboard side of *Purdy*, but bounced and slid into the side of the destroyer at frame 63. This aircraft was carrying an armour-piercing bomb which went through the ship's side plating like a knife through butter and detonated internally, blowing ten crew members overboard. Fortunately these men were all later picked up by one of the 'pall-bearers', *LCS(L) 114*.

All steering control was lost immediately after these twin blows as was almost all internal and external communications with the forward fireroom, while No.2 5in mount was rendered totally inoperative with both Nos.1 and 3 mounts reduced to local control only. Emergency stand-by power enabled all the 40mm guns to continue in automatic control, however. The dead-reckoning tracer (DRT) track[14] in the CIC could not be read due to the combination of blast smoke and steam. Further attacks were expected due to the crippled state of the *Purdy*, and to avoid any danger of warhead explosions, all ten torpedoes were jettisoned.

Ultimately *Purdy* survived this ordeal and reached the USA. She was subsequently repaired and later participated in the Korean War during the early 1950s.

The *Stanly* survives two *Ōhka* strikes

We left the damaged *Cassin Young* making her way back to safety while *Purdy* resumed the action. On Radar Picket Station 2, the *Fletcher* Class destroyer *Stanly* (DD-478, Lieutenant-Commander James M. Robinson, USN) received instructions from the Commander of Task Group 51.10, Captain R. H. Whitehead, USN, to go to the assistance of *Cassin Young*. *Stanly* was well equipped for this duty as she had been joined by RCM Underway Team No.4,[15] which had reported aboard the destroyer on 21 March for temporary duty. The RCM Officer of this team described how they readied for action. 'The RCM installation had just been completed by personnel from the USS *Prairie*[16] and advantage was taken of a brief opportunity to check the installed equipment. The training of RCM personnel

---

14. The DRT – was a movable circular apparatus encased in a wooden box with a glass top over which was spread a sheet of parchment tracing paper. The device itself had worm gears which controlled movement, fore and aft and side-to-side, and was coupled to the ship's gyro. As the ship moved, an intensely focussed light was automatically projected upward onto the underside of the paper and provided an instantaneous updated visible dead-reckoning position. Every 60 seconds or so the operator could mark the paper at the point of the dot and a series of dots, when connected up, revealed the ship's movements in action.

15. RCM = Aviation Radio & Radar Counter Measures Technician – See National Defense Research Committee (NDRC) *RCM in the Pacific Theatre of Operations*, Radio Countermeasures, Summary Technical Report, Vol 1, Ch 15, dated 1946. Office of Scientific Research & Development, National Archives, Civil Archives Division, Washington DC, pp 315; also US Navy Manual CSP 1765(CA), dated 30 March 1943, Naval Security Group Library, Ch 8, pp 33, for more details on introduction of these teams.

16. *Prairie* (AD-15, Captain J. B. W Waller, USN) was a *Dixie* Class Destroyer Tender based at Ulithi since October 1944.

began from 25 March onward, but due to the fact that the ship was also preparing to join the Okinawa campaign, there proved barely sufficient time.

On receiving her orders, *Stanly* proceeded accordingly at 13.51 and while still *en route*, opened fire with her 5in battery at a flock of five *Vals* at high altitude heading southwest toward the Okinawa beachhead, dispersing but not halting them.[17] At 14.26 another lone *Val* was seen coming toward the *Stanly* from high off her port quarter. This aircraft immediately went into a steep suicide dive and was engaged by all guns and also by those of the *Benham* Class destroyer *Lang* (DD-399, Commander John Thomas Bland-III) which was at this time close by.[18] Although not hit, this Kamikaze was near-missed by 5in shell bursts and then hit from lighter weapons, which seemed to put it off course. The *Val* crossed over the *Stanly* amidships from port to starboard and pulled out of its dive, only to hit the sea off the destroyer's starboard quarter when engaged by the main battery. *Stanly*'s only damage was that the shock of her main armament firing broke a main gyro condenser, putting it out of action. Further enemy aircraft kept passing over in streams and *Stanly* went to a full thirty knots and took control of *Cassin Young*'s CAP and directed them onto yet another newly-sighted mass of enemy aircraft. Consequently, six *Vals* were shot down in quick succession by the fighters. Then, at 14.49, an *Ōhka* was launched at her. This attacker, was described thus 'approximately twenty feet long, had a fifteen foot wing span and no engine or propeller was observed.' This manned missile broke out of the aerial ruck and headed toward *Stanly* from off that ship's starboard beam, outpacing the defending fighters. The 5in battery took this device under fire and, as it approached, the 40mm guns joined in. Hit time and time again, the *Ōhka* kept on coming and struck the *Stanly* in her starboard bow, at frame 23, impacting some five feet above the ship's waterline. Such was the momentum of this strike that the attacker went right through the ship and exited through the port side and only detonated upon re-emerging. The remnants of the pilot were later found in compartment A-302-L along with some wreckage.

Within a few minutes a second *Ōhka* was launched against *Stanly*, which was making high-speed random turns. Two enemy aircraft had just been shot down by the CAP overhead when the missile suddenly came into view at 14.58 and approached rapidly at a speed in excess of 500 knots. The missile came in low on *Stanly*'s starboard beam and the main battery did not have time to engage, the light automatic weapons got in some bursts and hits were scored which knocked away small sections of its stubby wings. This machine passed across the destroyer just abaft No.2 funnel and tore away the ship's battle ensign as it passed through. Fire was resumed to port and the *Ōhka* was seen to attempt to bank but instead it struck the water some 2,000 to 3,000 yards from the port bow, where it 'bounced once, hit the water again and disintegrated.' The Captain of the *Stanly* reported that their approach was almost silent, 'only a 'swishing' was heard.'

---

17. *Battle Experience – Radar Pickets and Methods of Combating Suicide Attacks off Okinawa – March –May 1945.* Secret Information Bulletin No. 24. United States Fleet- Headquarters of the Commander in Chief, Washington DC.
18. In 1945 *Lang* and two of her sisters, *Sterett* (DD-407) and *Wilson* (DD-408), had received emergency AA modifications, whereby her torpedo-tubes had been removed and replaced by extra 40mm mountings.

Emerging from this attack with just three wounded crewmen as casualties, *Stanly* was verbally ordered by ComDesDive 4 to proceed to join the transport area off Okinawa Jima and, while complying, another fierce dogfight was observed at 15.30, a rather one-sided clash between fourteen F4Us of the CAP and a further group of mixed Japanese aircraft, during which five enemy machines, identified as *Vals* were destroyed. One single-engined aircraft broke away from the aerial fighting at 15.48 and made a suicide run at *Stanly*. For the third time the destroyer was forced to open fire and one Corsair, which was following, broke away to allow the ship's guns to have their chance and the aircraft, a *Zeke*, was struck by 40mm fire all the way in. Even so, the Kamikaze released a single bomb which detonated just fifteen yards from *Stanly*'s port bow, abreast frame 26, while the *Zeke* hit the sea at about the same distance from the starboard bow.

After this third attack *Stanly* proceeded to Kerma Retto (known colloquially as 'Busted Ship Bay') to effect repairs, where she remained for ten days. Captain Robinson recalled that, 'Just prior to the period covered by this report, additional radio equipment was installed in CIC and radio central in order to handle all phases of destroyer fighter direction. All equipment functioned well and remained in operating condition even after the ship had been hit by a suicide plane and shaken badly by a plane that crashed just off the port bow. SGA and SC-4 were in full operation during and after the attack. The Mark 12 antenna was hit by shrapnel when the suicide plane crashed into the ship, but the remainder of the installation was completely operational.' He did note, however, as others had done, that, 'The noise level in CIC became excessive when ship's tactical and fighter direction circuits were in use.' Washington's response to this was to note, 'Every effort should be made to monitor such circuits with headphones.' On the same day the former four-piper destroyer converted to high-speed transport, *Gilmer* (APD-11, Commander John S Horner) took a Kamikaze into her galley deckhouse, killing one crewman and injuring three others. She stayed on station.

Another common problem was the difficulty in sorting out friendly aircraft from hostiles when a whole circus of different types were milling around over the ships and dog fighting was taking place. The Japanese took advantage of such chaotic conditions by suddenly breaking off from the aerial combat and making fast Kamikaze dives against the ships. The target ships were often reluctant to engage such aircraft immediately lest they prove friendly. *Purdy*'s captain put much of the blame on bad IFF (Identification-Friend or Foe) procedures, a complaint as old as the war itself. He wrote: 'In general, the greatest offenders of IFF doctrine were the PBM's. (One common phrase over the Inter-Fighter Director (IFD) circuit is 'Tallyho one friendly PBM' – referring to the Martin PBM Mariner flying boat.) *Purdy* was closed once only by a friendly showing no IFF.' Washington commented that, 'Repeated failure to use IFF after so many warnings seems to warrant drastic corrective measures.' *Purdy*'s captain continued, 'Much reliance is placed on IFF with the great multitude of aircraft present at all times. With experienced operators, friendlies mixing with enemies are easily discernible. At no time did combat fail to impress upon bridge, lookouts, or gun control the location of enemy planes, as all friendlies were showing IFF. If the enemy is making any attempts at reproducing IFF signals, none has so far been apparent to this vessel.'

The *Purdy* later resumed radar picket duty and was then despatched to Ulithi on 5 May for more permanent repairs. An accident there required her to leave for Guam to replace a damaged gun turret and this placed her out of service for the rest of the war.

RCM Intercepts

The RCM officer aboard the *Stanly* recorded that he was given very little chance to provide the full training he considered necessary before the ship was hustled out to the combat area. He recalled that there were insufficient skilled operators to both train others and maintain regular on-board duties, although he did manage to both lecture and briefly discuss with the ship's officers on the basics of 'RCM doctrine, CIC duties and required reports.'

There proved just enough time to organise the enlisted personnel into intercept watchers, using TN-2 tuners across 75–300 megacycles[19] and to prepare to carry out jamming should they be ordered to do so, but, in the event, this requirement never arose. The team kept continuous intercept watches until 12 April, but although some suspected Japanese radar signals were intercepted and reported, following the laid down routine,[20] none were intercepted during the actual attack on the *Stanly* on 12 April itself.

To illustrate the wide range of enemy broadcast wave-length interceptions identified by *Stanly* during this period, the following table is of relevance.

Date	Location of *Stanly*	Zebra [Zone] Time	Signals
31 March	25 00' N, 127 48' E	1130	162/500/15–18
31 March	25 00'N, 127 48' E	1200	404/2000 or greater
31 March	25 56'N, 127 44' E	1835	97/300–400/30–40
31 March	25 56'N, 127 44' E	1910	160/1600/2–3
02 April	27 35' N, 126 59' E	1725	212/1500–2000 Unobserved
04 April	27 25' N, 126 59' E	1400	190/700–1000/4–8
05 April	56 40' N, 127 40' E	1845	74/450/30–35
05 April	26 40' N, 127 40' E	1915	97/400/35
06 April	26 55' N, 127 06' E	0005	202/60 or 70 in excess 100
06 April	25 45' N, 127 18' E	0930	202/-/20
08 April	26 00' N, 127 -0' E	1115	221/600/12–15

The SC and Mark 12 radars both picked up the use of 'window' by the Japanese aircraft on several occasions prior to the actual attack date. On each of these occasions the aircraft approaching *Stanly* dropped 'window' and withdrew at once, so it was inferred that ECM 'window' was used in these instances to cover the retreat of the observation aircraft itself. However, the Japanese use of 'window' was dismissed as 'not very effective' because it lacked sufficient density to block the screen and could be read through in every case.'

---

19. Later replaced by TN-2b tuner. For the full details on the shipboard radar countermeasures system, set-up, equipment and operation as developed by the end of the war, see – Radar Bulletin No.11 (RADARELEVEN) – *The Shipboard Radar Countermeasures Operator's Manual*, (Opnav 34–P-802), United States Fleet, Headquarters of the Commander –in-Chief, Navy Department, Office of the Chief of Naval Operations, Washington, dated 18 February 1946.
20. Outlined in Pacific Fleet Confidential Letter 7CL-45.

Another destroyer with RCM fitted was the *Fletcher*-Class destroyer *Colhoun* (DD-801, Commander G. R. Wilson, USN); it is reported that this equipment performed two registered actions. In one instance it detected a friendly airborne radar signal when the aircraft itself was not showing any IFF. This stopped *Colhoun* from shooting this aircraft down and avoided a 'friendly fire' casualty. On a second occasion it established the fact that Japanese shore-based radar was located on Yuron Shima.

Concerted Kamikaze attacks off Okinawa on 12 April 1945

The determined efforts of the Japanese to inflict maximum damage on the invasion fleet and offshore shipping continued throughout the 12 April. Among the many ships damaged this day were the destroyer *Zellars* (DD-777, Commander Leon Samuel Kintberger) which was screening the battleship *Tennessee* (BB43). Three *Jills* singled her out and although she managed to destroy two of them a third struck the ship, badly damaging her. Only one man aboard was killed and repairs were carried out that enabled her to return to the West Coast.

The *Cassin Young* (DD-793) was hit for the first time on the 12th, five suicide aircraft attacking her, of which she destroyed four, but was badly hit by the fifth despite which, and the loss of a crew member, her damage was repaired locally and she was soon back on duty once more. She was not to escape the further attentions of the Kamikazes for much longer though! Also on 12th April, the destroyer escort *Riddle* (DE-185, Lieutenant-Commander Roland H Cramer) was attacked by two Kamikazes and hit once, but she too was also able to continue her work within a short period. Another victim this day was the destroyer escort *Walter C. Wann* (DE-412, Lieutenant-Commander John W Stedman, Jr.) attacked by two *Vals*, damaged but able to continue after local repairs. Likewise the 12th saw the destroyer escort *Whitehurst* (DE-634, Lieutenant-Commander Jack Carter Horton) hit after an attack by four *Vals*. Her damage proved more serious and casualties were high; she had to return to the West Coast for major repairs. Nor was this the end of this grim day's toll.

The ordeal of the *Lindsey*

The destroyer-minelayer *Lindsey* (DM-32, Commander Thomas Edward Chambers, USN) was operating with Task Group 51.5 off the Hagushi beachhead Okinawa on 12 April, and was *en route* to Zampa Misaki to lend assistance to the destroyer-minesweeper *Jeffers* (DMS-27, Commander Hugh Quinn Murray, USN)[21] when she was hit by two Kamikazes in the space of a minute. The first hit was made at 14.50 by a *Val*, one of a group of four, which approached from astern and crashed along the starboard side of the ship as far forward as frame 69. The small bomb it carried detonated and fragments penetrated some depth-charges. The second hit took place within one minute and was by another *Val* which made a steep dive forward hitting the port frame 30 at first platform level. This strike blew up the forward magazine with 'a heavy dull explosion' followed by

---

21. She was the former *Bristol* Class destroyer DD-621, converted after Normandy in 1944 – she was later re-converted to destroyer configuration post-war.

'heavy brown smoke. Observers also identified a sharp report believed to have been due to the detonation of the second plane's bomb.'[22] 'Evidence indicates that the magazine explosion consisted of a mass deflagration of 5in powder cartridges in A-404–M on the third platform level, frames 18 to 26. This magazine was separated from the group two magazine by the refrigerated spaces.' This explosion blew the entire bow of the ship off, including the fore 5in gun mount and *Lindsey*'s keel was sheared at frame 30, the main deck hinged upward at about frame 60. Flooding extended to bulkhead 72. The captain rang off the engines in order to slow the ship down thus preventing an inrush of water throughout the ship. Even so, the ship's trim at the bow increased by about 18 inches. Fortunately the main propulsion plant and gyro remained unaffected and fully functional. Casualties were eight men killed outright, forty-six missing and sixty wounded. The remaining guns of the after battery were undamaged and were taken under local control after just a few minutes. The *Lindsey* was finally towed to the anchorage at Kerma Retto stern first by the fleet tug *Tawakon*i (ATF-114, Lieutenant-Commander Clarence L Foushee). Bulkhead 60 was made water-tight and then the cripple was towed stern-first to Guam where a false bow was fitted in the Auxiliary Repair Dock *ARD-26* (Lieutenant-Commander Irving B. Smith, USN). With this in place the *Lindsey* steamed all the way back to Norfolk, Virginia, Navy Yard under her own power. Here she was fully repaired and survived in the Atlantic Reserve Fleet until 1970.

Other ship casualties on 12 April included the *Jeffers* (DMS-27, Commander Leo William Nilon) while the next day the destroyer escort *Connolly* (DE-309, Lieutenant William A Collier) was damaged. On the 14th the old battleship *New York* (BB-34, Captain K C Christian) was struck and damaged as were the destroyers *Sigsbee* (DD-502, Lieutenant-Commander Gordon Patea Chung-Hoon), *Dashiell* (DD-659, Commander Douglas Lee Lispcomb Cordiner) and *Hunt* (DD-674, Commander Frederick Earle McEntire, Jr.). Next day another destroyer *Wilson* (DD-408, Commander Willis L Roberts) and two landing vessels, *LCS-51* and *LCS-116*, were added to the long list of damaged ships while on the 16 April the destroyer *Pringle* (DD-477, Lieutenant-Commander John Lawrence Kelley, Jr.) was sunk west of Okinawa, with 71 dead, including her CO.

Intrepid struck once more

The *Intrepid* (CV-11) had shrugged off several suicide attacks over the previous months, but on 16 April it felt like that this time they had her number. This aircraft hit her flight deck and part of its fuselage, and the aircraft's engine went right through and into her hangar deck. If you visit her moored in New York you can stand, as I have, and take photographs on the exact spot that this Kamikaze ended up, and it is sobering indeed. Eight of her crew died and a further twenty-one were injured in this attack which spread flaming petrol through the ship. Yet so efficient were her teams that in under an hour the fires had been contained, and within three hours from the hit the *Intrepid* was once more landing her aircraft. Ultimately she returned once more to San Francisco for repairs,

---

22. War Damage Report No. 51, Destroyer Report: *Gunfire, Bomb and Kamikaze Damage, including Losses in Action 17 October, 1941 to 15 August 1945*, dated 25 January 1947, Preliminary Design Section, Bureau of Ships, Navy Department, Washington DC.

arriving on 19 May. She was ready for service again on 29 June and sailed for the Pacific once more, undaunted, but too late to see any more service other than a 'live fire' exercise at Wake Island on 6 August.

Even the biggest and toughest ships were not totally ignored. A *Zeke* made an attack along the port hand side of the 'Mighty Mo' that day. Absurd to think that it could have done any harm to this armoured monster, the battleship *Missouri* (BB-63, Captain William McCombe Callaghan), and indeed her paint was hardly scratched, but it was an audacious attempt. The more vulnerable destroyer types *Bryant* (DD-665, Commander George Cameron Seay), *Harding* (DMS-28, Commander Donald Brewster Ramage) and *Hobson* (DMS-26, Commander Joseph Ignatus Manning) were damaged as were *Taluga* (AO-101, Commander Hans M Mikkelsen), *Bowers* (APD-40, Lieutenant-Commander Frederic W Hawes), *LCI-407* and *LCS-116*, while on 17 April they were joined in Cripples Creek by the destroyer *Benham* (DD-796, Lieutenant-Commander Frederic Seward Keeler).

On 16th April, the destroyer *Laffey* (DD-724, Commander Fredrick Julian Beckton, USN) earned itself the journalistic sobriquet 'The Ship That Would Not Die' after surviving hits by no less than the enormous total of seven Kamikazes and four bombs, resulting in the loss of thirty-two crewmen killed and seventy-one wounded. She was credited with shooting down eleven aircraft from the attacking force. When asked to abandon the vessel Beckton answered, 'We still have guns that can shoot.' She was saved and remains preserved today as a museum ship and National Historical Landmark site at Patriots Point, Charleston, South Carolina.[23] Still it continued, day after day, as waves of Kamikazes tore in. On 22 April both the minesweeper *Swallow* (AM-65, Lieutenant-Commander Whitefield F Kimball) and *LCS (L) (3)-15* were sunk while damaged ships included the destroyers *Hudson* (DD-475, Commander Richard D Rockwell Pratt), *Wadsworth* (DD-516, Commander Raymond Dennis Fusselman), *Isherwood* (DD-520, Commander Louis Edward Schmidt, Jr.) and the minelayer *Shea* (DM-30, Lieutenant-Commander Charles Cochran Kirkpatrick). On 25 April, the destroyer escort *England* (DE-635, Commander John Alexander Williamson), famous for sinking a whole flotilla of Japanese submarines single-handed in a few days, was damaged by a Kamikaze strike. The 27 April saw the *Canada Victory* (APA-441, Master William MacDonald) sunk, and destroyers *Rathburne* (APD-25, Commander Richard L Welch) and *Ralph Talbot* (DD-390, Commander Winston Seaborn Brown) damaged. They were joined the following day by the destroyer *Wadsworth* (DD-516), which had already been slightly damaged on the 22nd when she took a hit from a bomber that missed with its torpedo, but then went on to crash into the ship. Other ships that suffered were *Daly* (DD-519, Commander Richard Rumel Bradlley, Jr,), *Bennion* (DD-662, Commander Robert Henderson Holmes) and *Brown* (DD-546, Commander Robert Rutherford Craighill) as well as the fast minesweeper *Butler* (DMS-29, Lieutenant Robert Messinger Hinckley, Jr.) – all being damaged to varying degrees.

---

23. Beckton, Rear Admiral F. Julian & Morschauser II, Joseph, *The Ship That Would Not Die*, New Jersey:1980, Prentice Hall.

Hospital ships targeted

A new low was reached with an attack on the night of the 28th against a fully illuminated hospital ship which saw heavy loss of life. The *Comfort* (AH-6, Captain Adin X. Tooker)[24] was attacked south-west of Okinawa by a single-engined Kamikaze at 20.41. The ship was crammed with 700 wounded and a full complement of doctors and nurses, and was *en route* for Guam. There was a full moon and her international markings were fully visible but the attacker made a deliberate approach, crossing over the *Comfort*, pulling round and making a deliberate dive straight into her. A warning signal was sent by *Comfort*'s skipper, 'Kamikaze Red – Smoke Boat Make Smoke' but it was too late. The plane ploughed on down through three of the superstructure decks and into a surgery where an operation was underway. Thirty died, including six nurses and most of the surgical team under Major Alexander Silvergrade, while a further forty-eight were wounded.

Some claim that this attack was a deliberate retaliation for the sinking of the unarmed Japanese Red Cross relief vessel the 11,249–GRT *Awa Maru*, Captain Hamada Matsutaro, by four torpedoes from the American submarine *Queenfish* (SS-393, Lieutenant Commander Charles Eliott Loughlin, USN) on 1st April 1945, in which more than 2,003 Japanese civilians were killed and only one man, Kantora Shimoda, survived. The *Awa Maru* was fully illuminated and her route was frequently transmitted, and US submarines were notified not to attack. This led to the court martial of Loughlin later, at Admiral Nimitz's request, but he claimed he thought his target was a destroyer and received only slight punishment and went on to make Admiral.[25]

Such serious incidents were compounded by similar damage inflicted upon the hospital ship *Pinkney* (AH-10, Captain A L Hutson). She was laying off Hagushi embarking wounded when, at 17.30 on 28 April, she was struck by a low-flying Kamikaze aft. The explosion tore a 30ft hole in her, and killed sixteen patients in their cots and eighteen crew members. Fires broke out and raged for three hours, burning out all the wards and caused a heavy list to port. She was eventually salvaged and returned to the States for repair. A further casualty of the Kamikaze was *LCI-580*.

On 29 April, the destroyers *Hazelwood* (DD-531, Commander Volckert Petrus Douw) and *Haggard* (DD-555, Commander Verner Jensen Soballe), and the fast minelayers *Shannon* (DM-25, Commander Edward Lee Foster) and *Harry F. Bauer* (DM-26, Commander Russell Champion Williams, Jr.) were put out of action, while on the 30th *Bennion* was struck again and the minelayer *Terror* (CM-5, Commander Horace W Blakeslee) suffered damage on 1 May. It almost seemed, at least to the uninformed at this time, that the Americans were losing destroyers faster than they could build them.

---

24. *Comfort* was the former passenger ship *Havana* See Jackson, Kathi, *They Called Them Angels: American Military Nurses of World War II,* Westport, Conn: 2000. Praeger/Greenwood Press and also Harper, Dale P, *Too Close for Comfort*, Victoria, B.C;2001, Telford Publishing.
25. The full story is given in the National Security Agency document (b) (3) – P.L.86–36, *The Sinking and the Salvage of the* Awa Maru – *A Strange and Tragic Tale,* (Washington DC, May 1986), That the attack on *Comfort* was a revenge mission can only remain as speculation at this distance in time, but the body of the Kamikaze pilot was found aboard with papers detailing Allied hospital ships and locations – suggesting deliberate targeting.

Chapter Nine

Okinawa: the Second Phase

'... I received the thankful command to depart tomorrow. I am deeply emotional, and just hope to sink one. Already hundreds of visitors had visited us. Cheerfully singing the last season of farewell.'

Corporal Kazuo Araki, 72nd *Shinbu* Squadron

The new month began as the old month had ended. On 3 May the destroyer *Little* (DD-803, Commander Madison Hall, Jr.) was sunk by the Kamikazes as was the rocket landing ship *LSM(R)-195*, while the destroyer *Bache* (DD-470, Commander Alan Roberts McFarland) was among those hard-pressed ships that was damaged. On the plus side one of the most famous duels between destroyer and Kamikazes also occurred that day.

The incredible survival of the *Aaron Ward*

On 3 May the destroyer-minelayer *Aaron Ward* (DM-34, Commander William H. Sanders, Jr., USN), an *Allen M. Sumner* Class destroyer conversion,[1] was hit no less than six times. Acting in a radar picket capacity, she was in partnership with the destroyer *Little* (DD-803), on Station No.10, when set upon by a whole series of Kamikazes.

The ships' gunners managed to knock down two attackers, both of which were *Vals*, albeit the first impact was from one of this pair which achieved a near-miss off the starboard quarter, its engine and propeller being driven inboard from the explosion to hit the aft 5in gun mounting.[2] The second hit was by a *Zeke* which dove into the same gun mount while the 500lb general-purpose bomb it released just prior to impact blew out the side of the after engine room. This hit jammed the ship's rudder, and she began to slow down and turn to port. Even so she managed to destroy two more enemy aircraft, a *Betty* and a *Val*.

The third impact was also by a *Val* which came in over the ship's bow and bridge, narrowly avoiding both, then clipped the fore funnel as it passed and damaged the ship's

---

1. This destroyer should not be confused with two previous USN destroyers of the same name – the old four-piper (DD-132), built in 1919 and transferred to the Royal Navy in the 'destroyers for bases' deal, and scrapped in 1948; and DD-483, a *Livermore* Class destroyer built in 1941 and sunk in an air attack off Guadalcanal in April 1943.
2. Destroyer Report No. 50– *Gunfire, Bomb and Kamikaze Damage, including Losses.* Action Report of *Aaron Ward*, letter DD4583/A16–3, Serial 0025, dated 16 April 1945 (Action Report with endorsements).

rigging before finally impacting in the water close alongside the starboard quarter in close proximity to the first impact. It was now 19.00.

Strike number four was a hit by yet another *Val* which, diving almost vertically toward the bridge, missed slightly abaft of it and struck the main deck at frame 81, its 500lb GP bomb – dropped just prior to impact – being a near miss which blew in the side of the forward fireroom. The destroyer was now dead in the water and a sitting duck. True to form and smelling blood, further aircraft homed in on the cripple.

She was then struck again, almost in the same place, by another *Val* which came in over the bridge and crashed into the starboard deckhouse at frame 90. Another aircraft came in at 19.21 following a shallow trajectory from dead astern and impacted the after funnel, while its 500lb GP bomb detonated in the after uptakes. The funnel, searchlight, gun mountings 26 and 28 were all blown aloft by this explosion and the debris rained down aft on the few survivors in that area.

Aaron Ward shipped about 1,650 tons of water, and free surface water flooded through five major compartments. Her GM[3] was reduced to approximately 1 foot. The blasts caused huge gasoline and ammunition fires throughout the amidships but these were eventually brought under control with the aid of *LCS (L)-83* which came alongside and *LCS (L)-14*. Fortunately the fire main pressure and forward power stayed on line via the forward emergency diesel generator. With many of her crew dead or dying, *Aaron Ward* had become a stationery target and almost levelled to the waterline, but eventually the *Shannon* (Commander Edward Lee Foster, USN) managed to get a towing cable aboard her and brought her slowly back to safety.

*Aaron War*d struggled into Kerama Retto on 4 May with nil freeboard aft, an eighteen foot draft forward and a 5–degree list to starboard. She was given emergency repairs and was even able to sail under her own power to Pearl Harbor and then via the Panama Canal to New York Navy Yard, where she arrived in August 1945. She made this passage halfway around the world using her starboard shaft only. Despite her horrendous upper deck appearance she survived, although following her decommissioning she was not considered worthwhile repairing and was scrapped in July 1946.

The case of the *Aaron Ward* emphatically demonstrated the tremendous resilience of these long-hulled destroyers, although her casualties included forty-five officers and men killed, and forty-nine wounded.

Meanwhile her erstwhile companion, *Little* (Commander Madison Hall, Jr., USN), had worse fortune. She was hit by four Kamikazes, two simultaneously, and had her back broken. She was abandoned and went down at 18.55 with heavy loss of life; thirty men killed and seventy-nine injured.

Also damaged in a suicide attack was *LCS (L)-25*, while on 4 May Kamikazes sank the destroyer *Luce* (DD-522, Commander Jacob Wilson Waterhouse, she sinking with 150 of her crew including her CO) as well as *LSM(R)-194* and *LSM-190*.

On 4th May the destroyer *Morrison* (DD-560, Commander James Richard Hansen, USN) moved to Radar Picket Station No.1, some fifty miles north of Okinawa and in the

---

3. GM = Metacentric Height – The measurement of the initial static stability of a floating body, calculated as the distance between the ship's centre of gravity (CG) and the metacentre of the vessel.

flight path of many Kamikaze planes from air bases in southern Kyushu. The destroyer *Ingraham* (DD-694, Commander John Francis Harper, Jr. USN), and four smaller landing craft, were at this same picket station when about twenty-five enemy planes were sighted on radar at 07.15. Although CAP fighters downed many, several Japanese planes penetrated to the picket station. One hit *Morrison* at 08.32, and another at 08.33. Two floatplanes then hit the destroyer in quick succession at 08.35 and the ship started to sink. It had gone under by 08.40. The four Kamikazes hit so rapidly, and the ship sank so quickly, that most of the men below deck were lost. Her casualty list was heavy; 155 dead and 87 wounded – among the 127 survivors rescued by *LCS-21* was her skipper. *Ingraham* was also damaged and was eventually sent back to Hunters Point for repairs.

Escort Carrier *Natoma Bay* hit

The escort carrier *Natoma Bay* (CVE-62, Captain Bromfield Bradford Nichol, USN) was damaged on 7 May. At 06.35 two *Zeke*s were reported approaching the ship at high speed from abaft the beam, strafing with incendiary ammunition as they came and both were taken under fire from the carrier and her escorts. The leading Kamikaze aimed at the bridge then rolled over and into the flight deck, which was penetrated, its bomb exploding inside and blowing open a hole 12 x 20 feet in the fo'c'sle. One aircraft was set ablaze and the ship's anchor windlass wrecked. Almost immediately the second *Zeke* arrived but was hit by AA fire and crashed into the water close alongside. Total casualties were just one officer killed and one airman from VC-9, and three sailors wounded. The fires were almost instantly put out by a very efficient damage control team. Just a single scheduled air strike was cancelled as a result of this attack and by 1030 'normal service was resumed.' She was detached for Guam on 20 June and reached San Diego by 19 August. *Natoma Bay* was later repaired and used to repatriate POWs before being decommissioned in 1946.

HMS *Formidable* damaged

At 11.30 on 9 May, while off Sakishima Gunto, the carrier *Formidable* (R1, Captain Philip Ruck-Keene, RN) was hit by a *Zeke* armed with a single 500lb bomb which made a steep diving attack. *Formidable* and the three accompanying carriers carried out a succession of emergency turns while the incoming target was reported as being repeatedly hit, to no avail. The aircraft approached from port, crossed the flight deck, flew along the starboard side where the guns were 'wooded', turned over and impacted the flight deck alongside the island, causing much damage and some casualties among the exposed gun crews there. The explosion of this machine was devastating enough but in addition its bomb pierced the flight deck leaving a hole measuring about two square feet with a two-foot deep depression in the armoured flight deck, some 24 by 20ft across. A large fire was started among the aircraft parked on deck. Three steel shards went down into the hangar deck of which one continued into the central boiler room, rupturing a steam line *en route* and unleashing a jet of scalding steam, then proceeded yet further down to rupture a fuel tank in the ship's double bottom.

The loss of the boiler reduced the ship's speed to 18 knots and she was unable to operate her aircraft for five hours. Eleven aircraft, ten Avengers and one Corsair, were destroyed and her crash barriers and radar rendered inoperative. Casualties amounted to eight dead and forty-seven wounded. With the fires brought under control, burned-out aircraft ditched, the flight deck repaired (by the application of quick-drying cement with a steel plate welded over the top), *Formidable* was quickly operational once more.

Anti-aircraft protection for the carriers had been fatally weakened by the earlier departure of battleships *King George V* and *Howe* (37, Captain Henry William Urquhart McCall), the AA cruisers *Black Prince* (Captain Gerald Vaughan Gladstone) and *Eurylus*, (Captain Richard Oliver-Bellais) and the six destroyers of the 25th Flotilla, all of which had been detached to conduct a bombardment of the air strips on the island of Miyako situated between Okinawa to the north and Yaeyama to the south, leaving only eight destroyers to shield the carriers. It was felt that a heavy naval gun bombardment would cause more damage in a hour than repeated bombing had done in many days, and, while this is very probably true, the effects of the lack of heavy AA batteries provided by the battleships and cruisers was immediately apparent. The Japanese employed up to twenty aircraft of various types, some of which helped decoy the limited CAP away so the Kamikazes could go about their work.

It was not until post-war that it was discovered that *Formidable* had been much more severely damaged than first thought.

BPF, 9 May 1945

This day saw the BPF take some hard blows. Japanese snoopers had been in evidence all day and late in the afternoon and, at 16.45, five bogeys were detected approaching very low from the west. Four Seafires intercepted this group some fifteen miles out but were decoyed away by a single machine, which, although they duly destroyed, meant that the rest of the group bored in unopposed. These four also avoided a second section of Seafires and climbed to 3,000 feet, penetrating to the fleet and commencing their attack dives at 16.50. The British ships were being 'radically manoeuvred by emergency turns' at 22 knots. An emergency turn of 60 degrees starboard was being carried out when one Kamikaze made a 10 degree dive into *Victorious* from her starboard quarter. This aircraft was continuously engaged by the Oerlikons and hit repeatedly, being well ablaze and starting to break up, but at full speed this machine hit the carrier's flight deck close to the forward lift. Its bomb exploded and holed the flight deck, causing a fire. The accelerator was put out of action by the blast as was one of the twin 4.5in gun mounts and a lift hoisting motor. The fire-fighting teams managed to get the fire under control quickly. The captain of the *Victorious*, Michael Denny, when interviewed by the author, expressed the opinion that the Kamikaze attacks, far from being 'wasteful;' as some post-war historians have asserted, was, on the contrary, a very viable and effective method of attacking warships. Denny stated that they were 'a first class show from the enemy point of view.' He described the attack thus:

'Our anti-aircraft fire was pretty effective and the *Victorious* was an immensely handy ship to handle, with a big rudder. I could spin her around quite rapidly and

I managed to ruin both Kamikaze attacks. They aimed originally for between the lifts – with American ships they could open up the flight deck and go right through into the hangar space below; but eventually they found that this didn't work with the British carriers – they had armoured decks. Kamikazes successfully striking an American carrier could put her out of action with regard to operating aircraft, but this did not work with the British carriers. This was possibly the reason why, later on, they seemed to go for the bridges of British ships with a view to killing the command personnel – but this was a silly thing to do, because they could do far more by going for the hull of the ship. Damage to the actual lifts, while less spectacular, was a far more effective way of putting a carrier out of action.'

Captain Denny recalled that this pilot started his final attack almost directly astern but the hard turn placed him abeam. 'He tried to pull up and start again, but he was not quick enough. I crossed ahead of him pretty close and his wheels touched the flight deck at right-angles. The undercarriage sheared right off and the plane broke up, sliding eight feet across the flight deck to crash over the side on onto the 4.5in guns.'

'From the first moment I started to swing the ship, he had been trying to adjust and steer up the flight deck – which would have given him the whole length in which to drop his stick down and hit – but he didn't make it.'[4] At 16.56 a second suicide aircraft made a shallow power glide from astern against the same ship. Again it was hard hit by the defensive fire and was ablaze, but it struck the flight deck aft a glancing blow, and, still ablaze, passed over the side. Four of the Corsairs in the deck park aft were damaged, and a 40mm gun director was destroyed, and one arrestor unit was put out of commission. The third attacker followed at 16.57, also approaching *Victorious*, but, at the last moment, perhaps seeing the direct hits achieved by his two predecessors, switched target to the battleship *Howe* (B-3, Captain Henry William Urquhart McCall, DSO, RN) ahead of the carrier. This proved to be suicide in every respect as the much more powerful anti-aircraft batteries of the *Howe*, chiefly the quadruple-2–pdr pom-pom atop the after 14in gun turret, whose crew were nicknamed 'The Pirates', shredded the aircraft as it approached her starboard quarter in a long shallow dive. Continually hit throughout its approach, this machine was well ablaze when it passed over the battleship's quarterdeck and entered the water some 100 yards distant. The *Howe* was equipped with a range of anti-aircraft weapons, and just those capable of firing aft included eight 5.25 inch, two octuple 2–pdr pom-poms, eight Bofors and eight 20mm Oerlikons.

The last of the quartet approached at 17.05, feinting first against the *Formidable* and then *Indomitable* (Captain John Arthus Symons Eccles) and being engaged, and frequently hit, by both ships' gunfire but without any apparent result. The Kamikaze then made a sharp turn and conducted a dive into *Formidable*'s deck park. The 2–pdr pom-pom aft continued to engage this aircraft on its final run in and parts of this machine were visible flying off the wings and body of the aircraft before it hit. The resulting detonations were most spectacular, the resultant fire – stoked by the fuel and ordnance from the parked

4. Author Interview with Admiral Sir Michael Denny, GCB, CBE DSO, RN, reproduced in *Task Force 57*, London, 1969.

machines – caused a huge smoke trail – though happily its bomb failed to penetrate the flight deck.

The explosion destroyed six Corsairs and an Avenger on deck, and blew many rivets out of the flight deck, leaving holes through which burning fuel fell into the after hangar and this hangar had to have the fire sprinkler system activated, which damaged three further Avengers and eight Corsairs. Surprisingly the only fatality was the petty officer gun-layer of the pom-pom who was decapitated by an aircraft wheel. Another eight men were wounded. The American Liaison Officer opined that an American carrier thus hit might well have been lost, but *Formidable* reported herself able to land aircraft again by 17.55.

Watching this attack was Sub-Lieutenant R. W. Halliday. He told the Author:

'The Kamikazes always seemed to attack at a vulnerable moment, which aboard a carrier meant while the ship was committed to launching or recovering her aircraft. You are sitting, strapped in to the seat of your aircraft, on the flight deck awaiting take-off. Air Raid Warning Red is sounded: Kamikazes approaching. You can probably see them out of your cockpit. Everyone on the flight deck disappears to take cover, but you are left sitting in your aircraft and this is very unpleasant. The *Formidable* lost a large number of pilots and planes in this manner in one attack – a suicide pilot smashed straight into a deck park; a very effective attack on the Japanese part, but most unnerving from ours.'[5]

The following day, Vice Admiral Vian visited both *Victorious* and *Formidable* to inspect their damage and reported that both ships had conducted temporary repairs which would enable both to remain sufficiently operational to continue the planned strike programme. A conference was held which included Admirals Henry Bernard Hughes Rawlings, Vian and Rear-Admiral Eric James Patrick Brind, commander of the 4th Cruiser Squadron (CS4) to discuss how better protection might be given to the carriers. The Japanese change of tactics on the 9th appeared to have forsaken the hitherto normal high approach in favour of a low-level approach, which had the effect of reducing the warning time for the defending fighters.

Among the measures decided upon for adoption immediately were:

(a) To station two radar pickets, each consisting of a 6in cruiser and a destroyer, twelve miles to the northwest and southwest of the fleet in order to increase the range at which incoming aircraft were detected. Two fighters were to be allocated to each picket, and on initial sighting of an incoming enemy, further fighters were to be vectored out to assist.

(b) To bring the 5.25in cruisers in from the screen and to station them with the main body of the fleet to increase AA protection for the carriers whenever in the operational area.

---

5. Captain R. W. Halliday, DSC, RN to the Author, reproduced in *Task Force 57*, London, 1969.

The Australian Navy *County* Class heavy cruiser, HMAS *Australia* on 21 October, 1944, showing damage to her bridge as a result of being crash-dived by a IJA 6th Brigade Mitsubishi Ki-51 *Sonia* off Leyte Gulf. Among her many casualties was her captain who received fatal injuries. This was the first of five such attacks on the *Australia* and she survived them all. *(US National Archives, Washington DC, 80-G-291383)*

The first 'official' Kamikaze mission leaves its Philippines air base to strike at an American Task Group on 25 October 1944. *(Imperial Japanese Navy photo)*

Seen from the *Kalinin Bay*, the escort carrier *St.Lo* (CVE-63) is rent by an enormous explosion caused by her aircraft torpedoes blowing up 90-seconds after being hit by a Mitsubishi A6M *Zeke* Kamikaze flown by Lieutenant Yukio Seki, IJN, off Samar at around 10.30 on 25 October 1944. The detonation in the hangar deck resulted in a fireball up to 300 feet above the flight deck. The after elevator can be seen being tossed almost 1,000ft into the air. She became what was regarded as the first 'official' victim of the Kamikaze campaign. *(Official US Navy, NS0306308)*

Taken from the ships bridge, this photograph shows the explosion in the hangar deck erupting from the flight deck of the escort carrier *Suwannee* (CVE-27) after she had been struck by a Mitsusbishi A6M5 Navy Type 0 Carrier Fighter Model 52, *Zeke*, piloted by PO1c Tomisaku Katsumata on 25 October 1944. This particular aircraft had previously been flown by the Japanese ace Warrant Officer Hiroyoshi Nishizawa, but had been turned over to Katsumata because Nishizawa was scheduled to fly to Manila to pick up new aircraft. *(Puget Sound Navy Yard photo 4311-44 from National Archives and Records Administration, College Park, MD, NS0302710)*

Aboard the escort carrier *Suwannee*. Part of a Nakajima Sakae 21, 14-cylinder radial engine from the A6M5 *Zeke* Kamikaze that crashed into her starboard side at Frame 64, on 25 October 1944. The cylinder heads of the engine have been destroyed but the connecting rods and crankshaft can be discerned. *(Puget Sound Navy Yard, 4332-44)*

The *Independence* Class light carrier *Belleau Wood* (CVL-24) burning aft following a hit by a *Kamikaze* while operating off the Philippines on 30 October 1944. Flight deck crewmen are moving undamaged TBM Avenger torpedo planes away from the flames as others fight the fires. The fleet carrier *Franklin* (CV-13), which was bombed by the same aircraft just before it crashed into *Belleau Wood*, can be seen ablaze in the background. *(US National Archives, Washington DC, 80-G-342020)*

Lieutenant Yoshinori Yamaguchi steers his Yokosuka D4Y3 Type 3 *Suisei* (*Judy*) dive-bomber in a Kamikaze attack against the fleet carrier *Essex* (CV-9) at 12.56 pm on 25 November 1944, in the Philippine Sea. The dive-bombers dive-brakes hang down and the port non-sealing fuel tanks emit petrol vapour, both as a result of AA fire, as the kamikaze closes in on the carrier's deck. *(US Naval Archives and Administration, Washington DC, 80-G-270648)*

The USS *Ward* (APD-16) which, as a destroyer, fired the first defensive shots of the Pacific War at Pearl Harbor when she attacked a Japanese miniature submarine. *Ward*, later converted to a high-speed transport, was damaged off Okinawa and uncontrollable fires broke out. She had to be abandoned and was finally sunk by gunfire from the destroyer *O'Brien* (DD-725) which was commanded by *Ward's* former captain of 1941. *(US National Archives, Washington DC, 80-G-270773)*

It was not just the terror of the Kamikaze attacks themselves, but the constant strain of waiting for them to occur when within range of Japanese airfields. Despite radar, combat air patrols overhead and increasing the number of lookouts, many ships were surprised and attacked with lethal results. The continuing periods of full alert wore down ships' crews over a period of days, weeks and months. This can be seen in the expressions of the gunners aboard the light cruiser *Phoenix* off Mindoro on 18 December 1944. *(US National Records and Administration, Washington DC, 80-G-47471)*

Suicide pilots partake of the last briefing on their mission prior their final flight. *(Imperial Japanese Navy photo)*

The *Benson* Class destroyer *Gansevoort* (DD-608) showing the itemised damage she received when struck in the port side by a Kamikaze while in Mangarin Bay, Mindoro on the afternoon of 30 December 1944. This photo, from Mare Island, California repair base, lists the horrendous damage done when her main deck was blown upward. *(US Navy photo, NARA, San Francisco)*

One early victim was the battleship *New Mexico* (BB-40) which, while taking up her bombardment position off San Fernando to Poro Point, Lingayen Gulf, was struck on the port navigation bridge on 6 January 1945, by a Kamikaze. This attack killed several senior officers, including the ships' commander, Captain Robert Walter Fleming, USN, British Army officer Lieutenant-General Herbert Lumsden, Special Military Representative to General MacArthur, and Sub-Lieutenant (S) Morton, RN, as well as William Henry Chickering, a war correspondent with *Time* magazine, who were all killed instantly on the ship's bridge, but Admiral Sir Bruce Fraser, C-in-C designate of the British Pacific Fleet, standing on the other side of the bridge escaped without a scratch. *(US Navy Photo)*

The heavy cruiser *Louisville* (CA-28) is seen from the escort carrier *Salamaua* (CVE-96) as she heels over under attack as a Kamikaze strikes home at 17.14 on 6 January 1945 in Lingayen Gulf. As well as the aircraft itself the two bombs that the plane was carrying both detonated inboard and Captain R L Hicks, USN, was among the many casualties. *(US National Archives, Washington DC, 80-G-363217)*

Seen from the light cruiser *Miami* (CL-89), the fleet carrier *Ticonderoga* (CV-14) ablaze after two Kamikazes hit her off Taiwan at 12.08 on 21 January 1945. Loss of life was heavy, 143 men killed and 202 injured, among them Captain Dixie Kiefer, wounded, the Air Officer, (killed), the Executive Officer (wounded) and the Gunnery Officer (killed). *(US National Archives, Washington DC, 80-G-273151)*

Attack off Iwo Jima. On 21 February 1945 a burning Kamikaze slides across the flight deck of the escort carrier *Lunga Point* (CVE-94) before falling harmlessly into the sea alongside. *(US National Archives and Records Administration, 80-G-430121)*

The *Essex* Class carrier *Randolph* (CV-15) was hit by a Ōhka 750kg manned missile carried by a Yokosuka P1Y *Ginga* (*Frances*) twin-engined bomber, which struck her on the starboard side aft, just below the flight deck on 11 March 1945 while anchored in the 'safe haven' of Ulithi Atoll in the Caroline Islands. She is seen here, on 13 March 1945, with the repair ship *Jason* (ARH-1) alongside. *(US National Archives, Washington DC, 80-G-344531)*

Removing the debris with the Rising Sun emblem and remains of a Kamikaze pilot from the battleship *Nevada* (BB-36). This aircraft had one wing shot off by the ship's gunners but still impacted the battleship's deck and caused sixty casualties while off Okinawa on 27 March 1945. *(Official US Navy Photo from 'All Hands' – Bureau of Naval Personnel Information Bulletin – NAVPERS-O, August 1945)*

A Yokosuka MXY-7 Ōhka (Cherry Blossom) I-18, No.1049, christened *Baka* (Fool) by the Americans and also known as the 'Flying Warhead', found and photographed by US Marines at Yontan Air Base, Okinawa on 1 April 1945. *(US National Archives, Washington DC)*

The flight deck of the fleet carrier *Indefatigable* (R-7) after she had been struck by a suicide aircraft on 1 April 1945. The armoured deck was not pierced but merely "dished" to a depth of three inches over a 15 square foot area. Within 40 minutes she had resumed flying operations once more. *(Commander Pat Chambers, RN)*

Damage to the base of the Island structure of HMS *Indefatigable* (R-7) where she was struck by a Kamikaze. The detonation wrecked the sick bay where Lieutenant-Commander Pat Chambers and many others were preparing and caused eight deaths with sixteen wounded. *(Commander Pat Chambers, RN)*

The light cruiser *Pasadena* (CL-65) is near-missed by a Kamikaze aircraft that crashed just off her starboard quarter at 14.12 on 11 April 1945. She was undergoing five suicide attacks in six minutes as part of the Japanese *Kikusui* No. 2 operation. Photo taken from the carrier *Essex* by CphoM Paul Maddon. *(US Navy Official)*

A Japanese wartime propaganda photograph purporting to show Chiran High School girls of the volunteer *Nadeshiko* Maintenance unit, waving farewell to a Kamikaze pilot taking off on a suicide mission. The aircraft, photographed at the Chiran Air Base, Fukuoka Prefecture in southern Kyushu, used by the 6th Air Army suicide group and known as *Tokkou No Machi, Chiran*, is genuine but the girls have been superimposed on the original print. Such 'composite' overlaying was commonly used by both Japanese and Allied sources during the war and is not unusual. *(IJA Official Photo)*

This famous photograph of a Japanese Navy A6M *Zeke* Kamikaze about to strike the battleship *Missouri* (BB-63) off Okinawa on 11 April 1945, was taken by Seaman Len Schmidt. This aircraft, flown by Petty Officer 2nd Class Setsuo Ishino, IJN, struck the battleship's port side below the main deck, causing minor damage and just one injury. *(US Naval Historical Center NH62696)*

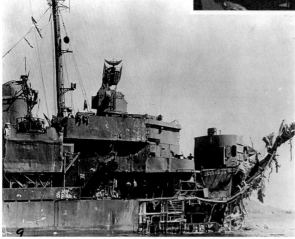

The Destroyer-minelayer *Lindsey* (DM-32), showing the extensive damage suffered to her forward hull and superstructure, which was caused by two Aichi D3A2 *Val* Kamikazes crashing into the ship off Okinawa at 15.40 on 12 April 1945. This photograph was taken at Kerama Retto anchorage 14 April 1945. There the ship received a temporary stub bow and returned to the States for full repairs. *(US National Archives, Washington DC, 80-G-330108)*

Seen from the battle-cruiser *Alaska* (CB-1) a *Fletcher* Class destroyer passes the burning aircraft carrier *Intrepid* (CV-11) which was hit by a Kamikaze on 16 April 1945. On this occasion the aircraft penetrated through to her hangar deck but the fires were rapidly brought under control. Despite numerous Kamikaze hits *Intrepid* survived the war and is now a museum ship at New York. *(US National Archives and Administration, 80-G-328441)*

A group of nurses examining the wreckage of the Kamikaze that hit the Hospital Ship *Comfort* (AH-6) off Okinawa on the night of 28 April 1945. It demolished an operating theatre and supply room, killed six doctors, six nurses, nine army medical corpsmen, one navy crewman and seven patients while injuring a further thirty-eight Army and Navy enlisted personnel. *(US National Archives, Washington DC, #80-6-315914)*

The British aircraft carrier *Formidable* heavily on fire after being hit by a Kamikaze off Sakishima Gunto at 11.30 on 4 May 1945. The impact left a dent in the armoured flight deck and sent a steel shard down through the hangar deck and centre boiler-room (where it ruptured steam lines) before coming to rest in a fuel tank. A large fire was started among aircraft parked aft on the flight deck which destroyed ten Avengers and one Corsair as well as killing eight crewmen and wounding forty-seven more. *(Sandra Meacock)*

Scene aboard *Formidable* immediately after this attack with debris scattered across the flight deck as the fire-fighting teams get to work. The crumpled remains of the Kamikaze lie at the base of the ship's island. *(Sandra Meacock)*

The fleet carrier *Bunker Hill* (CV-17) suffered the heaviest casualty list inflicted by the Kamikazes when two of them, piloted by Lieutenant Yasunori Seizo and Kiyoshi Ogawa respectively, hit her at 10.20 on 11 May 1945. A total of 396 crewmen died and 264 more were injured, many badly burnt in this attack. She is seen burning hard with most of her deck park wiped out and her after lift buckled. *(US National Archives and Record Center, Washington DC, 80-G-274266)*

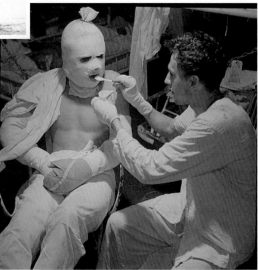

Badly injured crewman, pressure-bandaged after suffering severe burns when his ship was hit by a Kamikaze, being hand-fed aboard the USS *Solace* (AH-5), May 1945. *(US National Archives, Washington DC, # 80-G-346694)*

The battleship *New Mexico* (BB-40) is hit again by Kamikazes, on 12 May 1945 off Okinawa. This time she was struck on the gun deck and the fore funnel and a 200ft high sheet of flames left 58 dead from a total of 177 casualties. *(US National Archives, 80-G- 328653)*

Seen through the ship's rigging a Kamikaze, hit by AA fire dives into the sea close to the light cruiser *Vicksburg* (CL-86), off Okinawa, 14 May 1945. *(US National Archives, Washington DC, 80-G-490019)*

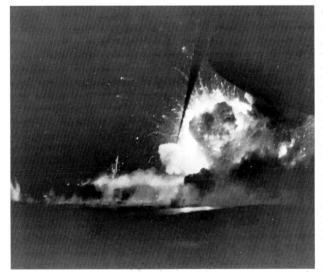

The escort carrier *Bismarck Sea* (CVE-95) became the last US Navy carrier to be sunk in the Pacific War when she was struck by two Kamikazes on 21 May 1945. The first came in low and hit the ship on the starboard side aft, abreast the after elevator and penetrated into the hangar deck to explode in the ship's magazines. Just as the fires were being brought under control the second aircraft made a vertical dive into the elevator shaft, detonating a torpedo store and destroying all fire-fighting equipment. The ship had to be abandoned with the loss of 318 crewmen killed. *(US National Records and Archives, 80-G-335103)*

Corporal Yukio Araki (age 17 years 2 months) from Kiryu, Gunma Prefecture, holding a puppy with four of his equally young companions of the 72nd *Shinbu* Corps at Bansei Air Base, in southern Kyushu, on Saturday 26 May 1945 prior their Kamikaze flight to the Okinawa area two days later. Flying *Vals*, ten aircraft took off, one of which aborted. The remaining nine did not return and it is thought that two of them were those that struck the destroyer *Braine* (DD-630) killing sixty-six of her crew and wounding seventy-eight more. *(Asahi Shimbun, Osaka)*

The destroyer *Braine* (DD-630) was hit by two Aichi D3A2 *Val* Kamikazes at 07.45 on 27 May 1945 and managed to reach harbour at Kerama Retto. The mangled remains of her 'midship's section are here seen being examined. The destroyer lost sixty-six men killed, some of them to sharks after jumping clear of the fires aboard, and seventy-eight injured. *(US Navy Official, South Boston Navy Yard)*

The *Fletcher* Class destroyer *William D Porter* (DD-579) sinks after salvage efforts failed. On 10 June 1945, this ship was taken by surprise by a single *Val* Kamikaze. Although hit and shot down the *Val* crashed close alongside the ship and its bomb detonated directly under her keel, breaking her back. Luckily there were no casualties. *(US National Archives, Washington DC, 80-G-49002)*

The Australian-manned destroyer HMAS *Nizam*, late in the war. This illustrates how her torpedo-tubes were taken out and replaced by two single 40-mm Bofors guns as an emergency measure against the Kamikaze attacks. The sky-arcs of both weapons were minimal however and can only have had limited effect. *(RAN Official)*

Lieutenant-Commander George Walsh, USN, while serving as an SB2C Helldiver dive-bomber pilot with VB-80 aboard the carrier USS *Ticonderoga* (CV-14) underwent an ordeal by fire when that carrier was struck by Kamikazes off Formosa on 21 January 1945. He provided the author with a graphic first-hand account of just what it was like to undergo such an ordeal, and try and find safety when blinded by fire and smoke. *(Courtesy of George Walsh)*

The destroyer USS *Braine* (DD-630) showing the devastation wrought by Kamikaze hits including the complete demolition of No.2 5-in turret and the deckhouse before and alongside her bridge that extended back to amidships. Despite suffering such damage, once repaired she continued to serve with the US Navy until 1961, and then went on to have a long service life with the Navy of Argentina. *(USN Official)*

The cruiser *Nashville* (CL-43) after she had been hit on her way to the Mindoro, Philippines, landings, by a Kamikaze in her port side 5in AA battery at 10.00 on 13 December 1944. The bomb carried by this aircraft flipped over into the starboard battery and detonated there. Losses among the US Marine gun crews were very severe. *(US National Archives and Records Administration, Washington DC, 80-K-6886)*

Very few ships that survived a Kamikaze hit still survive today. One is the aircraft carrier *Intrepid*, a museum ship in New York, and another is the *Fletcher* Class destroyer *Kidd* (DD-661) seen here. She was operating off Hagushi, Okinawa at 13.54 on 11 April 1945 when she was hit at the waterline in her starboard fireroom, while the bomb it was carrying passed clean through the ship before detonating. The *Kidd* suffered thirty-eight men killed and fifty-five injured, including Commander H G Moore, USN, the ship's captain. Repaired she later served on during the Korean War and on Taiwanese Strait patrols. She became a Memorial Ship in 1982 and over the years was fully restored to her August 1945 configuration. She is moored on the Mississippi River and Baton Rouge, Louisiana. This photo was taken on 26 August 1988 and has been placed by Cobatfor in the public domain. *(Cobatfor)*

Another view of the Royal Australian Navy manned destroyer *Nizam* seen alongside the US carrier *Shangri-La* (CV-38) off the coast of Japan during the closing stages of the war. She also features extra AA weapons aft in lieu of her torpedo tubes and enhanced radar arrays. *(US Navy Official 80-278801)*

The Royal Navy *Battle* Class destroyer *Barfleur*, coming alongside the US carrier *Shangri-La* (CV-38) to transfer stores in the closing stages of the war. The new 4.5-inch mountings carried forward were a huge improvement of earlier British destroyer weapons. Officially these guns had a 55° elevation but as can be seen here, were capable of far more than that. Aft they carried a heavy bank of 40-mm weapons. Although a flotilla of these ships were being formed, and four more were on their way to the Pacific, *Barfleur* was the one to see active deployment in the combat zone. *(US Navy Official 80-278810)*

The Author, Peter C Smith, and Japanese Historian Tetsukuni Watanabe, along with some veterans, at the Nagoya Kamikaze *Kusanagi* Unit Memorial. Some fifty-six Kamikaze pilots and crew who did not return are honoured here. This unit was first inaugurated on 1 April 1945 and not finally disbanded until 2 September 1945. The unit was formed with three squadrons, comprising thirteen, two and thirteen aircraft respectively, each with of D3A2 *Val* dive-bombers and moved to Kokubu Airfield in Kagoshima Prefecture for *Kikusui* Operations 1, 2 and 4. The inscription reads: "At a time when the land of Okinawa where they sleep has seen the day of the homeland's recovery, we Navy veterans who live in Toyota City with the cooperation of volunteers erect this monument to tell future generations forever of the loyalty of the Kusanagi Unit." *((c) Peter C Smith)*

Admiral Matome Ugaki flew the last known Kamikaze mission on 15 August 1945 in a Yokosuka D4Y *Suisei* (*Comet*) dive-bomber from Oita airfield. At the Yasukuni *Jinja* Shrine Museum in Central Tokyo one of these types has been carefully restored and is on display in the Central Hall. Here it was examined by the author (left), Yoshimitsu Komine, Section Chief of the Exhibition of the Museum (right), and famous *Suisei* pilot Lieutenant-Commander Zenji Abe (centre). *((c) Peter C Smith)*

(c) To station a destroyer astern of each carrier to afford more gun protection in what appears to be the enemy's favourite position for attacking carriers.

It should be noted that (c) was merely a reversion to established practice first adopted in the Mediterranean, following the dive-bombing of *Illustrious* by German Ju87 *Stukas* off Malta in January 1941. Also, during the *Pedestal* convoy operation which lifted the Malta siege in August 1942, three *Dido* class cruisers had been allocated, one each as close-protection to the carriers *Eagle, Indomitable* and *Victorious*. Why this well-established earlier practice had been abandoned earlier on in the Pacific was not revealed.

What *was* specified at this time was:

'In addition to the introduction of the closer formation, one destroyer is now stationed astern of each carrier whilst in the operating area to provide close gun support, particularly against fore-and-aft attack. Destroyers to close up to two cables during attack. Ideally these destroyers need a large 40mm armament aft as the most frequent direction of attack has been from astern. The *Battle* class destroyers should fill this role admirably, and it is hoped that extra Bofors guns can shortly be fitted in all destroyers of the British Pacific Fleet.'[6] It was also stated that the removal of the after bank of torpedo tubes in four *Napier* Class destroyers to enable the fitting of four additional Bofors was proceeding. As well as extra anti-aircraft firepower support, the question of radical manoeuvring was considered. There proved no real consensus on this, it being noted that although large alterations of course did not seriously hamper gunfire, once the targets had been indicated and the guns were on, they did add to the difficulty of fire distribution and identification. It was considered, however, that radical manoeuvre was 'a valuable means of defence against the suicider.' As for the accuracy of the fleet's gunfire and also the target tracking and the actual stopping power of the weaponry employed, some data from this meeting was enlightening. It was concluded that there had been a total of ten individual suicide attacks and of these there were four occasions that defensive gunfire had scored hits on the enemy which caused them to miss or glance off the target and were fully effective; three occasions when the aircraft were firmly and continuously hit, but weight of shell failed to stop the target aircraft crashing inboard, and three when no hits at all were made on the approaching enemy.

'From these results it is clear that the guns are not hitting hard enough. Harder hitting can be achieved by either:

(a) Bringing the enemy under accurate fire for a longer period.
(b) Bringing the enemy under a greater volume of accurate fire.
(c) Bringing the enemy under earlier, accurate fire from heavier guns.'

They concluded that all the above methods ultimately depended upon accuracy, which had to come from more and better training. 'In this connection it has been shown that the

---

6. ADM199/591, *op cit.*

automatic weapons' manually-laid gyro sights are still failing to lead the target and it is for consideration that all lead-generating sights be fitted with a control which will cause the sight to overcompensate for the speed of the target.' This report went back to the Admiralty and was duly pontificated upon, but too late to affect the outcome of wartime operations.

On 5 October the Director of Air Warfare and Training (DAWT) produced a pithy statement. In it he commented that he, 'has always contended that the relatively slow avoiding action of a ship cannot influence the aim of a suicide pilot who is himself unimpaired by wounds and whose aircraft is unscathed, and that in the cases where aircraft have narrowly missed their target, the cause has been damage inflicted on pilot or aircraft. Nevertheless, the fact remains that ships continue to be narrowly missed when under wheel, and there seems to be no reason why such manoeuvring should not be continued, (if only to give the feeling that everything possible is being done) so long as it does not complicate the gunnery problem, and, through the excessive heel of the ship, handicap other personnel who are involved in its defence. DAWT, however, is unshaken, in his view that avoidance of a suicider by manoeuvring is a matter of luck rather than good management, at least in the case of major units.' The Director Gunnery Division (DGD) concurred entirely with these remarks with regard to avoiding action. It was, however, pointed out that the US Navy had a different opinion. Their *Anti-Suicide Action Summary* observed that 'statistics show that suiciders obtained a greater percentage of success against large vessels which did not resort to radical manoeuvre.'[7] It was stated that, 'the adverse effect on target indication may outweigh the effect of radical manoeuvre, which must also effect the control of gunfire to some extent, if only due to the considerable increase in vibration.' Also, 'Even with Remote Power Control (RPC) of the guns, the increase of training rates by violent manoeuvring and the difficulties of ammunition handling with the ship listed must have an adverse effect on AA gunnery.'

With regard to using *Battle* Class destroyers as close AA support for aircraft carriers it was stated that: 'While the large 40mm armament aft in the *Battle* class is said to make these destroyers admirable for close AA support to carriers, it has been generally accepted that the large gun with a VT fuse is the most lethal weapon for Kamikaze or *Ōhka* manned missile. Particularly with light fleet carriers with no medium-range armament aft, it would appear essential to employ a destroyer with 4.5in armament aft.' The experience of the *Howe* and the recommendation of a barrage set at 1,000 yards to engage suicide aircraft had been approved by Admiral Sir Bruce Fraser and the DGD concurred. It was felt that twelve miles was insufficient for early-warning pickets.

With regard to gyro sights it was suggested that possible causes for the general impression that gyro sights fail to give sufficient lead were considered to be:

(a) Engaging aircraft which are well outside effective range
(b) Engaging aircraft before the gyro sight has had time to run up.

---

7. *Anti-Suicide Action Summary*, August 1945, Cominch P-0011, dated 31 August 1945.

The DGD was opposed to fitting the suggested control to overcompensate for target speed, but the captain of the Gunnery School, HMS *Excellent,* was asked to investigate the possible causes of shooting astern. Commander David Owen had reported that, 'fortunately the Japanese have not yet learnt that the most vulnerable time for a carrier task force is at dusk.' The Director of Training and Staff Duties division (DTSD) seized on this and his comments were also quite scathing. He, 'did not understand and certainly cannot agree with Commander Owen's remark.' He continued: 'There have been innumerable instances of dusk and dawn attacks, and in fact the Americans were last winter compelled to station a cruiser and destroyers on the dark (east or west according to sunset or sunrise) side of their Groups as an additional picket. There have also been some night attacks and there is evidence to show that such attacks are on the increase' He warned against underestimating their opponents. 'The Japanese are in fact adept at changing their tactics according to conditions. They make the fullest use of all cover, whether cloud or land, they are improving the co-ordination of their suicide attacks and, being familiar with the fade charts of U.S. radar, they are constantly bringing off surprise attacks as on the *Bunker Hill.* Full overhead air cover is considered essential.'[8]

Sangamon badly hurt

Also on this bad day, the escort carrier *Sangamon* (CVE-26, Captain Alvin Ingersoll Malstrom, USN) was targeted and damaged. At 19.33 a fully bombed-up Kamikaze hit the ship, and both went through the flight deck and exploded inside her with devastating effect. Raging fires broke out on both the flight and hangar deck, and even as deep in the vessel as the fuel deck. All contact with the bridge was cut off as these fires took hold and the *Sangamon* careered out of control. As she veered around the compass rose, the wind sweeping through her randomly fanned the flames in unpredictable directions, hampering the already hard-pressed firefighting teams and spreading the destruction. In the end, by gallant effort, the steering of the ship was re-established using the after control position at 20.15 and she was steadied on an optimum course to assist the fire teams. Gradually progress was made until, by 22.30, all fires were reported to be under control. Unsurprisingly the casualty toll was high with eleven dead, twenty-five missing plus twenty-one badly wounded. She was very badly damaged and although sent back to Norfolk Navy Yard for rebuilding, work on her, which commenced on 12 June, was ceased on the Japanese surrender as uneconomical and she was never fully repaired, being taken out of commission on 24 October 1945. Effectively the *Sangamon* became a delayed Kamikaze victim and never served again.

More May casualties

The light cruiser *Birmingham* (CL-62, Captain Harry Douglas Power) was badly damaged on 4 May; destroyer *Bache* (DD-470, Commander Alan Roberts McFarland) was slightly damaged on 3 May, and again on 13 May when she lost forty-one dead and

---

8. ADM199//591.

had to be sent home for repair. The destroyer *Brown* (DD-546) destroyed a Kamikaze on 5 May and received slight damage from fragments of the exploding aircraft, while *Cowell* (DD-547, Commander Charles Luther Wertz) suffered similar discomfort on both the 4 and 25 May. On 5 May *Ingraham* (DD-694) was attacked by five Kamikazes, shooting down four before the fifth smashed into her causing many casualties, including fifteen dead, and had to be sent to the West Coast for repairs. The *Shea* (DM-30) was heavily damaged by an *Ohka* on 4 May losing thirty-five dead and ninety-one wounded, necessitating her return to the USA to repair, while the *Gwin* (DM-33, Commander Fredrick Samuel Steinke) was attacked by six Kamikazes; she shot down five in six minutes before the sixth hit her although her damage was repaired locally and she later continued in action. The ancient destroyer-minesweeper *Hopkins* (DMS-13, Lieutenant-Commander Douglas P Payne) was struck a glancing blow from a Kamikaze that killed one man on 4 May, while *Oberrender* (DE-344, Lieutenant-Commander Samuel Spence) was hit by a Kamikaze on 24 May and suffered twenty-four dead. Subsequently, upon her return to the USA, she was deemed not worth repairing and was scrapped; the same fate attended the destroyer escort *England* (DE-635), which was hit on 9 May suffering the deaths of thirty-seven crewmen and extensive damage. The seaplane tender *St George* (AV-16, Captain Robert Gordon Armstrong), hit on 29 April, was hit again on 4 May and the survey vessel *Pathfinder* (AGS-1, Captain Boscom H Thomas) was hit on 6 May suffering slight damage.[9]

Bunker Hill put out of the war

On 11 May Task Groups 58.1 and 58.3 were in the vicinity of Point 'Eagle', ninety miles east of Okinawa. Both US Task Groups had been shadowed from around midnight and at 09.40 five Japanese aircraft had already been destroyed close to the picket ships. However, the radar screens had remained clear over the Groups until 09.58 when a bogey was picked up at twenty miles range. *Bunker Hill* (CV-17, Captain George A. Seitz, USN)[10] had been stood down to cruising quarters from General Quarters at 09.50. There was a deck park of aircraft on the flight deck aft which was about to be moved forward, while twenty-eight more were airborne. Fortunately none of the aircraft on deck were bombed up but all had been refuelled. Although the crew were relaxed from action stations, two hostile aircraft had escaped detection and were hidden in a blanket of cloud 2,000ft above the ships. They thus achieved considerable surprise when both dove into the *Bunker Hill* without any warning at 10.00. One of the CAP fighters spotted them as they appeared at steep angles through the only hole in the cloud and gave a warning, consequently General Quarters was being sounded as the first machine, a *Judy*, struck the ship. The guns' crews had no time to register on the first attacker, which, unimpeded, struck the truck (a wooden or metal cap at the top of a mast) which tipped it over and into No.3 elevator. The

---

9. The minesweeper *Gayety* (AM-239), claimed sunk by German and Japanese sources, was not even commissioned until September 1945.
10. Captain Seitz was the second captain of the *Bunker Hill*, having relieved her first CO Captain John Jennings Ballentine during the ship's stateside refit earlier.

40mm and 20mm guns fired just a few rounds at the second machine, a *Zeke*, piloted by Ensign Kiyoshi Ogawa, who, undeterred, crashed into the carrier twenty seconds after the first to detonate abreast the Island and the deck-edge elevator. This second machine released a bomb just before the aircraft itself struck the flight deck and ripped open a gap measuring roughly 40 x 20 feet. Ogawa's bomb, however, continued on, penetrating deep inside the ship and detonated in VF-84's ready room killing thirty fighter pilots instantly. The resultant explosions resulted in huge blazes and heavy smoke which in the words of the British Liaison Officer's report, 'penetrated everywhere at surprising speed, the ventilation fans being full on at the time.'[11] As a result, two boiler rooms and one engine room had to be abandoned, although water pressure on the fire mains, after a brief interval, was restored, which was just as well because hatches had been left open on the hangar deck that enabled a fire to commence amidships on No.2 deck, the dense smoke making access for the fire-fighting teams very difficult. The suffocating pall spread through the ship and resulted in the loss of 352 officers and men with a further forty missing, the majority being caused by asphyxiation. Many men were trapped with no safe exit other than to jump from the ship and almost three hundred had to be picked out of the water by rescuing destroyers. Some seventy aircraft were burnt out in *Bunker Hill* and, as related, a high casualty rate was taken of her pilots killed by the explosions in the gallery deck ready room.

There was extensive fire damage on Deck 2 with machine shops, officers' quarters and living accommodation all burnt out. Fires here proved difficult to put out and although other blazes were reported as extinguished by 12.00, fires were still burning on Deck 2 at 15.30 when Mitscher was forced to shift his flag to *Enterprise*, along with a skeleton staff of two dozen officers and four dozen men. Ogawa's body was found inside the ship having remained largely intact. He had sent two signals back to his base prior to the attack: at 09.58 'I found enemy vessels' and, at 10.02, 'Now I am nose-diving into the ship.' A final death poem was found on his body.

It could have been even worse, for a third Kamikaze made a dive on the already stricken ship, but was taken under fire and shot down by the light cruiser *Wilkes-Barre* (CL-103, Captain Robert Lee Porter, Jr., USN). Even so, now Task Force 58 had been reduced by five big carriers, *Franklin, Wasp, Hancock, Intrepid* and *Bunker Hill*, as well as thirteen destroyers, since the start of *Iceberg*.

The *Ōhka* analysed

Designed by Ensign Ohta Mitsuo, serving with 405th *Kokutai*, in conjunction with the University of Tokyo's Aeronautical Research Institute, the *Ōhka* (Cherry Blossom) was in essence, a piloted, rocket-powered suicide weapon. Sailors in the US Navy dubbed this device *Baka* ('Fool') but in doing so did it a grave injustice for it was one of the first effective anti-ship missiles, systems that have dominated sea-air warfare ever since.

---

11. ADM199/590.

The concept was simple in that this flying bomb, instead of a technical solution to the complex problem of steering the missile into the target, had the computer replaced by the far more efficient human brain of the volunteer. It was at once more effective than any artificial device of the time, and Japan had an unlimited supply of young men willing to carry out that function. After examination at the Yokosuka, *Dai-Ichi Kaigun Koku Gijitsusho* (Naval Air Technical Arsenal), the device was deemed a practical weapon of war and proper planning commenced to produce it as such. The design accordingly became the Yokosuka MXY-7 Suicide Attacker and work commenced in earnest. Several variants were ultimately built but the only one to see active combat service was the Model 11. This aircraft had a total weight of 4,718lb of which the warhead itself comprised 2,646lb. The weapon was equipped with short, stubby wooden wings with a nose cone of high-explosives, a small pilot compartment and a power plant that comprised a three-stage acceleration sequence with three Type 4 Model 1 Mark 20 solid-fuel rocket motors. The whole device was carried under the belly of a specially-adapted twin-engined bomber, usually the Mitsubishi G4M2e Model 24J *Betty*, which had to close to within less than fifty-five miles, its maximum horizontal range, (approximately two miles per each 1,000ft of altitude at release) from its intended target. The optimum release height of the Ōhka was 27,100ft to achieve even this distance, and normal release, and therefore range, was lower, around 23,000ft with release at around twenty nautical miles. Once released the pilot would glide toward its selected objective as the rocket power was only good for three miles.

The approach was therefore almost silent, which added to its deadliness, but at the same time this glide period made it vulnerable to intercepting fighter attack although, as a target, it was very small. Once close enough the pilots activated the rockets which had a combined burn time of just 24 seconds. These could be fired in stages or all at once, and accelerated the bomb at high velocity. The acceleration sequence was calculated thus:

	Average speed (mph)	Yards covered
1st Rocket	350	1,368
2nd Rocket	450	1,760
3rd Rocket	550	2,152

The final three miles of an Ōhka's descent were covered in 24 seconds, an average acceleration of 12.5mph per second of flight and an impact speed of 600mph. This meant that it was virtually immune to AA fire at this time – with the 5in/38, the Ōhka would only be within firing range for 53 seconds; with the 40mm just 13 seconds and the 20mm only 5.5 seconds, and its own momentum would carry it into the target. On the limited plus-side was the fact that its wings and tail were made of plywood, the Ōhka would trigger a VT-fused projectile at a radii of from thirty to forty feet (9 to 12.2m). A defending fighter would, of course, have no chance of interception once the rocket was fired so the obvious aerial defence was to chop down the mother ship which, weighed down by the bomb, was slow, or shoot the Ōhka down during its glide period. As no conventional fuel tanks, engine nor propeller existed to either ignite or damage, its vulnerability was further reduced.

With an assumed rocket thrust of 1,763lb and a minimum glide angle of 5 degrees 35 minutes, they could achieve a maximum impact speed of 525 mph in horizontal approach and 618 mph if gliding at a 45 degree angle. The speed increased by 25 mph for each

5 degree increase in the down angle. The warhead consisted of 1,136lbs of Trinitro-Anisol. Two further variants – the 22, with a TSU-11 jet engine, and the 43, with an NE 22 turbo-jet, both with 1,763lb warheads, never reached operational status. The training of Ōhka pilots actually preceded the Kamikaze programme. However, the Ōhka was not invincible. A report[12] listed its weaknesses as, 1) a heavy wing loading of 70.6lbs per square foot, meaning that even minor damage could be fatal, and, 2) the stiffness of controls at high speed made accurate aiming by the pilot very difficult which was compounded by the low-level approach. We have already seen some cases of actual attacks where this was demonstrated.

In ten Ōhka attacks between April and May 1945, three resulted in hits, one in a damaging near miss and six in non-damaging misses. One of the more successful missions took place on 8 April 1945, when a group of nine *Betty* bombers with their Ōhka rocket bombs were sent against the American fleet. This time they achieved results and the destroyer *Mannert L. Abele* (DD-733), Commander A. E. Parker, USN) was struck by two of these weapons – one piloted by Lieutenant (j.g) Saburo Doi – and the ship was split in half and sank. The destroyer-minesweeper *Jeffers* (DMS-27) managed to hit another incoming rocket with AA fire at fifty yards (45.72m) range, preventing an impact, although the resulting aerial detonation caused widespread devastation of her upperworks.

Results such as these were sparse, but it was acknowledged by Allied intelligence that production numbers, estimated then at 200 per month, would rapidly increase and the only limiting factor was sufficient mother aircraft. One major setback to Japan's Ōhka programme was the sinking of the large aircraft carrier *Shinano* (Captain Toshio Abe, IJN) by the US submarine *Archerfish* (SS-311, Commander Joseph F. Enright, USN), on 28th November 1944. *Shinano*[13] sank the next day with fifty Ōhka on board, while thirty more were lost when the carrier *Unryu* (Captain Khnishi Kaname, IJN) was sunk by the submarine *Redfish* (SS-395, Commander Louis D. McGregor, USN) on 19 December 1944. Both carriers had been attempting to supply Manila with *Ohkas* and other material, though all were lost before they could be used.

The report also admitted:

'The *Baka* (Ōhka), Japan's first such weapon, presents the most difficult target our surface forces and aircraft have encountered in the war to date. It is also potentially the most dangerous anti-shipping weapon to be devised, being a guided missile with the best possible control – a human being.' The Achilles'-heel of this weapon remained the fact that while being deadly itself, the aircraft that had to carry it to the vicinity of the target were comparatively slow and vulnerable. As a result of generally meagre operational results, production and development ceased within a few months of introduction and were replaced by other concepts.

---

12. 'Baka – Flying Warhead', *C.I.C. (Combat Information Center)*, US Office of the Chief of Naval Operations, Washington DC, June 1945 Issue.
13. *Shinano* had been laid down as the third of the *Yamato* Class battleships, but after the Battle of Midway had been completed as an aircraft carrier. She was lost due to the inexperience of her crew, few of which had served afloat before and lack of training they received before being ordered to sea against her captain's protests.

Chapter Ten

Two Notable Radar Picket Actions

'I think of springtime in Japan while soaring to dash against the enemy.'

Lieutenant (j.g.) Nobuo Ishibashi

During the Okinawa campaign 25 ships were sunk and just over 250 were damaged by Kamikaze aircraft. In the sixty-one days between 16 January and 17 March 1945, suicide attacks in which Kamikaze pilots lost their lives occurred on only seven days. It is worth examining some of the many destroyer actions that took place while on radar picket duty at this time in detail.

What has been described as, 'A striking example of success by personnel whose controlling thought was, "Don't Give up the Ship"' was the action fought on 11 May by the radar pickets *Hugh W Hadley* DD-774, (*Allen M. Sumner* Class) whose captain, Commander L.C. Chamberlin, was senior officer of a small group of ships including the *Evans*, DD-552, (*Fletcher* Class) commanded by Commander F.C. Camp, USN. It is worthwhile quoting verbatim from the official reports of this stirring action to show exactly what odds were faced by such exposed pickets off Okinawa at this time. It also conveys, in stark reality, how their electronic equipment really worked in practice rather than theory.[1]

Commander Chamberlin reported:

'The USS *Hugh W. Hadley* (DD-774) was OTC [Officer in Tactical Command][2] of a force consisting of two destroyers, three LCSs and one LSM. In order to achieve manoeuvrability and concentrated gunfire, the following formation was ordered: the four small support ships in a diamond formation on a circle one thousand yards in diameter speed ten knots, reversing course every half hour; the two destroyers, in column, distance fifteen hundred yards, speed fifteen knots. When attacks commenced, both destroyers increased speed to twenty-seven knots and manoeuvred in vicinity of their support [vessels – author's note] to concentrate gunfire.

---

1. Secret Information Bulletin No. 24 – *Battle – Experience – Radar Pickets and Methods of Combating Suicide Attacks off Okinawa – March–May 1945* – United States Fleet, Headquarters of the Commander in Chief, Navy Department, Washington 25 DC, dated 20 July 1945.
2. It is normal naval practice to regard the name of the ship as being synonymous with her current commander at the time a report is referring to – all navies do it. The rationale being that, while commanding officers can change during an operation or battle (being killed or wounded and replaced), the ship remains integral and constant.

'On the morning of 11 May at 06.05, the Combat Air Patrol of twelve planes reported on station. At about 07.40, bogies were reported to the northeast. At 07.45, a large enemy float plane appeared through the mist and was taken under fire by both ships. Soon this plane headed away from the *Evans* and came directly for the *Hadley* which was about one mile and a half from the *Evans*. The plane was shot down by the *Hadley* at a range of 1200 yards. At about 07.55, numerous enemy planes were contacted by our instruments as coming toward the ship (and Okinawa) from the north, distance about 55 miles. One division of CAP was ordered out to intercept. Shortly thereafter, several enemy formations were detected, and the entire CAP was ordered out to intercept. Our Fighter Direction Officer in CIC has estimated that the total number of enemy planes was 156 coming in at different heights in groups as follows: Raid One: 36, Raid Two: 50, Raid Three: 20, Raid Four: 20 to 30, Raid Five: 20. Total 156 planes.

'At about 0755 the entire Combat Air Patrol was ordered out in different formations to intercept and engage the horde of enemy planes closing us and shortly we received reports from them that they had destroyed twelve planes. Then they were so busy that they could not send us reports, but we intercepted their communications to learn about forty to fifty planes were destroyed by them. CIC reported that there were no friendly planes within ten miles of this ship.

'From this time on the *Hadley* and the *Evans* were attacked continuously by numerous enemy aircraft coming at us in groups of four to six planes on each ship. During the early period, enemy aircraft were sighted trying to pass our formation headed for Okinawa. These were flying extremely low on both bows and seemingly ignoring us. *Hadley* shot down four of these.

'The tempo of the engagement and the manoeuvre of the two destroyers at high speed was such as to cause the *Hadley* and the *Evans* to be separated by distances as much as two and three miles. This resulted in individual action by both ships. Three times the *Hadley* suggested to the *Evans* that they close for mutual support and efforts were made to achieve this, but each time the attacks prevented the ships from closing each other. The *Hadley* closed the four small support ships several times during the engagement.

'From 0830 to 0900 the *Hadley* was attacked by groups of planes coming in on both bows. Twelve enemy planes were shot down by the *Hadley*'s guns during this period, at times firing all guns in various directions. The *Evans*, which at this time was at a distance of about three miles to the northward, was seen fighting off a number of planes by herself, several of which were seen to be destroyed. At 0900 the *Evans* was hit and put out of action. At one time toward the close of the battle when friendly planes were closing to assist us, the four support ships were prevented from shooting down two friendlies that they had taken under fire. One plane was seen to splash inside their formation due to their own gunfire. However, I am not able to give an accurate account of their action. They were very helpful in picking up my crew who were in the water, in coming alongside and removing wounded, and in helping us to pump.

'From this time on, the *Hadley* received the bulk of the attacks and action became furious with all guns firing at planes on all sides of the ship. CIC reported that the

Sugar George [SG] was filled with enemy planes. The Commanding Officer saw that the situation was becoming too much for one ship to handle and he ordered the Combat Air Patrol to close the formation and assist us. With outstanding courage, our planes fearlessly closed the ships and attacked enemy planes. They achieved great results and when the *Hadley* was finally helpless in the water our crew was sparked with renewed courage by the sight of our airmen driving off the remaining enemy aircraft.

'For 20 minutes the *Hadley* fought off the enemy single handed, being separated from the *Evans*, which was out of action, by three miles and from the four small support ships by two miles. Finally, at 0920, ten enemy planes which had surrounded the *Hadley*, four on the starboard bow under fire by the main battery and machine-guns, four on the port bow under fire by the forward machine-guns, and two astern under fire by the after machine-guns, attacked the ship simultaneously. All ten planes were destroyed in a remarkable fight and each plane was definitely accounted for. As a result of this attack, the *Hadley* was (1) hit by a bomb aft (2) by a *Baka* bomb seen to be released from a low-flying *Betty* (3) was struck by a suicide plane aft (4) hit by a suicide plane in the rigging.

'The ship was badly holed and immediately both engine rooms and one fireroom were flooded, and the ship settled and listed rapidly. All five-inch guns were out of action, a fire was raging aft of number two stack, ammunition was exploding, and the entire ship was engulfed in a thick black smoke which forced the crew to seek safety, some by jumping over the side, others by crowding forward and awaiting orders. The ship was helpless to defend herself and at this time the situation appeared hopeless. The Commanding Officer received reports from the Chief Engineer and the Damage Control Officer which indicated that the main spaces were flooded and that the ship was rapidly developing into a condition which would capsize her. The exploding ammunition and the raging fire appeared to be extremely dangerous. The engineers were securing the forward boilers to prevent them from blowing up. The order 'Prepare to abandon Ship' was given, and life rafts and floats were put over the side. A party of about fifty men and officers was being organized to make a last fight to save the ship, and the remainder of the crew and the wounded were put over into the water.

'From this point on, a truly amazing, courageous and efficient group of men and officers, with utter disregard for their own personal safety, approached the explosions and the fire with hoses and for fifteen minutes kept up this work. The torpedoes were jettisoned, weights removed from the starboard side, and finally the fires were extinguished, and the list and flooding controlled and the ship was saved. Although the ship was still in an extremely dangerous condition, one fireroom bulkhead held and she was finally towed safely to the Ie Shima anchorage.

'The total number of enemy planes destroyed by the *Hadley* in this period of one hour and thirty-five minutes of continual firing was twenty-three. This number includes twenty shot down to the water and three suicide hits.

'Our mission was accomplished. The transports at the Okinawa anchorage were saved from an attack by one hundred and fifty-six enemy planes by the actions of our ships. We bore the brunt of the enemy strength and absorbed what they had to throw at us. It was a proud day for destroyer men.'

The comment inserted by Washington was pertinent. 'The ship's mission was gallantly completed but inadequate air support was evident. Proper air support was necessary and urgent. Was the system in use too inflexible? Our fighters were outnumbered over 5 to 1. A picket should be part of a system and not just an uncoordinated unit.'

The report of the OIC of *Hugh W Hadley*'s fighter direction team stated:

'The action lasted from about 0750 until about 0915 at which time all enemy planes were shot down and both DDs of RP No.15 were out of action.

'Action began when high CAP intercepted and shot down one *Frances* by Viceroy 1. At the same time two float type planes were sighted by ship's lookout and low CAP. One *Paul* shot down by ship's five-inch battery. No further reports on the other, presumably shot down in the melee. Both pontoons of this plane exploded when it hit the water. Presumably it was specially prepared as a suicide plane, with pontoons filled with explosive, and equipped with contact detonators. This plane crashed 300 yards off the starboard beam while making a very low run on the ship.

'About 0800 this ship picked up a large bogey, 345 degrees, 100 miles from *Bolo*. Viceroy 11 and 13 at Angels 15 over Pt. Uncle was vectored out for an intercept as a single flight. Raid split at 30 miles from ship and CAP was split to intercept each half. Viceroy 13 tallyhoed six planes, Viceroy 11 tallyhoed 30 planes. Viceroy 13 quickly disposed of his six and went to the aid of Viceroy 11. Few, if any, of these planes escaped them. This is designated as Raid 1 on attached diagram. Raid 2, estimated fifty planes, flew directly over Pt. Uncle where *Panamint's* CAP of eight planes engaged them.[3] Heine 1 was asked to send help and his planes orbiting Pt. Tare were directed to proceed to Pt. Uncle and vicinity, and join the fray. No vectors were necessary.

'Raid 3 also appeared at this time and was on a course to pass to westward. Information was passed to *Lowry* (DD-770) in RP station 16 and he was asked to intercept it, which he did. His four-plane CAP tallyhoed twenty enemy planes and effectively disposed of them. At the height of the combat, Raids 4 and 5 appeared. Raid 5 flew directly into the melee to the northeast of us and was engaged. It was impossible to vector any planes to meet it as none were left unengaged.

'At this time Viceroy 11–1 reported he was out of ammunition but he was staying on to do what he could. He shortly reported forcing one *Betty* into the water and set the pace for all planes to standby. Several more planes were also forced down in this manner by pilots unknown. Raid 4 came in at the same time, passed by the melee intact and when 10 miles north of the ships, fanned out, circled the

---

3. *Panamint* (ACG-13), Captain E. E. Woods, USN, was a *Mount McKinley* Class Command and Air Control Ship (officially – General Communications Vessel) crammed with specialised electronic and radio equipment, and during Okinawa was the flagship of Rear Admiral Lawrence F. Reifsnider, USN, commander of Amphibious Group 4.

formation and attacked from all sides. This raid was opposed by Ruby 15 (two-plane RP patrol) only. Some enemy planes were shot down and a coordinated attack was partly broken up, but the majority of these planes got through to the ships and were mostly destroyed by AA gunfire.

'Both Ruby 15 planes began picking off stragglers at the beginning of the action, then opposed Raid 4, estimated twenty to thirty. When enemy planes closed, these two planes came in with them. One very outstanding feat by one of these two planes (believed to be Ruby 15–1, but not verified) was that though out of ammunition, he twice forced a suicide plane out of his dive on the ship and the third time forced him into such a poor position that the plane crashed through the rigging but missed the ship, going into the water close aboard. This was done while all guns were firing at the enemy plane. The highest award for flying skill and cool courage would not be too much for this pilot.

'His wingman also stayed at masthead height in the flak and assisted in driving planes away from the ship. At the time the ship was hit below the waterline, power failed, our VHF radios were already inoperative from antennas carried away by a diving plane, and all communications were lost except on SCR 610 battery operated emergency set on 34.8 MC. However, only three bogies were left airborne and they were all being harassed by the original CAP, now out of ammunition and low on fuel. It is believed these last planes were shot down by fighter reinforcements coming from Bolo under control of Ringtail Base. None escaped to return to Japan.

'First plane shot down was a *Frances* over Pt. Uncle by Viceroy 11, quite possibly the coordinator, as he was 20 miles ahead of the main bodies of planes and alone. There seemed to be an assortment of all types of planes, including many torpedo planes which were all destroyed before they launched torpedoes. Air traffic on the fighter net was too heavy to keep track of splashes. Before fighting became general, the CAP had shot down fifteen planes, ships' gunfire had hit and destroyed eleven for *Hadley*, four for one small craft, others unreported. After the big melee began no further attempt was made because all nets were already overcrowded with tactical traffic alone. No raids attacked the ships unopposed, and except for raid 4, stragglers from the melee were the only ones who were able to close the ships.

'From beginning to the end, the *Hadley* was under attack by planes attempting suicide dives. The ship was manoeuvred so that maximum battery fire was always presented. At one time this ship had seven different air targets under fire simultaneously. The Commanding Officer of this ship deserves special commendation for an exceptional job of defending his ship against terrible odds. Enemy planes were taken under fire many times without harm to friendly planes attacking the same target.

'Communications on IFD [Inter-Fighter Director] net were excellent. Gunfire shocks knocked loose patch panel connections repeatedly, but a man in radio control stood by and kept them operational. TBL[4] transmitter was used and it stayed

---

4. TBL was a HF radio transmitter with a frequency range of 175–600kc; 2,000–18,100 kc with a power output and emission of 200 watts A1; 200 watts A2, 200 watts A3.

functional even after terrific shock which knocked out most radios, until power failed. AN/ARC1 – Receiver[5] – failed after a few minutes of firing 5in batteries. SCR 624 – stayed functional during battle. SC 610 functional and used to call support ships for assistance and to pick up survivors after all other communications were a casualty. TCS – Both failed from shock of explosion in engineering spaces. TDQ transmitter, RCK receiver[6] perfect performance until diving plane tore down antennas. Net discipline very good on IFD (Inter-Fighter Director). Net discipline by all planes and most stations on fighter nets was very good. Ringtail Base had a tendency to talk too much and crowded more important tactical traffic off the air.

'Radar performance – Excellent performance was given by both SC and SG radars. Fire control was not available for other purposes than gunnery. Fighter Direction Team – The CASCU (Commander Aircraft Support Control Unit) radar-men manned the air department of CIC and gave the best performance I have ever witnessed. All raids were picked up at maximum range and perfect track; estimates of composition and altitude were put on the board by this crew without prompting.

'Enemy tactics – Each raid seemed to split up into general melee as soon as attacked by our planes. Most stayed in plane-to-plane combat, but many from each raid, and especially Raids 2 and 4, bypassed the dog-fighting and came on in to attack the ships. One common approach was for two planes to come in close as a formation, then, when within machine-gun range, to split and each attempt a dive at the ship. Nearly all attacks on ships were potential suicide attacks, but the same plane would give way to avoid collision with one of our planes which was attacking it without ammunition. Little, if any, window was observed although unused window was recovered from wreckage aboard the *Hadley*. Raid 4 made a good coordinated attack. They came in and when 10 miles from the ship fanned out into several groups which circled the formation and then pressed home simultaneous attacks from all directions. They were not diverted by our planes but pressed home attacks on shipping until shot down by AA or forced into the water by CAP planes which were by now were nearly all out of ammunition.'

The Headquarters comments from Washington DC annexed to this report were critical. 'These tactics make it obvious that the best accepted principles of Fighter Direction must be followed. Could the simultaneous attacks from all directions have been prevented by breaking up the initial circling of enemy planes for advantageous positions? Were all raids opposed by adequate fighters? Were the fighters kept between the raid and base? The Pickets were harassed and finally hit by unmolested enemy planes.'

This criticism is notable in that that not a single word was said about the fact that earlier raids had used up all the CAP aircraft available save for two, and that these had no

---

5. A ten-channel, crystal controlled transceiver for fighter control with 100–157 megacycle frequencies, 6 watts A3 emissions.
6. VHF Ship to aircraft with 115–156 megacycle frequencies, crystal controlled, 45 watts A1 power.

ammunition! Nor that two destroyers had diverted the best part of fifty aircraft from the main targets and destroyed almost all of them.

Commander Chamberlin also included comments on particular facets of the action. 'The ship was put out of action by a *Baka* Bomb. It was released from a large lumbering *Betty* which came in from astern during the final attack, altitude about 600 feet. The bomb appeared to be about one and one half times as large as a 21in torpedo. On each side were very short stubby wings about one-third the usual normal wing length of a plane. There was no engine. The bomb struck the ship on the starboard side at frame number 105, which is the bulkhead between the after engine room and forward fireroom. The explosion from this bomb was terrific and some decks were lifted about 20 inches causing ankles and knees to be broken or strained. Three large engineering spaces were immediately flooded and the ship settled in the water rapidly.'

Washington commented that, 'Three large engineering spaces were flooded but the ship was saved. The training and familiarisation of effective damage control procedures by the entire crew were demonstrated in this action. It will be remembered that the damage control parties were fighting raging fires, exploding ammunition, and flooded compartments, and taking care of the wounded.'

Chamberlin wrote too that, 'It can be recorded that the aviators who comprised the Combat Air Patrol assigned to the *Hadley* gave battle to the enemy that ranks with the highest traditions of our Navy's history. When the leader was asked to close and assist us, he replied, "I am out of ammunition but I am sticking with you." He then proceeded to fly his plane at enemy planes attacking in attempts to head them off. Toward the end of the battle I witnessed one Marine pilot attempting to ride off a suicide diving plane. This plane hit us but not vitally. I am willing to take my ship to the shores of Japan if I could have these Marines with me.' Washington merely noted – 'It was unfortunate that we had an insufficient number of fighter planes to do the job at hand.'

Vice-Admiral Marc Mitscher of Task Force 58 added his comments thus. 'Experience gained in this operation indicated that with improved radar equipment, the radar patrol line operating 30 to 40 miles in the direction of the enemy will be able to detect and destroy low-flying enemy planes before they sight the main force. This may very well be the answer to the suicide plane. For the present, planes approaching above 10,000 feet will be handled by the CAP over the task group. However, it is conceivable that with the introduction of SP radar, the radar patrol line will be able to handle a greater number of interceptions. If this condition materialises, a greater percentage of the CAP will be turned over to the radar patrol line FDO.'

With regard to lighter cannon, referred to throughout the report as 'machine-guns', Chamberlin's comments were in marked contrast to the majority of reports from the fleet. 'I was amazed at the performance of the 40mm and 20mm guns. Contrary to my expectation, these smaller guns shot down the bulk of the enemy planes. Daily the crews had dinned into their minds the following order: 'Lead that Plane.' Signs were painted at the gun stations as follows: 'Lead that Plane'. It worked; they led and the planes flew right through our projectiles.

'The fire discipline was strict, gunnery communication rapid and effective. Ammunition expended:

509 rounds of 5in/38 Calibre VT
292 rounds of 5in/38 Calibre AA
8950 rounds 40mm HET [high explosive tracer.]
3980 rounds 20mm HEI [high explosive incendiary]
2010 rounds of 20mm HEIT [high explosive incendiary tracer]
801 charges smokeless powder.'

The magnificent fight of the *Evans*

The part played by the *Evans* was related by Commander Camp.

'The *Evans* and *Hadley* departed from the Hagushi anchorage on the afternoon of 10 May 1945, under orders of CTG 51.5, and arrived on Radar Picket Station #15 about 1500. Other ships in support on that station were *LSM 193*, *LCS 82*, *LCS 83* and *LCS 84*. The latter four ships were disposed in a diamond formation 1000 yards on a side, their course reversed about every half hour by signal, speed maintained at 10 knots. *Hadley* and *Evans* were in column in that order, speed 15 knots, distance 1500 yards, circling the support formation at a distance of about one mile. *Hadley* was Fighter Direction Ship and controlled a small Combat Air Patrol. *Evans* was Fire Support Ship. At 1934 that evening a *Kate* was shot down by this ship.

'From 0151 until 0343 11 May 1945, remained at General Quarters as there were enemy aircraft in immediate vicinity on reconnaissance missions. Early in the morning of the 11th, a general warning was received from Commander Fifth Fleet to expect heavy air raids during the day.

'Enemy aircraft were again in the area from 0640 to 0654, after which we were in the clear until commencement of the action which this report covers.

'During this action the sea was calm, wind 12 knots from 170 degrees T [True] barometer 29.90" starting to rise, air temperature dry bulb 74 degrees F [Fahrenheit] , wet bulb 71 degrees F, main injection temperature 78 degrees F. There were low scatter stratocumulus clouds at about 5000 feet, and a higher layer of altostratus clouds, total of sky covered about seven-tenths. Visibility moderate to good, from 5 to 10 miles. The calm sea and light wind were very favourable factors in rescuing men blown overboard and in saving the ship itself.

'At 0745 there were radar indications of a bogie coming in from the north, and at 0751 a seaplane was sighted about 10 miles on the port quarter own formation base course 055 degrees T. Although from the side view it appeared possible that the seaplane was friendly, the ship went to General Quarters, set Condition ' Able' and increased speed to 27 knots. By 0753 the plane had been identified as a twin-float *Jake* and the main battery opened fire, followed by 40mm and 20mm guns as range closed, target angle zero; the ship was manoeuvred to bring as many guns as possible to bear. At 0757 the plane was shot down 1000 yards on the starboard quarter, a tremendous explosion out of all proportion to its size resulting when it hit the water.

'During the following account it should be borne in mind that it is impossible to give true bearings in most cases due to the fast pace of the action, and because the ship was being manoeuvred at maximum available speeds of from 28 to over 30 knots, with the purpose of bringing as many guns as possible to bear, and at the last moment to take violent evasive action, reversing the direction of a well-outlined turn if possible. Whenever opportunity offered, the *Hadley* was closed for mutual fire support, but the action was too furious to be entirely successful in this.

'There were no further contacts until 0830, when three low-flying planes were picked up by SG radar bearing 350 degrees T (off port quarter) at 10 miles. Commenced tracking immediately and opened fire with main battery at 0831. Shot down leading plane, a *Kate* at 6000 yards. The second *Kate* coming in 1500 yards directly behind the first received direct 5in hit and disintegrated at 4000 yards. The third *Kate*, which had changed course to its left and was closing on a bearing of 030 degrees T, went down in flames as a result of 40mm fire 500 yards off *Evans'* port beam. All three of these planes were shot down within two minutes. A severe enemy air attack was developing and planes closing from all directions.

'At 0835 with *Evans* closing *Hadley* from 3500 yards on his starboard quarter, *Evans* and *Hadley* both opened fire with 5in on an enemy aircraft (type undetermined) closing on *Hadley*'s starboard beam and ahead of *Evans*. Hits were observed and the plane blew up dead ahead of *Evans*, and about 3000 yards on beam of *Hadley* (an assist with *Hadley*). At 0839 a *Zeke* approached from high on starboard quarter in steep dive, taken under fire by *Evans'* 5in battery at 7000 yards, by 40mm at 3500 yards, and shot down in flames at 2500 yards. At 0841 a *Zeke* approached from high on starboard quarter in steep suicide dive and was shot down by 40mm and 20mm fire, hitting the water 800 yards on starboard beam. At 0845 a *Tony* approached on *Evans'* port bow toward *Hadley* (then on *Evans'* port bow 3000 yards. Hits were observed and plane crashed close to the port quarter of the *Hadley* (an assist with *Hadley*).

'Less than two minutes later a *Tony* approached from high and deep on port quarter in a very steep dive, was taken under fire by 40mm and 20mm, and set on fire. It dropped a bomb close aboard on starboard bow, and was shot down by 5in battery at 1500 yards off the starboard bow going away. At 0849 an *Oscar* approached from port quarter in shallow dive at high speed. Taken under fire by 5in battery at 6000 yards and 40mm battery at 4000 yards, it crashed in flames 1000 yards off port quarter of *Evans*. Less than a minute later, without ceasing fire and with 5in guns in automatic, the director was slewed forward from port quarter to port beam and an approaching *Jill* was taken under fire at 10,000 yards. This *Jill* was shot down at 7000 yards.

'At 0851 a *Kate* was observed closing *Evans* rapidly on a bearing of 330 degrees relative and taken under fire at 5000 yards by main battery. The enemy plane, although hit and burning severely, continued to close until at about 200 yards broad on port bow it launched a torpedo. Hard left rudder was applied, with the ship making about 10 knots, and fortunately the torpedo crossed just ahead of bow [at] less than 25 yards. The *Kate*, already on fire, was shot down going away 2000 yards off starboard bow by 5in fire.

'At 0854 a *Tony* approaching from *Evans'* port bow was taken under fire by *Hadley* and *Evans'* main batteries at 7000 yards, with hits observed from both ships. Plane was shot down an equal distance from *Hadley* and *Evans* at 3500 yards (an assist with *Hadley*). 0856 observed a *Val* coming in from high and deep on port quarter. It was taken under fire by main battery at 6000 yards, by machine-guns at 4000 yards (3657.6m). Numerous hits were scored and the enemy plane set on fire. Although he attempted to suicide, it appeared the plane was out of control as it crossed over ship and crashed in water 2000 yards off starboard bow.

'0901 *Oscar* approached from deep on port quarter in shallow high speed dive. Taken under fire by main battery at 6000 yards, hit and set on fire at 4000 yards. This *Oscar* dropped a bomb which landed 400 yards off *Evans'* port quarter. It then made an unsuccessful suicide attempt, and finally crashed 1500 yards on port bow.

'By 0902 two more boilers had been cut in and *Evans* was making speeds in excess of 30 knots as we manoeuvred radically to avoid suicide planes. At the same time the main battery was downing the *Oscar*, a low-flying *Jill* approached from port beam directly toward *Evans*, taken under fire by the 40mm at 5000 yards. Machine-guns shot off port wing and the *Jill* crashed barely 500 yards from ship on port beam. At 0904 a *Tony* coming in port quarter at an estimated altitude of 2500 feet was shot down by *Evans'* first salvo at 9000 yards.

'At 0907 *Evans* received first hit by suicide plane when a *Judy*, approaching from the port bow, although hit and damaged by *Evans'* gunfire, struck at water line port side frame 16. Hit resulted in a hole 3ft by 4ft, which flooded lower sound room and forward crew's living compartment. No power was lost, although telephone communications with CIC went out temporarily due to breakage of telephone junction box caused by shock.

"The next enemy plane encountered was a *Tony* at 0909 at about 2000 feet altitude and in a shallow dive, approaching on port beam, was taken under fire by *Evans*, main battery at 8000 yards and was destroyed as direct 5in hit was scored at 3500 yards.

'Less than two minutes later an enemy aircraft (type undetermined) approached from port beam in high speed glide dive from approximately 3000ft. Taken under fire by main battery and machine-guns which set him on fire, he succeeded in suiciding aboard in vicinity of frame 122 below waterline. This plane was carrying a bomb or torpedo which, from divers' reports, exploded just outside the after fireroom hull. The pilot's body was found on the fantail. The after fireroom and after engine room flooded instantaneously as a large portion of the bulkhead between them was blown out. Steering control was lost temporarily at this time but quickly shifted to trick wheel.[7] Speed was reduced to approximately 18 knots.

---

7. Hand-operated steering wheel used as emergency steering gear on destroyers when electromechanical steering fails or if there should occur any signal failure between the steering wheel on the bridge and the receiving unit. In such instances the helmsman standing by at the after steering position operates the trick wheel and receives steering orders on the sound-powered telephone.

'At 0913 enemy *Oscar* in steep dive from high altitude out of sun, on port quarter, was taken under fire by 5in battery and after 40mm. Although hit by gunfire, this plane was successful in suiciding *Evans*. This suicide *Oscar* was carrying a bomb which was released just before plane crashed through superstructure deck over galley. The bomb penetrated main deck and exploded in the forward fireroom, causing both boilers to explode. At the same time, a second enemy suicide, also an *Oscar*, approached from the starboard bow, under fire and being hit by machine-gun batteries, struck the after starboard boat davit, crashed to the main deck just forward and outboard of the other *Oscar*, and resulted in gasoline fires on main deck, bridge and director deck. One of the pilots was found in the galley, the other on the main deck. All light, power, steam, water pressure and most communications were lost and *Evans* was dead in the water. The diesel generator cut in, but was secured as fuel oil and water covered part of the switchboard in that compartment.

'At 0925 the final attack of the action occurred when an unidentified enemy aircraft was sighted dead ahead at 4000 yards, diving on the ship, with two F4Us of the Combat Air Patrol in hot pursuit. The enemy was taken under fire by 40mm machine-guns and hits by #2 40mm at 2500 yards were observed on port wing. These hits, with perhaps others by the Combat Air Patrol, disturbed the plane's flight attitude sufficiently to cause it to miss the bridge. The plane passed down the port side and crashed astern, close aboard.

'As there was no pressure on the fire main, it was necessary to form bucket brigades. Using 40mm cans, buckets, CO2 extinguishers and gasoline handy billy pumps, progress was being made in extinguishing the fires then the USS *LCS 84* came alongside to starboard at 0929. The assistance rendered by the *LCS 84* was invaluable. By 0950 all fires were extinguished and, with salvage gear furnished by *LCS 84* plus handy billies *Evans* had in operation, pumping was started in the forward engine room and compartment A-302–C. At this time the ship's draft was 22 feet (6.70m) forward and 17 feet 6 inches aft (5.33m) Twenty-seven of the wounded were treated aboard *Evans* and transferred to *LCS 84* for further transfer to USS *Ringness* (APD-100), Lieutenant Commander William G. Meyer, USN.[8] The latter also took off 120 of our personnel not required for salvage work.

'Although there had been a maximum list of 3 degrees to starboard, topside weights were a source of concern. The port anchor had been jettisoned earlier when we were taking water from the hole in the port bow. All depth-charges, smoke screen generators, and a considerable amount of topside ammunition were jettisoned. Eight torpedoes were fired, the remaining two torpedoes and tubes having been damaged by suicide plane crash.

'At 1045 the USS *LCS 82* completed picking up personnel blown overboard, came alongside to port and immediately commenced pumping flooded compartments. All bulkheads in compartments adjacent to those flooded were shored by *Evans'* repair parties.

---

8. Light Transports converted from Destroyer Escorts while building. *Ringness* was the former *Crosley* Class destroyer DE-590.

'*LCS 84* shifted to the port side and at 1108 USS *Harry E. Hubbard* (DD-748), Commander Arthur Montgomery Purdy, USN, came alongside to starboard. The ship rendered great assistance by lending pumps and salvage equipment, in addition to furnishing impulse charges which enabled us to fire five of the eight torpedoes which were jettisoned. At 1110 *LCS 82*, making no headway in pumping after engineering spaces, shifted suctions to forward engineering spaces.

'At 1300 when *Hubbard* cleared the side, the USS *Arikara* (ATF-98), Lieutenant John Aitken,[9] came alongside, commenced pumping forward engineering spaces, and furnished additional pump for the forward living compartment. From this moment on, definite progress was made. At 1350 the *Arikara* cast off from alongside and commenced towing from ahead for the anchorage at Ie Shima. The draft had been reduced forward by two feet and aft by one foot. At 1450 USS *Cree* (ATF-84), Lieutenant P. Bond, came alongside to starboard and assisted in towing and salvage. From 1630 to 1900 *Evans* pumped fuel overboard. With *Cree* alongside to starboard, *LCS 82* and *LCS 84* to port and the *Arikara* towing, the *Evans* made the remainder of the trip to Ie Shima without incident. The long day was brought to a close when the *Cree* dropped her anchor at 1915.'

The Official comment here was more enthusiastic 'Radar Pickets and their associates are deserving of the highest praise for their outstanding performance of duty.'

The gunnery officer of the *Evans* added his comments thus:

'During the attack I observed thirty to thirty-five enemy aircraft shot down and crash into the sea. Under such a rapidly developing and sustained attack, detailed data covering the action in places is obscure, but the planes accounted for by this vessel (fifteen unassisted, three assists with the *Hadley*, one assist with CAP, plus four which through damaged were successful in suiciding the *Evans*) have been verified by the ship's officers and other personnel.

'Japanese suicide tactics remained more or less unchanged as reported by other ships that have undergone suicide attacks, *with one notable exception*[10] that is, not until the closing minutes of the action, when practically all of their aircraft had been expended, was there any indication of a coordinated attack. The final attack, however, was well coordinated and in the moments just prior to the *Evans* being hit, this vessel had three aircraft under fire simultaneously.

'The first suicide, which hit the port bow (frame 16) at the water line, did little damage; the entire gun battery remained in full operation. The second plane, whose bomb exploded in the after fireroom (frame 122), severed all power and fire control cables to the after guns (5in guns 3–4–5, 40mm 3–4–5). Power to these guns was never regained but they continued to fire in manual. The third and fourth suiciders, which hit almost simultaneously in the forward fireroom, destroyed all power to the forward guns (5in guns 1–2, 40mm 1–2, Main Battery Director,

---

9. An Ocean Tug of the *Abnaki* Class.
10. My italics.

Computer and stable Element). All guns were operative in manual. The last plane
to attack was hit in the port wing by #2 40mm (firing in manual) and passed down
the port side, crashing approximately 250 yards astern.

'After all power had been lost, the Gunnery Officer ordered the Main Battery
Director abandoned and its crew to assist in salvage work as he, himself, proceeded
to assume duties as Executive Officer, taking charge of Damage Control and
Salvage Operations. This was done since the Executive Officer had been critically
wounded. Also at this time the Assistant Gunnery Officer assumed duties as
Gunnery Officer, taking over control duties of the 5in guns which were still
operative in manual power local control as well as machine-gun control. These
batteries were kept manned and alert until arrival at Ie Shima anchorage.

'During this attack *Evans* fired approximately 800 rounds of 5in/38, 3400 rounds
of 40mm and 5500 rounds of 20mm ammunition. In addition, all depth-charges,
smoke screen tanks and eight torpedoes were jettisoned to improve stability as the
ship was rapidly settling.

'The performance of the ordnance equipment was magnificent, with not one
casualty in the 5in battery until the ship was struck by the second suicide.

'The conduct of personnel was outstanding. Despite the fact that three aircraft
were shot down within 800 yards of the ship and that there were near misses by a
500–pound bomb and a torpedo dropped within 200 yards of the ship, all hands
remained at their stations and continued to fire their mounts until cease firing was
ordered.'

The captain of the *Evans* fully agreed with comments made by officers from both the
Newcomb (DD-586) and the *Mannert L. Abele* (Commander Alton E Parker) in that
he thought that, 'ships assigned radar picket duty have torpedo mounts removed and
replaced by quad 40mm batteries, thereby reducing the hazard of exploding torpedoes
as well as increasing ship's anti-aircraft armament.' Washington commented that, 'The
present 2200–ton destroyers fitted for Radar Picket duty have this feature.'

The CO of *Evans* made a list of pertinent points concerning air attacks on pickets.
'Each air attack presents its own peculiar problems. In this one there were a total of about
fifty planes attacking *Hadley* and *Evans* over a period of an hour and a half. It was our
good fortune that during most of the action the planes came in singly or in a group from
one bearing at a time. We were thus enabled to concentrate guns on one attack, shoot
it down, and shift immediately to the next attack. In the final stages, when planes were
diving from three directions simultaneously, one out of the sun, we could only continue
to shoot and manoeuvre at maximum speed, and hope for the best.

'*Hadley* and *Evans* attempted to remain in close support of each other, and succeeded
several times in rendering mutual assistance. The frequency and varied direction of
attacks was such that some separation was inevitable as we manoeuvred at high speed and
turned radically to bring all guns to bear.

'It is felt that the following points should be stressed in this type of action:

(a) Lookouts: Use all available bridge and control personnel, and insist on a strict sector
     watch, especially when a plane is being flamed elsewhere.

(b) SG Radar: Invaluable for early warning on low-flying bogies.

(c) When under observation, change course frequently ten, twenty or thirty degrees.

(d) When attack begins, or before if possible, increase speed to maximum.

(e) Manoeuvre to bring maximum number of guns to bear on each attack. Then, when possible, change direction of turn at the last moment.

(f) Use rapid continuous fire, with ammunition ratio four VT to one AA Common (HQ noted– 'The experts recommend 100 percent VT fused projectiles.'

(g) Although against doctrine, it was found necessary in many cases to shift fire from one target flamed to the next attack, keeping guns in full automatic and continuing to shoot while slewing director.

(h) Use of Mark 53 ammunition: Excellent performance in every way, especially in that no premature were observed on very low flying bogies.

(i) Use of push buttons and synchro motor on computer for rapidly changing target angle. (Note from HQ read 'This computer will be under consideration by the Bureau of Ordnance'.'

The two destroyers had certainly made a splendid fight of it and both ships survived. Sadly both were so damaged that, ultimately, they were deemed surplus for the requirements of the post-war fleet, and both were scrapped in 1947 as not worth full repair. A sad end for a gallant duo.

Chapter Eleven

Okinawa – Fight to the Finish

'My greatest concern is not about death, but rather of how I can be sure of sinking an enemy carrier. Ensigns Miyazaki, Tanaka and Kimura, who will sortie as my wingmen, are calm and composed. Their behaviour gives no indication that they are momentarily awaiting orders for their final crash–dive sorties. We spend our time in writing letters, playing cards, and reading. I am confident that my comrades will lead our divine Japan to victory.'

Ensign Susumu Kaijisu, Genzan Air Group

The failure of the US Army ashore to bring the stubborn resistance of the defending Japanese to an early resolution led to some recriminations and much adverse press coverage at the time. Army commanders had already amassed a hefty casualty list, and were reluctant to press the pace and raise their casualties still higher. Understandably, the sailors offshore, undergoing almost daily poundings from Kamikazes, with an ever-rising butcher's bill of their own and a whole lagoon of damaged ships, saw things rather differently. On 12 May 1945 the old battleship *New Mexico*, now commanded by Captain John Meade Haines, took a Kamikaze from astern which crashed into her gun deck and knocked a 30ft hole in her funnel. Blazing petrol sent a 200ft flame plume into the sky and AA ammunition tumbled down into her fireboxes. She was heavily damaged with fifty-eight of her crew killed, three missing and a further 119 wounded. She remained on station for a further fortnight before leaving to repair at Guam. The following day the destroyer *Bache* (DD-470) and destroyer escort *Bright* (DE-747, Lieutenant-Commander William A McMahan) were both damaged.

Enterprise (CV-6) finally stopped

An early morning Kamikaze attack was mounted on the 14 May by a force of twenty-eight A6M5 Model 52C *Zeke*s from the 6 *Tsukuba*, 11 *Kenmu* and 8 *Shichisho* units. They took off from Kanoya NAS in two groups, twelve at 05.25 and sixteen more at 06.19 with orders to strike targets of opportunity. They had a fighter escort of forty planes designed to clear the way for them to the target. Six of the Kamikazes turned back and failed to complete the mission but the remaining twenty-two carried on. Two US Task Groups were sighted at 07.18, some 140 nautical miles from Miyazaki by the escorting fighters.

Having resumed operations after earlier Kamikaze damage, the *Enterprise* was in the thick of it again on 14 May. She had gone to General Quarters at 03.57 when reports were received of bogeys in the area but even so was taken by surprise when, at 06.53, a Kamikaze appeared from out of the cloud base at an altitude of 1,500 feet in a 30–degree dive. The carrier's AA guns commenced firing and the rudder was put over hard left for an emergency turn, but it was all too late. The *Zeke*, piloted by twenty-two-year-old Lieutenant (j.g.) Shunsuke Tomiyasu[1], and with a 1,100lb armour-piercing, delayed-action bomb aboard, continued in toward the *Enterprise* and it appeared it had misjudged the dive and would narrowly miss astern, but, when about 200 yards from the carrier, the young pilot made an instant correction and, in the words of the report, 'flipped the plane over in a left-hand snap roll to steepen the dive to about 45–degrees' and, in this inverted posture, "crashed" the flight deck, 'just abaft the forward elevator, slight to port of the centreline.'[2] The impact punched a hole about twelve feet long by twenty feet wide through the flight deck temporarily rendering aircraft operations impossible. Continuing their penetration further into the ship, both aircraft and bomb destroyed a bank of transformers that lay in their path whose immobilisation immediately knocked out the power to group I and II 5in batteries and the Mk.14 sights of Nos.1, 2 and 4 20mm batteries. Also rendered inoperative were Nos.1, 2, 3, 4 and 6 40mm mountings and their Mk.37 directors, as both normal and alternative power supply cables housed in the trunk of the elevator were cut by their passage. Additionally, two controllers for the 5in ammunition hoists were wrecked in a similar manner.

The Kamikaze, engine and pilot came to rest at the base of the forward elevator pit, the bomb having separated as they brushed the transverse bend at frame 40. The bomb's path took it through the elevator pit at second deck level and on into compartment A-305-A at third deck level where it exploded in a rag storeroom. This started a big fire in the elevator pit which then set fire to the aircraft in her deck park. The most spectacular external visual manifestation of the detonation was the blasting of a huge section of the forward elevator 400 feet into the sky above the ship, along with a plume of smoke and debris from the rendered decking which fell back into the sea. Other pieces of the elevator, decking girders and bracket parts rained down on the flight deck on both sides of the smoking aperture that remained. The remaining segment of the elevator was entirely inverted by the blast and fell back into the elevator pit upside down. In the hangar space the blast, far from wholly venting with the elevator itself, caused enormous damage and bulged the flight deck upward right across the whole width of the ship by as much as 3½ feet at its centre on frame 46. Hangar deck curtains were demolished as far along as frame 140 and disabled both flight deck bomb elevators on the starboard side.

Nor was the damage confined to blast, for a 6in fire-main loop and 3in damage control main riser were wrecked with the water flooding from both. Other air-lines and water pipes, both fresh and drainage were also fractured. The power cables for the forward catapults were cut, electrical damage was widespread with all forward lighting and

---

1. Commander Edward Peary Stafford , USN, Rtd., in his book *The Big E,* calls this pilot 'Tomi Zai', and claimed this was the name on a calling card found on the body, and even named Chapter 24 that way. This seems to be a corruption of Tomiyasu. Fortunately, some very dedicated research by Kan Sugahara has established the truth. See *Who Knocked the Enterprise Out of the War, Naval History* Magazine, April 2008, Volume 22, Number 2. Stafford's account was published in New York 1962.
2. USS *Enterprise* (CV6) *War History Narrative.* Damage Report No. 59: 14 May 1945, Bureau of Ships, Navy Department, Washington DC.

telephonic communications with the rest of the ship extinguished forward of frame 38. Amazingly her engines remained intact and she was able to maintain her position in the formation while the damage control parties went about their business very efficiently.

With regards to the human losses, relative to the physical destruction wrought it might be regarded as surprisingly small. Some fourteen men died and a further sixty-eight of her crew were injured, many being badly burnt. As for the attacker, the body of Shunsuke Tomiyasu was found at the bottom of the elevator well – along with the engine of his aircraft. Crew members later salvaged as war mementos parts of the aircraft's propeller and fuselage. Like *Saratoga* earlier, the 'Big E' survived this attack, but never operated aircraft again as her repairs at Puget Sound Navy Yard were not completed until 13 September 1945, when, although once more fully battle worthy, her war was finally over.

Other Kamikaze damage inflicted on 17 May was to the destroyer *Douglas H. Fox* (DD-779, Commander Raymond Maurer Pitts). The following day the *Sims* (APD-50, Lieutenant-Commander Charles Greif Raible) was damaged and on 20 May the destroyer *Thatcher* (DD-514, Lieutenant-Commander Charles Richardson Chandler) was damaged as were the *Chase* (APD-54, Lieutenant-Commander George Osmon Knapp II) and *Register* (APD-92, Lieutenant-Commander J R Cain, Jr.). On 24 May, the destroyer *Guest* (DD-472, Lieutenant-Commander Marvin Granville Kennedy) was damaged while high-speed transport *Bates* (APD-47, Lieutenant-Commander Augustus Wilmerding) and her CO killed, *LSM-135* were both sunk.

Stormes damaged

Few warships can have received their baptism of fire as swiftly as the brand-new *Allen M. Sumner* Class destroyer *Stormes* (DD-780, Commander William Naylour Wylie, USN). She had only arrived at Hagushi as part of the escort of the heavy cruiser *Louisville* (CA-28, Captain Rex Legrande Hicks) on 23 May to join the 5th Fleet. She was immediately assigned to Radar Picket Station No.15 and sailed on that duty early on the 24th, and experienced the first enemy attacks without incident that day and during the night. At first light the following morning the weather was bad, with poor visibility and intermittent rain squalls. The weather steadily deteriorated as the day wore on and by 09.00 heavy and low overcast dominated, with visual range down to 4,000 yards. *Stormes* was in company with the destroyers *Ammen* (DD-527, Commander James Harvey Brown Jr.) and *Drexler* (DD-741, Commander Ronald Lee Wilson, USN), supported by the pall-bearers LCS *(L) 52, 61, 85* and *89* in position Lat 27–22.5N, Long 127–48E north of Okinawa.

All ships went to General Quarters at 08.00 when reports were received of enemy aircraft closing from the north-west. A strong CAP of fourteen F4U Corsairs was overhead and they duly deployed to intercept the bogeys. At 08.25 observers aboard *Stormes* saw the Corsairs knock down an *Oscar* at a distance of around 10,000 yards on a bearing of 340 degrees (True). But other Japanese aircraft were constantly probing and were difficult to spot. At 09.03 another bogey was recorded closing the group from the south. The outer ring of the CAP apparently missed this aircraft coming in from this unexpected direction and, although the enemy was picked up in the CIC, there were so many friendly aircraft contacts on the SG-1 that they saturated the radar scope with their IFF. Control was on the bearing but could not define the contact sufficiently. Here was a classic case of too many cooks spoiling the broth and confusing the defence. By 09.04 *Stormes* was on course 045 degrees and was making twenty knots when a brief glimpse was caught at a mere 4,000 yards of the Kamikaze bearing 160 degrees relative through the rain and overcast. The target angle was 060 degrees and was closing at an altitude of around 1,500ft. At 09.05 she was sighted again, seen to pass between two F4Us heading in the opposite direction and then lost to sight again. However, Control now acquired this target and 'commence fire' was ordered, but there was a delay in doing so for fear of hitting the two friendly aircraft and also for the fact that the target's trajectory, which was crossing astern of the ship, was such that fire would have to be opened over friendly ships. As the hostile appeared to head away from *Stormes* across her stern, Commander Wylie swung his command hard to port enabling all guns to bear. The aircraft came out of the murk bearing 280 degrees (Relative), in a 30–degree dive at about 2,000 yards and seemed to be deliberately targeting the *Ammen*, the next ship ahead, in a shallow diving attack. All three twin 5in batteries opened fire and their bursts were close to the target. Number 3 mounting (aft) was controlled by the Mk.37 Director and of the two forward mountings, No.1 was controlled by Director 1 (due to the high elevation of the attacker) and No.2 by Director 2. *Drexler*, astern, apparently did not fire, but *Ammen* joined in with main batteries and automatic weapons. *Stormes* got off six rounds AAC[3] while the light weapons, in the brief interval allowed, contributed 120 rounds of 40mm and 150 rounds of 20mm, some of which hit and the enemy was burning during its final approach.

However, the enemy pilot suddenly threw his machine, identified now as a *Tojo*[4], into a half-loop at bearing 315 degrees (Relative) and 'came down in a twisting turn overhead at an angle of 60–70 degrees; turned on its back and struck the *Stormes* on the after torpedo mounting at 09.05. At the time of the hit *Stormes* was accelerating to 25 knots and executing a hard left turn. The 500lb bomb it released just prior to impact, plunged through the superstructure deck just abaft the torpedo mounting at frame 171, emerged through the after deckhouse at frame 172, and pierced the main deck at frame 173 and Berth deck at frame 176 before exploding in magazine C-305M, under her No.3 5in mount – having travelled twenty-eight feet internally through the ship. The detonation blew big holes in both the Berth deck and upper handling room, causing very heavy casualties, and demolished No.3 5in mounting. Simultaneously the downward blast blew open a large hole in the ship's bottom on the centreline, which extended from frame 176 to frame 186. The ship's back was broken, her keel being severed along with three longitudinal ribs on each side, and *Stormes*, stern sagged by six inches. The Gyro compass tumbled and severe fires were reported on the fantail (stern), and in the after deck house, which necessitated jettisoning the depth-charges. At the point of impact the after torpedo mount was demolished totally and a gasoline fire broke out. Two of the torpedo air flasks exploded blowing two tubes overboard complete with their warheads. The other three were knocked to the deck and jettisoned. The Japanese aircraft was totally destroyed by impact and fire with only a bit of one wing, the tail, a machine-gun barrel, housing and part of a connecting rod being identifiable.

---

3. AAC = anti-aircraft shells- common – as distinct from VT-fused AA shells.
4. A later study of the available evidence tended to indicate that it was, in fact, a *Zeke*.

Commander Wylie estimated that his ship had taken the impact well, suffering, (other than the temporary disabling of the Gyro) some loss of defensive fire power aft and a reduction in maximum speed, just twenty knots being maintained. Both forward mountings remained operational and were soon in action again. Personnel casualties were twenty-one men killed and fifteen wounded. All fires were brought under control within twenty minutes and were out within two hours. By noon, repair parties had shored up the threatened sections aft and plugged the holes. It was noted that *Stormes* was just one of many *Allen M. Sumner* Class destroyers that were able to promptly subdue a serious fire. 'The effectiveness of the fire protection system in the 2200–ton class has been repeatedly demonstrated.'[5] Matters were probably helped by the fact that the bomb exploded so deep inside the ship that the fire main remained unaffected and pressure was available from the forward pumps. The destroyer was low in the water but salvageable, her draft aft being 14ft 8ins before the hit and 17ft 6ins afterwards, while forward her draft was 13ft 4in prior to being struck and approximately 14ft subsequently with the waterline just below the first platform deck level. She was close-guarded by *Ammen* ahead and *Drexler* astern.

A fire broke out in No.2 engine room at 10.43 and steering control was lost, and she had to be steered by her engines, but within ten minutes this blaze was out and she regained steering control with her rudders. As usual with a damaged ship, her vulnerable state attracted further enemy attention. The two forward 5in mountings had again been in action at 09.20 against five unidentified aircraft which suddenly appeared out of driving rain at 4,000 yards range, but this ceased a minute later when they were identified as friendly. The same thing happened at 11.15.

At 12.27 the *Fletcher* Class destroyer *Sproston* (DD-577, Commander Fred R Stickney, USN) arrived and took over as her escort, and so began a long haul back to Kerama Retto for emergency repairs. *Stormes* finally arrived at Hagushi Anchorage, Okinawa Shima, and anchored in 27 fathoms, close to the *Crescent City* (APA-21, Captain Donald Loring Erwin), to transfer her dead and wounded. In his report Commander Wylie paid generous tribute to the skill of his adversary: 'The enemy pilot was an excellent flyer. He handled his plane quickly and executed an attack which presented an ever changing deflection problem at difficult position angles. He took full advantage of his tremendous speed without ever losing control of his plane. He executed a half roll to ensure a hit in the last 500 feet of his dive.'[6]

Due to the demands from the abnormally high number of damaged ships, *Stormes* was unable to enter the floating repair dock (*ARD-13*, Lieutenant-Commander Clarence S Williams), at Buckner Bay until 17 July where she was fully assessed. Her damaged hull was cut away and renewed to repair the rupture in her hull. The hull was cut at frame 182 and the stern was jacked up 7.5ins in order to align the after port shaft strut with the shaft line. The starboard strut was too far out of alignment and so *Stormes* had to return home

---

5. War Damage Report No. 51, Destroyer Report: *Gunfire, Bomb and Kamikaze Damage, including Losses in Action 17 October, 1941 to 15 August 1945*, dated 25 January 1947, Preliminary Design Section, Bureau of Ships, Navy Department, Washington DC.
6. Commander W. N. Wylie, USS *Stormes* DD 780, Serial 072, Action Report, dated 1 June 1945. pp 2.

on her port shaft only. She was floated out on 13 August and got underway two days later, being deemed sufficiently seaworthy. She reached Hunters Point on 17 September after a long, slow voyage via Saipan, Eniwetok and Pearl Harbor, during which she survived heavy weather conditions off California which saw her rolling up to 50–degrees, and began a three-month overhaul. She proved a tough old bird and was still serving as late as 1971 when she was sold to Iran.

Further Kamikaze victims 22–28 May

The minesweeper *Spectacle* (AM-305, Lieutenant G B Williams) was hit by a Kamikaze on 22 May and suffered twenty-five dead among her casualties. Sent back to the West Coast she was considered too badly damaged to repair and was subsequently written off. On 25 May the destroyer-minesweeper *Butler* (DMS-29) was hit by a Kamikaze suffering nine crewmen killed: damaged she was sent home to the States where she was considered to be not worth repairing and was later scrapped. Also on the 25th the destroyer escort *William C. Cole* (DE-641, Lieutenant Clay Harrold) was attacked by two Kamikazes. She shot down a *Tony*, and an *Oscar* that attempted to dive into her, but because of the ship's quick manoeuvring it only grazed a torpedo tube mounting as it passed low across the vessel. On the same day the former '4–piper' destroyer *Barry* (APD-29, Lieutenant-Commander Clemens Francis Head), which had been converted as a high-speed transport, was attacked by two Kamikazes – one of which hit and severely damaged her. She was patched up locally to be used as a 'decoy' target but was only too successfully sunk soon afterward as will be related. Similarly, also on 25 May, her sister ship *Roper* (APD-20, Lieutenant-Commander Ulysses Brooks Carter) was hit by a Kamikaze and so badly damaged that she was not considered worth repairing on return to the States.

On 26 May the destroyer escort *O'Neill* (DE-188, Lieutenant-Commander David Spence Bill, Jr.) was heavily struck, badly damaged and, after being patched up locally, was sent home to effect proper repairs. The following day, 27 May, *Forrest* (DMS-24, Lieutenant-Commander Sanford Elza Woodard) was targeted by three Kamikazes, two of which she shot down, but the third got through, badly damaging her and killing five of her crew. She too, upon return to the States, was written off as uneconomical to repair and scrapped. The same day saw the minesweeper *Dutton* (AG-8, Lieutenant F E Sturmer) hit and damaged, although in this case she was deemed worthy of repair and post-war was converted into a survey ship. Finally, on 28 May, the destroyer *Drexler* fought an epic battle, being singled out by several Kamikazes, and hit by one which knocked out all motive power and started large petrol fires aboard. Her guns continued in action, however, and she shot down several more attackers until a twin-engined *Francis* got through and struck her very hard – the impact immediately rolled the vessel right over and she sank in less than a minute taking with her 158 of her 357–man crew.

Equipping Destroyers for Radar Picket Duty

The first American destroyer fitted for Fighter Direction duties had been the *Fletcher* Class vessel *Trathen* (DD-530, Commander John Randolph Millett, USN) in the summer of 1943 and she had vectored fighters out against aerial targets with some success and was later joined by a sister in the same configuration. However, the importance of this in efficiently controlling the CAP had grown enormously in importance in the intervening eighteen months and that duty was part-and-parcel of the Advanced Radar Picket (or 'Tomcats') role at Okinawa. Their duties were not only to assist in controlling the returning air strikes from the fleet, but to give advance warning of incoming bogies and try and identify enemy aircraft infiltrating the fleets' air space by the favourite Japanese tactic of following them home.

Following the experience in the Philippines a conference held on the last day of December 1944, with representatives of both 5th and 7th Fleets, and Destroyer Command Pacific, the need for specialist ships was accepted. They were to be equipped with SR (search radar) on the foremast and SG with radar direction finding (RDF), and additional VHF radio equipment, talk between ships (TBS) tactical radio communication sets and other refinements. YE and YG homing beacons were fitted and they acted as reference markers for the CAP and Mk.III (Identification – Friend or Foe) IFF interrogators to sort out the CAP from the enemy. The favoured radars included SA, which was an air-search radar designed for destroyer-sized vessels and derived from the much larger CXAM used on carriers early in the war. It had a 1.36m wavelength, a 5 microsecond pulse width and a 60Hz pulse repetition frequency, and a maximum air range of about 40 nautical miles. Introduced from 1942 onward about 1,500 sets were produced. The SC-2 (and later SR) types of Air Search types became the standard destroyer radar fit during the war and for a considerable time afterwads. It was basically the same configuration as the SK but had smaller antenna to reduce weight, an important factor in small ships. It incorporated the PPI display, integral IFF, and at Okinawa, anti-jamming devices were introduced. It had a 1.5m wavelength, 4 microsecond pulse width and 60Hz pulse repetition frequency, with a maximum air range of 80 nautical miles; almost 1,000 were produced by the war's end. For fighter direction the 10cm SP radar, with a 1 or 5 microsecond pulse width and 120 or 600 Hz pulse repetition frequency, was a destroyer adaption of the CXDT type fitted to battleships, carriers and cruisers. It was only fitted to a limited number of destroyers especially tasked for this duty, their version weighing 9039lbs and it had a range of 40 nautical miles.

Surface search sets were usually of the SG centimetric type which first became practicable in 1940 after the British handed over their magnetron which enabled the use of microwave operation. They had the advantage of smaller size and antenna weight, and was the first to build in the PPI capability. The SG was first tested on the trials vessel *Semmes* (AG-24, Lieutenant-Commander Frank L Followay), a former old 'four-piper' destroyer, in June 1942 and was quickly rolled out to the whole fleet of destroyer size and above. It had an air range of 15 nautical miles, operated at 50kW and had a 775 pulse repetition frequency. While the later SC-3 version utilised the shorter 8.6cm wavelength, it appeared too late to see combat use.

It is important to know that the well-known radar jamming technique of dropping aluminium foil strips to jam radar screens with a multitude of false blips, known to the Allies (as related earlier) over Europe as 'Window', was fully familiar to the Japanese, who termed it *Giman-shi* (deceiving paper). Invented by Lieutenant-Commander Sudo Hajime, IJN, it was first successfully used in combat during the Solomon Islands campaign in 1943. Okinawa marked the first mass use of this electronic counter-measure (ECM) by the Japanese as the material was in scarce supply for them. It was found effective at jamming metric band radars and confusing radar-controlled AA, but not efficient against centimetric radar.

The SP pencil-beam height-indicating sets were valued for accurate valuation of both high-altitude and wave-skimming aircraft location.

When batches of the long-hulled *Gearing* Class were converted to radar pickets, they shipped a tripod mast to carry the extra gear aloft including SP height-finding radar to advise the CAP and aid interceptions. The after bank of torpedo-tubes was replaced by jamming gear. Of course, after Leyte Gulf and the sacrifice of the *Yamato*, surface targets for the torpedoes had suddenly become few and far between anyway, although the change was only accepted with great reluctance by died-in-the-wool Navy men, of which Fleet Admiral Ernie King was one. But even he did eventually relent in the face of the Kamikaze onslaught and twelve ships were initially selected for the six-week conversion at Boston and Norfolk Navy Yards.[7] Later the Fleet Admiral sanctioned the conversion of a dozen further such destroyers.[8] The destroyers had Mk.56 automatic-weapons reaction with radar and Blind-Fire capability for 40mm and 5in weapons, but these were superseded progressively by the Mk.57, and especially the Mk.63 types, following the anti-Kamikaze programme, which had radar antenna mounted on the gun mountings themselves.

The installation of the Combat Information Centre (CIC) as a central clearing house for all location/detection/identification data proceeded apace. Here all information came in via the various radars and radio reports continuously, which were co-ordinated and updated on a master plot. The changing and updated picture was repeated to the bridge on the PPI scope, but many commanders began to use the CIC to fight the ship in some circumstances. The very limited size of destroyers of course with their cramped hulls packed with the essential requirements of their breed, guns, torpedo-tubes and depth-charges, and the need for the captain to have all this knowledge at his fingertips, biased the location of the CIC in the bridge structure itself, usually taking the place formerly reserved for the CO's day cabin on the main deck immediately below the bridge. This, of course, made them vulnerable as the main aiming point of the Kamikaze when attacking such ships was the bridge structure itself.

With all these reports coming in from a single echo contact the CIC position was tolerably able to cope, but with multiple echoes and the activities of the CAP it tended, during heavy raids, at times, to resemble a modern Tower of Babel. Extra specialist operators were, of course, required and the very complexity of the problem, the urgency of its solution and the multiplicity of its functions, placed extra strain on the limited

---

7. These were the destroyers *Frank Knox* (DD-742), *Southerland* (DD-743), *Chevalier* (DD-805), *Higbee* (DD-806), *Benner* (DD-807), *Dennis J. Buckley* (DD-808), *Myles C. Fox* (DD-829), *Hawkins* (DD-873), *Duncan* (DD-874), *Henry W. Tucker* (DD-875), *Rogers* (DD-876), and *Perkins* (DD-877).

8. These destroyers were the *Everett F. Larson* (DD-830), *Goodrich* (DD-831), *Hanson* (DD-832), *Herbert J. Thomas* (DD-833), *Turner* (DD-834), *Charles P. Cecil* (DD-835), *Vesole* (DD-878), *Leary* (DD-879), *Dyess* (DD-880), *Bordelon* (DD-881), *Furse* (DD-882) and *Newman K. Perry* (DD-883).

accommodation of destroyers and also, of course, although not so immediately obvious at the sharp end, of the training programmes.[9]

The ordeal of the *Braine*

The fitting of specialist gear to facilitate radar picket work was initially done as and when possible. One such ship was the *Fletcher* Class destroyer *Braine* (DD-630, Commander William W. Fitt, USN). In mid-May 1945 *Braine* arrived at Kerama Retto anchorage where she was joined by three new officers especially added to her complement to operate her new radar and fire-control equipment. On 25 May she sailed to relieve the *Bennion* (DD-662, Commander Robert Henderson Holmes, USN), on duty at Picket Station No.5, where she found her team mate, the destroyer *Anthony* (DD-515, Commander C. J. Van Arsdall, USN) in place, along with the supporting 'pall bearers' *LCS(L) 13, 82, 86* and *123*.

Air attacks were constant on her arrival at this hot-spot, with all manner and type of aircraft, and forms of attack, Kamikaze, conventional torpedo-, dive- and low-level fighter-bombers and *Ōhka*'s launched from heavy bombers, of which the two destroyers shot down one 'mother ship' as well as fighting off other enemy aircraft that night and early morning. A short lull followed due to bad weather, but on Sunday 27 May the weather cleared and all hell broke loose again. This day, the 40th Anniversary of Admiral Heihachirō Tōgō's overwhelming victory against the Imperial Russian Navy at the Battle of Tsushima, it was natural that such a pivotal date (equivalent of Trafalgar Day for the Royal Navy) should see a major effort being made. And so it proved. Admiral Soemu Toyodo, IJN, sent a powerful strike force of 175 aircraft, *Kikusui* No.8, with the expenditure of twenty-six advanced training aircraft as a dusk spearhead, fifteen converted seaplanes, six *Gingas*, eleven heavy bombers, four *Tenzans (Jills)* and four land-based bombers against the fleets off Okinawa, with an accompanying stirring speech to remind the pilots of the deeds of their forefathers. Admiral Ugaki was bewailing the anniversary in his diary in pessimistic tones. 'I don't think we have lost any of our naval traditions, but why have we been pressed into such a tragic plight?'[10] His young pilots were expected to turn the tide on Japan's Navy Day or die in the attempt.

Braine had just secured from General Quarters at 07.45, there was an overcast sky and no CAP was visible, ideal conditions for the attackers. Without any warning four

---

9. Similarly, British aircraft-carriers utilised the aircraft direction room (ADR) for talking to and directing their CAP. When bogies were intercepted the fighter pilots would 'Tally Ho' their interceptions. The plot was a large vertical circular transparent map of the area, dissected by grid references of 360–degrees. The radar reports would give the bearing of hostiles and estimate the range. The plotting rate would then mark these on the map with wax crayons, red or blue. The flight direction officer (FDO), either port or starboard, would then home the nearest fighters to this target. There was a repeat plotter on the bridge for the ship's captain in exactly the same way, but of course these were much bigger ships and well-protected, not exposed like the pickets.'

10. Ugaki, Admiral Matome, *Fading Victory: The Diary of Admiral Matome Ugaki 1941–1945*, Annapolis.MD 1991.Naval Institute Press.

aircraft, identified as *Vals*, commenced attack dives out of the cloud cover. The two destroyers engaged and destroyed the first machine; the second was hard hit, set ablaze and went into the water close to starboard of the *Anthony*. Debris and the pilot's body came inboard, but the only damage amounted to small splinter holes in the destroyer's after funnel. The third attacker flew right across *Anthony* already on fire from flak hits. Commander Van Arsdall later related how it only narrowly missed his ship and feathered the sea before it pulled up in a left climb to about 1,400 feet, and then tipped over and made a dive into the *Braine*.

Braine's captain had ordered right full rudder and then rang down to the engines for flank speed to no avail. This aircraft dove in right across the destroyer's bow, just above main deck level, aiming for the bridge. The approach at the end was too low and the Kamikaze's wing was chopped off as it struck No.1 5in mounting which tipped it into No.2 mounting's shell handling room where it blew up. The gun's crew was wiped out as were those of the forward 40mm mountings save for one man, who was blown into the water, and the gun's captain, Arnold Papanti, who survived despite having his clothes burnt off, the foam inside his helmet melted to his head and a compound fracture of the left leg. The bomb, estimated at 500lb with a delayed-action fuse, was hurled forward and entered the ship's Wardroom where it detonated wiping out the CIC, killed the doctor, the new XO, the fire control officers, forward medical aid station and forward repair party teams. Gunnery Officer David Manning, who was stood on the port side of the flying bridge, later recalled seeing this aircraft coming right at him. 'I could count the cylinders on the engine!' He dived behind the fire director, which saved his life, and later made his way aft to assist with fire-fighting.

This first devastating hit was followed within minutes by another as the fourth aircraft, which was following hard astern of the first, came in over the starboard bow. Again one wing was lost as it sheared off on the starboard boat davit while the aircraft itself struck the starboard 'midships deck, ending up in the ship's sick bay and supply office. Again the bomb skidded along under its own momentum and detonated in the intakes of No.2 funnel, the blast blowing overboard this stack and the fighter directors, and wiping out the amidships medical unit and repair parties. A high-pressure steam line was ruptured, adding to the din and carnage, and scalding men alive in the fire room. The explosions and fires cut off water pressure so that the forward magazines could not be flooded, nor the resulting enormous fires fought. Blazing aviation fuel once more contributed to the blaze and all 40mm ammunition cooked off, while the torpedoes were shaken loose of the mountings and also threatened to ignite. *Anthony*'s engineering officer recalled seeing No.2 torpedo mount still intact, but with one of the warheads hanging directly above the damaged area with 'shredded orange stuff' hanging from it. He was 'reassured' by a torpedoman that although this was TNT it could explode if set off 'by a black powder booster and a little detonator.' All communications with the bridge were severed. The *Braine* careered around at twenty knots in a wide arc while the aft steering party attempted to bring her under control. After an hour *Braine* was finally brought to a halt and *Anthony*, along with *LCS(L)-86* and *LCS(L)-123*, managed to get alongside to help fight her fires and tend to the injured, while other men in the water were rescued by *LCS(L)-82*, and ten more were saved by a Martin PBM-5 Mariner amphibian of Rescue Squadron VH-3, one of the wounded dying *en route* to the hospital ship from his burns.

Marine Corsair fighters which arrived overhead protected this aircraft from attacks by Japanese fighters on the way back to base. The sea was choppy ('moderate swells and an eight-knot wind'), and the water was full of sharks – not everyone who went into the water came out. Men in the rescue boats had to use rifles to drive the sharks away as they lifted men out of danger. It took four hours hard work in dreadful conditions to finally snuff out *Braine*'s inferno while other vessels sailed from Kerama Retto to assist, one of which, the destroyer escort *Reeves* (DE-156, Lieutenant-Commander Matthias Stanley Clark), put both her Doctor and Chief Pharmacist Mate, Darrell Helton, aboard *Anthony* to help tend to *Braine*'s wounded. As was to be expected, the casualty toll was very high, in fact *Braine* suffered the highest number of casualties from any 'Kamikazed' destroyer that managed to survive. Eight Officers and fifty-nine enlisted men were killed or died of wounds and 102 were wounded, fifty of which required hospitalization. But survive she did – and *Braine* was eventually got into the Kerama Retto anchorage and moored alongside a tender for damage assessment, where examination revealed that her hull itself was undamaged. The topside, however, was a fire-ravaged shambles, her engine rooms and fire-rooms had been badly damaged and required a lot of work to make her seaworthy for the long voyage back to the States. Those killed were buried at sea with a memorial service held on 19 June before departure.

What of the attackers? They found the body of the first pilot along with the aircraft's engine, where it had buried itself, in the officers' quarters. 'He was wearing Texas-style cowboy boots, and carried several ceremonial dolls with him to his death. His wallet was later found. In it was a carefully-placed picture of the pilot's wife and child. One of the planes had a Pratt & Whitney engine and was equipped with Goodyear tyres.'[11] The motor of the second Kamikaze was located in the *Braine*'s deck amidships. The destroyer survived and after repair remained in the post-war fleet until 1971 when she became the Argentine ship *Almirante Domeca Garcia* (D-23), being finally scuttled in 1983.

Further Kamikaze Victims 27 May to 16 June

Night Kamikaze attacks drew blood just before midnight on 27 May. The two high-speed transports *Rednour* (APD-102, Lieutenant-Commander Roland H Cramer) and *Loy* (APD-56, Lieutenant-Commander James Voight Bewick) were in company when so attacked. Both avoided direct hits but both were damaged by the aircraft being shot down and detonating close alongside causing damage. *Rednour* lost three men killed and had to be sent back to San Pedro, California, to repair, while *Loy* survived and carried on patrolling, only to be damaged again by another Kamikaze on 29 May. On 28 May the attack transport *Sandoval* (APA-194, Commander R C Scherrer) was attacked by a *Tony* which smashed into her bridge killing three of her officers, while on the same date *LCS(L)-52* was also attacked by a night-time Kamikaze which was hit by AA fire and exploded directly above the ship showering her with debris. She lost one man dead and ten wounded, but continued working.

---

11. Okinawa – *A Fiery Sunday Morning* – USS *Braine* (DD630).

An attack was made on the *Tatum* (APD-81, Lieutenant-Commander William Cotesworth Pinchney Bellinger), a former *Buckley*-Class escort converted into a high-speed transport, at dusk on 29 May by four Kamikazes. One of these machines got through to the target, but fortunately the bomb she was carrying turned out to be a dud. *Tatum* was repaired locally and resumed operations. Among the big transport ships which received varying degrees of damage from Kamikaze attacks on 28 May off Le Shima were the *Brown Victory* (MC-0171, Master Terje Andreas Johannsen) which suffered four men killed, *Josiah Snelling* (MC-0541, Master Peter Grimstad), but without casualties, and *Mary A. Livermore* (MC-2292, Master Robert Deschamps) which suffered eleven men killed including her captain.

The bombarding ships also received unwelcome attention early in June on the 5th the battleship *Mississippi* (BB-41, Captain Jerauld B Wright) took a Kamikaze into her starboard side, but shrugged it off and carried on without pause. The much-tried heavy cruiser *Louisville* (CA-28), having repaired her earlier damage, was targeted by them once more on the same date and damaged again, although she was quickly repaired and back on duty again by the 9th. On 6 June the destroyer minelayer *Harry F. Bauer* (DM-26) was attacked by eight Kamikazes while in company with the *J. William Ditter* (DM-31, Commander Robert Roy Sampson). Both ships shot down three aircraft apiece, but both received damaging hits from the remaining pair of aircraft. The *Bauer* was repaired at Leyte and resumed operations, but *Ditter*'s hurt was greater and she had to be sent back to New York via San Diego. With the end of the war it was decided not to bother repairing her. On 10 June the destroyer *William D. Porter* (DD-579, Commander Charles Melville Keyes) shot down a *Val*, but the aircraft went into the water close by and the bomb it was carrying detonated directly below the ship, breaking her back. After a brief struggle to keep her afloat she sank – a unique case. The destroyer *Twiggs* (DD-591, Commander George Phipps, Jr.) was attacked by a torpedo-bomber on the 16th and the torpedo that this aircraft was carrying was for some reason not launched, possibly because the crew were killed or incapacitated and it thus failed to enter the water and, instead, fell free from the burning aircraft to strike the ship amidships. The parent aircraft almost immediately followed its missile into the ship and she quickly sank with 152 dead including her captain, Commander George Philip.

The attacks continue at a lower rate – 21 June to 20 July

After a short pause serious casualties re-commenced on 21 June with *LSM-59* being sunk while acting as escort for the decoy ship *Barry*, Commander Clemens Francis Hand; also on the 21st the destroyer-escort *Halloran* (DE-305, Commander James George Scripps) shot down a Kamikaze but one of its bombs exploded in the process and severely damaged the ship's upperworks, killing three of her crew. Two large targets were the Seaplane Tenders *Curtiss* (AV-4, Captain Scott Earnest Peck) and the *Kenneth Whiting* (AV-14, Commander R R Lyons); both were acting as command ships and both were damaged on 21 June, the *Curtiss* taking a Kamikaze into her third deck which killed thirty-five men and she had to be sent home to repair at Mare Island; the *Whiting* was more fortunate, she shot down an *Oscar* and part of the exploding aircraft fell on the ship, causing only slight damage.

Next day, 22 June, the destroyer-minelayer *Ellyson* (DMS-19, Commander Robert W Mountrey) was slightly damaged by an incoming (and inverted) *Oscar*, and on the same date *LSM-213* and *LSM-534* were also damaged. There followed another relative lull, before, on 19 July the destroyer *Thatcher* (DD-514), having already been badly damaged on 20 May by an *Oscar* which killed fourteen of her crew, was hit once more. On her return to the States she was scrapped.

Barry's prolonged demise

An interesting loss was the high-speed transport *Barry* (APD-29, Lieutenant-Commander Clemens Francis Hand, USN). As related above, she had been hit by shore fire off Okinawa on 25 May and was towed into Kerama Retto on the 28th, and beached, but the old ship was found not worth repairing. All useful equipment was stripped out of her and her innards filled with empty 5in ammunition containers as makeshift floatation devices, remote-controlled flashing lights to simulate AA gunfire and smoke pots – all controlled by the accompanying *LSM-59*, (Lieutenant D. C. Hawley, USNR), which already had one engine disabled from a previous attack and was not therefore fully operational. On 21 June the *Barry* was towed out of harbour as a decoy by the fleet tug *Lipan* (ATF-85, Lieutenant Fred N. Beyer, USN). In this guise she proved only too successful and attracted the attentions of two Kamikazes, one of which crashed aboard the accompanying *LSM-59* and blew her to smithereens along with many of her crew, while the second crashed into the empty bridge of the *Barry*. Attempts to tow her back to Ie Shima failed as her old hull gave out and she sank that night.

The first 'Stealth' bomber attack?

Just what could be achieved, even with old and obsolete aircraft, was illustrated on the night of 29 July. Some criticisms of the Kamikaze form of attack centred on the feeling (in post-war Western eyes at least) that it was 'wasteful'. If one can in any way think that any kind of warfare is not wasteful, in both terms of lives lost and waste of national treasure and resource, then surely the criteria must be a comparison with what was achieved against what was thrown away. The idea has taken hold over the past decades that all suicide missions that ended in ships being sunk were mounted by the very best and most modern aircraft the Japanese had at the time. How wrong that assumption was could not be better illustrated than in this attack.

Far from fielding the latest technological examples of their aviation assets, the attack launched by the volunteer pilots of the Special Attack Corps 3rd *Ryuko* (Flying Tiger) Squadron consisted of fragile old biplane trainers, more akin to World War I aviation than the cutting edge of the second global conflict. Described in many reports as 'seaplanes' they were nothing of the sort. The Japanese had certainly employed seaplanes as Kamikazes, as we have seen in these pages, the last occasion being on 3rd July, but not on this occasion. The actual machines employed that night were known to the West by the code name *Willow* – Yokosuka K5Y, two-seat, IJN, land-based trainers. As training aircraft they followed the usual custom of being painted in high-visibility colours, in their case a vivid orange, which earned them the Japanese pilots' sobriquet *aka-tombo*

(Red Dragonfly), a common Japanese winged insect species.[12] The unit itself was a Navy Training formation, and at the time was based on the island of Miyakojima, which is situated on a line between Formosa and Okinawa. As such it was ideally situated to launch short-range attacks. Such a formation would have a very poor chance of surviving long enough to evade the CAP or the heavy AA fire of the target ships if deployed during daylight hours, but it was considered that they stood a good chance if used in a night attack. Two sorties were made, among the last by any Kamikaze unit, five aircraft being sent off on 29 July and three others on 30 July.[13] The pilots of these eight aircraft were: Chief Flight Petty Officer Hiroshi Mimura, Flight Petty Officer 1st Class Tamio Iori, Flight Petty Officer 1st Class Kiyotada Kondo, Flight Petty Officer 1st Class Yu Hara, Flight Petty Officer 1st Class Shojiro Sahara, Flight Petty Officer 1st Class Shozo Matsuda, Flight Petty Officer 1st Class Hoichi Yagi and Flight Petty Officer 1st Class Makoto Kawahira.[14]

Each aircraft in the group that took off on the night of 28/29 July was carrying a single 200lb bomb, the heaviest they could carry. They flew south and soon located American ships, and succeeded in achieving a large measure of surprise. Some American sources attribute the surprise achieved to the fact that this type of aircraft, 'an antique biplane,' got through because they 'didn't show up clearly on radar because it was made mostly out of wood and cloth.'[15] This was pure hyperbole, because the reports indicate that the incoming enemy aircraft were in fact picked up at half-an-hour past midnight, at a range of thirteen miles. The closing speed was estimated at a very modest ninety knots, and this in itself gave evidence that a training type of aircraft was employed. The ships they found were three *Fletcher*-Class destroyers of Radar Picket Station 9A, operating to the west of Kerama Retto. The ships concerned were *Callaghan* (DD-792, Commander Charles M. Bertholf, USN), some of whose previous encounters with Kamikazes we have listed already, and she had the Commander of Destroyer Squadron 55, Captain A. E. Jarrell, USN, embarked. Other destroyers in company were the *Pritchett* (DD-561, Commander Cecil T. Caulfield, USN), and *Cassin Young* (DD-793, Commander John W Ailes III, USN). They were accompanied by the 'Pall Bearers' *LCS(L)-125, -129* and *-130*. The leading aircraft was engaged by the main armaments of both *Callaghan* and *Pritchett*, but

12. See Commander Charles M. Bertholf, USS *Callaghan* (DD-792) Revised *Form for Reporting AA Action by Surface Ships*. Commander Bertholf stated that the aircraft which struck his command was a, 'bi-plane, single engine, fixed landing gear.'
13. (Katsuhiro Hara, Shinsou Kamikaze Tokkou: *Hisshi Hitchuu No.300 Nichi* (*Kamikaze Special Attack Facts: 300 Days of Certain Death*); Tokyo: 2004, KK Bestsellers; and Tokkotai Senbotsusha Irei Heiwa Kinen Kuchukai (Tokkotai Commemoration Peace Memorial Association 1990 – Tokbubetsu Kougckta (Special Attack Corps) Tokyo 1990.
14. See inscription on the Kamikaze Special Attack Corps Ryuko Squadron Monument, erected close to the Miyakojima City Athletic Field, on the 50th Anniversary of the mission, 29 July 45, by Keizo Sasai, a former member of the unit, at Minakuchi Town, Shiga Prefecture. 1995. The name of Hoichi Yagi, who died off Formosa during the 30th July sortie, rather than off the coast of Kadena, Okinawa, is omitted from this monument.
15. See David Boldt, *At WW II Reunions, Ex-enemies Share Memories and Golf Course*, internet post-dated August 6, 1999.

to no effect and it continued on to strike the former ship on her main deck where it folded up into matchwood. However, its bomb continued on, piercing the deck and detonating in the ship's after engine room. The detonating bomb wrecked the engine room and jammed the ship's rudder. Worse, the blast caught the damage control and fire-fighting parties who had reacted promptly to the aircraft crash and were thus mown down. Fierce fires broke out and engulfed the ship in the vicinity of her rear stack, flames roaring out of control from frame 118 back to frame 150.

Commander Bertolf signalled to the LCS(L)s to close his command and help fight these fires, but it soon proved hopeless and the ship's stern was soon under water as far forward as the forward depth-charge throwers, themselves awash. All the LCSs could do was evacuate the wounded, of which there were a large number and this was completed by 01.55. *LCS(L) 130*, Lieutenant William H. File, Jr. alone pulling twenty-seven men who had been blown overboard out of the sea. Things worsened quickly for within five minutes the ship's magazines began cooking off. The *Callaghan*'s uncontrollable inferno led to a mass detonation of seventy-five rounds of 5in projectiles in her No.3 upper handling room and a 15–degree starboard list. *Callaghan* was rocked by further explosions which negated all hope of getting her back to a safe anchorage. Finally 'Abandon Ship' was ordered and the survivors were got clear. At 02.34 *Callaghan* sank by the stern.[16] While these dramatic events were taking place, the fires aboard the burning and sinking *Callaghan* had, unsurprisingly, attracted the remaining Kamikaze aircraft to the scene likes moths to a flame.

A second *Willow* also managed to penetrate and was engaged by the *Pritchett*, which had been selected as its target. This aircraft was hit continuously from a range of 5,000 yards and eventually crashed into the sea about six feet from *Pritchett*'s port side. The aircraft's bomb carried on with the momentum and hit the destroyer's thin side plating aft where it detonated. The explosion heavily damaged the ship's superstructure aft, demolished her port side depth charge racks and dislocated her radio and electrical leads. Despite this injury the destroyer stayed on station for two more hours assisting in the rescue of *Callaghan* crewmen before retiring to effect emergency repairs. A third *Willow* also approached and was promptly shot down while a fourth attacked *Cassin Young*, although it too was equally swiftly disposed of by that ship without more ado. *Cassin Young* then closed with the LCS group and took aboard all of *Callaghan*'s survivors, a ship that had been fatally attacked and lost less than two hours before she was due to be relieved by the destroyer *Laws* (DD-558, Commander Lester O. Wood, USN) as she was due to return to the States for a refit.[17]

The attackers of 30 July made their dives into *Cassin Young* at 03.26 causing serious damage and the loss of twenty-two of her crew, including her Captain designate, Lieutenant-Commander Alfred Brunson Wallace, USN, with a further forty-five wounded, including Commander Ailes.

---

16. Commander Destroyer Squadron 55, Serial 0023, *Anti-Aircraft Action Report for Action of 29 July, 1945– Loss of USS* Callaghan (DD792), dated 7 August 1945. Enclosure (A).
17. See Barry Foster, *The Last Destroyer*, 2002, Infinity Publishing, West Conshohocken, PA.

A monument to the Japanese attackers, almost but not quite the last to sacrifice themselves in this manner, contains the following poignant description of their final moments.

> *With back hunched, pushing forward the control stick*
> *Now comes an end to many countless hopes*

The training aircraft also came close to sinking the high speed transport *Horace A. Bass* (APD-124), Lieutenant Commander F. W. Kuhn, USN.[18] She was working off Hagushi in the early hours of 30 July when the radar again picked up a bogey closing at slow speed. Even so, the night lookouts were taken by surprise when one of the 'sticks and wire' Kamikazes suddenly appeared out of the night making straight for her. The attacker was not taken under fire and was virtually given a 'free shot' but even so the pass was ineffective. The biplane crossed over *Bass* brushing her close enough to shred some life-rafts and parts of some boat's davits. The attacker went into the water just off the ship's port side and the 220lb bomb detonated on impact with the water. Fragments came inboard striking down sixteen of the crew, one of whom was killed and damage was done to her hull, but not enough to cause her withdrawal.[19]

Pause for much thought – The US Navy Anti-aircraft Summary

On 30 April 1945, under the name of Rear-Admiral Charles M. Cooke, Jr, USN, Chief of Staff,[20] United States Navys issued a detailed summary of their reaction to the Kamikaze threat as undergone up to the end of January 1945. It was concerned with what was known through Intelligence and Action sources of the Japanese methods and how best the AA defences of the fleet could counter them. It was issued widely to the fleet from May 1945 onward.[21] The summary began with a brief historical review and the statement that 'Suicide attacks are not new to the fleet. Periodically since the beginning of the war fanatical Japanese pilots have deliberately crashed their planes into fleet units, although usually not until after their aircraft had suffered critical damage.' Contrary to the accepted view that the Kamikaze tactic had taken the Navy by surprise when it was first introduced in the latter part of October 1944, Cooke expressed the opinion that, 'The development of suicide tactics to an intensive degree was to be expected.' He cited the reasons for this as they stood 'Piloting a Japanese aircraft was tantamount to being slated for certain death sooner or later as a victim of our aircraft or AA fire. The psychological tendency of

---

18. The former *Rudderow* Class destroyer escort DE-691.
19. USS *Horace A. Bass* (APD124), Serial 024, Action Report– *Defense of Okinawa*, 30 July 1945, dated 9 August 1945.
20. Rear Admiral C. M. Cooke, Jr, known as 'Savvy' Cooke for good reason, was a highly intelligent naval officer who had replaced Rear Admiral Richmond Kelly Turner, USN, in mid-1942 and moved up to become Deputy Chief of Staff in October 1943, and then Chief of Staff under Fleet Admiral Ernest J. King.
21. COMINCH P-009 –*Anti-aircraft Action Summary – Suicide Attacks April 1945*. United States Fleet, Headquarters of the Commander in Chief, Washington 25, D C. Dated 30 April 1945.

the Japanese toward self-sacrifice made logical the inauguration of aerial 'Banzai' raids against our shipping'.

The normal bomb and torpedo attacks against ships had latterly proved 'both ineffective and costly to the enemy.' At the time of the introduction of the Kamikaze ('Storm sent from Heaven') units the enemy had suffered the almost complete elimination of his surface fleet in the Leyte Gulf battle, but, Cooke asserted, 'Intensive suicide attacks against our surface forces were planned some time before the first units were placed in action. It is believed that training of suicide pilots was initiated as early as last summer, and that fourteen pilots were killed and twenty-one aircraft destroyed in early practice sessions directed at improving techniques. It is reported that in the pilot's pre-crash sensations 'fainting is inevitable in such cases'.' Cooke provided further details as learned from interrogations of survivors including the fact early Kamikaze crews were volunteers and averaged in age from nineteen to twenty-four and that they were more prevalent in the Navy than in the Army. Some POW's revealed that this soon changed and that, 'commanding officers 'volunteered' whole squadrons and that squadrons were now drafted. Cooke also stated that 'One recent report was to the effect that a pilot had been found with his feet manacled to the rudder controls, evidently to ensure that the 'Kamikaze' phobia was retained.' Cooke also alleged that 'Women have been reported as being in training as suicide pilots.' He concluded: 'There is no reason to believe that there will be a shortage of pilots as long as this form of attack proves profitable to the enemy. Training of such pilots should prove much simpler than the development of skilled fighter and bomber pilots, as their only objective is to evade interception and dive into ships.'

Of course, although this report does not specify, the willing volunteer stage had long since been surpassed by coercion or shaming tactics. One example of how effectively this was applied was given by Flight Officer Motoji Ichikawa, who survived the war. He recalled that one day an announcement was made for all the pilots to line up in front of headquarters. The commander then dismissed all those men who had single parents or who were only children. He then dismissed those who were first sons before calling the remainder into a semi-circle closer to him. He then announced that the war was going badly and that an offensive was being planned, 'that will bring excruciating pain and damage to the enemy.' The CO then stated that a new and very special instrument of certain death to the enemy had been developed but, 'in order for this kind of special attack to succeed, the weapon has been designed as a one-way trip.' He then told the pilots they could choose to take part in this mission by writing "Yes" or "No" on their ID card and then drop them in a special box. Ichikawa's first inclination was to write "No" but he did not. His conscience overcame his reluctance. He felt that peer pressure would judge him as weak, unmilitary, and unmanly, should he object. Therefore rather than be shamed, or branded a coward, he wrote "Yes" on his ID card. Later whole units were to be "volunteered" by their COs without even that level of consultation.[22]

---

22. Naito, Hatsuho, *Thunder Gods: The Kamikaze Pilots Tell Their Story*; Translated by Mayumi Ichikawa. New York, NY 1989. Kodansha International/USA Ltd.

Having set the scene with varying degrees of accuracy and speculation the summary then spelt out the problem faced by AA gunnery which was the final line of defence. It was obvious, and admitted that 'The psychological value of AA, which in the past has driven away a large percentage of potential attackers, is inoperative against the suicide plane. If the plane is not shot down or so severely damaged that its control is impaired, it almost inevitably will hit its target.' It was starkly spelt out that – 'Expert aviation opinion agrees that an unhindered and undamaged plane has virtually a 100 percent chance of crashing a ship of any size *regardless of her evasive action.*'[23] How then to counter such an attack? More than 50 per cent of all attacking suicide planes were being destroyed by the ship's guns (which compared favourably with a success rate of 33.6 per cent against dive- and torpedo-bombers earlier in the war) and it was considered that with 'time, study and intensive training' this percentage would increase. The question was, with major amphibious operations planned at Iwo Jima, Okinawa and ultimately, mainland Japan, these things were a future option and the solution was required immediately. For there was no doubt about the success of the Kamikaze method, at least not at COMINCH. They stated clearly that, 'From the Japanese point of view, suicide attacks are a profitable tactic' and used the following two tables to illustrate this viewpoint.

Table I: Conventional Dive- and Torpedo- bombing attacks.

300 planes sortie.
180 lost to Combat Air Patrol (60%)
120 attack ships
40 lost to AA (33.3%)
12 achieve hits or damaging misses on ships (10%)
80 return to base
220 lost to CAP and AA to score 12 hits.

Table 2: Suicide Attacks.

60 planes sortie
36 lost to CAP (60%)
24 attack ships
12 lost to AA (50%)
12 get hits on ships (50%)
0 return to base
60 lost to score 12 hits.

Thus the Japanese only required one-fifth the number of sorties to score a specific number of hits by suicide crashes as were needed in the standard forms of attack. At the same time the Japanese plane and pilot losses were only 27% as high as in the former methods. Combat Air Patrols were one key factor, and it was revealed that among points receiving

---

23. My italics.

considerable attention here were air defence in depth, stacking of CAP, fighter direction and air discipline. 'The use of planes equipped with radar to assist in the detection of enemy planes has been proposed.' This was the origin of the AWAC (Airborne Warning & Control) solution adopted by the US and Royal Navys post-war.[24] More primitive methods were suggested as stop-gaps including firing 5in shell bursts in the direction of incoming Kamikazes to attract the attention of the CAP. Also, increasing the number of fighter aircraft carried in each carrier at the expense of offensive aircraft like dive-bombers and torpedo-bombers – which was certainly a good outcome from the Japanese perspective as it reduced the power of the Allied fleets. There was considerable criticism of the tendency to withdraw the CAP from over the ships at dusk and at dawn, often it was noted 'friendly aircraft were completely absent, leaving the entire defence problem to ships' guns.'

From the strictly AA perspective it was clear that the Kamikaze introduced a whole new problem. Certainly, on the positive side, 'The probability of shooting down a suicide plane was found to be relatively high,' but 'Unfortunately it is not high enough and consequently the AA defence against these aircraft cannot be considered satisfactory.' Nor were the Japanese standing still; as Okinawa unfolded it was seen that their basic philosophy was that self-destruction was justified in that it produced the greatest elimination of a greater number of enemy personnel and a greater amount of enemy equipment. 'One of their basic motivations is that even so great a nation as the United States cannot long withstand such attrition.' New variations were expected such as a full load of explosive or napalm instead of the light bombs currently being carried; jet or rocket propulsion to increase hitting power and night attacks. The use of the flying bomb (which had already scored successes for the Luftwaffe in the Mediterranean and the Bay of Biscay) was predicted. The cases of the *Jeffers* (DMS-27) on 12 April, which was attacked 'by a flying bomb released by a *Helen* at a range of 14,000 yards and an altitude of 4,000 feet; and of the *Stanly* (DD-478) on 12 April attacked by two flying bombs, were cited. In the first instance the bomb was shot down fifty yards off the port beam 'after absorbing many 20mm hits' while in the second instance both were shot down by repeated hits from 40mm guns, but one clipped the ship's after funnel and detonated in the water. 'Parts of one pilot were recovered.' It was noted that in these attacks there was co-ordination with conventional forms of attack. In the case of the destroyer *Mannert L. Abele* she destroyed a *Val* making a standard dive-bombing approach and was then attacked by two *Ohkas* which both hit, breaking the ship's keel. Her Captain reporting that after one had struck her, 'immediately thereafter a flying bomb struck the starboard waterline at frame 115. The ship broke in two and sank immediately.' It was emphasised in Cooke's summary that, 'Heavy firepower, first at the launching plane and then at the bomb, using a high percentage of VT fuses, is the best answer to this new weapon. Fire control should emphasize compensation for a rapidly accelerating target.'

---

24. Although this was subsequently abandoned by the British due to short-sighted defence cutbacks in the 1970s, the scrapping of the big carriers and the resultant casualties inflicted on British personnel during the Falklands War soon afterward.

It was admitted that reports of Kamikaze attacks made between 1 October 1944 and 31 January 1945 were not yet complete but it was felt that enough were available to draw some conclusions. Although the emphasis was on Kamikaze attacks, it was revealed that although 312 suicide crashes were made in that period, another 1,132 aircraft did *not* make suicide attacks, of which 936 were conventional attacks and NOT suicide missions, while 196 were uncertain as they were shot down before their final intentions became obvious. A summing-up of AA effectiveness revealed the following statistics:

1,444 suicide and non-suicide planes were taken under fire

352 suicide planes approached within gun range

40 (or 11%) of these were shot down before committing themselves to a crash attempt

312 suicide attempts actually were made on ships

191 (61 %) were shot down or deflected, but of these 53 (17%) landed close enough to ships to damage them

1,092 non-suicide planes were taken under fire

156 (14%) were shot down

23 (1.2%) scored hits on ships

How various warship types came off in defending themselves against the Kamikaze in this period was also revealing. Despite the almost universal post-war disparaging of the battleship by historians the world over[25] Cooke's analysis revealed that, 'Battleships have been more successful in protecting themselves from damage by suicide planes than any other type of ship.' He concluded, 'This is unquestionably due to the greater firepower of these ships, better distribution of guns and less distraction from the AA problem.' He might have added, although he did not, that the effect of a Kamikaze hit on a heavily-armoured battleship was almost negligible in most cases, other than on exposed bridges. At the other end of the scale merchant ships achieved a very low defence success rate. This demonstrated that defence in the later stages of any suicide attack was dependant on the target ship, and that, unless the volume of AA fire met was very high, they were virtually certain of hitting their targets.

These facts were, perhaps, self-evident, and so was the point made that aircraft-carriers, 'especially CV's,' had proved more susceptible to damage than any other types of naval vessels. 'Two out of every three planes attacking managed to score a hit or damaging near miss on one of these ships. Always the primary target of suicide planes, CVs present a target so large that an attacking plane is almost certain to hit unless it suffers severe structural damage. CVEs, comparatively slow and lacking in the fire power of their larger sisters, have nevertheless given a creditable performance.' The summary omits all references to ships of the British Pacific Fleet, and in this mirrors most post-war

25. See for example Hamer, David, *Bombers versus Battleships; the struggle between ships and aircraft for the control of the surface of the sea*. London; 1998 Conway Maritime Press; where even the jacket shows not a battleship at all, but a small freighter under masthead attack from an A-20 Boston bomber.

American accounts, being totally self-absorbed in the usual parochial way we have long become accustomed to from both historians and Hollywood, but it *is* better than these in that it does include the ships of the Royal Australian Navy in its figures. The reason for this Cooke gave as 'Suicide planes attacking these ships were taken under fire by US Naval Vessels, and they also assisted in the destruction of enemy aircraft.'

As for the type of weapon most suitable for the fleets' defence against the suicide attacker, the summary stated that two features stood out.

1. The success of the automatic weapons, which were credited with approximately 80% of all plane kills (50% to 40mm and 27% to 20mm), leaving only 20% to the 5in batteries.
2. The poor performance of 5in batteries, especially during suicide attacks. These guns fired 'disappointingly small quantities of ammunition at the many targets presented.' This performance was put down to the 'result of failure to open fire at maximum range.' Also there was deemed a failure to use a sufficient proportion of VT fuses. Whenever a 5in burst was close enough to a Kamikaze it was noted that it was liable to cause the target plane to crash at a safe distance whereby it inflicted no damage on the ship.

Defining a 'typical' suicide attack was found to be difficult to do. 'No two are exactly alike; the only thing each has in common being either the planes' crash into a ship or its 'splash' on interception.' The Summary itself divided the Japanese tactics into the following elements.

The Approach

This was apparently designed to exploit weaknesses in the Allied search radar and avoidance of the CAP. Many have already been noted from the Philippines campaign, the use of the land to shield the attacker; the trailing in the shadow of the IFF of the Allied aircraft returning to their carriers; low-level, high-speed approaches; splitting defences with small groups approaching from different points of the compass; the use of cloud cover to avoid visual sightings; rarely flying a straight course but diving and climbing until in among the ships and then making unpredictable 'wing-overs' into ships not on the original approach course. Two points were noted. 'It is believed that suicide planes are accompanied by radar-equipped control planes, which vector the suicide pilots to our ships from a long range.' Another factor noted was that, as in the case of the *Judy* which smashed into the *Essex* on 25 November for example, 'instances are on record where dive flaps have been used to restrict speed and increase accuracy.'

The Attack

If surprise was achieved, a dive angle of 75–degree angle was made from out of the clouds straight on to targets; otherwise the attacking formations of aircraft usually split into smaller groups upon nearing the maximum range of the 5in gun defences. In doing this they aimed to confuse and fragment the defences. This was also achieved by continual alteration of course; with low-level final approaches into the ships' hulls; with highly-aerobatic manoeuvres, even inverse final approaches. When taken under close-range fire they made unexpected nose-ins from unexpected angles. The tactic of releasing their bomb just before the aircraft hit the ship spread the damage effects of. It was noted that about 60% of bombs were carried into the ship by the aircraft as against 40% being released prior to final impact of the carrier. This method had changed by January when 88% of the bomb load was carried into the ship and only 12% released prior to the hit. It may be that the more skilled pilots were dead by that time.

Type of aircraft employed

There was no one type favoured over any other, it depended much on availability, fast, single-engined fighters, *Oscars* and *Zekes* were widely employed, but so were slower types like the *Val* and the *Jill*, while very vulnerable machines such as twin-engined *Betty* and *Frances* were also employed. Only four-engined types failed to be so utilised. Of course as time went on this became part of the attraction of the use of the method, for even obsolete and training aircraft could be impressed to deliver lethal damage into enemy fleets while the skill to pilot them was elementary.

The bombs carried were relatively small 500lb weapons, for the most part under the belly, or two, one under either wing. In truth they were too small to be fully effective, but larger bombs were either unavailable or incapable of being mounted on the types employed. Several POW reports were studied. The tendency of aircraft to catch fire was noted. And it was suggested by a prisoner that the wings of suicide aircraft were rigged so that the pilot could ignite them, but this was dismissed completely. 'There is no concrete evidence to indicate that the fire is caused by any source other than anti-aircraft fire.' Another POW stated that 'Wooden suicide planes are being manufactured with a speed of 410 knots and a ceiling of 18,200ft. They will carry dynamite, equipped with an electric fuse, and also will be capable of carrying one bomb. The purpose of the plane is to sink one ship at the expense of one such plane.' Other trends were noted. The carrier was obviously the prime target at this stage of the war, but, failing that, troopships and transports presented the minimum resistance with the maximum potential cull of combatants. However, just about any ship would be targeted as the opportunity arose. Picket destroyers had already been singled out and the Okinawa campaign was to reinforce that lesson most emphatically. Any crippled vessel that looked like it was in trouble tended to be the focus of repeated attacks, (a sort of 'feeding frenzy' to finish off the weakling). Some ships attracted attention for unknown reasons and became subjected to repeated attacks (HMAS *Australia* being the prime example, while her almost identical sister ship, HMAS *Shropshire*, was by comparison, virtually ignored). As for the point of aim, with aircraft carriers the deck park was almost irresistible and the concentration of flammable aviation gas and ordnance ensured a maximum effect from any hit here. Failing that, the ship's elevators, communication's hub, or island structure attracted much attention. On less vulnerable, better armoured and defended ships, ie battleships, heavy and light cruisers etcetera, the bridge was the invariable aiming point as it was just about the only area where significant damage could be inflicted and had the attraction of potentially killing or at least wounding senior enemy officers too! Smaller warships, destroyers and escorts, presented thin hulls and fragile upperworks, but are more evasive and required more skill to hit when at speed. But even the smallest vessels, PT-boats and landing craft, were targeted when the opportunity presented itself.

There followed a detailed examination of the various gun batteries and the effectiveness of each. For the 5in the requirements that were stressed were – Early engagement – it was stated that a Kamikaze would have a 47% survival chance from three 5in/38 twins using Mark 32 fuses at 10,000 yards range, but if fire was not opened until it had penetrated into 4,000 yards range, 'there is a 70 percent probability that it will survive'. It was also stressed that 'there is no substitute for volume of fire.' Another recommendation was that the maximum percentage of VT fuses practicable should be used. The use of lead–computing directors (Marks 51, 52, 57 and 63) were recommended as improving efficiency.

As for the light automatic weapons it was noted: 'The ability of some planes to survive an incredible number of hits and still land on board has resulted in the conclusion that the plane has to be disintegrated to prevent its causing damage.' But it was admitted that only 20% of Kamikazes had been taken apart in this manner and of these successes 63% was achieved by the 40mm battery.

Confusing the defence

On the effectiveness of radar, Vice-Admiral J. S. McCain, the Commander of TF38, submitted a detailed report that made for sombre reading. He reasoned that by combining the suicide dive with the lessons gained in past actions and a careful analysis of our defensive system, particularly our use of radar, *the enemy have developed the latest and most threatening problem that has yet confronted the US Navy.*[26] These attacks, McCain wrote, show not only the 'fanatical mind' of the Japanese, but 'what is far more dangerous, the application by the pilots and operations personnel of a complete understanding of radar and the complexities of air defence and air control'. The enemy totally understood several basic principles and McCain enumerated them. In brief some of these were – that a small group of aircraft drew less radar response than a large one; that following returning US strikes back to their carriers made detection difficult; that many small targets was difficult to differentiate; that altitude was a weak point and constant alterations of height and course were difficult for SM Fighter Direction Set to track; that a high, fast power glide in particular presented estimation problems.

Further confusion was sewn among the defenders by the fact that, 'The use by enemy of an IFF that looks like Mark III Code 1, 2, or 3 is definitely established.' This reference was to the IFF Mark III which was replacing the Mark II. The latter had the advantage of having a separate 'A' radar band which interrogated on demand by the operator. The signal automatically triggered a return pulse from the aircraft's transponder. The radar return and the 'A' band response appeared on the scope enabling instant recognition. A further refinement, 'G' band, enabled friendly fighters to be distinguished from other Allied types.

26. My italics.

British electronics

Although much radar and radio equipment was interchangeable between the two main Allies, the British Pacific Fleet used its own terminology to a large degree. The principle radar types on Royal Navy ships during 1944/45 included: Type 276, which was introduced as it gave good warning for low-flying aircraft below 5,000ft, and was backed up by the Type 291;Type 277 Surface Search/Height Finding radar, operating at 10cm (3 GHz); Type 279 Air Search radar, which featured twin synchronised antenna, 7.5m (40MHz) with the associated 'Hayrake' interrogator; Type 291 Air Search radar with a Type 243 IFF interrogator; Type 286 Metric Target Indicator set with ATQ aerial with 214 MHz frequency which first appeared back in 1940 and was replaced by the Type 290, a 100kW set with 214 MHz frequency; Type 291 Air Search radar; Type 293 Fire Control centimetric Mark V radar, a Target Indicator set with a 6ft diameter 'Cheese' antenna (a thin parabolic antenna between reflector plates, 'double cheese' comprising one stacked above the other as a transmitter and receiver pairing). The 293M with AUR aerial, the 293P with AQR aerial and the 293Q ANS all were of 500kW peak power, with 2,997 frequencies, 100 mm wavelength and all were introduced in 1945 working with a Type 242 IFF interrogator; Type 281 Air Search radar with Type 243 IFF and Type 252 IFF transponder as well as VHF/DF transmitters, TBS etc.[27] [It is interesting to note that the development of British Searching Control (SLR) Gun Predictor (nicknamed 'Elsie') owed much to the work of Japanese scientists. This device, which proved so highly-effective in shooting down V-1 flying bombs over southern England in 1944, utilised five Yagi aerials which employed a 10ft wavelength, two pairs directionally (up/down and left/right) while the fifth transmitted a steady radar beam.

The Yagi antenna was the invention of Japanese physicist Dr. Hidetsugu Yagi of Tohoku Imperial University and his assistant Dr. Shintaro Uta, and was first patented as far back as 1926, and was introduced to improve the gain of the antenna concentrated in one direction. This was accomplished by adding directors and reflectors. This type of unidirectional antenna has a frequency bandwidth inversely proportional to antenna gain. Increasing the diameter of the conductor diameter, the wider the band and the greater physical strength of the antenna. Ignored in his homeland, Yagi's device was taken up in Europe and North America with results that came home to roost for Japan in the Pacific War.

Improved defensive weapons

A plethora of ideas of how to combat them followed the first suicide attacks, some practical, some rather less so (amongst them searchlights, hand-held bazookas and chain shot). But the principle that remained valid was that 'a new weapon is of value only if it can be demonstrated as being several times superior to the weapon it replaces, if it can be made available in quantity, and if it is sufficiently versatile to retain its value in the face of changing tactics.' None of the new ideas could approach the increase in effectiveness of existing AA defences by weapons already in place. However, the development of a 3in AA gun was pressed forward, but it was obviously a long-term project. On the principal of making better use of what they had, it was noted that VT Fuses were in the process of being replaced by Mark 53, Mod 3 type, which had considerably increased sensitivity, higher operability and shorter arming time (450 yards as against 800 yards for the Mod 1 and Mod 2) than before. It was estimated that it would double the effectiveness of the 5in guns. 'This ammunition is now en route to the Fleet.' A Mark 47 fuse was being developed for the 6in/47 gun that was under test but there was said to be "no possibility" of developing a VT fuse for the 40mm.

Although the concept of using rockets for defence showed "considerable promise" it was still in its infancy. The development of the 5in spinner with VT fuse was considered 'an attractive possibility for anti-suicide work.' Similarly the development of an automatically-loaded twin 5in gun with a 90 rpm rate of fire, were in the design stage, but was still a long way from production. The wholesale disillusionment with the value of 20mm Oerlikons in stopping a Kamikaze was acknowledged, but the summary still considered it a valid weapon and while twin 20mm were being installed in quantity, testing of a quadruple 20mm power-driven mounting was underway as were studies into the feasibility of a 37mm gun. As for fire control it was considered that the introduction of the Mark 57 and Mark 63 directors for 40mm mounts would increase three- or four-fold the chances of destroying aerial targets over the existing Mark 51.

Finally it was acknowledged that, 'Suicide tactics not only nullify the psychologically-deterring effects of AA; they also place a strong psychological weapon in the hands of the enemy. Reports from the fleet indicate that, although officers and men have the greatest respect for the suicide plane for the most part, they have not permitted the new enemy tactics to decrease their gunnery efficiency.' Nonetheless some exceptions to the general rule was acknowledge. 'Several gunners have leaped overboard when a hit on their ships appeared imminent. Others have developed severe cases of hysteria and other emotional disturbances after their ships underwent particularly violent attacks. Personnel aboard ships which have been sunk by suicide planes are most affected.'

It is salutatory to see the solutions put forward to counter these effects and to build and maintain morale; they were:

1. Assign duties to occupy each individual before, during and after an action, and convince him of their importance. Hysteria will not develop if a person is busy and faced with definite responsibilities before, during and after an action.
2. So indoctrinate men in their assigned duties that they do them almost automatically in an emergency.
3. Convince gunnery department personnel, through movies, lectures, etc., that a suicide plane will fall if accurate fire is continued until the target appears to be 'coming down the barrel of the gun'.
4. Imbue in personnel a hatred of suicide pilots which will inspire aggressiveness and supreme courage on the part of the gunners.
5. Assure personnel that their very lives depend upon their best performance, and that the suicide problem resolves itself into one of 'kill or be killed'!'

Just how this analysis played out in future combat was already under test even as the document was being distributed to the fleet, for off the shores of Okinawa the Kamikaze attacks were already reaching a new intensity, and losses were mounting.

Chapter Twelve

On To Japan?

'As an engaged man, as a man to go, I would like to say a little to you a lady before I go. I only wish your happiness. Do not mind the past. You are not to live in the past. Have the courage and forget the past. You are to create a new future. You are to live from moment to moment in the reality. Anazawa no longer exists in the reality.'
Second Lieutenant Toshio Anazawa to his fiancé.

Last fight of the *Bush*

Typical of the ordeal faced by the defending ships was the experience of the destroyer *Bush* (DD-529, Commander Rollin Westholm, USN). She was part of Carrier Task Group 51.5, under the Commander Transport Screen under Captain F. Moosebrugger, USN, Commander of DesRon 63, in the Amphibious Force Flagship *Biscayne* (AGC-18). The *Bush* was allocated to Radar Picket Station No.1 on 5 April, her duties being described as maintaining, 'alert air and surface radar and sound searches to give early warning of enemy forces attempting the area.' Every enemy or unidentified contacts registered had to be reported to Commander Task Force (CTF) 51. Standing instructions established that each picket destroyer was supported by two Landing Craft Support (Small). These little craft, displacing just ten tons, were equipped with rocket launchers, smoke pots and machine-guns. Each pair was instructed to remain in close contact with their parent destroyer at all time. (The LCS(L)'s which performed such duties later received the unwelcome sobriquet "Pall Bearers" due to the fact they were called upon to evacuate survivors from Kamikaze victims throughout the campaign.) Each picket destroyer was given a patrol area within a 5,000 yard circle which they were to circle at fifteen knots and any enemy aircraft that came within 12,000 yards range was to be engaged.

The enemy was active after dark on 6th April 1945 and between 02.45 and 03.45, *Bush* fired on four different aircraft and claimed to have destroyed one of them. This target was tracked at a height of 6,000 feet in level flight when first engaged, presumably heading for the transport anchorage. Once firing commenced the aircraft continued briefly on its course and then descended in a steep dive passing over the destroyer. Its descent was described as sounding as if it were out of control, but the radar picked it up again as the range opened and lost it completely at ten miles range. At 04.00 a light was seen on the water on a bearing where radar contact had been lost. The *Bush* was equipped with Mk.4 radar equipment, although it was later noted that had Mk.12 and Mk.22 radars been fitted instead, better results would have been obtained during night operations.

Apart from an abortive submarine alert, the morning passed peacefully and it was not until 14.30 that the radar picked up a group of hostiles some 35 miles north and rapidly closing, and the *Bush* went to General Quarters in readiness. At 14.35 a second group was on the screen and by 14.45 two further bogeys were approaching at the same speed, direction and height. These aircraft were also located by the nearby picket destroyer *Cassin Young*. These four groups were designated as Raids 1, 2, 3 and 4 by the task force flagship, and *Cassin Young* allocated four of the patrolling CAP to *Bush* to control and carry out an intercept. Raid 1 consisted of a formation of *Val*s and *Bush*'s gunfire destroyed two of these before the Fighter Direction Officer (FDO) homed the fighters onto the remainder at 14.55.

Raid 2 then bored in and was taken under fire by the 5in armament at 15.00 on the 6th which drove them off to the west as further friendly fighters were vectored in by other pickets from the east. The sky was now full of both hostile and friendly aircraft, and the 5in battery switched target to engage Raid 3. After this had been broken up, the *Bush* turned left and came onto a westerly course, and a hostile was sighted approaching fast from dead ahead low down on the wave crests. Speed was rung down for 27 knots and the rudder was increased to full left in order to bring the Kamikaze onto the starboard beam so all guns could engage. When the 5in battery was thus unmasked all guns opened fire at a range of between 7,000–8,000 yards. The Japanese pilot responded with what was described in *Bush*'s Action Report as, 'rollercoaster tactics, climbing and dipping, combined with a slight weave during its approach.' The oncoming aircraft's height varied from between ten to thirty-five feet. The ship's 5in battery and any 40mm that could be brought to bear were firing at their maximum rate. The 2,100–ton *Fletcher* Class destroyers were equipped with five single 5in/38 guns controlled by a Mk.37 Director firing variable time (VT) proximity-fused shells. They also had twin 40mm and 20mm light AA weapons for last-ditch, close in swamping barrages, but these proved inadequate in deterring an aircraft piloted by a man determined to give his life for his Emperor and his nation.

The Action Report notes, with some incredulity, this fact: 'All batteries were firing at maximum rate, and despite heavy and what appeared to be accurate 5in and 40mm gunfire, the plane kept coming in. At the time it seemed unbelievable that it could do so. At a range of 2,000 yards, when it appeared as if a suicide crash were probable, the rudder was shifted hard right in an attempt to swing the stern clear. The plane (a *Jill* carrying a large bomb or torpedo), however, changed course to the right at the same instant and at 15.15 crashed with a terrific explosion at deck level on the starboard side between #1 and #2 stacks.' The bomb itself exploded in the forward engine room. An idea of the force of the explosion may be gained from the fact that a six foot section of engine room blower, weighing 300–500lbs was blown into the air high enough to knock off the SC-2 antenna and land on the port wing of the bridge.' It was also recorded that the starboard plating from the forward fire-room forward bulkhead right back to the after engine-room forward bulkhead was blown out. The water flooded into the ship through this gaping hole and the *Bush* listed ten degrees to port as the forward fire-room, forward engine room and after fire-room rapidly flooded. Every man in the after engine room died, and just four men from the forward fire room and eight from the after fire room survived, most badly burnt or scalded.

There was massive damage elsewhere with the forward quintuple 21in torpedo mounting being blown overboard, the main starboard deck blown away, and the SC-2 gunnery control radar set and all the radio antenna wrecked. Of her 5in armament Nos.2, 3 and 4 mounts were jammed and would not train, Nos.43 and 44 40mm mountings were put out of action by the blast. Below decks there was widespread damage to the ship's sick bay, galley, supply office and laundry. The emergency diesel generator kicked in for a short period enabling the transmission from the CIC of a brief signal that the ship had been hit. Attempts to contact the escorting *LCS (L) 64* were initially unavailing and *Bush* was on her own save for a CAP of four aircraft overhead for a while.

Stringent measures were taken to maintain seaworthiness after this catastrophic damage including the shoring up of the damaged bulkheads, jettisoning of much 5in ammunition, torpedoes, depth-charges and wreckage to reduce topside weight. Several small fires were put out by the combined efforts of the crew and escaping steam. It was hoped that these prompt actions might yet save the ship, which was threatening to break in half.

The CAP departed at 16.35 and was not replaced, but from Radar Picket Station No.2 the *Colhoun* (DD-801, Commander George R. Wilson, USN) was seen closing to assist. Unfortunately around the same time a group of between ten to fifteen Japanese aircraft were sighted at cloud level some ten to fifteen miles off. *Colhoun* began engaging these aircraft at the same time, sending a visual signal that she would close *Bush* as soon as they had been driven off. *LCS 64* also appeared from the south-west and she was asked to close the *Bush*'s port side to evacuate the wounded and *Colhoun* was asked to request the despatch of two tugs to assist *Bush* back to base.

The next attack now commenced with a pair of *Val*s circling nearby preparing to dive and the *LCS64* was shooed off out of harm's way. *Colhoun* was meanwhile still engaging another enemy group and the two *Val*s had a free run. As there were 150 men crowded on the fo'c'sle of the *Bush*, orders were given for them to go over the side if or when the attack developed. There were by this time an estimated fifteen to twenty hostiles in view and, at 17.00 one of the two *Val*s made an attack run in toward the *Bush*'s starboard side. This aircraft was engaged by two of the 40mm mounts that remained operational and this forced the aircraft to turn away and cross the ship's stern. This *Val* then circled the *Colhoun* which was three or four miles south-east and made a Kamikaze attack into her, striking her amidships. The *Colhoun* continued steaming and gradually drew away. *Bush* was now a hapless target and on her own once more, and the Japanese lost no time in trying to finish her off completely. Three *Zeke*s were sighted at 17.15 circling the ship ten miles out and taking advantage of cloud cover. The first one broke formation at 17.25 and climbed up into the sun dead ahead of the wallowing *Bush*. 'He did a wing-over and commenced a 25–30 degree dive from ahead, strafing as he came in. The forward 40mm guns took him under fire and personnel on the forecastle went over the side.' This *Zeke* pilot picked his spot, crossing from starboard to port before dipping his left wing and diving toward the ship's bridge. He missed and instead impacted between the ship's funnels amidships on the port side. A large fire broke out at the point of impact and, in the words of the action report, 'The crash almost cut the ship in two. It is believed that the bottom and keel were the only things holding it together.' This attack effectively cut all communications between the forward and after parts of the ship as well. Seeing she remained afloat, a second *Zeke* broke away from the circling enemy formation and made his attack in a shallow run, strafing as he came and weaving. Taken under fire and hit by the Bofors and Oerlikons, he crossed the *Bush* amidships about five feet up, then gained height, dropped one wing and headed for the destroyer's forecastle, engaged by the forward port 40mm to no avail. This aircraft impacted the superstructure near No.2 5in mount and the ship's wardroom. The resulting explosion and fire engulfed the latter, which was being used as an operating room and caused terrible carnage among those in there. This fire rapidly spread, being fanned by the gun's ammunition which began to cook-off in the heat.

The report continued:

'It is believed that this plane must have been carrying extra gasoline for incendiary purposes as it seemed as if the entire forecastle were enveloped in flames. The forecastle was abandoned and the gig sent to pick up the badly wounded. At just about the same time the *Colhoun* was struck by a second suicide plane. All these attacks were carried out with skill and determination.'

Only the after section of the vessel remained relatively unscathed at this point, but she was expected to break in half at any time. A third Kamikaze circled overhead, and evidently felt the *Bush* was doomed and so flew away eastward, and dove into the *Colhoun*. The inevitable commenced at 18.30 on the 6th when a heavy swell caused the *Bush*'s battered hull to fold up like a pocket-knife before she went down. The survivors, many terribly burnt, were left in the water over a wide area with no small boats in the water able to assist other than the ship's gigs. The long evening passed as groups tried to become more organised for mutual support, but the Report makes almost unbearable reading in places as men died from shock, despair and exhaustion. Eventually a small flotilla of vessels gathered from 21.30 onward and between them they hauled from the ocean 246 survivors and twelve dead bodies. Among those killed in this assault was Commander Willis, the Commander of DesDiv 48.

Meanwhile the *Colhoun* was undergoing a similar ordeal by fire. Having placed herself between the incoming Kamikazes and the *Bush*, she drew the enemy to her like moths to a flame. She claimed the destruction of three Japanese aircraft, a *Val* and two *Zeke*s but, as related, took a heavy hit from one suicide aircraft that impacted the ship and destroyed a 40mm mounting, killing its crew and that of the neighbouring mounting, while the bomb which was released just prior to the crash penetrated through to *Colhoun*'s after fire room before detonating. All personnel on duty there were wiped out.

Despite these blows the destroyer remained under control via the emergency steering system while one engine and one set of boilers, along with her remaining armament, remained in action. She was capable of fifteen knots. Two further *Val* dive-bombers were claimed destroyed before a second *Zeke* struck her to starboard. Again the heavy bomb carried by this aircraft exploded below the ship's water-line, breaking her keel and opening her up to the sea via a gap estimated at 20 feet by 4 feet. Both boilers were wrecked and both her oil fuel and her electrical circuits ignited fires. Power to all guns ceased and they had to be trained manually. Even so she claimed the destruction of another Kamikaze, and damage to another from yet a third group that now approached her while she was still in this parlous state.

The third aircraft of this trio (a *Val*) was undeterred and bored in to strike the ship on the after starboard side. The bomb struck the fantail at a shallow angle and skidded over the side of the ship to explode close alongside her. A further hole, estimated at about 3 feet in diameter, was opened up, further increasing the amount of water pouring into the ship.

The *Colhoun* had withstood this assault with great fortitude but yet a fourth Kamikaze, a *Zeke*, making what appeared to be an impromptu suicide run for it carried no bomb, approached in a dive. Hit, on fire and smoking, this aircraft smashed into the destroyer's bridge as a final blow. The ship's captain was near missed and several crew members knocked unconscious, but none were killed and the damage was not serious. But there was no need for it to be, the ship had already been fatally damaged.

The majority of the ship's survivors were taken off by *LCS-48* at 18.00 leaving just a small number aboard in a last ditch effort to take aboard a towing wire from a rescue tug in the hope of salvaging her. The tug attempted to tow *Colhoun* to Okinawa, but fires continued to rage and the last members had to be evacuated. With nobody left to fight the blazes or check the inflow of water, the list of the ship steadily increased until it became critical. It became clear that *Colhoun* was doomed and the remaining men were taken off before the destroyer, heavily listing, and with uncontrolled flooding, was finally sunk by the *Cassin Young* with gunfire in position 27° 16' N., 127° 48' E. Incredibly, despite the number of Kamikaze hits, she lost just thirty-four officers and men killed or died of wounds, and had a further twenty crewmen injured including many suffering from burns.[1]

Mullany survives – just

Meanwhile, also on 6 April, another *Fletcher* Class destroyer, the *Mullany* (DD-528) underwent a similar ordeal to the *Bush* and *Colhoun*, but somehow managed to survive. She was part of the anti-submarine screen patrolling to the east of Okinawa Shima, Nansei Shoto covering stations

A-1 and A-3 were assigned also as the radar pickets for that area along with the destroyer *Purdy* (DD-734), destroyer minesweeper *Gherardi* (DMS-30, Lieutenant-Commander William Wade Gentry), motor gunboat *PGM-10*, Lieutenant-Commander James W Collins and *LCI-41*. At 17.43 on 6 April, *Mullany* was steaming at fifteen knots on a course of 145 degrees, under an overcast sky, a 4,000 feet ceiling with ten miles visibility, when anti-aircraft fire was observed about five miles off the starboard bow. The ship went to flank speed and full right rudder was applied as she sounded off to General Quarters.

---

1. National Archives, Washington DC, Record Group 28, World War II War Diaries 12–7–1941 – 1231–1945. Action Report of USS *Colhoun*- Report of operations in the invasion of Okinawa Jima, Ryukyu Islands, 4/1 – 6/45 including enemy suicide crash dives and resulting loss on 4–6–45. Micro Serial 118138, dated 4–127–1945 Reel A1548.

An attack by a single radial-engined fighter developed immediately, its type being reported variously as an *Oscar*, *Tojo* or *Zeke*, although it later transpired that it was indeed an *Oscar* piloted by Takeichi Minoshima. It was noted in the Action Report that: 'There seemed to be no co-ordination amongst the three Japanese aircraft which were in the area at the time of the attacks, and with a fourth aircraft which appeared later.'

This first attacker flew across the destroyer's starboard bow at 9,000 yards range, circled and then commenced its dive. The entire 5in battery, in automatic control, had opened fire on this machine at a range of 8,000 yards with *Mullany* still turning hard to starboard, which put the Kamikaze 330 degrees relative which rapidly changed to zero deflection as the aircraft approached, 'the director was employing direct range keeping semi-automatic control, with optical pointing and ranging, spotting direct. 'The ship had reached about 20 knots and when the aircraft was about 2,000 yards off, the Captain tried to swing the ship's stern clear by stopping and backing the port engine.'

The 40mm and 20mm joined in the barrage with the former also under automatic control by individual heavy machine-gun directors, and they were seen to be hitting, while some 5in bursts from the forty-five rounds she managed to get off were near misses, and flame and then smoke was seen coming from the aircraft engine cowling. But it was not stopped and seemed to be aiming at the destroyer's bridge. It was later observed that: 'There are indications that the plane which crashed into this ship was not a suicide plane, nor a member of the "Special Attack Corps". The pilot, found burned and mangled on the side of the ship opposite from the hit, wore a complete parachute rigging, and was not elaborately dressed similar to other suicide pilots. The gunnery officer is of the opinion that the pilot was killed by gunfire as he dove in his strafing attack, or that the plane was knocked out of control when very close aboard and thus crashed into the ship.'[2] Just before final impact this aircraft suddenly turned to starboard and, at 17.45, struck the after deckhouse on the port side, detonation taking place between Nos.3 and 4 turrets, penetrating into No.3 mount's handling room. An officer on duty was blown clean out of the forward door of the handling room by 5in powder explosions. There were no indications of any bomb being carried.

The after bulkhead of the after engine room was pierced, and scalding oil and water forced the duty men out, although none were lost. The resulting explosion spread burning aviation fuel over the after deck and 40mm ammunition began igniting as big fires broke out. The deckhouse, the 40mm mounting and the director were smashed up, depth charge rack No.2 was destroyed and direct steering control went out. The torpedoes were jettisoned as were some of the depth-charges but others were already unreachable because of the blaze. Fighting the fires was hampered with the loss of the after repair party under Machinist Wood, all of whom were dead or badly burnt, and by the putting out of action of the fire main and damage to the control valves. As a result neither the after magazines nor handling rooms could be sprinkled. The ship switched to emergency power which brought the two forward 5in mountings and four of the 40mm groups back into action. At 18.09 the depth-charges overheated and blew up with a terrific explosion, killing many of the fire-fighters and blowing others overboard. It was later found that

---

2. Action report USS *Mullany* DD528. 15 March to 6 April 1945. Dated April 16 1945.

the forward starboard corner of No.4 handling room that lay adjacent to the starboard depth-charges had been bent inward and perforated by many fragment holes. *Mullany*, like many of her class, had all her depth-charges stowed above deck, with an estimated 600lb of explosives in each of the twenty-six Mk.7 charges carried on reserve racks and in six projectors with five charges each. It all made for a considerable external detonation which was mainly (but not exclusively) vented upward and outward.

Eight minutes after this tragedy another Kamikaze came in from the port bow and commenced circling *Mullany* at 8,000 yards. She was engaged by the two forward 5in mountings which with six rounds of AA common [i.e. orthodox rounds] and AA special [VT fused shells] knocked her down. There was no respite for within a minute yet a third attacker materialised some 6,000–8,000 yards off the port bow. Fire was shifted to this target by the 5in guns and again, with the expenditure of 39 rounds, one wing was shot away and it also went into the sea. All this was done with excellent style and efficiency and emphasised the efficiency, of the American 5in/38 calibre yet again, showing that only it had the stopping power necessary against a determined foe.

Aft, the *Mullany* was still ablaze despite the best efforts of the survivors, but they incurred further losses as, from 18.25, more detonations occurred among the 5in ammunition in the handling room and more crew were blown into the water or killed outright. Desperate attempts were made to flood the after magazine but in vain, nor could fires near the No.2 magazine's lower ammunition hoist that threatened further carnage be controlled.

Several supporting vessels gradually closed the stricken destroyer. *LCI-461* aided in the fire-fighting efforts from the starboard quarter as did *Gherardi* following its arrival on the scene. Ultimately a small flotilla of vessels came to her aid and surrounded the *Mullany*, with the arrival of the destroyer *Purdy* and the minesweeper *Execute* (AM-232, Lieutenant R E Brenkman); even the diminutive *PGM-10* rescued seventy-five men from the water. *Gherardi* (DMS-30) attempted to take the place of *LCI-461* to use her hoses, but there were so many men in the water with boats trying to rescue them that *Gherardi* was unable to close with *Mullany*, whose decks in some places were glowing and the bulkhead of one of the magazines was reported to be red-hot. Another Japanese aircraft made an approach from dead ahead at 18.28, thinking perhaps the burning *Mullany* was easy pickings, but fifteen rounds of 5in disabused the pilot of such thinking and he turned away.

At 18.29, with this threat removed, *Mullany*'s captain now ordered that the ship be abandoned, which was done efficiently and without further loss. The *Purdy* signalled for both fighter protection and tugs to be sent as it was still hoped to save the ship while the Captain went aboard *LCI-461* to organise volunteer salvage parties to go back aboard and he led the first of these at 23.00. Meanwhile *Purdy* had closed the blazing ship and at great risk, attempted to play her hoses on the area of the after magazines, as did *Execute* which made two abortive attempts to take *Mullany* under tow. The salvage teams, equally bravely, and despite the risk of more explosions, set to work with a will and gradually *Mullany* was transformed, step-by-step, into some semblance of a working ship once more as the long night passed. Numbers 1 & 2 boilers were relit at 00.30, and No.1 turbo-generator brought back into service at 01.00, and the gyro-compass half-an-hour later. *Mullany*'s First Lieutenant made a damage-control inspection and reported back to the

CIC. A manual steering party got to work in the after steering compartment; at 01.45, *Mullany* began to move again on just her starboard engine and worked up to 11 knots steering by magnetic compass. By 08.30 the following day, the destroyer was approaching Kerama Retto anchorage and the steering engine was operational again. The expected tug never did arrive so *Mullany* entered the anchorage on one engine by herself and anchored in berth K–11. It had been a magnificent achievement.

Japanese Army Kamikaze Bases

The main base for the Imperial Army suicide pilots, who represented about 40% of the Kamikazes attacking Allied shipping off Okinawa, was Chiran, Kawanabe, Kagushima, along with its two satellite airfields, Kikaijima and Tokunoshima, from whence Army flyers flew missions with the Ki-43 *Oscar* and Kawasaki Ki-61 *Tony* fighters. But the Imperial Army flyers also operated out of other air bases, including Bansei at the southern tip of Kyūshū, home of the 72nd *Shinbu* [Military Might] Squadron equipped with Type 99 bombers (which badly damaged the destroyer *Braine* on 25 May); Kengun, Kumamoto Prefecture, with both Mitsubishi Ki-67 *Hiryu* bombers [Flying Dragon, *Peggy*] of the *Sakua-dan* type and *Tony* fighter-bombers operating from there; Miyakonojo, Miyazaki Prefecture, with both East and West airfields utilised between 6 April and 1 July by the squadrons of the *Shinbu* Corps, flying *Frank* fighter aircraft; and from Formosa [now Taiwan], from the airfields of Giran, Shinchiku, Taichu and Tainan.

Approximately 400 Army suicide pilots were killed off the Philippines and over 950 more off Okinawa. Allegedly precise figures are offered up, but different sources vary and total reliance cannot be placed upon them, but this estimate suffices to show the scale of the effort mounted by the Army, in what, to this day, many westerners seem to believe was an exclusively Navy operation.[3]

The remarkable Torihama Tome

The very young men, aged between 17 and 25 for the most part, were often very far from home when, as they sincerely believed, they came to offer up their lives to save the country and their families in sacrifice. From their touching poems and memories the natural need for a "mother" figure in their final days of life was often prominent. One remarkable woman, Torihama Tome, along with her daughters Reiko and Miako

---

3. The Chiran Museum itself cites *Tokkotai Irei Junshukai* (Tokkotai Commemoration Memorial Association) own publication *Tokkou Kougekitai* (Special Attack Operations), as 1,036 and exhibits photos of them all, while a latter edition gives a figure of 1,019, but it is far from clear if all these made actual attacks which led to their deaths, or whether these were aerial attacks or other forms of suicide ventures like the ground assault on Yontan airfield. (At Yontan field, on Okinawa, five Mitsubishi Ki-21 *Sally* bombers of 3 *Dokuritsu Chotai*, each carrying eight special suicide commandos under the overall command of Captain Chuichi Suwabe, crash-landed on the night of 24/25 May 1945. They managed to totally destroy nine Allied aircraft and badly damage twenty-nine others before all, save one, were killed by the startled defenders. The lone Japanese survivor managed to escape and join Japanese forces still fighting on the island.)

who made small items of clothing for their guests, offered a substitute matriarchal figure to help lessen the pangs of their final hours. Torihma was the proprietor of the famed *Tomiya* Restaurant in the township of Chiran itself which opened after the base was inaugurated in 1942. Her dedication continued during the post-war years when families of the fallen visited and were equally kindly received, and this touching care later earned her the Sixth Order of Merit from the Japanese Emperor.

Since 2001 the restaurant itself has become the *Hotaru [Firefly]* Museum run by the grandson of Torhma, who died in 1992, and dedicated to the memory of a few of these young men with their last letters home, and shows short movies of her life and memoirs

The 'Battleship Buster'

The one type of warship most immune to the Kamikaze crash was the heavily-armoured battleship, whose decks were designed to resist armour-piercing shells. In order to defeat such sturdy resistance, the Japanese attempted to produce an aerial–delivery weapon that would, in theory, make even this type of vessel vulnerable. They took for their inspiration from the German *Luftwaffe*'s SHL-6000 *Hohlladungsbombe* (SHC- Special Hollow Charge bomb) which had been designed to achieve the same objective. Although the two systems were by no means identical of course, in that the German was electronically guided while the Japanese was piloted, they were to be delivered to the target area in rather a similar manner. The German *Mistel* weapon consisted of an adapted Junkers Ju 88 bomber packed with explosives, with a guiding fighter plane and pilot 'piggy-back' mounted on top. The brainchild of Siegfried Holzbauer, the weapon had a copper-core penetrator and tests showed that it could pierce 24ft of steel armour plate or 60ft of reinforced concrete. The Germans planned to use this weapon against selected Soviet targets beyond the Urals under Operation *Eisenhammer* (Iron Hammer), and also later attempted to use it against Allied battleships off Normandy in 1944, (Operation *Beethoven*), but failed. They scored a near-miss on the frigate HMS *Nith* (K-215, Lieutenant-Commander Donald Emberton Mansfield), which had been converted to a Brigade Headquarters Ship, which slightly damaged her and caused a few casualties, but she was quickly repaired and put back into action again. Rumours that they also hit the scuttled hulk of the old French battleship *Courbet* (which was being used as a breakwater offshore) appear to have little or no foundation in fact.[4] The Japanese had comparable ideas and also planned to use a potentially devastating weapon against Allied capital ships and carriers, and so produced, not a copy, but their own unique solution. It was an awesome weapon, in short, a 3–ton thermite bomb, the *Sakura-dan*.

The Germans certainly contributed to the development of this weapon sending plans of their own bomb, as then yet to be tested in actual combat, to Japan aboard the *B-1* Class Japanese submarine *I-30* (Commander Shinobu Endo, IJN), in October 1942 as part of Operation *Yanagi*. The *I-30* left L'Orient submarine base in France with a variety of top-secret equipment and plans, and reached Singapore on 13 October, only for her to be

---

4. Fleischer, Wolfgang, *Deutsche Abwurfmunition bis 1945* (German Air-Launched Weapons to 1945); 2003; Motorbuch Verlag Pietsch.

sunk off Keppel Harbour in a British minefield that same day. Some of her precious cargo was rescued however and reached Japan without being ruined by seawater, but exactly what is not clear as great secrecy was exercised. Tucked away far from prying eyes, or any hope of snooping, the weapon was developed by the Pai-Chengzi complex at Shandung, in their vassal state of Manchukuo (Manchuria). Whether influenced by the Germans or not, the *Sakura-dan* was produced and was used in combat as a suicide weapon.

Rather than using the hollow-charge principle, the Japanese weapon was in essence a thermite-based directional incendiary charge. It had a 5ft 3in diameter with a 15–degree downward-angled base which faced forward. The parabolic rear casing of this weapon was strongly-constructed from 1.7 inch thick material designed to channel the blast forwards on impact. This projected an enormous blast of flame 3,280ft ahead of the detonation point. It was estimated that such a strike impacting at a distance of 985ft from a medium army tank would completely annihilate it. This 6,393lb device was imbedded into a specially-adapted Ki-67 *Hiryu* [*Peggy*] bomber. To accommodate the weapon and locate it exactly at the centre of gravity (CG) of the host aircraft, thus enabling it to fly correctly with such a burden, the upper fuselage had to be sliced away and the projection then faired over with plywood to maintain airflow and balance. The whole crew compartment on the starboard side of the aircraft was deleted as was all defensive armament, thus the remaining flight crew was honed down to five, a pilot, engineer, navigator and radio operators. It was flight-tested at Kagamigahara air base in Gifu Prefecture, in February 1945. The first unit to take delivery of this weapons system was the 62nd *Sentai* based at Nishi Tsukuba, which received two. The unit then transferred to Tachiarai on the island of Kiushim, and one machine, piloted by Lieutenant Kato Kozaburo, flew over to Kanoya, in northern Kyushu, from where the first combat mission was despatched on 17 April, the other machine having been destroyed in an accident. The intended targets were the fleet carriers of Task Force 58 off Okinawa and the *Sakura-dan* machine was accompanied by two Ki-67 *Tokubetu Kougeki* (Special Attack Units – *To Go*) aircraft, part of a force of forty-nine suicide aircraft despatched that day, of which thirty returned to base. So what happened to Lieutenant Kato?

The three '*Peggys*' had taken off independently from 07.13 and, at 09.50, managed to elude F6F Hellcats of the CAP patrolling south-east of the island of Tokunsoshima. Twenty minutes later Kato radioed that he had located a carrier and was about to attack it. One of the navigators of the other *Peggy* duo, Commander Maemura, allegedly saw a trail of flame pouring from Kato's aircraft. It suddenly climbed abruptly into the clouds and vanished. Nothing more was heard and the assumption was that this aircraft had either been hit or that the weapon had malfunctioned and had somehow self-destructed along with its host. Whatever the reason no attack was made or reported. Two further *Sakuran-dan* conversions were delivered to the 62nd *Sentai*. These were again joined by two *To-Go Hirtu* machines and took off from Kanoya on 27 May for a second strike attempt. Once more both *Sakuran-dan* reported that they were attacking specific targets but were never seen again, while their accompanying *Peggys* aborted.

Meanwhile a second unit, reported to be commanded by Major Katano Isamu, had been formed in June. At the ceasefire the aircraft were determined to carry on and launch an attack on Saipan, scheduled for 16 August. One special aircraft was said to have been sabotaged and whether the other did succeed in taking off is unsure, but no *Sakura-dan* machines were ever found after the surrender.

Further Attacks

On 7 April 1945 another mass attack took place with fifty-four Naval Kamikaze from 5th Air Fleet of which twenty-four returned without completing their missions. In addition in this two-day period the Army Kamikaze pilots launched 125 sorties. Their successes included a dusk attack on the battleship *Maryland* (BB-46) when a Kamikaze crashed atop her No.3 turret, destroying the 20mm gun batteries mounted there, with the loss of sixteen killed and 37 wounded, but she continued in action. The other casualty this day was the destroyer escort *Wesson* (DE-184) which was hit amidships by a Kamikaze that crashed into her torpedo-tubes, resulting in eight dead and twenty-three wounded. The engine rooms were flooded and she was taken in tow by the destroyer *Lang* (DD-339) but she later made Kerama Retto under her own power and was subsequently sent back to San Francisco for proper repairs.

On the 11th Kamikaze attacks were lighter than previously, with the first breaking over the Task Groups at 13.30. Individual aircraft were reported overhead in the cloud cover by radar. Rear-Admiral Frederick Carl 'Ted' Sherman's Task Group 58.3 had a British liaison officer (LO) embarked, and his report revealed how the Japanese were learning how even economical use of such tactics could keep the Allied crews continuously on the alert for long periods and contribute to exhaustion. It was noted that the Japanese 'were ingenious, using window, coming in singly, using cloud and the sun, co-ordination of their dives very ably and obviously aware of the deficiencies of present radar installations.'

He continued: 'Plenty of practice was had by all in countering the suicide type of attack – twelve suiciders being shot down by gunfire by Task Group 58.3 without a ship being hit, although damage was caused by near misses. The shooting was excellent – particularly impressive being the quick sighting and opening fire, and the rapid training and firing of *Bunker Hill*'s 5in turrets controlled by Mk.51 directors. Nevertheless the suiciders once in their dive were persistent blighters and took a lot of punishment before being deflected from their targets, and as there were about eight misses within 100 yards of the bigger ships of the group it would seem that the problem of the suicider is not entirely solved.'

'The attacks continued in bursts for the remainder of the day, but fortunately the Japanese have not yet learnt that the most vulnerable time for a carrier Task Force is at dusk – the force being undisturbed during this period. The total bag for the day was thirteen shot down by gunfire and seventeen by fighters.'

The Japanese despatched sixty-four Kamikazes against the US Fleet, of which thirty-four, more than half, returned without result. Of the damage inflicted by the remaining thirty machines, the battleship *Missouri* (BB-63) with Task Group 58.4 was stuck by a Kamikaze but brushed this off without any damage at all. The *Enterprise* (CV-6) was near-missed by a total of four Kamikazes, and had some of her forward tanks pierced, distorted one of her shafts, and damaged power supplies and radars. She had to return to Ulithi to effect repairs. The *Essex* (CV-9, Captain Carlos Wilhelm Wieber) had a forward fuel tank pierced and one radar knock out. The destroyer *Kidd* (DD-661, Commander Harry Grimshaw Moore) was damaged and the destroyer *Bullard* (DD-660, Commander Eigel Thornton Steen) – slightly damaged by Kamikazes. Off Okinawa the destroyer escort *Samuel S. Miles* (DE-183, Lieutenant-Commander Henry G Brousseau) was damaged.

Flooding as a destroyer loss

The US destroyers which had borne the brunt of the Kamikaze attacks and which would continue to do so, proved remarkably resilient. The main reason for this is that the suicide attackers mainly inflicted damage above the waterline rather than below it. Because of this very few destroyers sank quickly. So far there were just two proven exceptions to this and the results were sobering.

The destroyer *Reid* (Commander Samuel Aldo McCornock) was hit in Ormoc Bay, Leyte on 11 December 1944, and lost 103 men killed and 45 more wounded. Twelve aircraft attacked her and number seven, a Zeke, scored a direct hit on her fantail which detonated the after ammunition magazines blowing her entire stern off. Water immediately flooded through the ship and she sank by the stern before rolling over. She vanished beneath the waves two minutes after the first blast. There were only 120 survivors, one of whom, a seventeen-year old, when interrogated with "How was your ship sunk – torpedoed?" because she went under so quickly, responded "Well – that's what we were told to say." Asked why he replied, "They don't want information to leak out how effective suicide bombing is. The way I look at it is, it's not only the damage to ships that is effective, it's the mental impression that it makes on those it hits."

On the 28 May the new destroyer *Drexler* (DD-741, Commander Ronald Lee Wilson) was patrolling to the north-west of Okinawa when she was hit by two Army Kawasaki Ki-45 *Toryu (Nick)* twin-engined fighters, each carrying two bombs under their wings, in quick succession at 07.02 and 07.04. The ship was immediately opened up and the sea flooded in so quickly that, within just 49 seconds after the second aircraft struck her, she sank. Such a rapid loss naturally meant very heavy casualties, some 158 men were lost, the majority of which went down with the ship as there was no time to escape. Of the rest who got clear, two were found dead on recovery, and fifty-four were wounded. There have been several published accounts of her loss, which included some harsh recriminations from survivors.

On the 12th the Japanese threw their main weight against the ships off the anchorage and their escort, and only one attack was directed at the Task Force that day. The Japanese were now throwing in all manner of aircraft, including many obsolete types, including biplanes, and these were easily dealt with by patrolling fighters who claimed to have destroyed 154 machines. In fact the Japanese despatched eighty-three naval and sixty army Kamikazes. The escort carrier *Bataan* (CVL-29, Captain Valentine Hixon Schaetfer) was near-missed but remained undamaged. Following which the Task Force re-organised again after losses to three Groups, with TG 58.2 dissolved while TG 58.3 withdrew to refuel.

The casualties taken by the pickets gave pause for thought. 'In future, owing to Japanese preference for attacking outlying destroyers, the Task Force destroyer pickets were to be concentrated in one unit of six to twelve destroyers and furnished with a CAP of eight fighters, to be increased to sixteen fighters as soon as enemy aircraft showed intentions of attacking,' wrote the British Liaison Officer.

Kamikaze results against Okinawa Support Force

While the attacks on Task Force 58 and 57 were serious, the Japanese had also devoted a considerable percentage of their Kamikaze attentions on the ships offshore from the invasion beachheads. In total forty-three ships were damaged by Kamikazes compared to just six ships damaged by orthodox bombing, three by mines, one by aerial torpedo, one by gunfire and one by suicide boat. Among the ships sunk by Kamikazes were three destroyers, two APD, three AE and two small craft. Ships damaged and irreparable at forward bases included one battleship, one escort carrier, one heavy cruiser, eleven destroyers, three destroyer escorts, five Attack Transports, a minelayer and two LSTs. Ships damaged but repairable in the forward area were listed as one battleship, one light cruiser, seven destroyers, one LST, two LCI, 3 AKA Cargo Ships Attack and two APD High Speed Transports.

The Allied Fighter Defences

The main culling of the Kamikazes was in the air, and the Allied forces used a mixed bag of single-engined fighter aircraft to oppose their implacable enemy. Aboard the US Navy carriers the principal interceptor was the Grumman F6F Hellcat, a big, strong airplane, well-proven by this stage of the war. As the suicide pilots took their increasing toll, the ratio of the aircraft types maintained aboard the aircraft carriers changed to reflect an increasingly defensive posture. That alone was a tribute to the effect of the Kamikaze. The three main types of aircraft, the defending Hellcats, and for offensive operations the dive bombing Curtis SB2C Helldiver and the torpedo-bombing Grumman/Goodyear TBF/TBM Avenger, hitherto had approximately one-third of the embarked complement of aircraft each. This rapidly changed and at Okinawa offensive power was reduced by a third as more fighters were carried.

The United States Marine Corps used the powerful Chance-Vought F4U Corsair from airfields ashore, both in the Philippines, flying from Guiuan airstrip on Samar, and at Okinawa where they used Kadena airfield. Once such shore bases could be established on the Marine flyers made a large contribution to the aerial battles and some seventeen different USMC squadrons were involved, the fighters claiming 506 "kills" at Okinawa alone. Typical of these was Marine Air Group 14 (MAG-14), commanded by Colonel Edward A Montgomery, which comprised three squadrons equipped with F4U-4 Corsairs, VMF-212 ('The Hellhounds'), under Major John P. McMahon, VMF-222 ('The Flying Deuces'), commanded by Major Harold A. Harwood, and VMF-223, ('The Bull-Dogs') under Captain Howard E. King, USMC. They had transhipped bases from the Philippines to Okinawa aboard the *Hillsborough County* (LST-827), Lieutenant R. L. Olander, USN, and soon made their mark. Between them the three Corsair squadrons alone claimed 410 enemy aircraft destroyed. Some Marine units were transported aboard escort carriers, the *Commencement Bay* Class ship *Block Island* (CVE-106), Captain Francis Massie Hughes, USMC, hosting VMF-511, and her sister ship *Gilbert Islands* (CVE107), Captain Lester Kimme Rice, USMC, had VMF-512 aboard.

One Marine flyer, Major Vernon E. Ball of the VMF-323 ('Death Rattlers') squadron was dubbed an 'instant ace' by the American press corps after being catapulted off the escort carrier *White Plains* on 9th April to fly ashore to Ruby Field, the Allied code name for Kadena, on Okinawa. During a brief, but very eventful flight, Ball managed to survive an unintentional mid-air collision which destroyed one Japanese aircraft and then, with his damaged Corsair, destroyed a second, before landing.[5] F4Us also began serving with shipboard Navy fighter squadrons as well and proved to be one of the best aircraft of the period, going on to do good work in the Korean War many years later. Night-fighters also featured in the USMC line-up, and Captain Robert C. Baird, USMC, of VMF(N)-533 flying a Grumman F6F night-fighter shot down a *Betty* at 03.51 and then a G3M *Nell* at 05.01 on a single mission on 16th June. By day VMF-223 claimed some of the last Japanese aircraft destroyed in the Okinawa campaign when they accounted for four Ki-44s over Amami O Shima at 18.30 on 21st June.

Finally, in contrast to the standardised composition of the American units involved, the Royal Navy flew their usual mish-mash of types, of varying effectiveness. Historically crippled by a long period under RAF control between 1918 and 1939, the Royal Navy's Fleet Air Arm, from being at the forefront of naval aviation development in the former year had, through an almost total lack of interest and crippling limitations of funding, fallen far behind both the IJN and the USN by the outbreak of war. Churchill's obsession with strategic bombing had ensured that the bulk of British wartime expenditure had gone to producing thousands of heavy bombers, which meant the Fleet Air Arm had to make to do with either conversions from current RAF aircraft, a tiny number of new British-built naval types or, principally, on obtaining American naval aircraft from Lend-Lease.

So the British fighter aircraft at Okinawa included the delicate Supermarine Seafire, a 'navalised' version of the famous Spitfire – sleek, elegant, but far too fragile for the rough and tumble of sea warfare, and with a pathetically short range. The Seafire was mainly used for the immediate CAP but suffered more damage from deck landings than combat. On occasions it proved itself capable of outfighting the Zero, as when *Indefatigable*'s Seafires knocked down three out of four *Zeke*s on 4th May, without loss to themselves, but this aircraft proved a constant anxiety to keep operational. The Chance-Vought Corsair was the most efficient and tough fighter. The British pilots had no trouble operating this powerful aircraft from the decks of their fleet carriers, which were smaller than the US Navy flight decks, but whose own navy had, initially, rejected them for this purpose. However, due to its strength and its ability to carry larger bomb-loads than most other naval aircraft, they were mainly used as fighter-bombers rather than in the interceptor role. Luckily the BPF also had the Grumman F6F Hellcat and they proved as effective in British hands as in American, even if their numbers were comparatively paltry.

Home-built aircraft included the Fairey Firefly, but again she was used mainly as a ground strafer and rocket-firing attacker. An excellent British Naval fighter aircraft was in the process of being prepared, the superb Hawker Sea Fury, which would have finally given the Royal Navy an aircraft to equal, or outclass any other naval fighter, but, alas it arrived too late on the scene to affect anti-Kamikaze operations.

During *Iceberg 1* the BPF had destroyed just thirty Japanese aircraft but had themselves lost fifty-nine, many of them in accidents. The same pattern was shown in phase 2, with ninety-six Japanese aircraft being destroyed (mainly on the ground) for the loss of no less than ninety-eight British aircraft on operations and a dreadful sixty-two in accidents. It was a sobering experience.

5. Wolf, Dr William, *Death Rattlers: VMF 323 over Okinawa*, Atglen, Penn: 199. Schiffer Publishing.

Liaison Officer Opinions

The British Pacific Fleet Liaison Officer commented that: 'The defences ashore still appear to be deficient of an effective radar warning system and the heavy losses suffered by picket destroyers in bolstering up this system would appear to be excessive. Task Force 58 has achieved greater success in this respect by concentrating the pickets into one body and giving them a very adequate CAP. As a result of losses at Okinawa, the number of picket stations have been reduced and brought closer in, but the strength of the pickets (2 DDs and 2 LST or LCIs) has not been increased. The need for these pickets to carry out the double duty of radar pickets and anti-submarine screen has presumably been the root of the trouble because of the large number of positions required for the latter.' He added: 'The pickets were heavily attacked, four being sunk and many others damaged. In the inner areas mutual support when practicable was of great value. In general, fighter direction was far more effective than in the Lingayen operation. This was particularly so when the presence of all available Fast Carrier aircraft permitted real defence in depth. Relatively few aircraft reached the transport area, but the price paid by the pickets and screens was very high. The gallantry and devotion of these ships was beyond praise.'

'Gun defence was probably better than in the past with the 40 mm particularly accurate. There were, however, many cases when repeated hits from these weapons failed to stop the suicide. A hit or VT burst from a 5in was the only certain killer. The writer would find the proceedings less tedious if we had a gun capable of firing a 20lb, VT-fused shell every second from a mounting remote power controlled by a Mark 51 Director.'

The question of equipping the British Pacific Fleet with VT fuses, which after all British scientists had helped to develop in the first place, was one of several subjects where the generally good Anglo-American relationships met friction points, mainly due to the hostile attitude of Admiral Ernest King.

The British Premier, Winston Churchill, who constantly prodded his military chiefs on the every detail of the day-to-day running of the war, had, a year before, sent one of his infamous 'Action This Day' notes to the First Lord of the Admiralty, Albert V. Alexander, and the First Sea Lord , Admiral Andrew Browne Cunningham, on the matter.[6] Captain Stephen Roskill, RN, later to become the official British Naval Historian, but at that time an acknowledged anti-aircraft expert and in 1945 Chief Staff Officer for administration of the British Admiralty Delegation (BAD) in Washington, DC, was later to recount how he had first-hand knowledge of this particular difficulty with King and how his chief, Admiral Sir James Somerville, was able to overcome it.

'When I went to negotiate with King's staff for the BPF's allocation I came up against a brick wall of refusal, so I raised the issue to Somerville at one of his weekly staff meetings. He asked for a brief on the subject, which I quickly provided, and the very next evening when we met at a cocktail party he said to me "Well, Stephen, I've got your VT fuses." I was so astonished that I asked how he had done it. He said "Well, as today was a public holiday I thought it would be a good chance to catch Ernie, so I asked for an appointment and got it. I then said to Ernie "Look here, this VT fuse business in which we helped you with the design, has always been on a fifty-fifty basis when they got into production. Your

---

6. Churchill to 1st Lord and 1st Sea Lord, 10 January 1945, and their reply dated 21 January 1945. National Archive ADM.205/35.

staff is quite willing [which was not at all true] but they say there's a funny old bugger up top that's stopping it – and that's you!" Whereupon King had yielded- perhaps in astonishment at Somerville's mode of addressing him.'[7] This was done on 27 March 1945, as Somerville's pocket diary entry for that date confirms, he and Lieutenant-General G. N. Macready, the latter representing Chief of the Imperial General Staff, met with King that day and that King said 'he'd have it looked into at once.'

The BPFLO also submitted a series of notes on air attacks at Okinawa between 23 March and 18 April 1945.[8] In this report he stated that about 80% of all daylight attacks on Task Force 58 were Kamikazes. The principal means of delivery was by single-engined types, *Vals* and *Oscars*. The bomb load was one or two 500lb bombs and it was rare for no bombs at all to be mounted. Approaches were made in small groups of one to four aircraft, the exceptions to this rule being mass attacks received on 6, 12 and 16 April when groups of ten to thirty aircraft were received. Heights varied from 10,000ft to 20,000ft until about thirty miles out from the target where, even if *not* intercepted, a steep power glide brought the Kamikaze down to less than 5,000 ft. The favoured target for the Kamikaze pilot was always the aircraft carrier, but, where no carrier was immediately available, single ships were selected for obvious reasons (weaker defence capability, no supporting fire) and the radar pickets suffered accordingly.

Each Kamikaze's final approach was also made individually, no matter how strong the group it belonged to, although on occasions attacks consisting of up to ten machines would approach in rapid succession, generally from the same sector in a conveyor-belt type of delivery. As the battle progressed the Japanese achieved better co-ordination, especially against lone targets, and combined *Viper (Ōhka)* attacks with both suicide attacks and dummy runs by the target co-ordinator.

'Comparatively little use was made of sun and cloud cover though it was not unusual to see a plane circling outside effective gun range for several minutes while it selected a target. Most of the attacks were of the very low type, with a corkscrewing approach, and a final climb and pushover on to the target. The remainder of the attacks were made in shallow dive with last minute wingover sometimes onto a target adjacent to the one originally aimed at. No attacks were observed in which the initial angle of dive exceeded 30 degrees.'

In a supplementary report submitted after the second stage of the operation, the BPFLO stated that there had been few marked changes to the Japanese tactics. Those changes that were made were:

(a) The number of high reconnaissance flights increased.
(b) The variety of aircraft types devoted to Kamikaze operations widened to include *Jacks* and *Georges*, and even twin-float seaplanes were observed.
(c) There was the first suicide aircraft attack made against Task Force 57.
(d) A few night suicide attacks were attempted.

---

7. *Churchill and the Admirals*, Roskill, Captain S. W. 1977. Collins, London, pps 270–271.
8. ADM199/591; *Operation Iceberg – Report of BPLO to Commander 5th Fleet. Annex 'A' – Notes on Air Attacks at Okinawa. 23rd March – 18th April.*

Okinawa Attacks – BPFLO Analysis.

Type	Sunk	Damage Severe	Damage Moderate	Damage Slight
Fleet Carrier (CV)	0	5	3	1
Light Fleet Carrier (CVL)	0	0	0	2
Escort Carrier (CVE)	0	2	1	0
Battleship (BB)	0	2	4	4
Heavy Cruiser (CA)	0	1	1	1
Light Cruiser (CL)	0	0	2	2
Destroyer (DD)	8	29	14	13
Destroyer Minelayer (DM)	0	4	1	4
Destroyer Minesweeper (DMS)	1	4	1	3
Destroyer Escort (DE)	0	9	7	3
Minesweeper (AM)	2	2	1	1
Transport (APA & AP)	0	0	4	4
HIGH Speed Transport (APD)	1	0	4	1
Hospital Transport (APH)	0	1	0	0
Hospital Ship (AH)	0	0	1	0
Surveying Ship (AGS)	0	0	0	1
Dry dock (ARD)	0	0	0	1
Seaplane Tender (AV & AVD)	1	0	1	0
Attack Transport (AKA & AK)	0	2	1	2
Ammunition Ship (Army) (XAK)	3	1	0	2
Oiler (AO)	0	0	1	0
Minelayer (CM)	0	1	0	0
Motor Gunboat (PGM)	2	0	1	0
Motor Minesweeper (YMS)	1	1	4	0
Landing Craft (LCI,LCS,LSM,LST)	9	7	5	16
TOTAL	28	71	57	61

The use of window was continued on a lavish scale and even window-filled bombs were postulated. This use of window was not to protect themselves, but deliberate attempts to shield the approach of low flying Kamikazes.

As to changes in the Fleet's defence posture, the BPFLO stated unequivocally that: 'The most notable feature has been the gun defence put up by the destroyer pickets. They claim no special methods in achieving their astonishing results, but it is noteworthy that all strongly urge holding fire until the enemy is within effective range. This is an old precept which has tended to fall into disrepute.'

Okinawa Attacks – BPFLO – Loss by Type of attack comparison.

Type Of Attack	Sunk	Severe Damage	Moderate Damage	Slight Damage	Total
Kamikaze Hit or Near Miss	19	62	33	37	151
Bomb Hit or Near Miss	0	1	2	6	9
Ōhka Attack	1	1	1	1	4
Aerial Torpedo	0	1	0	0	1
Strafing	0	1	0	0	1
Suicide Boat	1	3	0	3	7
Mine	4	0	1	0	5
MTB	1	0	0	0	1
Ramming Submarine	0	1	0	0	1
Booby Trap	0	0	1	0	1
Shore Batteries	0	0	2	2	4
Grounding & Beaching	1	0	7	7	15
Weather, Collision etc	1	3	5	1	10
Friendly Fire	0	0	3	6	9
TOTAL	28	73	55	63	219

Against the Ōhka – of which only half-a-dozen had been launched at that time – tracer control of 40mm and 20mm is recommended, with a mixture of two-second fixed barrage and VT for the 5in. It was noted that what was termed "the old Guadalcanal trick" was employed by some destroyers and this was described by veterans as going full ahead, putting the rudder hard over and swinging round the anchor to bring all guns to bear on a suicider.'

The best defence against the Japanese use of window was careful correlation of radar reports from pickets to sort the wheat (incoming Kamikazes) from the chaff (defending fighter patrols).[9]

The COMICPAC, Admiral Chester William Nimitz's views on the matter were revealed at a meeting aboard the yacht, *Dauntless*, early in March. During a discussion with Somerville he expressed the following opinion. 'Referring to suicide attacks he said that these do affect morale to some extent and the main thing was to have as few men as possible on the upper deck and exposed to such attacks. It was the sight of subsequent casualties which seemed to upset officers and men more than anything else. *Saratoga*'s heavier flight deck [it was built of teak] undoubtedly saved her after she had been hit by four suiciders.'[10]

---

9. ADM199/591– /458/BPF/026.
10. *The Somerville Papers*; Simpson, Michael, 1995: London. Scolar Press for The Navy Records Society, pp 637.

These figures were, of course, only provisional, but even at that early date they were far more accurate than the grotesquely exaggerated figures of Allied losses quoted by the Japanese at the time, or even decades later! One Japanese publication claimed that during the final phase of the war Kamikazes sank 57 aircraft-carriers, while 108 other warships and escort carriers were so badly damaged that they took no further part in the war, while another 84 were less seriously damaged and 221 lightly damaged, a total casualty list of 470 warships. This claim was still being made over four decades after the true figures were widely known![11]

BPF Aircraft Direction and Radar Intercepts

Although it was usual for the British to find themselves the pupils and not the teachers in adopting the new form of air/sea warfare as perfected by the Americans during the period 1943/45, in one particular field of expertise they felt themselves, rightly or wrongly, superior to their ally in respect of fighter control.

Learnt the hard way via hard-fought European operations like Operation *Pedestal* in 1942 in which three fleet carriers had operated together against land-based German and Italian high-performance aircraft, this was an asset hard to quantify but of the utmost importance.

The British Pacific Fleet's experiences during Operation *Iceberg* was salutary when they examined how successful, or otherwise, they had been in intercepting incoming Kamikaze attacks with their much lighter fighter defences and weaker anti-aircraft weaponry in comparison to their American opposite numbers. The report stated that ten separate attacks were made against the BPF in this period. Of these seven were intercepted and their attacks thwarted before they could be delivered. Three of the attackers penetrated the CAP and delivered their attacks as described above. In total the BPF made forty-three ship-controlled interceptions resulting in twenty-eight kills and some "possibles". Shadowing aircraft were also located and fighters vectored out, but in at least seven instances the intercept failed. This was put down to a combination of errors in height-finding, violent evasive action by the target aircraft and, in the case of the *Dinah* aircraft, by their greater speed and clever use of cloud cover. The British also itemised Japanese methods as used against the BPF and these were summarised thus:

'Attacks have been made by small groups of four to six suicide bombers which are usually single-engine aircraft escorted by one twin-engine 'Pilot' (*sic*) [Guide]. Suicide aircraft do not rely upon mutual support.'

'On interception or on sighting the force, the group breaks formation and each aircraft seeks to approach and attack individually.'

'Intruder tactics have been used by aircraft which follow in behind returning strikes.' [This was an old Japanese ploy and was used as early as the Battle of Midway in 1942]

'To ensure immunity [of the ships being attacked] each aircraft has to be shot down.'

---

11. Kamikaze Kankō Iinkai, eds., *Shashinshū – Kamikaze: riu, Kaigun tokubetsu kōgekitai, jō*, pp19. (KK Besutoseraazu, 1996.

'Suicide attacks may be made at any height according to weather conditions. Attacks low on the water offer the greatest difficulty owing to the short range at which they are detected.'

On the performance of various British radar outfits in detecting incoming Japanese aircraft it was stated that Types 281 and 798 'performed satisfactorily within their known limitations.' The Japanese dispersal tactics 'aggravate the difficulty in distinguishing between different aircraft at approximately the same range.' The Type 277 was said to have 'lived up to expectations as a low cover set' and provided reliable low cover out to distance of between twenty-five to thirty miles, with occasional ranges of thirty-five to forty-five miles on aircraft flying at heights of between 1,000 and 3,000ft. It was noted that correct height-finding had been "disappointing" and that was probably due to 'the difficulty in picking up the right aircraft without an azicator.'[12]

Phase II of *Iceberg* brought further debate. On the disposition of the fleet it was appreciated that close mutual support between the ships was essential if the suicide bomber which broke through the outer defences was to be destroyed before reaching its target. The accepted policy of having the heavy ships and carriers well separated, in order to provide ample room for manoeuvring and for operating aircraft, was modified. The new thinking called for much closer station-keeping which reduced the distance and a new cruising plan, 5F, was introduced to reflect this. With this the carriers were placed around a 2,000–yard radius circle, each with a destroyer astern of her and the battleships and cruisers within 2,000 yards of the carriers. It was thought that these distances might be reduced yet further.

It was noted that *Formidable* and *Indomitable* had both been hit by suicide aircraft when only shielded by destroyers, the heavy ships being away conducting a shore bombardment. The delivery of much heavier ordnance over a shorter period into the target area by this method was offset by the vulnerability of the carriers in leaving them thus exposed. The pros and cons were discussed at length and the decision was that when the next shore bombardment took place, the 5.25in cruisers would be left with the carriers. Another point, perhaps obvious, was that the greater the distance from the target the fleet was, the less attacks developed against it. Here again a balance had to be struck between this fact and the

---

12. ADM199/1041; Appendix V to VABPF No. 1092/4 of 9th May, 1945–Secret. Operation *Iceberg*, pp1. An Azicator was a modified form of PPI (Plan Position Indicator) and consisted of a PPI displaying Type 281 radar with a mechanical bearing cursor which was coupled to the Type 277 bearing control. *Very* briefly, the Azicator was placed so that it could be viewed by the Type 277 bearing operator who could thus make the Type 277 aerials follow in Azimuth a moving target while searching in elevation. See – Report on Radar Type 277, Commanding Officer escort carrier *Campania*. The Commanding Officer of the light cruiser *Emerald* also sent in a Radar Report which revealed that with this new equipment, 'Aircraft are frequently tracked across the plot at ranges over 50 miles which have not been detected by Type 281 and a height therefore not obtained.' With this equipment *Campania* was able to achieve a series of 'Best Seen' fixes that varied from aircraft as low as 50ft being picked up at 26 miles distance, through aircraft at 1,500ft being located at 55 miles and aircraft flying at 10,000 feet being located at 73 miles. See also *Azicators and Allocators, 1944–1945*, (AVIA 7/2400 (D2753), and *Warning Radar Displays – PPI – Part 1, Revolutionary Effect of Radar*. Naval Instruction Film, ADM 2579–1 1948–07. National Archives, Kew, London.

extra distance the strike aircraft from the carriers would have to fly to conduct their own missions. It was noted that American opinion varied considerably on this dilemma, one report advocating a distance of 150 miles, another of only sixty miles. Both Allies agreed on the essentialness of stationing a destroyer close astern of each carrier.

Gunnery needed to be improved. The replacement of the after set of torpedo-tubes on the *Napier* Class destroyers by Bofors guns was in progress. In the end the four ships, *Napier* (D13), *Nepal* (D14), *Nizam* (D15) and *Norman* (D16) were thus modified and had a single Mk.II 40mm mounted on the amidships searchlight platform to give a clear field of fire, with a quadruple 2–pdr pom-pom abaft the funnel, two twin 20mm Oerlikons amidships and two singles in the bridge wings.

Admiral Vian also commented that, against the Kamikaze, 'It was painfully evident (and discouraging to the guns' crews) that the Oerlikons have not the necessary stopping power.'

What this meant in practice was described by Petty Officer Telegraphist Terry Morgan who was serving aboard the destroyer *Grenville*, the Flotilla Leader of the 25th Destroyer Flotilla (DF).

'When an attack was imminent certain destroyers left the screen and steamed in close support of the carriers. *Grenville* was one of these (KK) Kamikaze Destroyers as they were called. During the launching or recovery of aircraft was when the Japanese seemed to choose to attack and I had to go to the Bridge on one occasion when *Grenville* was in her Kamikaze support position, and it was frightening. The Fleet was steaming into wind at high speed and looming up on one side about a cable away was the battleship *King George V* and on the other the carrier *Formidable*, both dwarfing little *Grenville*. What it must have been like when everyone was firing, goodness knows, we in the Wireless Office could only hear the gunfire and feel the shudders as our guns fired. But to beat a Kamikaze it had to be destroyed and there was an opinion that the 20mm projectile would knock bits off the aircraft, but a heavier shell was needed to destroy it.'

'In one case the Kamikaze pilot in his white robes was blown into the mast of the carrier he had attacked. The medical staff removed his remains and carried out a post-mortem on the body to ascertain if the Kamikaze pilots were perhaps under the influence of drugs when committing suicide. *Grenville*'s close-range weapons were kept busy during these attacks supporting the carriers. Looking back I cannot remember the day's battles being discussed in the Mess, we seemed to accept it as normal routine.'

'On our previous visit to Ulithi our Captain had visited an American warship that had been hit by a Kamikaze with two crew onboard. Our Captain suggested that the extra man was 'A man under punishment'.'[13]

USN thinking at this stage

The American thinking on pickets was continually refined in the light of bitter experience. There was an exchange between the Commander, Third Fleet, and CTF 31. Spruance

13. Morgan, Terry – *A Tel's War*, Lee-on-Solent, 2001. pp 86. Self-published, reproduced by courtesy of the author.

wrote: 'Continued heavy damage to pickets call for constant study and re-evaluation, and justifies giving serious consideration to radical changes in dispositions, composition and techniques.'

'Desire you consider the following and make appropriate experiments having regard for all calculated risks and informing me of your plans and estimates:

(a) Reduce number of manned picket stations to four.
(b) Increase strength of each exposed picket station by adding homogenous types which will about double 5in and AA weapons on station.
(c) Maintain CAP of 4 to 8 fighters over each picket station.
(d) Orbit the CAP elements in such position as to enable them to deal with Nip planes threatening pickets, before attack on pickets can develop.
(e) Employ PT's on picket duty to give warning of approach of low flying planes both remote from and close to anchorage.
(f) Reduce transport area screen to reinforce pickets on basis of lesser present danger from enemy submarines and surface craft.'

The establishment of radar warning stations on the smaller islands of the group where they could perform a similar function to the pickets at sea was also under consideration, but this was dependant on ships and men being available to occupy suitable sites.

Halsey replied:

'The security of pickets and other isolated units of force has been the subject of the most careful and constant consideration. Many of the excellent suggestions contained in your 290231 are already in effect and have proved effective. Specific comment follows:

(a) Five picket stations now in use and is present minimum, pending satisfactory development of station on Tori Shima. Further reduction may be made after establishment of stations on Ineya and Aguni.
(b) Relief picket ships now arrive prior sunset and remain until after dark, thereby augmenting picket strength during critical twilight period. During recent heavy attacks picket strength was increased to 3 DD and in some cases to 4.
(c) and (d) – TCAP [Target Combat Air Patrol – a CAP over the target zone] of 8 to 12 planes has been provided each picket for a considerable period and has been most successful. Plan provides 2 planes at picket and remainder to be vectored by picket as required.
(d) Ship warning close to anchorage now provided by inner screen which also provides A/S coverage. Possible use of PT's [PT boats – an American equivalent of British motor torpedo boats (MTB) – light, fast wooden-hulled small craft.] with pickets will be explored.

(e) During dusk periods and periods of probable attacks, transport area is pulled in to permit doubling up screening units for mutual protection. This has proved effective. Plans now being studied for reducing screen.'[14]

The American Intelligence evaluation

On 20 July 1945, as the Okinawa operation was drawing to its conclusion, the Office of Strategic Service s (OSS) issued its own evaluation of the Kamikaze phenomenon.[15]

After a review of what apparently was the motivation behind this tendency and a review of the various methods known to be prepared, the study moved on to examine the Kamikaze form of aerial attack. They stated unequivocally that: 'The suicide planes and piloted bombs are the most glamorous of the suicide weapons yet devised. Implementation of the idea of self-immolation, via a crash in flames on the deck of an enemy battleship for the undying glory of self and for Emperor, results in a serious threat to Allied surface operations. Despite the serious attrition of Japanese aircraft and pilots, the threat is likely to continue.'

It was acknowledged that, 'Japanese suicide air tactics have been improved and refined since their first appearance large-scale during the Leyte operation and attacks by Japanese suicide aircraft against Allied shipping have increased sharply in the last few months.' The study thought that, while the earlier missions were "somewhat improvised" and that the flyers themselves were 'spurred on by propaganda' a change of tack was apparent. 'The Japanese High Command now appears determined to exploit these unorthodox tactics to the utmost and has taken steps to improve the training, planning and accomplishment of suicide missions.' The ethos remained, as it always had, belief in the ultimate triumph of Japanese, 'spiritual forces over the enemy's material power.' The indoctrination of pilots was examined. 'No deviation from duty is possible, for the pilot's ancestors, his family, and his name would be forever disgraced. Attacking in steep high-altitude dives or low along the water, these Kamikaze pilots have inflicted considerable damage on Allied shipping.'

The importance of Damage Control

In an examination of destroyer damage during World War II, the US Navy produced the following interesting statistics which compared those ships hit by gunfire, bombs or Kamikazes (ie mainly above the waterline damage) with those damaged by torpedoes or mines (ie below the waterline damage) plus accidental damage victims. The results were predictable, of the former, (a total of 192 destroyers) thirty destroyers were sunk as a result but 162 survived; of those suffering underwater damage, a far smaller number overall 48

14. ADM199/591 – Signals Com3rd Fleet to CTF 31 – Appendix "A" – Despatches Relating to Pickets.
15. Post-war the OSS was re-structured and emerged as the Central Intelligence Agency (CIA); They released this document into the Public Domain as Intelligence Study Number 31, *Japan's "Secret" Weapon: Suicide.*

destroyers, twenty-seven were sunk and only twenty-one survived. Of the miscellaneous damage causes (strafing, suicide boats, ramming etc.), just eleven destroyers suffered damage and only three were sunk as a result.

The new American destroyers were regarded as four-compartment ships, by which it was meant that four major compartments extending from one main transverse bulkhead to the next could be flooded before the main deck became awash. Even a Kamikaze hit at one such junction was therefore unlikely to bring about the loss of the ship, although, as with extreme cases like the *Lindsey*, whole sections might break away through subsidiary damage (the detonation of a main magazine), but still the ship survived. Kamikazes certainly inflicted extensive topside damage, with gasoline fires and bomb explosions spreading the carnage, but although this caused high casualties among the exposed upper deck personnel, it rarely threatened the total loss of the ship, despite appearances.

Damage control, and the training of personnel to deal with all eventualities, played as great a part in survival as that of stout and sturdy construction. The US Navy defined damage control at that time as comprising 'the maintenance of fire power, mobility, manoeuvrability and floatability.' They also defined that this was to be achieved by 'the preservation of stability and buoyancy, by control of list and trim, by the rapid repair of structure, vital systems and equipment, by counteracting the effects of fire, and by facilitating the care of personnel casualties.'[16] It is obvious from the cases involving the Kamikaze attacks that these small ships were able to absorb such impacts to a far greater degree than expected, mainly because they were almost always impacted above the waterline rather than below it. It was flood, rather than fire, horrendous though the latter was for personnel, that was the ship killer.

Analysis of destroyer loss by type of damage from Kamikaze attack

By extracting data produced by this report, the following details are revealed on just how effective, or otherwise, Kamikaze attacks were.[17]

Fourteen destroyers were lost by flooding during the war, and of these, Kamikaze attack brought about two, *Reid* (DD-369) and *Drexler* (DD-741), of six ships lost as a result of loss of buoyancy aggravated by radical list. Of six further destroyers whose sinking was attributed to loss of buoyancy aggravated by radical trim, four, *Callaghan* (DD-792), *Luce* (DD-522), *Morrison* (DD-560) and *W. D. Porter* (DD-579) out of six were caused by Kamikazes. Six more destroyers were sunk due to structural failure, of which five were sunk after having 'Jack-knifed', with Kamikazes being responsible for four of these, namely: *Bush* (DD-529), *Mannert L. Abele* (DD-733), *Pringle* (DD-477) and *Little* (DD-803), while another, *Colhoun* (DD-801) was lost when she sagged at the stern after a suicide strike. Magazine detonations brought about the sinking of five destroyers, of which two, *Abner Read* (DD-526) and *Mahan* (DD-364), were as a result of Kamikaze attacks.

Nonetheless it was a fact that almost half the US Navy destroyers that were damaged in the war by above-water weaponry were victims of the Kamikaze. It was conceded

---

16. See Chief of Naval Operations, Washington, DC – *Damage Control Instructions*, F T P 170(B) – 1945.
17. See *Statistical Analysis of Japanese Suicide Effort Against Allied Shipping During Okinawa Campaign*, OPNAV-16–V A118, dated 23 July 1945.

that destroyers bore a disproportionate share of Kamikaze attacks due to the vulnerable, outlying and unsupported positions in which they were thrust compounded by the fact that they had the least amount of armour protection and defensive gun-power to mitigate this. Their only asset was speed. The most frequent suicide attack mode was a steep glide at the bridge or other prominent upperworks feature.[18] The conclusion was that although the Kamikaze form of attack 'was undeniably more accurate' than orthodox forms, they were considered 'inefficient, however, when compared in effectiveness to coordinated dive-bombing and torpedo attacks as conducted by the Japanese carrier groups early in the war.' The achievements were that Kamikaze or *Ōhka* attacks brought about the damage of ninety-five destroyers, but only 13 (13.7 %) actually sank, whereas 38.9% had been sunk by conventional aircraft attacks.

But of course, this begged the question that it was not comparing like-for-like, because the accuracy of the Japanese aerial attacks in the period 1941–42 far exceeded those of the 1944–45 period, due to lack of training, superiority of Allied air and gun defences, and other matters. The conclusion was that the study of Kamikaze attack turned out to be very relevant to the post-war fleet because of impending widespread future threats from pilotless aircraft or guided missiles.

Japanese Weapons

One interesting fact to emerge was that only 60% of the aircraft types that were involved in Kamikaze attacks were able to be identified. This seems an incredibly low figure for aircraft that actually impacted on ships and left substantial hardware behind them, but such is the case. Of the identified types 50% were either Aichi D3A1/2 *Val* dive-bombers with a 47.5ft wing span, all-up weight of around 8,000lb or Mitsubishi A6M *Zeke*s of various marks, a 6,000lb fighter with a 36.2ft wing span. Also prominent was the Mitsubishi *Betty* twin-engined bomber or torpedo-bomber, often used as the "mother-ship" for launching rocket-powered piloted *Ōhka* suicide planes. This weapon could be launched at heights of up to 30,000ft and had a range of sixty miles from this altitude.[19] The Americans felt that the warhead was inefficient and as far as could be estimated, only three US destroyers were struck by this weapon, the *Mannert L. Abele* (DD-733), *Stanly* (DD-478) and *Shea* (DM-30), and only one of these actually sank, but the damage caused by the *Ōhka* was only a contributory factor added to several Kamikaze hits.[20]

The last Picket casualties: 9 August 1945

The *Allen M. Sumner* Class destroyers *John W. Weeks* (DD-701, Commander William Lockhart Harman, USN), *Hank* (DD-702, Commander John William Myers Montgomery, USN) and *Borie* (DD-704, Commander Noah Adair, Jr., USN), and the *Gearing* Class destroyer *Benner* (DD-807, Commander John Munholland, USN), all of DesRon 62, were assigned *Tomcat* duties positioned about fifty miles to the south-west

---

18. Two reports applied, OPNAV-16–V A106, dated 23 May 1945 and OPNAV-16–V A118 dated 23 July 1945.
19. TAIC Summary N. 31, OPNAV 16–V T131, dated June 1945.
20. See Japanese *Aircraft*, TAIC Manual No. 1, OPNAV-16–VT, No. 301.

of the Task Force 38 carrier groups, who were striking at targets in northern Honshu on the early afternoon of 9 August. This group was attacked successively by at least five Kamikazes that had successfully evaded the CAP, the first of which, initially identified as an Aichi B7A1 *Grace* Carrier Attack Bomber, but later thought to be a *Val* dive-bomber, made a diving attack. This Kamikaze flew across the destroyer line under heavy anti-aircraft fire, passing so low over the *Hank* that fuel from its damaged tanks drenched the bridge personnel. This aircraft then banked sharply and dove into rear of *Borie*'s after bridge superstructure, striking the ship between the 5in gun director and the mast, and started large fires. The impact knocked many men overboard who were never seen again, while the bridge communications were all knocked out and control had to be shifted to the after steering position. The bomb it carried, estimated to be a 500lb weapon, passed through the ship before detonating off her starboard side and peppering her hull with fragments. Eventually these blazes were brought under control although 40mm ready-use ammunition continued to explode. The damaged destroyer was able to return to the fleet, but *Borie* had suffered forty-eight men killed and missing, and a further sixty-six wounded. She subsequently took aboard medical teams from the battleship *Alabama* (BB-60, Captain William Bernard Goggins) and the destroyer *Abbot* (DD-629, Commander Francis Walford Ingling) to help with the many injured. Many of the wounded were subsequently transferred to the Hospital Ship *Rescue* (AH-18, Captain Robert Barber Twining). *Hank* suffered one man missing in action and had five more injured when they were drenched by flammable fuel and debris from one damaged Kamikaze that passed low overhead as it went into the ocean.

Over the course of the next four hours another four attacks were made. *Benner* then searched diligently, without success, for *Borie*'s missing crewmen before the hunt was abandoned.

The Last Victim

The dubious distinction of being the last ship to be *hit* by a Kamikaze belongs not to the *Callaghan*, but to the 6,873–ton Attack Transport *Lagrange* (APA-124, Captain Frank R. Walker). She was a Victory Ship of the *Haskell* Class, built in 1944 and trained for amphibious operations; she was part of Transport Squadron 17 and had taken part in seven amphibious operations, including the occupation of Kerama Retto, a small group of islands off Okinawa, on 26 March 1945. She returned to Okinawa and anchored in Nakagusuku Bay (at that time temporarily re-named as Buckner Bay) to discharge her war cargo. Here, at 19.47 on the evening of 13 August, she was taken under attack by two Kamikazes, thought to be *Zekes* or *Tojos*, each carrying a 500lb bomb. Both planes were hit by anti-aircraft fire but both got through. The first hit the ship with its bomb still in place at an angle of ten degrees, with one wing hitting No.3 forward boom while its bomb struck *Lagrange*'s port kingpost and ploughed into her after port superstructure where both plane and bomb detonated. All electrical power was knocked out and there was no power to fight the enormous fires that resulted, with flames reported pulsating up to 200 feet high.

Almost immediately after this devastating blow, the second Kamikaze arrived. Again, one wing caught the ship's kingpost which spun it into the sea to port some twenty yards out; fuel and debris came inboard to add to the blaze and general carnage. A third attacker failed to connect. Much damaged was inflicted, the superstructure amidships being unrecognisable, with most of the bridge decks, communications officers and navigation aids destroyed. *Lagrange* lost twenty-one crewmen killed and eighty-nine wounded in this strike, but she remained afloat and after hostilities had ended she was repaired and returned to San Francisco on 21 September 1945.[21, 22]

The final gunnery action against the Kamikazes

On 15 August 1945, the day after the Japanese formal acceptance of a cease-fire, a destroyer picket station belonging to Task Group 38.3 was in position with four *Fletcher* Class destroyers, *Heermann* (DD-532, Commander Dwight M. Agnew, USN), *Black* (DD-666, Lieutenant-Commander E.R. King, USN), *Bullard* (DD-660, Commander Eigel Thorton Steen, USN) and *Chauncey* (DD-667, Lieutenant Commander Preston B. Haines, Jr., USN), some 100 miles south-east of Honshu. The sky at the time was in total overcast but the radar picked up an approaching bogey at a range of seventeen miles. It was tracked in toward the pickets and briefly broke out of the cloud cover some eight miles distant, presumably to make a visual check, before hiding in the murk once more. Within a minute, having orientated itself, the aircraft emerged once more having already entered into its attack approach in a 20–degree glide. Speed was estimated to be 200 knots, coming down toward the pickets from a height of about 8,500 feet. The four destroyers increased speed to 25 knots and the first ship to open fire, with the range now down to 8,000 yards, was the *Heermann*. Identified as a Yokosuka *Judy*, a VT burst knocked away part of this aircraft's wing or tail, sending it into a slow spin. By this time both *Black* and *Bullard* had also opened fire with their 5in batteries and claimed further hits. The *Judy* was knocked to the right and went into the water about 200 yards from the *Bullard*. *Heermann*'s captain later reported that 'In accordance with verbal instructions from Commander, Third Fleet, the *Judy* was shot down 'in a friendly manner'.'[23]

21. *Lagrange* APA 124 – Serial 043 War *Damage Report*, dated 29 August 1945.
22. A former crew member gave an account of this ship's experience, see. Gerald M. Yankee, *My Crew and I: The Story of the Last Navy Ship Casualty of World War II*, River Heights, Palm Beach, Florida. 2011. Some people also think that the 1956 Hollywood Universal Studio movie, *Away All Boats* starring Jeff Chandler, Lex Barker and Richard Boone, was based, in part at least, on this incident, although the novel by Kenneth M. Dodson from which the film was adapted, was based on his war service aboard the *Pierce* (APA-50). Unlike the vast majority of such Hollywood efforts, this movie was widely acclaimed for its accuracy and included notable live colour footage of Kamikaze attacks.
23. Information Bulletin No 29– *Anti-aircraft Action Summary – World War II*, Headquarters of the Commander in Chief, United States Fleet, United States Fleet Headquarters of the Commander in Chief Navy Department, Washington DC, promulgated by Vice-Admiral Charles Maynard Cooke, Jr, Chief of Staff, dated 8 October 1945.

Ugaki's Last Mission

At Fifth Air Fleet Headquarters on Wednesday 15 August Admiral Ugaki made his final diary entries. The first lines still reflected his, and many of his contemporaries, thinking, that the final battles still lay just ahead of them. 'Late at night, the Grand Naval Command alerted *Ketsu* Nos.1, 2, 11, 12, and 13 too. With this order, the whole country has been alerted.' But it was all over and the suspension of all the planned attacks was ordered. Ugaki wrote 'I completely disagreed with the order, as I believe that we should fight until the last moment.' He steeled himself. 'So I made up my mind to ram enemy vessels at Okinawa, directly leading special attack aircraft, and gave an order to prepare *Suisie* planes at this base immediately.' At midday came the Emperor's broadcast decreeing the ending of all Japanese war activities, the die was cast. Ugaki was in despair. 'I've never been so ashamed.' As he had not officially received the cease-fire order Ugaki was resolved to carry out his last mission. 'I'm going to follow in the footsteps of those many loyal officers and men who devoted themselves to the country, and I want to live in the noble spirit of the special attack.'[24]

Ugaki went to Oita airfield where eleven *Suisei* dive-bombers were ready with their volunteer crews and their engines warming up. The Commander of 701 Air Group told him that all were ready to accompany him with his whole unit, and they duly took off and headed south. *En route* to oblivion Ugaki sent a last stirring message by radio in which he announced, 'I am going to proceed to Okinawa, where our men lost their lives like cherry blossoms, and ram into the arrogant American ships, displaying the real spirit of a Japanese warrior.' Thus passed the last Kamikaze.

---

24. Ugaki, Admiral Matome – *Fading Victory – The Diary of Admiral Matome Ugaki 1941–1945*, Annapolis, MD: Naval Institute Press, 1991.

Chapter Thirteen

Reflections and Reactions

'There are persons we love, we think of, and many unforgettable memories. However, with those we cannot win the war. To let this beautiful Japan keep growing, to be released from the wicked hands of the American and British, and to build a 'freed Asia' was our goal from the *Gakuto Shutsujin* year before last: yet nothing has changed. The great day that we can directly be in contact with the battle is our day of happiness and at the same time, the memorial of our death.'

Second Lieutenant Shigeyuka Suzuki

Some American accounts of the Kamikaze campaign describe the method as 'wasteful' and 'Ineffective' and many more passing judgements with the benefit of over seventy years of hindsight declare it 'immoral'. Perhaps it was all those things from a modern, western standpoint, but perhaps one must consider both the conditions that faced Japan at that time and the culture of the nation that carried it out. Such a debate would, of course, be endless, and the computer 'expert' huddled over his PC in the Mid-West of the United States in 2015 might have a different perspective of the young men who sacrificed themselves in the vain hope of protecting their homeland and families back in 1945.

Leaving aside the moral standpoint, what of the charges of ineffectiveness and wastefulness? A large number of young men died, some say needlessly, and caused other young men to die, some say pointlessly. But that is the nature of war as it ever was and ever will be. Everyone and every nation at some point draws a line in the sand and says thus far and no further in conceding to other peoples 'or nations' demands. The hundreds of thousands of British boys that went over the top at the Somme, Passchendaele and a dozen other futile trench warfare battles were ultimately sacrificed totally without purpose – for their sons had to do it all again twenty years later and today Germany still dominates Europe, albeit via her commercial might rather than military, but she still dominates it. The Kamikaze pilots numbered but a fraction of those multitudes who paid the supreme sacrifice, but laid down their lives in the firm belief they were doing the honourable thing.

As for wasteful and inefficient, well the Allied navies and the politicians were shaken by this campaign. So much so that a special force was set up to examine how to counter it should the invasion of Japan proceed as planned.

Task Force 69

The former Commander of the Pacific Fleet fast battleships, Vice-Admiral Willis Augustus 'Ching' Lee, Jr., USN, was appointed to head up Task Force 69 in 1945.

Working under the direct operational control of the Commander-in-Chief, United States Fleet, he was charged with testing methods, procedures, and all types of material in the combat of Japanese suicide attacks. The Task Force itself was centred on the former battleship, converted to a trials ship, *Wyoming* (AG-17)[1] and also had the *Baltimore* Class heavy cruiser *Bremerton* (CA-130, Captain John Boyd Mallard, USN), two *Gearing* Class destroyers, the *Henry W. Tucker* (DD-875, Commander Bernard Henree Meyer, USN), and the *Dennis J. Buckley* (DD-808, Commander Kinloch Chafee Walpole, USN), two *John C. Butler* Class destroyer escorts, the *Edward H. Allen* (DE-531, Lieutenant Commander Merrill Merrett Sanford, USN), and the *Tweedy* (DE-532, Lieutenant Commander Thomas Donald Cunningham, USN), plus *LSM-435* fitted with radar equipment, three LCS(L)s: *LSC (L)-1, LCS(L)-5* and *LCS(L)-6*. Furthermore, on 15 June, two experimental Navy aircraft squadrons were established to work with these ships, they were: Experimental Development Squadron XVF 200, with Commander Dean S. Laird, USN,[2] as Operations Officer for VF-200/VL-1L, with thirty F6F-5s, four F4U-4s[3] two captured Mitsubishi *Zeke*s and (later) twelve Curtiss SB2C-4E Helldivers on strength, and Experimental Utility Squadron XVJ 25 with some of the unit's aircraft distributed to the Naval Auxiliary Air Facility (NAAF) Rockland, Maine, which was equipped with drones, tow-planes and simulated bogeys.[4] Both these units were initially based at Naval Air Station (NAS) Brunswick, Maine, operating under the direct control of Commander-in-Chief (COMICH) with the brief of 'evaluating and testing tactics, procedure, and equipment for use in

---

1. The former battleship had had her 12in gun mountings removed and replaced by twin 5in/38 calibre mounts. As such, *Wyoming* was nicknamed 'The Chesapeake Raider' as all she did was steam around Chesapeake Bay giving AA practice to gunners. She also featured single 5in mounts to port and starboard. After a refit at Norfolk Navy Yard late in the war, her smaller weapons included four single 3in/50 calibre; twelve 40mm Bofors (one quad, three twin and two single), eight single 20mm Oerlikons, and two experimental Mk.17 rocket launchers. See – US Navy Ordnance Document OD 5272 – AG17 USS *Wyoming* – Location of 5" guns, Directors and 36" Searchlights (PARALLLAX DATA), dated 12th April 1945. A future President of the United States, one Ensign Jimmy Carter, served aboard her between 8 August 1946 and 23 July 1947 as Deck Division Officer, Radar Officer and CIC Officer.
2. Dean 'Diz' Laird was a Utility Test Pilot, at this time having recently served afloat aboard the carriers *Ranger*, *Bunker Hill* and *Essex*. The only US Navy ace to have shot down both German and Japanese aircraft, he later earned fame as commanding the Navy's first jet aircraft squadron in 1947.
3. The powerful Goodyear-built F2G Corsair, powered by the Pratt & Whitney R-4360 engine, although later reputed to have been designed as an anti-Kamikaze fighter, had begun development before the Kamikaze attacks had begun and only a handful were operational at this time.
4. Establishment was – two WF6–3, sixteen Curtiss SB2C-4B Helldiver dive-bombers, one Grumman TBF-1C Avenger torpedo-bomber, five General Motors TBM-1C Avengers, eight Lockheed PV-1 Venturas, one Douglas R4D-5 Skytrain transport aircraft, two Martin JM1 Marauder target-tugs, two Martin JM-2 Marauder target-tugs, one Beechcraft Expeditor JRB-3 twin-engined light transport, one Beechcraft Expeditor JRB-4 twin-engined light transport, one Beechcraft SNB-2C Twin Beech trainer and five Culver TB3C-1 Cadet target drones.

special defence tasks particularly those concerned with defence against the *Kamikaze*.'[5] The naval side of the Experimental Force was based at Casco Bay, Portland, Maine and administered by the Atlantic Fleet. It began operating on 1 July 1945. The initial efforts Willis and his team were directed to solve were:

(a) Improvement of early detection and tracking of enemy aircraft by:

1. More efficient operation of present radar and CIC installations.
2. Improving these installations by modifications which can be accomplished quickly in the fleet.

(b) Increased effectiveness of anti-aircraft fire by:

1. Anti-aircraft fire coordination.
2. More rapid control.
3. Increased rate of fire.
4. Early target acquisition and identification.

(c) Testing new weapons and facilities to evaluate their effectiveness, and working out initial operating procedures for their use.

A whole list of experimental projects were formulated for test and evaluation, including the evaluation of Army SCR 270/MTI in LSMs to determine whether long-range MTI-equipped (Moving Target Indication) search radar would assist in the detection and tracking of Japanese aircraft over land areas near the beachheads; evaluating the Mark 32 radar IFF interrogator for fire control radar; evaluating Field Change 50 for SG-1 radar; determining the best procedures for operating Mark 37 director at various ranges in 'surprise' and 'no-surprise' conditions; evaluating whether SCR-720 would provide adequate overhead coverage; evaluating SC-lc MTI to determine effectiveness of tracking aircraft through 'clutter'; evaluating VJ (Barrage Jammer) equipment to determine its usefulness in fighter direction and target designation; developing procedures for testing 5in/38 control systems under 'surprise' conditions; evaluating performance of director systems to increase chances of hits from the 5in batteries; evaluate comparative performance of Mark 8 and Mark 1 computers with Mark 37 directors; evaluate performance of Mark 57 and 37 director systems; evaluate relative performance of Mark 37 and Mark 57 directors; evaluate performance of Mark 15 Mod 1 20mm quadruple mount and Mk.22 Mod 0 quadruple 20mm mounts; evaluate effectiveness of high-speed cranks in VF in designating targets for main battery director; evaluating SG zenith watch antenna to determine the extent of its effectiveness; evaluate relative performance of experienced and inexperienced Mark 37 director and Mark 1 computer teams, and evaluating utility of coloured bursts as indicators for shipboard or CAP target designation.

---

5. See ODF3F/8/45.

Such a programme would involve a considerable amount of work and not all the results would have been ready in time for the first phase of the invasion of the Japanese home islands themselves, Operation *Olympic*, had it taken place.[6] It was promised that, 'Special emphasis will be placed on the dissemination of information which appears to be of immediate value to the fleet.' The Royal Navy considered the setting up of this Task Force to be essential and considerations were given at the Admiralty in London to establishing a similar organisation.[7]

Tragically 'Ching'Lee himself had hardly taken control of this Force when he was struck down by a heart attack and died on 25 August 1945. His replacement was Admiral Robert Pearce Briscoe, USN, who assumed control in September 1945 when the force became known as the Operational Development Force. The lessons no longer became so urgent then for the war was over, but was the Force set up in vain? Probably not, many of the problems they were established to examine with regard to tackling the Kamikaze had relevance in the post-war world of the Cold War and anti-ship missile defence, and indeed the Operational Development Force itself subsequently proved to be the originator of the US Navy's Test and Operational Development Force (OPTEVFOR) which still continues today.

How much relevance did the Kamikaze have in effecting the post-war defence thinking against the threat of missile strikes? In 1971 a detailed study[8] was undertaken by the Operations Evaluation Group of the Center for Naval Analysis.

---

6. Operation *Olympic* was scheduled to commence in October 1945, the aim was to invade and occupy the southern third of Kyūshū,. If successful, this was to be followed by Operation *Coronet*, a landing at Honshū, on the Kantō Plain near Tokyo. The whole series of landings was code-named Operation *Downfall*. The Japanese, in their turn, planned to concentrate all available defences on repelling, at any cost, the Kyūshū landing, under their Operation *Ketsugō*.
7. *Formation of US Experimental Fleet (Task Force 69) to test prototypes of armaments etc under sea-going conditions: remarks on possible formation of a similar British Fleet*, National Archives, Kew, London, ADM1/18514 – MO9657/1945. The only result, due to lack of money, was that the heavy cruiser *Cumberland* was converted to a trials ships post-war.
8. Nicolai Timenses, Jr. – *Defense Against Kamikaze Attacks in World War II and its Relevance to Anti-Ship Missile Defense*, Vol 1, *An Analytical History of Kamikaze Attacks against Ships of the United States Navy during World War II*. Washington DC: November 1970.

Chapter Fourteen

Learning the Lessons

'As a man I will courageously go. Now, I have no special nostalgic sentiments. However, I will go regretting that although being born a man, I have not had filial piety. To give this young self for the protection of the Imperial nation, I believe is piety. I hope that you will forgive my sin of being undutiful and that you may live in happiness.'

Corporal Shinji Ozeki to his mother.

The advent of the Kamikaze was often regarded as a special circumstance with regard to sea warfare; a 'one-off' peculiar to the special circumstances of a unique culture that had been manipulated; even an aberration, that would never recur. In fact many facets of the Kamikaze attack would be duplicated in sea warfare as the decades rolled on with the advent of the sea-skimming missile and in the need for defensive capabilities able to plot, scan and react at speeds unheard of scant years before.

Post-war evaluation for future warfare lessons

Were there any lessons for today, with suicide terror attacks again high on the agenda on the enemies of western civilisation? The Japanese pilots who gave their lives would vehemently deny any such similarity – their targets were the legitimate ones of war, the opposing enemy military forces, whereas militant Islam deliberately targets innocent civilians, even babes-in-arms, indeed, their warped ideology seems to prefer such soft targets. This is the difference between the modern terrorism, with its wholly evil intent and base motivations, and the desperate but forlorn actions of the Japanese. But even if the motivation behind each was widely different, the development of guided weapons and stand-off missiles has been enormous over five decades and just from that strictly military viewpoint alone, the Kamikaze attacks of 1944–45 merit some modern consideration. One cannot stop a determined suicide attacker, so how can one lessen the dangers? This problem was appreciated very early in the post-war era.

One post-war study, which appeared a year after the Japanese surrender acknowledged that: 'It now appears doubtful that the Japanese Kamikaze type of attack will again become a major factor in naval warfare, but is rather a forerunner of the development and application of pilotless aircraft and guided missiles.' Looking back across fifty years and in the light of the Falklands War and the Israeli–Arab conflicts, and similar incidents, this can be seen as a very perceptive forecast. The report continued: 'Viewed in this respect, it is apparent that much additional information of possible future significance can be obtained by a careful study of the wealth of war damage experience resulting from Kamikaze attacks.'[1]

One debate on warship design and construction, especially with regard to aircraft carriers, centred on the question of whether or not the fitting of an armoured flight deck was a good or a bad thing. Superficially, at the time, the oft-quoted statement by a US Naval liaison officer with the British Pacific Fleet seemed to sum the whole argument up as whereas an American carrier would be incapacitated for many weeks by a Kamikaze hit, in the case of the British carriers it was merely a case of 'sweepers man your brooms!' It was recognised as a good quote, but an over-simplification, common, at the time it was made, although it made for excellent copy in British circles ever afterward. But deeper post-war studies have revealed that it was just not a simple case of trading protection for aircraft capacity between the two ideals. Indeed modern American internet experts are sneeringly contemptuous of the whole British "armoured box" concept of carrier design and likewise the contribution of the Royal Navy off Okinawa as well.

Hard hit and suffering heavy personnel losses though they undoubtedly did, the *Essex* Class carriers were, for the most part, repaired and back in action in a remarkably short space of time, whereas the British ships, while still able to operate aircraft[2] could only do so with their already much smaller air groups reduced to mere cadres. Nor was every British carrier fitted with an armoured deck – the four light fleet carriers which joined the BPF for instance, had no such protection, and, moreover, had even smaller air groups. Additionally these light carriers were much slower even than the British battleships which escorted them, the *Anson* (B-1, Captain Alexander Cumming Gordon Madden, RN), and *Duke of York* (B-2, Captain Angus Dacres Nicholl, CBE, DSO, RN). These light carriers had been deliberately crash-built to mercantile standards with the intent of handing them over to civil usage after the war. The four ships, *Colossus* (R-61,Captain Graham Henry Stokes, CB, DSC, RN), *Glory* (R-62, Captain Anthony Wass Buzzard, DSC, OBE, RN), *Venerable* (R-63, Captain William Alexander Dallmeyer, DSO, RN), and *Vengeance* (R-64,Captain Douglas Mortimer Lewis Neame, DSO, RN), later to be joined by the *Ocean* (R-65, Captain Caspar John, RN), which was being especially equipped for night-fighting operations, would most certainly have no more been able to withstand Kamikaze hits than the equivalent US *Independence* Class vessels.

Even in the case of the fully-armoured fleet carriers they did not escape scot-free in the end, *Victorious* for example, had repairs that required a month to carry out and others suffered long-term problems. In mitigation of their early demise post-war, many of the British carriers had already received severe poundings and heavy damage earlier in the war, *Illustrious* in particular surviving hits from no less than six 1,100lb and three 551lb bombs off Malta in January 1941. *Formidable* survived two 1,100lb hits off Crete

---

1. USS *Franklin* (CV13) Suicide Plane Crash Damage Formosa – 15 October 1944. War Damage Report No.56. Preliminary Design Section, Bureau of Ships, Navy Department, dated 15 September 1946.
2. With the exception of the *Illustrious*, which had to return all the way to the United Kingdom to repair after underwater shock detonations from a near-miss Kamikaze exacerbated existing propeller shaft defects and opened up her outer hull, cracking several frames and reducing her speed to nineteen knots.

in May the same year which permanently distorted her hull, and *Indomitable,* also in the Mediterranean, took two hits and three near misses from 1,100–lbs bombs in 1942, and a torpedo hit in 1943, which almost caused her loss. Nonetheless the inherent damage caused by Kamikaze hits did cause long-term problems far deeper than initially realised and only *Victorious* was, in the end, deemed worthy of modernisation post-war. Even the relatively new carrier *Implacable* (R5, Captain Cecil Charles Hughes-Hallett, RN), the only BPF carrier specifically to receive three additional four-barrel 2pdr pom-pom mountings to combat Kamikazes, and *Indefatigable* were scrapped very prematurely, although in the latter case their design limitations certainly contributed to their fates.

At the time, however, British armoured decks appeared to be the answer. Admiral Somerville noted when being shown around the *Coral Sea* (CVB-43), one of the new *Midway* Class carriers then under course of construction, 'Armoured flight deck being fitted.'[3] However, on another occasion he expressed surprise that while the Americans were adopting this practice for their new ships, the Royal Navy was abandoning the idea. It is assumed he was thinking of the proposed big British *Malta* Class fleet carriers [*Malta, Gibraltar, New Zealand* and *Africa* – none completed due to post-war austerity], which abandoned the armoured flight deck concept and opted for just 1in steel and an open hangar in the US manner, and with a 6in armoured citadel to protect the ship's vitals.

The advent of the Kamikaze cast some doubt on this radical (for the British) idea and a reversion to deck armour for the design was raised by the Assistant Chief Naval Star (Air). However Admiral Cunningham, the First Sea Lord, refused to change the X1 design to incorporate such armour, noting 'I consider it best to abandon it in this open hangar design, and treat the Japanese suicide bomber, against which it is a defence, as a passing phase.'[4]

The Americans compared the cases of *Victorious* and *Formidable* on the one hand, and *Franklin* and *Intrepid* on the other, before these longer-term effects of the British ships were general knowledge.

'The damage experiences of several British carriers, which unlike our own were fitted with armoured flight decks, demonstrated the effectiveness of such armour in shielding hangar spaces from GP bombs and vital spaces below the hangar deck from SAP bombs. Accordingly, the CVB Class (*Midway* Class) was designed with an armoured flight deck consisting of 3½in STS from frames 46 to 175 with a hangar deck consisting of two courses of 40–pound STA between frames 36 and 192. Although none of the CVB Class carriers were completed in time to take part in war operations, the effectiveness of armoured flight decks against Kamikaze attacks was demonstrated by various carriers attached to the British Pacific Fleet.'

'The *Victorious* was struck by three Kamikaze aircraft, two of which ricocheted off the armoured flight deck and over the side, causing no important damage. The third carried a bomb which detonated at frame 30 starboard at the butt of the 3in flight deck armour with 1½in 'D' quality (equivalent to HTS) steel. It does not appear that the Kamikaze

---

3. Somerville Pocket Diary, entry for 5 April 1945, Churchill College Archives, Cambridge.
4. DNC718 – *New Carrier Design,* 1944. National Maritime Museum, Greenwich, London.

actually struck the ship. The bomb detonation, however, depressed the 3in deck slightly but did not tear it open. On the other hand, the 1½in 'D' quality deck plating was ripped open over a total area of about 25ft². Two days were required for temporary repairs, at the conclusion of which the ship was fully operational.'

'HMS *Formidable* was hit by two bombs, the first of which struck and detonated on the flight deck 9 feet to port of the centre-line at frame 79, directly over a deep bent and at a juncture of three armoured plates. The armoured deck was depressed over an area 24 feet long and 20 feet wide. Maximum depression was 15 inches. Adjacent bents spaced 12 feet forward and aft of the point of impact were slightly depressed. A hole 2ft² in area was blown in the 3in deck. Three fragments penetrated downward through the ship into the centre boiler room. The damage in this boiler room, which was not described *(sic)*, temporarily reduced speed to 18 knots. The second bomb struck and detonated on the centre-line of the flight deck at frame 94. The 3in deck was deeply 'dished' directly below the point of impact by about 4½ inches and one rivet was knocked out. However, the ship was fully operational within about five hours, including flight operations.'

On the other hand American carriers suffering heavy damage mainly had it confined to above the hangar deck level. '*Franklin* did not sustain any direct structural and machinery damage in main or auxiliary machinery spaces. This has generally been true of other CV9 (*Essex* Class) carriers which have been damaged by suicide planes and bombs. It is attributable primarily to the effectiveness of the armoured hangar deck 2½in stainless steel – STS and to a much lesser extent to the armoured fourth deck 1½in STS which forms the overhead of the machinery spaces.' It was smoke and heat entering via ventilation supply systems which presented the greatest problem further down in the carriers and it was admitted that, 'As a matter of fact, this hazard has not been limited to carriers alone, for battleships, cruisers, destroyers and other classes of ships have experienced similar difficulties.' It was also, 'That the gallery deck spaces are death traps is unquestionable' and this was not due to the original design which had comparatively few gallery deck spaces in the way of the hangar, other than squadron ready rooms, that were occupied by personnel during General Quarters, but to subsequent alterations 'notably CIC and air plot' Because of the high location, gallery deck structures have been, lightly constructed.' It was revealed that in one case, on 19 March, 'Only one man escaped from CIC and air plot,' the rest being either immediately killed or else stunned, and then asphyxiated and burned before they could recover.'[5]

Prospects for *Downfall*

The dropping of the Atomic Bombs on Hiroshima and Nagasaki are often alleged to have given the Japanese leaders the excuse they required to end a war which everyone knew they had lost. However, this was by no means a clear-cut decision and there were many

---

5. USS *Franklin* (CV13) Suicide Plane Crash Damage Formosa – 15 October 1944. War Damage Report No.56. Preliminary Design Section, Bureau of Ships, Navy Department, dated 15 September 1946. NB In later *Essex* Class carriers the CIC was moved from the gallery deck down to below the armoured flight deck.

in senior positions who wanted to fight on. Had the Allies actually mounted an invasion of the Japanese home islands, one thing that is clear is that casualties would have been enormous, on both sides. The mobilisation of a large percentage of the civilian population was already under way and suicide missions of all kinds and natures were planned, much of it of a desperately naive and hopeless variety, but as far as airborne Special Attack Forces, Allied estimates of what was available made for grim reading.

Operation *Downfall,* the Allied codename for the invasion of Japan, had two facets. In October 1945 the seizure of southern Kyūshū would take place under the auspices of Operation *Olympic.* Once that had been achieved then the spring of 1946 would see the mounting of Operation *Coronet,* the landing of Allied armies on the Kantō Plain near Tokyo. The Japanese counter to these plans was Operation *Ketsgō* meaning Combine (as in a combination of all arms in defence), and the Kamikaze featured strongly in that strategy which, put simply, was to halt the invasion at the beach.

Admiral Matome Ugaki was placed in command of the Fifth Air Fleet and charged with the defence of Kyuhsu. Initially they hoped to deploy at least 13,000 aircraft to the task. Like in the Philippines, but on an enormously larger scale, it was hoped that by taking advantage of the land mass to hide behind, they could mount mass attacks sufficient to take out between one third to one half of the invasion troop transports. One hit in six attacks was what they were aiming at compared to one in nine achieved at Okinawa, but there were to be five times as many attacks!

One US Navy source prepared by the Navy Department in Washington, DC, spelt out in graphic detail just what could be expected and what preparations were being undertaken to counter the Kamikaze threat.[6] In terms of numbers of Kamikaze aircraft available to the Japanese defenders this report, if anything, *under-estimated* the forces that would oppose them.

The report began: 'That the Japanese will intensify their suicidal effort in the coming months is certain. The pattern of the enemy's defence is taking predictable form. The following may be expected:

1. The Japanese air force of an estimated 8,000 to 9,000 combat and training planes will be conserved for suicidal attacks on our surface forces. Carriers and land-based air strikes will meet little or no air opposition. Even bombardments of Japanese coastal cities, such as those by ships of Task Force 38 in mid-July, will not draw the Japanese air force out of hiding.

---

6. CominCh Secret Information Bulletin N. 22, *Anti-Suicide Action Summary,* USF 10B, Rad1A, Rad 6, Washington, August 1945 – This incorporated findings and estimates from the following publications and reports: OpNav-16–V No. A106, *Observed Suicide Attacks by Japanese Aircraft Against Allied Ships;* TAIC Summary No. 31– *Baka*; CinCPac-CinCPoa Bulletin No. 129–45 – *Suicide Force Combat Methods*; ComPhibs Pac Serial 00406, dated 16 June 1945, *Information on and Comments Concerning Suicide Plane Attacks*; ComPhib Grp 7 Serial 00123, dated 16 June 1945, *Counter-Measures Against Suicide Planes* ComBatRon 1 Memorandum 4–45, dated 2 June 1945, *Kamikaze Attacks, Defeating of*; CinCPac Con. Ltr. 15CL-45, Suicide Bombing Attacks.

2. The supreme suicidal effort of the enemy will coincide with the next amphibious operation. Rather than picket stations, as in the Okinawa campaign, suiciders will concentrate on troop and cargo transports, and large amphibious craft, in an effort to defeat the landing operation at the beachhead

3. Float and training planes, as well as combat types, will be employed in large numbers. To avoid losing a large proportion of their planes to our fighters, attacks will be made chiefly at dusk and night, when our air cover is weakest. Dawn attacks in diminishing numbers may be expected.'

Taking the figures of Okinawa as a base, 45% of attempted Kamikaze attacks were either destroyed or turned back by the Combat Air Patrol. Therefore it was thought that defending fighters would play a far less important role against the new expected Japanese tactics and the ships would have to rely more on their own defences. Again, at Okinawa, 38% of the attackers missed their targets as a result of AA fire while 17% scored hits. This was during a campaign when only 63.5% of enemy aircraft fired upon by Allied ships were actually suicide attackers. This percentage was expected to increase significantly at 'an accelerated rate.' Against this, the actual efficiency of such attacks decreased enormously from April when 123 suicide attacks took place and sank fifteen ships to May 1945 when ninety-eight suicide attacks sank ten ships, and to June 1945 when eighteen suicide attacks sank just three ships. This was attributed to the inability of the enemy to achieve surprise as they had done in the Philippines campaign due to distance from land and early warning by radar pickets; the vulnerability of obsolete aircraft to AA defences and the increasing lack of skill displayed by the suicide pilots, and the effectiveness of VT fusing and long-range barrages. There was no gainsaying of the effectiveness of the Kamikaze attack over the conventional air attack and in the period October 1944 to April 1945. The report summarised this thus:

'The enemy lost 784 suicide planes to score 216 hits on ships, and 356 non-suicide planes to obtain 58 hits. On a basis of this performance, had he devoted the entire effort of 2,936 planes coming within ship's gun range to suicide attacks, he would have scored about 792 hits on ships as compared with 79 hits had he used non-suicide attacks exclusively.' This ten-to-one ratio in effectiveness was the best support that the Japanese would concentrate on this tactic to the exclusion of all other in any forthcoming invasion.

The anticipated developments from the Japanese Kamikaze flyers in the months ahead included more such attacks conducted at night, dawn or dusk; the use of single-engine aircraft, medium bombers being restricted to carrying Ōhka, the use of heavier bomb loading with only enough fuel for one-way trips; 'The Japanese are estimated to have 5,000 training-type aircraft – all of which will very probably be employed to the maximum extent of their capabilities in suicide attacks.'

Attacks on pickets as at Okinawa had demonstrated that such tactics were futile in trying to defeat amphibious operations – in future pickets would be ignored, and attacks concentrated on troop and cargo transports and large amphibious craft before they have discharged their troops. Aircraft would be concealed and held ready, and a greater reliance on float planes working from rivers, lakes and harbours, which would avoid losses from the expected Allied destruction of conventional airstrips. Night attacks would increase.

How to counter such a vast effort? Early warning remained vital but the vulnerability of picket ships was obvious. The requirement would be to establish early-warning radar sets ashore at the earliest opportunity. Experiments with airborne early warning (AEW) radars were already underway but had not yet been proven. It was hoped that the first such aircraft would be deployed to the fleet carriers by October 1945. If these proved successful, they would enable interceptions to be made at greater distance from the target ships.

The AEW radar concerned had the ability to detect aircraft at up to seventy miles distant. The radar returns were relayed from the aircraft to a surface display console on any command ship with AEW receiving equipment. It was being trialled on US Navy/Marine Corps Avengers adapted to carry two radar operators, as well as on Boeing B-17 four-engined Flying Fortress heavy bombers fitted with an airborne CIC. It was hoped to have the first four-plane TBM unit ready by 1 October and five more such units ready a month later, with the first B-17s appearing in December. Four *Essex* Class carriers were being equipped with the necessary receiving equipment to act as command ships, along with the necessary trained personnel. The trouble was, *Olympic* was scheduled for 1 October!

As for the CAP, this was at its weakest at dusk and dawn, 'when it was most neede.' Night attacks were expected to increase and to counter this was a hope that the introduction of the new twin-engined Grumman F7F(N) Tigercat fighter would improve night airborne interceptions. The first of these aircraft was expected to join land-based USMC squadrons on 1 October, these planes being equipped with the long-range SCR-720 radar. They were also to have the APA-48 radar homing device from 1 August onward.[7] The use of airborne searchlights on night fighters was being tested. These searchlights had a one-mile range, although its most effective range varied from three eighths to one half of a mile.

The adoption of long-range 5in barrages at ranges of 10,000 to 12,000 yards, instead of the 4,400 yards generally employed in the Philippines, was also expected to improve defences. The use of submarines as radar pickets was also under consideration (the virtual elimination of the Japanese mercantile fleet was almost complete leaving vast numbers of US submarines with no useful mission). Fire Control radars needed IFF interrogators to sort out friend from foe in crowded skies, but, 'Technical difficulties have delayed the development of this project, and no immediate solution is available. The Mark 32 interrogator with the Mark 12 fire control radar shows most promise.' The use of rockets as AA weapons and experiments were, again, underway, utilising rockets with VT fusing. Even the use of 'Q' ships and other decoys was considered as they lured some less knowledgeable Kamikaze pilots away from valuable targets.[8] Barrage balloons were also considered. They had been used extensively, by many combatants, from defending

---

7. Described as 'essentially an APR-1 with a homing antenna of the lobe-switching type, which receives enemy airborne radar and provides homing indications by means of a direction indicator.'

8. 'Q' ships had originated in the First World War – disguised merchant ships with strong concealed gun armaments were deployed to lure German submarines in and then destroy them. The tactic only ever had very limited success even then. It was revived in World War II by the Royal Navy with even less success. Its proposed use as an anti-Kamikaze weapon seems almost, aside from the *Barry*, an act of desperation.

fleet bases like Scapa Flow and Taranto, and cities like London in Europe, to protecting the Normandy beachheads, those in the Mediterranean and to a limited extent, in the Solomons, but had never been very effective anywhere. The report was luke-warm, 'they interfere with air and AA defence, and serve as designators for enemy shore batteries, particularly off assault beaches and for enemy aircraft then they protrude above smoke blankets. The Japanese used them, 'to create a mental hazard for our pilots.'

As for the ships themselves some radical suggestions were thrown up from analysis. One would have expected that for high-speed, lightly-armed warships like destroyers, fast turns and zig-zagging at flank speed would have been the best answer to the Kamikaze, while larger ships, battleships and the like, with enormous fire power, but larger and less manoeuvrable, a steady course would have enabled the gunners to engage their attackers. In fact, the exact opposite was shown to be the case and the conclusions reached for warships under suicide attack was for:

'1. All ships should attempt to present their beams to high-angle approaches, and to turn their beams away from low-angle attacks.
2. Battleships, cruisers and carriers should employ radical changes of course in order to present the proper aspect.
3. Destroyers and smaller fleet units, and all auxiliaries, should turn at high speed to present the proper aspect to the attacking plane, but should not turn so sharply as to affect the accuracy of their AA fire.'

CAP defence emphasised the importance of continuing the existing policy of intercepting as far out as possible, the doctrine being to vector out the nearest CAP division when a bogey approached within 100 miles. It was the intent of the Kamikaze to avoid aerial combat, it was the intent of the CAP to force it upon them and the greater the range this was done, the more the chance of success. When large enemy raids were intercepted, however, they immediately broke up into smaller sections, a large percentage of each, taking advantage of cloud cover or the confusion of so many aircraft cluttering screens, tended to get through to make their final dives.

Other developments then imminent included the Moving Target Indicator (MTI), a modification for the SG-series radars which blanked out the 'pips' from stationary targets and displayed only moving targets. This facilitated detection of aircraft over land masses or during operations when the enemy used window in 'saturation' quantities.

So much for warships but as was conceded, the invasion of Japan would see the suicide pilots targeting not fast, heavily-armed fighting ships, but concentrating their efforts on APAs, AKAs and larger amphibious craft, all packed with troops presenting a high body count and influencing the public back home with horrendous casualty lists. Had such a policy have actually taken place, Allied leaders would have been presented with a serious problem of morale, not only of the soldiers themselves, unable to affect their own fates, but of civilians at home. The Japanese were perhaps still counting on a 'war-weary' nation negotiating a more favourable peace. This was probably as much of an illusion in 1945 as it had been in 1942, but the hindsight effects of Korea, Vietnam, Iraq and Afghanistan in later years illustrate just how successful such a policy might become. It was perhaps fortunate for many millions on both sides that the invasion of Japan never took place and that the Kamikazes never got their final showdown with the Allied fleets.

Assessment of the effectiveness of Anti-Aircraft Gunnery

One of the most interesting of the immediate post-war summaries was that issued in October 1945, which was in fact the final one of a series of 'Anti-Aircraft Summaries' which had been issued as Confidential CominCh Information Bulletins and as Secret CominCh publications. This particular issue ranged across the whole spectrum of the war in the Pacific, from Pearl Harbor in December 1941 to the surrender of Japan on 14 August 1945.[9] The breadth of the report was wide-ranging but we are here of course principally concerned with its findings with regard to the Japanese suicide attacks. However, comparison with results achieved (on both sides) with and against more conventional dive- and torpedo-bomber attacks, is illuminating and some of that is accordingly included here as a yardstick of measurement.

After claiming that it was the Allied invasion of Philippines that had 'inspired' the enemy's use of suicide tactics, a debateable conclusion, and also stating, on equally controversial evidence, that this method had 'proved effective, although no more so than conventional air attacks by our own planes,' the report stated that 481 enemy aircraft had been destroyed by AA gunnery during the course of 1944. This figure increased considerably for 1945, the fourth year of the war as far as the United States was concerned (although of course it must be remembered this was the *sixth* year of the war for their British and Australian counterparts) with the 'increasing tempo' of suicide attacks increasing at the conclusion of the maritime phase of the Philippine campaign, the occupation of Iwo Jima in February, and the Okinawa invasion, admitted to be 'the most difficult of the war' from March onward. The report stated bluntly, 'More [enemy] planes were knocked down by AA during this operation than in any previous year of engagements with the enemy.' Although the US fleet also operated against mainland Japan in this period, these raids had failed to provoke a similar response, 'Few enemy aircraft opposed this operation.' The feeling, left unstated, was that the enemy was husbanding his strength for the invasion proper.

The scale of air attack on warships accelerated enormously during the second half of 1944 (310 kills) and the first half of 1945 (964) with these two totals amounting to 50% of all anti-aircraft successes in all theatres for the entire war. Definitely identifiable suicide attacks totalled 999 (and that figure includes those discounted as Kamikazes by some). Of this enormous total 314 (31%) actually scored hits on ship targets, while a further 160 (16%) failed to hit their target vessels but caused damage to them, while 525 (53%) failed to do any damage whatsoever. The table for suicide attacks is revealing.

9. Information Bulletin No 29– *Anti-aircraft Action Summary – World War II*, Headquarters of the Commander in Chief, United States Fleet, United States Fleet Headquarters of the Commander in Chief Navy Department, Washington DC, promulgated by Vice-Admiral Charles Maynard Cooke, Jr, Chief of Staff, dated 8 October 1945.

Suicide Attacks October 1944 to August 1945

Date	Attempts	Hits	Damaging Near-Miss	Non-damaging Near Miss	AA success	Ships sunk
October 44	42	17 (40%)	6 (14%)	19 (46%)	25 (60%)	3
November 44	76	28 (37%)	12 (16%)	36 (47%)	48 (63%)	2
December 44	111	34 (31%)	17 (15%)	60 (54%)	77 (69%)	11
January 45	97	41 (42%)	22 (23%)	34 (35%)	56 (58%)	3
February 45	17	8 (47%)	2 (12%)	7 (41%)	9 (53%)	1
March 45	35	11 (31%)	7 (20%)	17 (49%)	24 (69%)	1
April 45	354	87 (25%)	52 (15%)	215 (60%)	267 (75%)	13
May 45	214	72 (34%)	31 (14%)	111 (52%)	142 (66%)	8
June 45	40	12 (30%)	7 (17%)	21 (53%)	28 (70%)	3
July 45	4	2 (50%)	2 (50%)	–	2 (50%)	1
August 45	9	2 (22%)	2 (22%)	5 (56%)	7 (78%)	0
TOTAL	999	314 (31%)	160 (16%)	525 (53%)	685 (68%)	46

Of course many aircraft were destroyed by the CAP or AA fire before their final method of attack (suicide or conventional) were clear. It was estimated from the data available, those of 3,924 aircraft attacking the Allied fleets, 1,192 (30%) were on suicide missions and of these, AA fire destroyed 878 of them (74%). In return Japanese suicide pilots made 314 hits on Allied ships against just 62 by conventional means of air attack.

Other figures of interest include the fact that whereas the number of rounds per gun required to destroy an enemy aircraft steadily increased as the war progressed, this trend was reversed in 1945 at the time of the peak suicide activity. The decline in accuracy prior to 1945 was accounted for by a number of factors, which were itemised as follows: the increase in the total number of AA weapons installed on warships; the increase in the number of ships firing at each target as operations increased in size; an increase in the number of night attacks in which fire control was less accurate; an increase in the speed, manoeuvrability and protection of enemy aircraft; the adoption of a doctrine which established fire being opened at extreme ranges (12,000 yards) and finally, a lack of sufficient opportunities for the training of the vast numbers of new gunners to man the fleet. In 1945 approximately half the wartime total of aircraft kills were made, and the ratio of rounds per destruction fell dramatically. The introduction of VT-fusing, the use by the enemy of increasingly more outmoded aircraft types for suicide missions, the corresponding lack of skill of the pilots due to the higher wastage and increase in the defending gunners skill and expertise, all contributed to this reversal of the trend.

The US Navy's adoption of the 5in/38 calibre gun as the standard main weapon for destroyers and the standard secondary weapon for battleships, *Alaska*-Class battle-cruisers[10] carriers, and heavy and light cruisers, proved a most successful move. This

10. The US Navy rated these ships, *Alaska, Guam, Hawaii, Philippines, Puerto Rico* and *Samoa*, of which only the first two were completed in time to participate in the war, as Large Cruisers, but their armament, size and speed put them firmly in the battle-cruiser category along with the German *Gneisenau* and *Scharnhorst*, the French *Dunkerque* and *Strasbourg*, the Soviet

weapon destroyed 30% of all confirmed aircraft 'kills' of the war, of which VT-fused projectiles accounted for just 35% of rounds fired but accounted for 50% of 'kills' achieved. The 20mm gun, considered the most important AA weapon in 1941–42, was soon eclipsed by both the 5in and the 40mm in efficiency during 1944 and 1945. While the 20mm was regarded almost universally as totally inadequate in this latter period (save by a few), the 40mm was acknowledged as the most effective AA weapon in regard to number of 'kills' made.

The suicide method of attack accounted for sinking 46 and damaging 306 ships which was approximately 14% of those sunk or damaged during the war, but only operated for the last year. In response, by 1945 the US Navy had developed a highly-organised strategy to deal with the suicide attackers. The fast carrier task groups had developed AA co-ordination plans, which provided long-range 5in gunfire protection against targets at maximum range via a Task Group AA Co-ordinator. All target information was channelled through this central control point via a dedicated VHF circuit. Each Group was sub-divided into four sectors, and ships in each sector, on an alert being triggered, supplemented search radars with fire control radars. The plan still left unrestricted freedom of action to individual ships in repelling air attack.

This method proved fine for the carrier task groups out to sea, but protection of the amphibious, bombarding, minesweeping and supply convoy forces, which of necessity were tied to the land, proved harder to maintain. The Japanese could lurk in the mountains and make surprise sorties with little chance of being detected. These ships were forced to anchor overnight and crowd together, so dusk and dawn attacks would find them vulnerable and smoke-screens were better protection for the majority than AA firepower. Pickets were employed to give them some protection and they doubled up as fighter-direction centres, but the tendency of the land-based Allied CAP to withdraw to its bases at twilight left such forces without the comfort of friendly aircraft overhead.

Individual warships operated their AA patrols to a tried-and-tested format. Once hostiles were identified as approaching, the ships went to General Quarters and maximum speed as quickly as they could; if possible the incoming attackers were placed abeam to enable maximum deployment of all available weapons, fire was opened at maximum range, the percentage of VT fuses steadily increased. The 5in batteries were placed under control of manually-operated auxiliary directors when ships were surprised, while long-range targets were controlled by the main director. The maximum possible rate of fire was maintained consistent with the safety of any friendly CAP aircraft or nearby ships, but inevitably there were mistakes, especially during mass attacks.

Guided rocket weapons – the German and the Japanese methods

The introduction of the suicide attack by the Japanese was important, in the American evaluation this tactic was rated the most effective method of all. Interestingly, Japan's German partners in Europe tried all types of air attack with dive- and torpedo-bombing

---

Kronshtadt and *Sevastopol*, and the proposed Nos *795* and *796* of the Japanese B64–type, and they are therefore so termed in this book.

being the most effective in the earlier years, then later, pilotless, directed glider- and rocket-bombs, which scored some notable successes in the Mediterranean area.[11] Lacking the scientific expertise of their ally, the Japanese equivalent of these in the Pacific was, of course, the piloted *Ōhka* bomb, rocket-propelled with a large payload as another facet of the suicide mission. Like their German counterpart, of course, such weapons had an Achilles' heel in that they had to be carried into battle by slow, medium bombers before being sent toward their targets. In the case of Japan most parent aircraft were *Betty* bombers and they had already been made obsolete as conventional bombers due to their tendency to catch fire easily. In other words while the *Ōhka*, once released, might be deadly, few of them ever got to that stage because they were lost with their parent aircraft to the CAP fighters, to whom they were sitting ducks. In addition, (again like their German counterparts but for different reasons) these weapons proved very difficult to control and manoeuvre once launched.

Night attacks were subsequently tried, but with low success. Indeed the whole *Ōhka* effort was one big disappointment to the Japanese, even when they believed their own hugely inflated figures of success. In truth the *Ōhka* was launched against ship targets on thirteen occasions and only four hits were scored, as we have seen, along with one damaging near-miss.

Rating of the Kamikaze method by the Americans

In the Philippines campaign the Japanese changed the deliberate crashing of aircraft into ship targets from a method of individual choice into a tactic in its own right. In that theatre 326 aircraft made suicide attempts and 120 (37%) actually impacted their target. There was a lull and then in the Okinawa campaign a supreme effort was made, and the sortie rate was much higher. But in the interim the defences had hardened and only 29% of the aircraft committed actually impacted the target, an 8% decline in effectiveness. Having conceded that, the fact remained that the Kamikaze tactic was three to four times more successful in scoring hits on ships than conventional aerial bomb and torpedo attacks, only 10% of which had resulted in damage to the ship target.

Allied innovations in the defence against the Kamikaze

As already detailed, the most telling invention in the defence against the suicide attacker had been the introduction and rapid spread of the VT for the 5in projectile. Once proven by the shooting down of a dive-bomber by the light cruiser *Helena* (CL-50, Captain Charles Purcell Cecil) off Guadalcanal 5 January 1943, this was eagerly embraced by the fleet and by eliminating fuse-setting errors was a major step forward in AA defence. VT

---

11. Notably the sinking of the new Italian battleship *Roma* and damage to several other large ships including the British battleship *Warspite*, cruisers *Spartan* (sunk), *Uganda* and *Savannah*, both damaged, and destroyers *Janus*, *Inglefield* and *Rockwood* (all sunk) in 1943–44. See – Peter C. Smith, *Ship Strike – The History of Air-to-Sea Weapon Systems*, Shrewsbury: 1998. Airlife Publishing.

fuses proved three times as effective as time fuses in the destruction of enemy aircraft. However, this was not the only Allied technical response that influenced the outcome.

The Mark 14 gun sight was another major development that added to the efficiency of the defence. The Mark 14 utilised two air-spun gyros to compute the lead angles in elevation and traverse, and introduced the principle of the disturbed line of sight. Beginning with 20mm guns in 1942, some 90,000 of these were produced during the war.

In parallel with the Mark 14, the Mark 51 Gun Director was introduced. This was a single-handed, hand-operated device which separated the director from the immediate effects of blast, smoke and vibration. Some 13,000 were produced and they were credited with making the 40mm gun which it controlled the most successful AA weapon, 'statistics indicated that guns controlled by this director shot down more aircraft than any other AA fire control combination in the fleet.' In addition, when the original Mark 50 lightweight, intermediate range, AA Director proved unsatisfactory for purpose, the Mark 52 was introduced followed by the Mark 57 director – an intermediate range, manually-operated, optical or blind-firing system for the 5in/38 and 40mm gun systems. By the end of the war the Mark 56 system arrived, being a 12,000–yard range director for 5in batteries with fully automatic radar tracking and fast solution timing, which was capable of handling targets closing at speeds of up to 600mph.

Improved defence weaponry

The AA equipment with which the US Fleet was equipped at the time of Pearl Harbor rapidly proved inefficient and ineffective, and this was equally true of both light and heavy batteries. Instead of the plethora of AA weapons of varying types, calibres, ranges and efficiency which so bedevilled the defence of Royal Navy warships throughout the war and beyond, the US Navy adopted a far more sensible and rational policy. They concentrated primarily on just three weapons – the 5in/38, the 40mm and the 20mm – ruthlessly casting aside as soon as practicable their existing AA weapons, namely; .30 and .50 calibre machine guns, the 1.1in, 3in/23 and, wherever possible, the 5in/25 by the new 5in/38. As well as providing the fleet with a more effective defence against air attack, this enormously simplified their supply and ordnance problems.

A lack of surface targets towards the end of the war also enabled destroyers to land at least one set of torpedo tubes and replace them with an additional quadruple 40mm mounting. At the same time AA weapons were crammed in wherever they might fit, both on both new construction and on older vessels, as they came in for refits. By August 1945 the AA firepower of the US Fleet far exceeded the entire AA defences of the entire United Kingdom! The 120 warships of Task Force 38/58 between them carried, in addition to 1,200 to 1,500 aircraft, 952 5in/38 barrels, 3,136 40mm barrels and 2,936 20mm barrels. Typical anti-aircraft weapon batteries were as follows:

Battleships (BB) – 165 barrels; Large Fleet Carriers (CVB) – 158 barrels; Fleet Carriers (CV) – 136 barrels; Battle-Cruisers (CB) – 102 barrels; Heavy Cruisers (CA) – 83 barrels; Light Cruisers (CL) – 50 barrels; Light Carriers (CVL) – 40 barrels; Destroyers (DD) – 42 barrels.

Okinawa – the ultimate test

The culmination of the Kamikaze effort was at Okinawa of course, and some interesting statistics came out. From a total of 2,027 enemy aircraft fired on between March and August 1945, 793 were suicide planes ie thirty-nine per cent of the total; this compared with 364 planes and twenty-six per cent at the Philippines. At Okinawa the Kamikazes tended to concentrate their attacks on smaller warships with eighty-six per cent hitting destroyers or lesser targets against sixty-one per cent in the Philippines campaign. In the latter, forty-three Kamikazes were taken under fire of which thirteen hit their target ships and four scored damaging near-misses. In comparing the effectiveness of the suicide attack against the conventional air attack, the Kamikaze was far more efficient. Thus to sink or damage an Allied ship it required fifty-one conventional aircraft to be destroyed against just 3.5 suicide attackers. A total of thirty-three suicide attacks were made of which thirty-one had aircraft carriers of various types as their main targets. 'Carriers are the most strategically important ships, and because of their size the most vulnerable targets in the fast carrier task force. Thus the enemy's concentration on carriers was highly to his advantage.'

As to which warships were the most effective in shooting down Kamikazes, one statistic which came as no surprise to the author – although no doubt it will to most of their legion of post-war detractors – is that it was the battleship. The summary states this baldly: 'Battleships are most effective in shooting down planes in suicide actions .' The following table illustrates this:

Kamikaze aircraft destroyed

Type of warship	Number of Actions	Aircraft destroyed	%
Battleships	37	7.9	21%
Carriers	88	9.8	11%
Cruisers	47	3.8	8%
Destroyers	92	2.5	3%

And, of course, battleships proved the most resilient of targets if hit. One facet of this was the determination of the so-called 'expected' distribution of aircraft kills by type of ship compared with the actual distribution. 'Expected' kills were obtained by assuming that in each ship's AA action, the 'rounds per aircraft' are the same as the overall average for the particular range of opening fire involved. Thus we have:

Type of warship	'Expected' kills	Actual kills	Ration actual to expected %
Battleships	3.8	7.8	200
Carriers	10.0	9.8	98
Cruisers	5.8	3.8	65
Destroyers	4.4	2.5	57
	24.0	23.9	

Such unexpected figures might possibly explain the retention of some battleships in the post-war fleets of both America and Great Britain. If this is truly the case, then this would be a most unusual side-result of the Kamikaze campaign.

Appendix 1

Statistics and Estimates

The United States Strategic Bombing Survey report estimated that a total of 2,550 Kamikaze sorties (excluding escorting fighters and observers) were flown in total by both Army and Navy flyers. The IJN carried out 2,314 sorties from the end of October 1944 until the end of the Okinawa operation, but this figure includes escorts and observers. From that total 1,086 returned without sighting a target, leaving 1,228 that actually made attacks. Of these, 475 made hits on targets or scored near misses which caused damage to US Navy targets. Almost 4,000 Japanese Army and Navy air crewmen died in *Tokkotai* (Special Attack Corps) missions between October 1944 and August 1945.

The breakdown of US Navy ships that were sunk or damaged by Kamikazes (including ships that were hit on several different occasions) are as follows:

	Sunk	*Damaged*
Battleships (BB)	–	15
Aircraft Carrier (CV)	–	16
Light Carrier (CVL)	–	3
Escort Carrier (CVE)	3	17
Heavy Cruiser (CA)	–	5
Light Cruiser (CL)	–	10
Destroyer (DD)	13	87
Destroyer Escort (DE)	1	24
Destroyer Minelayer (DM	–	13
Destroyer Minesweeper (DMS)	2	15
Submarine	–	1
(SC)	1	–
(AGP/AGS)	–	3
(AH)	–	1
(AK/AKA/AKN)	–	6
(AM)	–	10
(AO)	–	2
(APA/APD/APH)	3	30
(ARL)	–	2
(ATF)	–	–
(ATO)	1	–
(AV/AVP)	–	4
(CM)	–	1
(Landing Hip, Tank (LCT)	5	11
Patrol Craft (PC/PT)	3	3
(YDG/TMS)	1	7
Total:	33	286

It was estimated that the Japanese had in excess of 9,000 aircraft on hand at the time of the surrender and that over 5,000 of these had already been readied as Kamikazes had the Allied Invasion taken place. The emphasis would have been on the destruction of troopships and designed to inflict the maximum casualties in order to make America 'war-weary'.

Glossary

AB	Able Seaman
AAC	anti-aircraft – common
ABU	Automatic Barrage Unit
ACEM	Aviation Chief Electrician's Mate
ACM	Auxiliary Coastal Minelayer
ADP	Aircraft Defence Position
AE	Ammunition Ship
AEW	Airborne Early Warning
AG	Auxiliary Gunboat
AGS	Survey Ship
AH	Hospital Ship
AKA	Attack Cargo Ship
AO	Oiler
AM	Minesweeper
APA	Attack Transport
APD	High-Speed Transport (converted old destroyer)
APH	Hospital Ship
APL	Applied Physics Laboratory
APS	Active Protective System
ARD	Floating Dry-Dock
APR	Acoustic Pulse Reflectometry
ARL	Repair Ship, Landing Craft
ARP	Automatic Radar Plotting
AT	Ocean Tug
ATF	Fleet Ocean Tug
AV	Seaplane Tender
AVP	Seaplane Tender, Small
AWAC	Airborne Warning & Control
BB	Battleship
BNLO	British Naval Liaison Officer
BPF	British Pacific Fleet
BPFLO	British Pacific Fleet Liaison Officer
BS	Battle Squadron
CA	Heavy Cruiser (8in main armament)
CAP	Combat Air Patrol
CASCU	Command Aircraft Support Control Unit
CB	Battle-Cruiser (*Alaska* Class –12in main armament)

CG	Centre of Gravity
CIC	Combat Information Centre
CINCPAC	Commander-in-Chief, Pacific
CL	Light Cruiser (6in & 5in main armament)
CM	Minelayer
CO	Commanding Officer
CO2	Carbon Dioxide
COMPHIBSPAC	Commander, Amphibious Forces, Pacific Fleet
CS	Cruiser Squadron
CSF (AA)	Chief Shipfitter (Anti-Aircraft)
CV	Fleet Aircraft-carrier
CVB	Fleet Aircraft-carrier (Big)
CVE	Escort Aircraft-carrier
CVL	Light Aircraft-carrier (Independence Class)
CXAM	Search Radar – Long Wave
CXDT	Search Radar – Long Wave
CW	Continuous Wave
'D' Quality Steel	Flat production steel for cold-forming to British Standard quality.
DAWT	Director of Air Warfare and Training
DC	Director Control
DD	Destroyer
DE	Destroyer Escort
DESRON	Destroyer Squadron
DF	Destroyer Flotilla
DGD	Director Gunnery Division
DLCO	Deck Landing Control Officer
DM	Light Minelayer
DMS	High-Speed Minesweeper
DRT	Dead-Reckoning Tracer
DSC	Distinguished Service Cross
DSO	Distinguished Service Order
DTSD	Director Training and Staff Duties Division.
ECM	Electronic Counter Measures
FAA	Fleet Air Arm
FD	Fighter Direction
FDO	Fighter Direction Officer
GP	General Purpose
GQ	General Quarters
HEIT	High Explosive Incendiary Tracer
HTS	High Tensile Steel
ID	Identity
IFD	Inter-Fighter Director
IFF	Inter-Fighter Director/Identity – Friend or Foe
IX	Unclassified Miscellaneous Unit
j.g.	junior grade
K-guns	Depth-charge throwers

KIA	Killed in Action
KK	Kamikaze
LAW	Local Air Warning
LC (FF)	Landing Craft, Infantry (Flotilla Flagship)
LCI (G)	Landing Craft, Infantry (Gun)
LCI (L)	Landing Craft, Infantry (Large)
LCI (M)	Landing Craft, Infantry (Mortar)
LCI (R)	Landing Craft, Infantry (Rocket)
LCP (L)	Landing Craft, Personnel (Large)
LCV	Landing Craft, Vehicle
LCM	Landing Craft, Mechanised
LCS (L)	Landing Craft, Support (Large)
LCS(S)	Landing Craft, Support (Small)
LCT	Landing Craft, Tank
LCVP	Landing Craft, Vehicle & Personnel
LO	Liaison Officer
LSM	Landing Ship, Medium
LSM(R)	Landing Ship, Medium (Rocket)
LST	Landing Ship, Tank
LVT	Landing Vehicle, Tracked
LVT (A)	Landing Vehicle, Tracked (Armoured)
MAG	Marine Air Group
MARCOM	US Maritime Commission
MC	Megacycles
MCB	Motor Cargo (US Coast Guard)
MIA	Missing in Action
MTI	Moving Target Indicator
NAAF	Naval Auxiliary Air Facility
NAS	Naval Air Station
OPTEVAR	Operational Development Force
OSS	Office of Strategic Services
OTC	Officer in Tactical Command
PBM	Martin Mariner amphibian
PC	Patrol Craft
PG	Patrol Gunboat
PGM	Motor Gunboat
POW	Prisoner of War
PPI	Plan Position Indicator on a radar display
PT	Motor Torpedo Boat
PTC	Landing Ship for PC, PF & PT
Q Ship	Decoy Ships
Radar	Radio Detection and Ranging
RAN	Royal Australian Navy
RCM	Radio & Radar Counter Measures
RDF	Radio Direction Finding
RFD	Relief Fighter Direction

RN	Royal Navy
RNZN	Royal New Zealand Navy
RP	Radar Picket
RPC	Remote Power Control
RPS	Radar Picket Ship
SA	Search – Model A (1st series) radar – long wave
SC	Submarine Chaser
SD	Search – Model D (4th series) radar
SG	Search – Model G (7th series) radar – microwave
SJ	Search – Model J (10th series) radar
SK	Search – Model K (11th series) radar – long wave
SM	Search – Fighter Direction radar
SP	Short Pulse
SPA	Submarine Patrol Area
SPR	Short Pulse Radar
SR	Search- Model R (18th series) radar
SS	Submarine
ST	Search – Model T (20th series) radar
STS	Stainless Steel
(T)	(True) Course – True Course + Relative Bearing
TBM	General Motors version of the Grumman TBF Avenger torpedo-bomber.
TBS	Talk Between Ships
TCAP	Target Combat Air Patrol
TF	Task Force
TG	Task Group
TNT	Trinitrotoluene
TRANSRON	Transport Squadron
TU	Task Unit
USMC	United States Marine Corps
UXB	Unexploded Bomb
VC	Navy Composite Squadron
VHF	Very High Frequency
VF	US Navy Fighter Squadron
VB	US Navy Dive-Bomber Squadron
VJ	Barrage Jamming
VT	US Navy Torpedo-Bomber Squadron
VMF	US Marine Corps Fighter Squadron
VMSB	US Marine Corps Scout Bomber Squadron
VP	Navy Patrol Squadron
XAK	Army Ammunition Ship
XO	Executive Officer
XUF	Experimental Development Squadron
'Y' Stations	British Intelligence Interception and Direction Finding sites
YE/YG	US Aircraft Carrier Homing Beacons
YMS	Motor Minesweeper (Inshore)

The Aircraft

Japanese (with Allied reporting names)

Alf	Kawanishi E7K2	Trainer
Betty	Mitsubishi G4M *Hamaki*	Torpedo Bomber/Bomber
Dinah	Mitsubishi Ki-46 *Shiki*	Command Reconnaissance
Frances	Yokosuka P1Y1 *Ginga*	Torpedo Bomber/Bomber
Frank	Nakajima Ki-84 *Hayate*	Fighter
Grace	Aichi B7A1/2 *Ryusei*	Torpedo Bomber
Helen	Nakajima Ki-49 *Donryu*	Heavy Bomber
Irving	Nakajima J1N1–S *Gekko*	Night Fighter
Jake	Aichi E13A1	Floatplane
Jill	Nakajima B6N1 *Tenzan*	Torpedo Bomber
Judy	Yokosuka D4Y *Suisei*	Dive-Bomber
Kate	Nakajima B5N	Torpedo Bomber/Bomber
Lily	Kawasaki Ki-48 *Sōkei*	Light Bomber
Mavis	Kawasaki H6K	Flying Boat
Myrt	Nakajima C6N1 *Saiun*	Carrier Reconnaissance
Oscar	Nakajima Ki-43 *Hayabusa*	Fighter
Paul	Aichi E16A1 *Zui-un*	Floatplane
Peggy	Mitsubishi Ki-67 *Hiryū*	Bomber
Sally	Mitsubishi Ki-21	Heavy Bomber
Sonia	Mitsubishi Ki-51	Light Bomber
*Shiragiku**	Kyūshū K11W	Trainer
Tojo	Nakajima Ki-44 *Shōki*	Fighter
Tony	Kawasaki Ki-61 *Hein*	Fighter
Val	Aichi D3A1/2	Dive-Bomber
Willow	Yokosuka K5Y	Trainer
Zeke 55	Mitsubishi A6M	Suicide versions of Navy Type O (Zero-sen) fighter

*Never allocated an Allied code name.

Allied

Avenger	Grumman TBM	Torpedo Bomber/Bomber
Barracuda	Fairey	Torpedo Bomber/Bomber
Corsair	Chance-Vought	Fighter/Fighter-Bomber
Firefly	Fairey	Fighter/Ground Attack
Flying Fortress	Boeing B-17	
Hellcat	Grumman	Fighter
Helldiver	Curtiss SB2C	Dive-Bomber
Seafire	Supermarine	Fighter
Wildcat	Grumman F4F	Fighter

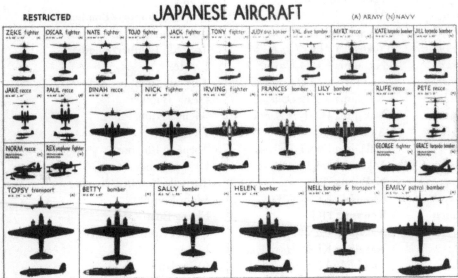

RESTRICTED   **JAPANESE AIRCRAFT**   (A) ARMY (N) NAVY

NOVEMBER, 1944

Appendix 4

A Conversion of Selected Measurements Aide

(N.B. This is a simplified list intended to provide a source of quick reference for readers who wish to convert, for instance, an Imperial measurement into metric. Some of the figures included are rounded up or down in order to avoid endless decimal points – it is not, of course, a definitive conversion chart.)

CENTIMETRES

Convert centimetres to inches	Multiply by (x)	0.3937008
Convert centimetres to inches	Divide by (÷)	2.54
Convert centimetres to feet	X	0.0328084
Convert centimetres to meters	X	0.01
Convert centimetres to yards	X	0.0109361
Convert centimetres per second to feet per second	X	0.0328084
Convert centimetres per second to kilometres per hour	X	0.036
Convert centimetres per second to miles per hour	X	0.0223694

FATHOMS

Convert fathoms to feet	X	6.0
Convert fathoms to meters	X	1.8288
Convert fathoms to yards	X	2.0

FEET

Convert feet to centimetres	Divide by	30.48
Convert feet to fathoms	X	0.1666667
Convert feet to inches	X	12.0
Convert feet to kilometres	X	0.0003048
Convert feet to meters	X	0.3048
Convert feet to yards	X	0.3333333
Convert feet per second to centimetres per second	X	30.48

Convert feet per second to kilometres per hour	X	1.09728
Convert feet per second to knots	X	0.5924838
Convert feet per second to metres per second	X	0.3048
Convert feet per second to miles per hour	X	0.6818182

GALLONS (US)

Convert gallons to cubic centimetres	X	3785.4118
Convert gallons to cubic feet	X	0.1336806
Convert gallons to cubic inches	X	231.0
Convert gallons to cubic metres	X	0.0037854
Convert gallons to litres	X	3.7854118
Convert US gallons to Imperial gallons	X	0.8326742

HORSEPOWER

Convert horsepower to pounds–feet per minute	X	33000.0
Convert horsepower to pounds–feet per second	X	550.0
Convert metric horsepower to kilowatts	X	0.7354988

INCHES

Convert inches to centimetres	X	2.54
Convert inches to metres	X	0.25
Convert inches to millimetres	X	25.4
Convert inches to yards	X	0.277778

KILOGRAMS

Convert from kilograms to pounds	X	2.2046224
Convert from kilograms to long tons	X	0.0009842
Convert from kilograms to short tons	X	0.0011023
Convert from kilograms per metre to pounds per foot	X	0.671969
Convert from kilograms per metre to pounds per inch	X	0.0559974

KILOMETRES

Convert kilometres to metres	X	1000.0
Convert kilometres to nautical miles	X	0.5399568

Convert kilometres to statute miles	X	0.6213712
Convert kilometres to miles	÷	1.61
Convert kilometres per hour to knots per hour	X	0.5399568
Convert kilometres per hour to miles per hour	X	0.6213712
Convert kilometres per litre to miles per Imperial gallon	X	2.8248094
Convert kilometres per litre to miles per US gallon	X	2.3521459

KILOWATTS

Convert from kilowatts to metric horsepower	X	1.3596216
Convert from kilowatts to horsepower	X	1.3410221

KNOTS

Convert from knots to feet per minute	X	101.26859
Convert from knots to feet per second	X	1.6878099
Convert from knots to kilometres per hour	X	1.852
Convert from knots to miles per hour	X	1.15077794

LITRES

Convert from litres to cubic feet	X	0.0353147
Convert from litres to cubic yards	X	0.0013079
Convert from litres to Imperial gallons	X	0.2199692
Convert from litres to US gallons	X	0.2641721
Convert from litres to pounds	X	2.2044903

METRES

Convert from metres to fathoms	X	0.5468067
Convert from metres to feet	X	3.2808399
Convert from metres to inches	X	39.3700787
Convert from metres to kilometres	X	0.001
Convert from metres to yards	X	1.0936133
Convert from metres per second to kilometres per hour	X	3.6
Convert from metres per second to feet per second	X	3.2808399

MILES

Convert from statute miles to feet	X	5280.0
Convert from statute miles to kilometres	X	1.609344
Convert from statute miles to nautical miles	X	0.8689762
Convert from statue miles to yards	X	1760.0
Convert from nautical miles to feet	X	6076.11549
Convert from nautical miles to kilometres	X	1.852
Convert from nautical miles to statute miles	X	1.1507794
Convert from nautical miles to yards	X	
Convert from Imperial miles per gallon to kilometres per litre	X	0.3540062
Convert from Imperial miles per gallon to US miles per gallon	X	0.8326742
Convert from miles per hour to centimetres per second	X	44.704
Convert from miles per hour to feet per minute	X	88.0
Convert from miles per hour to feet per second	X	1.4666667
Convert from miles per hour to kilometres per hour	X	1.609344
Convert from miles per hour to knots	X	0.8689762

MILLIMETRES

Convert from millimetres to centimetres	X	0.1
Convert from millimetres to inches	X	0.0393701
Convert millimetres to inches	÷	25.4
Convert from millimetres to metres	X	0.001

POUNDS WEIGHT

Convert from pounds to kilograms	X	0.4535924
Convert from pounds to metric tonnes	X	0.0004536
Convert from pounds per cubic foot to kilograms per cubic metre	X	16.018464
Convert from pounds per foot to kilograms per metre	X	1.488164
Convert from pounds per inch to kilograms per metre	X	17.857968

Convert from pounds per inch to pounds per foot	X	0.0833333
Convert from pounds per square foot to kilograms per square centimetre	X	0.0004882
Convert from pounds per square foot to kilograms per square metre	X	4.8824277
Convert from pounds per square inch to kilograms per square centimetre	X	0.070307

SECONDS

Convert seconds to degrees	X	0.0002778
Convert seconds to minutes	X	0.0166667

SQUARE CENTIMETRES

Convert from square centimetres to square feet	X	0.0010764
Convert from square centimetres to square inches	X	0.1550003
Convert from square centimetres to square yards	X	0.0001196

SQUARE FEET

Convert from square feet to square centimetres	X	929.0304
Convert from square feet to square inches	X	144.0
Convert from square feet to square metres	X	0.0929030
Convert from square feet to square yards	X	0.111111

SQUARE INCHES

Convert from square inches to square centimetres	X	6.4516
Convert from square inches to square feet	X	0.0069444
Convert from square inches to square metres	X	0.0006452
Convert from square inches to square millimetres	X	645.16
Convert from square inches to square yards	X	0.0007716

SQUARE METRES

Convert from square metres to square feet	X	10.76391
Convert from square metres to square inches	X	1550.0031
Convert from square metres to square yards	X	1.19599

SQUARE YARDS

Convert from square yards to square feet	X	9.0
Convert from square yards to square inches	X	1296.0
Convert from square yards to square metres	X	0.8361274

TONS & TONNES

Convert from long tons to kilograms	X	1016.-469
Convert from long tons to pounds	X	2240.0
Convert from long tons to short tons	X	1.12
Convert from metric tonnes to kilograms	X	1000.0
Convert from metric tonnes to pounds	X	2204.6226
Convert from short tons to kilograms	X	907.18475
Convert from short tons to metric tonnes	X	0.9071847

YARDS

Convert yards to centimetres	X	91.44
Convert yards to fathoms	X	0.5
Convert yards to feet	X	3.0
Convert yards to metres	X	0.9144

Index